Hans Müller-Casenov

The Humour of Germany

Hans Müller-Casenov

The Humour of Germany

ISBN/EAN: 9783337731274

Printed in Europe, USA, Canada, Australia, Japan

Cover: Foto ©ninafisch / pixelio.de

More available books at **www.hansebooks.com**

THE HUMOUR OF GERMANY

SELECTED AND TRANSLATED,
WITH INTRODUCTION AND
BIOGRAPHICAL INDEX, BY
HANS MÜLLER-CASENOV:
WITH ILLUSTRATIONS BY
C. E. BROCK.

LONDON
WALTER SCOTT, LTD
1893

NEW YORK
CHARLES SCRIBNER'S SONS
1893

CONTENTS.

	PAGE
INTRODUCTION	xi
MASTER FOX, THE CONFESSOR—*Hugo von Trimberg* (1260-1309)	1
ST. PETER'S LESSON—*Hans Sachs* (1494-1576)	4
A RAID ON THE PARSON'S KITCHEN—*Christoffel von Grimmelshausen* (1620-1676)	6
THE REVOLT IN THE THEATRE—*Ludwig Tieck* (1773-1853)	12
THE UNACCOUNTABLE STRANGER—*Ludwig Tieck*	24
VAN DER KABEL'S LAST WILL AND TESTAMENT—*Jean Paul Friedrich Richter* (1763-1825)	28
DIVISION OF LABOUR IN MATTERS SENTIMENTAL—*Jean Paul Friedrich Richter*	35
A TENDER-HEARTED CRITIC—*Jean Paul Friedrich Richter*	37
THE ACCIDENT OF THE DISTINGUISHED STRANGER—*August von Kotzebue* (1761-1819)	38
HOW THE VICAR CAME AROUND—*Heinrich Zschokke* (1771-1848)	49

CONTENTS.

	PAGE
THE MAN WHO SOLD HIS SHADOW—*A. von Chamisso* (1781-1838).	62
THE GHOST OF DR. ASCHER—*Heinrich Heine* (1799-1856)	66
TOURISTS AT THE BROCKEN—*Heinrich Heine*	70
MY APPRECIATIVE FRIEND—*Heinrich Heine*	72
"MADAM, DO YOU KNOW THE OLD PLAY?"—*Heinrich Heine*	73
VERSES FROM HEINE	100
ABOUT MONEY—*M. G. Saphir* (1795-1858)	105
A NIGHT IN THE BREMER RATHSKELLER—*Wilhelm Hauff* (1802-1827)	107
THE DUEL WITH THE DEVIL—*Wilhelm Hauff*	125
EDITORIAL CO-OPERATION—*Wilhelm Hauff*	130
MOZART'S JOURNEY TO PRAGUE—*Edward Mörike* (1804-1875)	133
A RABID PHILOSOPHER (AUCH EINER)—*Friedrich Theoder v. Vischer* (1807-1889)	146
HIS SERENITY WILL BUILD A PALACE—*Fritz Reuter* (1810-1874)	159
HIS SERENITY AND THE THUNDER-STORM—*Fritz Reuter*	167
THE LIEUTENANT'S DINNER—*Fritz Reuter*	177
THE HIGHER ALTRUISM—*Fritz Reuter*	181
MY PICTURES—*Fritz Reuter*	182
LISZT EXPECTED AT AN EVENING PARTY—*E. Kossak* (1814-1880)	188
A PRINCE IN DISGUISE—*Gottfried Keller* (1815-1887)	196

CONTENTS.

	PAGE
A DISREPUTABLE SAINT—*Gottfried Keller*	203
MILITARY INSPECTION—*F. W. Hackländer* (1816-1877)	221
THE KING OF MACCAROONIA—*Professor Volkmann* (1830-1890)	225
THE SAD TALE OF SEVEN KISSES—*Professor Volkmann*	232
A COUNTRY COMEDY—*Heinrich Schaumberger* (1843-1874)	235
HOW BLINDSCHLEICHER WENT COURTING—*P. K. Rosegger*	249
"WHOM FIRST WE LOVE"—*H. von Kahlenberg*	255
WOOING THE GALLOWS—*W. H. Riehl*	261
ELECTIVE AFFINITIES—*Franz von Schönthan*	274
HOT PUNCH—*Julius Stinde*	281
WOMAN—*Bogumil Golz* (1801-1870)	284
A CHRISTMAS TALE—*Eduard Pötzl*	288
THE CASE OF MINCKWITZ—*Paul Lindau*	293

STUDENTS' SONGS—

OLD ASSYRIAN-JONAH—*Joseph Victor Scheffel*	304
HEINZ VON STEIN	305
BRIGAND SONG	306
A FARTHING AND A SIXPENCE—*Count Albert von Schlippenbach*	307
THE TEUTOBURGER BATTLE—*J. V. Scheffel*	308
THE LAST PAIR OF BREECHES—*J. V. Scheffel*	311

CONTENTS.

STUDENTS' SONGS (*continued*)— PAGE

    ENDERLE VON KETSCH—*J. V. Scheffel*   313

    GOD AND THE LOVER—*Old German*   316

UNINTENTIONAL WITTICISMS OF THE ABSENT-MINDED GERMAN PROFESSOR   317

THE INCARCERATION OF THE HERR PROFESSOR—*Ernst Eckstein*   320

OUR WAR-CORRESPONDENT—*Julius Stettenheim*   335

SCHNORPS' SWALLOW-TAIL—*Fritz Brentano*   339

THE MAN OF ORDER—*Johannes Scherr*   352

THE LUXURY OF GOING ABOUT INCOGNITO—*Hans Arnold*   359

THE INNER LIFE OF THE SECOND-CLASS CAB-DRIVER—*Ernst von Wildenbruch*   382

BON-MOTS   404

THE EARLY DAYS OF A GENIUS—*Wilhelm Raabe*   408

NEWSPAPER HUMOUR   423

BIOGRAPHICAL INDEX OF WRITERS   431

INTRODUCTION.

In endeavouring to bring together examples of so significant and at the same time elusive a phase of national character—literary as well as psychological—as a nation's humour, it were of course vain to seek to make each selection typical in itself—typical, that is, in the sense of referring to the broad basis of a nation's individuality in respect of its humour as distinguished from other nations.

A general idea can only be obtained by scanning a broad field; here, as elsewhere, details have little meaning unless considered in their relation to the broader outlook. A constant interplay of varied influences has to be taken into account. The purely national aspect is obtruded upon by the individuality of each author, which nowhere expresses with such effect as in the literature of humour. The *time* of writing, considered historically, with its political tendencies, has also to be considered; its church dependence perhaps, and the peculiar trend of its social interests. It is intruded upon also by the time considered in its relation to literature as a whole, to the tendencies of form and style predominant at given periods.

Furthermore, there are strictly *local* peculiarities, subdividing Germany itself. It is more especially these that the student of literature, unless he be also a student of ethnological influences, is likely to wrongly estimate, while it is of the utmost importance that they be borne in mind to arrive at a just view of qualities that oversway minor differences, which are often the first to catch the eye. The more the Comic Muse is bound within the narrow limits of place, time, and personality, the more is she in her element. She of all muses is a painter of detail, versed in the art of reproducing punctiliously those petty traits which disengage her subject from all broader problems, and make it effective in proportion to its *unimportance* to the world's general affairs.

Writers upon the theory of humour are apt to deplore the absence of just such local land-marks in Germany as are strongly characteristic and still recognisable to the foreigner. It would appear to me that they have done so with some injustice. The *Volkscharacter* of southern and northern Germany, of the lowlands, and the Franco-Bavarian and Suabian districts, even of the various centres of civilisation, the large towns, is abundant in those differentiating qualities which go to make up originality of manner. The modes of thought and feeling characterising the population of different districts bear a stamp so distinct that one is inclined to consider them more strongly marked by provincial locality than by nationality.

In these days dialect proper, having gained the prestige of comparative rarity, like a peasant's national costume, or a bit of *bric-à-brac*, has been favoured by the humorist, although its reproduction in our literature has well-nigh insurmountable difficulties to cope with. The Low German, one of the most interesting of German dialects, because, historically, the most intact, and the most incapable of amalgamation with the language that has superseded it, had been left to grow rusty so far as literature was concerned, until Fritz Reuter rescued it from threatening oblivion, and made it the vehicle of a naïve and spontaneous *genre* of humour, to which it lent itself with singular charm and appropriateness.

The cause of the former neglect of Low German as a means of literary expression was very obvious, and there was no gainsaying the justice of it—viz., that it is used to-day only by the lower classes of Northern Germany, and that among readers there is but a very limited number to whom it is more comprehensible than a foreign language would be. It is this fact also which explains why Fritz Reuter, the most intimate and sympathetic of German humorists, although extensively read, has never attained the widest popularity.

Fundamentally, the German character appears to be averse to humour. Its mirth does not come to it spontaneously, a gift of the gods, arising out of the mere exuberance of being. This nation shares the temperament of all northern races, it moves more to the minor strains of feeling, to the *Adagio* which Richard Wagner found so aptly expressive of its character. It is quick to respond to things mystic, and yearns over the vague grace of twilight moods. It worships at the shrine of the hapless Prince of Denmark.—I say fundamentally, for, looking at the life of the nation as it appears to-day, in those pleasures of the lower and middle classes which have their scene of action in the out-of-door world, there would appear to be in plenty a spirit of merry-making and pleasure-seeking inherent in the German character. The mere primitive love of a good time, however, is inseparably connected with those classes representing, in a manner, a child-like stage of intellectual development the world over, and is not characteristic in any special sense of the German people.

It is safe to admit that a certain lightness of disposition, which seems indispensable to the humorous attitude, is absent among those race-qualities which go to make up the German nature pure and simple. If the nation has developed within itself those germs which have blossomed into a sense of the humorous; if it has passed through all those early stages of perception and expression which have culminated in a humorous literature of sturdy strength; if it has found at length a humorous literature (with Gottfried Keller for its prophet, and F. T. Vischer for its critic and exponent), it is due probably to a complexity of influences somewhat difficult to determine.

However free in its purely literary aspect humour may be from all ulterior purpose and aim, the tale of its growth with us is largely interwoven with impulses received from outside sources and sources didactic and philosophical. Outwitting the devil, the theme that recurs again and again as the oldest form of farcical expression in mediæval Germany, meant dealing with the stresses of adverse circumstance. This was the first step taken on the road to humour in Germany. The Powers of Evil had all the brute force upon their side; there was no coping with them, except by sharpening one's wits and irritating them by practical jokes until they might yield. The laugh that followed had all the hard ring of the victor's triumphant scorn. Early satirical writings were imbued with a like spirit. There was the lash to be swung at some enemy, and derision at his downfall was tempered by no kindlier emotion. There was a grim attitude of self-defence throughout it all. Indeed, it is only in going back painfully step by step that one is enabled to discern in this early literature the germs of humour at all.

The farces and puppet-shows at country fairs and the burlesques at the early theatre began to make room for the idea of retaliation. It became a question of clown against clown. The supremacy was never yielded long to one side. Laying aside all personal interest in the matter for the time being, there was an impartial shout of laughter at him who got the most kicks and cuffs. The popular mind began to rise above the situation, to put itself in the position of an unbiassed spectator, and to take delight in merely putting down whatever asserted itself. As an instance of this may be counted the practice of granting the devil, or a person disguised as such, a hearing in church on certain days of the year instead of the parish priest.

Then the sense of discrepancy between things great and small, things important and unimportant, the world of the senses and the world of the spirit, began to enter the popular perception, the impossibility of reconciliation, and, as a consequence, the pleasure of turning this world topsy-turvy, and so demonstrating the supremacy of the individual.

Side by side with this development, or partly perhaps based upon it, went the philosophic development. Thinkers, dreamers, and philosophers went on constructing a universe according to the laws of their individual minds, a universe containing nothing at all to be laughed at, and for many decades scholars were deeply buried in obstruse problems and finely-spun theories and systems, the lighter muse of poetry and art for the most part following but humbly and timorously from afar. But when philosophy and theology had spoken at large, and the mystery and fatal contradiction at the heart of things had not been unravelled, the pale brooding of some turned to melancholy, with others it turned to boisterous living and philosophic indifferentism.

Then it was that irony, directed upon the inordinate intellectual ambitions of man, removed him half imperceptibly into the sphere of the ludicrous. Self-irony may be the result of misanthropy, but it is certainly the beginning of a cure. One finds oneself to be made up of two absurdly contradicting hemispheres, as well as the rest of the world; the sense of the universal incongruity seems to make the case less tragic. To pass through this stage into the clearer atmosphere of conscious reconciliation with the actuality of things, of placid acceptance of the ups and downs, the shortcomings inherent in things, and in human nature withal,—into the atmosphere of pure humour, unperturbed by the possibility of personal disappointment, is a long step, easy to some, to others impossible. And it would seem that German Humour— taking the term in its widest sense as signifying subjective apprehension on the one hand and artistic expression on the other—is less the result of a temperamental predisposition than the culmination of a development. With a turn for flaccid sentimentalism, and by nature inclined to take themselves very seriously, it was a reaction, a bankruptcy in metaphysical methods that inaugurated and established something of a humorous *Weltanschauung*. The often oppressively heavy *Zeitgeist* has borne along its own corrective in the literature of two centuries as on an ever-strengthening under-current. There have been silent forces at play working imperceptibly through the innate robustness of the national character. It was this undeniable robustness which could not for long brook the extravagancies of weak emotionalism. Revolt was opened upon it on the one hand by the spirit of exact science, on the other by the need of æsthetic equilibrium. These two tendencies, the æsthetic and the scientific, are still contending for the field with much ado and bustle in some quarters.

Though a nation counting Heine and Lichtenberg among its own, it is not in the *spielende Urtheil*, as Jean Paul has called inspired sallies of wit, that German humour specially distinguishes itself; now and again there it has its moods of riotous absurdity; but where it is most characteristic is in the telling of the humorous tale, lovingly handled in its details, the pathetic verging very near upon the comic, finally succumbing in a ripple of good-natured laughter at somebody or other who is really not so very bad, but only very human, and for whose misfortunes—poor devil!—we may have a kindly feeling. Then we have a mastership in spectral stories, uncanny and imaginative, leaving the reader's mind in a delightful condition of doubt as to their actual meaning and significance; and we have also the expression of the spirit of poetic adventure,—a determination to have fun at all hazards, either *with* the public or else *at* the public, if perchance it should prove too dull to be taken into partnership. There is much of this in Chamisso's *Peter Schlemihl*, which, in the face of many dizzy structures of elucidation that have been based upon it, remains so truly humorous and so profoundly touching.

It is by no means always the *funny* element that predominates in German writings of a humorous tendency. Their office seems to be more to suggest the effect which these lighter moods of fancy have upon the serious affairs of life, and in studying the humour of Germany in a spirit of literary criticism it is indispensable to take these two aspects in their action and reaction upon each other. There is a psychical development of the individual which runs parallel to that of the nation. In confirmation of the theory of humorous development here faintly outlined, it may be said that in Germany, humorous perception is for the most part not the possession of youth. It is not until the need of a corrective to a habit of speculative brooding has been felt that imperceptibly and unconsciously healthful minds rise to those dispassionate heights whence the Occidental Brahmin gazes upon a motley world.

HANS MÜLLER-CASENOV.

[*For Acknowledgments to Authors and Publishers, see page* 430.]

THE HUMOUR OF GERMANY.

MASTER FOX, THE CONFESSOR.

THEY overtook the Ass, and so
    All three to Rome together go.
And when they saw the city near,
The Wolf said to his cousin dear:
"Reynard, my plan I'll name to you :—
The Pope, we know, has much to do;
I doubt if he can spend his time
To hear our catalogues of crime.
'Twill spare some trouble for the Pope
(And also for ourselves, I hope,
As we may 'scape with penance less),
If to each other we confess.
Let each describe his greatest sin,
So, without preface, I'll begin.
To notice trifles I disdain ;
But one fact gives my conscience pain.
'Tis this—there dwelt beside the Rhine
A man who lived by feeding swine.
He had a sow who rambled wide
While all her pigs with hunger cried.
I punished her in such a way
That never more she went astray.

Her little ones, deserted now,
Oft moved my pity, I'll avow;
I ended all their woes one night—
Now let my punishment be light!"
"Well," said the Fox, "your sin was small,
And hardly can for penance call;
For such a venial transgression
You've made amends by this confession.

"BUT NOW THE ASS MUST BE CONFESSED."

And now I'll do as you have done—
Of all my sins I'll name but one:
A man such noisy fowls would keep,
That no one near his house could sleep;
The crowings of his chanticleer
Disturbed the country far and near,

Distracted by the noise, one night
I went and stopped his crowing quite.
But this feat ended not the matter—
The hens began to crow and chatter;
And so (the deed I slightly rue)
I killed them and their chickens too."
"Well," said the Wolf, "to hush that din
Was surely no alarming sin;
Abstain from poultry for three days,
And, if you like, amend your ways.
But now the Ass must be confessed.
Donkey! how far have you transgressed?"
"Ah!" said the Ass, with dismal bray,
"You know I have not much to say;
For I have toiled from day to day,
And done for master service good,
In carrying water, corn, and wood.
But once, in winter time, 'tis true,
I did what I perhaps must rue:
A countryman, to keep him warm
(We had just then a snowy storm),
Had put some straw into his shoes;
To bite it I could not refuse;
And so (for hunger was my law)
I took, or stole, a single straw."

"There! say no more!" the Fox exclaimed;
"For want of straw that man was lamed;
His feet were bitten by the frost;
'Tis probable his life was lost.
'Twas theft and murder.—No reply!
Your penance is, that you must die."

Hugo von Trimberg (1260-1309).

"THE GOAT RUNS ON AND NEVER TIRES."

ST. PETER'S LESSON.

THE young goat had a playful mind,
    And never liked to be confined;
The apostle, at a killing pace,
Followed the goat, in a desperate chase;
Over the hills and among the briers
The goat runs on and never tires,

ST. PETER'S LESSON.

While Peter, behind, on the grassy plain,
Runs on, panting and sighing, in vain.
All day, beneath a scorching sun,
The good apostle had to run
Till evening came ; the goat was caught,
And safely to the Master brought.
Then, with a smile, to Peter said
The Lord : "Well, friend, how have you sped ;
If such a task your powers has tried,
How could you keep the world, so wide?"
Then Peter, with his toil distressed,
His folly, with a sigh, confessed.
"No, Master! 'tis for me no play
To rule one goat for one short day ;
It must be infinitely worse
To regulate the universe."

Hans Sachs (1494–1576).

A RAID ON THE PARSON'S KITCHEN.

THE commandant at Soest looked at me with approval, and said, "Tut, little huntsman, you shall be my servant, and wait upon my horses."

"Sir," I replied, "I should prefer a master in whose service the horses wait upon me. As it is not likely I shall find such a one, I am going to be a soldier."

"Hoity-toity," he said, "you have no more hair on your lip than a tree-frog. You are too young."

"Oh, no," I replied, "I will venture to brave any man of eighty. The beard does not make a man, else the he-goats would be in high esteem."

He said, "If you can show courage as well as you can wag your tongue, so be it."

I answered, "The first opportunity shall furnish the proof."

And so the commandant made over to me my dragoon's old trousers, in which my master had sewed a goodly number of ducats. Out of their vitals I provided myself with a good horse and the best fire-arms I could get; I thereupon polished up my belongings to their utmost possibility of brightness. I got me a new suit of green, for I delighted in the name of "huntsman," and gave my old garments to my boy, as they had grown too short and too tight for me. I sat on my horse like a young nobleman, and did not think small beer of myself. I took special delight in decorating my hat with a smart bunch of feathers like an officer. There were enough to envy me, and soon words and blows were the order of the day. But no sooner had I given proof to two of my enemies as to the nature of the thrusts I was skilled in, than I was left in peace, and my friendship was much sought for. In our raids upon the enemy I threw myself forward like bubbles in a boiling kettle, to be always the first in the fight. Whenever it was my good fortune to lay hands upon a desirable bit of pillage I shared it freely with the officers. The consequence was that I was allowed to plunder even in forbidden places, and could be secure of protection under all circumstances. So I was soon looked up to by friend and foe, and my purse grew as great as my name; even the peasants I managed to keep upon my side by fear and love, for I took vengeance upon those that tried to hinder me, and gave rich rewards to all who were helpful. I did not confine myself to large schemes, and never despised small ones if there was praise and admiration to be won thereby.

At one time we had been vainly hoping for some waggons with provisions to come into our way at the Castle of Recklinkhausen, and the pangs of hunger were upon us. And when I and my comrade, a student just run away from school, were leaning out of one of the windows, and hungrily gazing out into the country, my companion sighed after the barley-soup of his dear mother, and said: "Ah, brother, isn't it a shame to think that after having studied all the arts, I should not be able to supply food for myself? Brother, I know for certain, if I were only allowed to visit the parson in yonder village—you can see the church steeple just beyond the poplars—I should find a most excellent feast."

After a short parley the captain gave us permission; I exchanged my clothes with those of another, and the student and I betook ourselves to the village on a very roundabout way. The reverend gentleman received us civilly. When my companion had greeted him in Latin, accompanying his words with a profound bow, and briskly conjuring up a fine array of lies how the soldiers had robbed him, a poor student, of all his provisions, the parson gave him bread and butter and a drink of beer. I passed myself off as a painter's apprentice, and acting as if my companion and I had never met before, I told them both I should go down the village street to the inn for refreshment, and would then call for him, as we seemed to be going the same way. So I went away in search of anything that might be worth the trouble of coming for the following night, and I was so fortunate as to meet a peasant who was plastering up an earthen oven in which large loaves of brown bread were to lie and bake for twenty-four hours. I thought, "Go ahead; plaster away! I'll find you a customer for these delicious viands." I made but a short stay at the inn, knowing this cheaper way of getting bread, and returned to my companion, who had eaten his fill, and had told the parson that I was on my way to Holland to perfect myself in my art. The parson asked me to go and see the church with him, as he would like to show me some paintings that were in need of restoration. As it would not do to spoil the game, I consented. He conducted us through the kitchen, and when he opened the night-lock on the strong oaken door which led to the churchyard, I saw a wonderful sight. From the black heavens of this kitchen violins, flutes, and cymbals were pendent—in reality they were hams, sausages, and slices of bacon. I looked at them with happy forebodings, and they seemed to smile irritatingly upon me. I wished them in the castle to my comrades, but in vain; they were obstinate, and remained hanging where they were. I mused on ways and means of bringing them under my plan regarding the peasant's loaves of bread, but there were serious difficulties in the way, as the yard of the parsonage was surrounded by a stone wall, and all the windows were well protected with iron bars. Moreover, there were two large dogs in the yard that certainly would object to having that stolen the remnants of which was, in the course of time, to be the reward due to their watchfulness.

Once in church, it appeared that the parson generously intended to entrust me with the restoration of his old pictures. As I was exerting myself to find some plausible subterfuge, the sexton turned to me and said: "Fellow, you look more like a disreputable soldier-lad than like a painter." I was no longer accustomed to such speeches, and yet there was nothing for it but to swallow the taunt. I shook my head softly and replied, "Oh, you knave! give me a brush and colours, and I will paint a fool in a twinkling who shall resemble you throughout."

The parson made a joke of the matter, and reminded both

of us that it is not meet to tell each other unsavoury truths in so holy a spot. Then he gave us another drink, and we departed. But I left my heart with the sausages.

Returning to our people, I picked out six reliable fellows to help me carry home the bread. About midnight we entered the village and quietly took the bread out of the oven, and as we were about to pass the parsonage I could not bring myself to go on without the bacon. I stood still and looked up and down to discover some way into the parson's kitchen, but there was no opening except the chimney. We stored our guns and our treasured booty of bread in the charnel-house of the churchyard, managed to get a ladder and rope out of the barn, and I and my crony Springinsfeld climbed up on the tiled roof. I twisted my long hair into a top-knot, and let myself down by the rope to the objects of my desire. Once there, I did not delay, and tied ham after ham, and sausage after sausage to the rope. Springinsfeld fished everything out skilfully from his post on the roof and handed it down to the others. But, alack-a-day! as I was just going to give myself a holiday and come out, the pole that I was standing on gave way, and poor Simplicisimus was suddenly precipitated, and found himself in as bad a fix as need be—in fact, it was like a regular man-trap. Springinsfeld tried to help me by letting down the rope, but that also broke. I said to myself, "Now, huntsman, you are in for a chase in which there will be small mercy for your hide."

Sure enough, my fall had waked up the parson, and he called his cook and bade her strike a light. She appeared in night-attire, her petticoat around her shoulders, and stood close beside me. She seized a coal from the hearth, held her candle up close to it, and began to blow. At the same time I blew much stronger than she, which frightened the poor body so that she dropped both candle and coal, and retreated near her master. Now the parson himself struck a light, while the woman was telling him there was a horrible two-headed ghost crouching in the kitchen; she had probably mistaken my top-knot for a second head. When I heard this I quickly rubbed my face and hands with ashes and soot, until I doubtless bore small resemblance to the angel I had figured for at the nunnery. And if the sexton could have seen me thus occupied, he would certainly have given me credit for being a rapid painter. Thereupon I began to make as much noise as I possibly could, throwing pans and kettles about. I hung the ring of the large kettle about my neck, and took the poker in my hand, to have a weapon in case of need. All this did not put out the pious parson, who approached as if he were heading a procession, his cook behind him, carrying two wax tapers and a stoup. He was attired in his surplice, and had a book in one hand and his holy-water sprinkle in the other. He read some ritual of exorcism aloud before me, and then asked me who I was, and what was my business here. Seeing that he was labouring under the impression that I was the Evil One, I thought it but fair that I should act in accordance with my new *rôle*, and I answered him as I had once answered the robbers in the woods, "I am the devil, and I have come to turn your neck, and your servant's as well." He thereupon tried his most potent charm, "All good spirits praise the Lord! I conjure thee, return from whither thou comest!" I replied that this was impossible, happy though I should be to comply with his request.

Meanwhile my boon-companion Springinsfeld was indulging in spectral revelries upon the roof. When he heard what was going on in the kitchen below, and how I was passing myself off for the devil, he began to hoot like an owl, then barking like a dog, neighing like a horse, bleating like a sheep, crying like a donkey, cackling down the chimney like a hen about to lay an egg, and then again giving forth unearthly music like a hundred serenading cats; for this fellow was clever in imitating the voices of animals, and could howl as naturally as if a pack of wolves were standing about the house.

During the consternation of the parson and his charming feminine choir-boy I had time to look about me, and, to my joy, I made the discovery that the night-lock had not been put on the back door. Quick as a flash I pushed back the bolt, slipped out into the churchyard, where my companions were standing with triggers drawn, and left the parson to conjure devils as long as he pleased. And when Springinsfeld came down from the roof, bringing my hat along, and we had packed our spoils upon our shoulders, we returned to our party, not having anything more to do in the village, though I admit that we might have returned the borrowed ladder and rope.

Christoffel von Grimmelshausen (1620–1676).

THE REVOLT IN THE THEATRE.

(From Act I. of "A Topsy-Turvy World.")

SCARAMUCCIO.[1] POET.

SCARAMUCCIO.

No, Sir Poet, say what you please, talk as you wish, make as many objections as you can possibly make, it shall in no wise alter my purpose, to listen to nothing, to consider nothing, to insist upon having my own way,—so there!

POET.

Dear Scaramuccio!

SCARAMUCCIO.

I listen to nothing. Look, Sir Poet, how I am stopping up my ears.

[1] Scaramuccio and Pierrot represent species of buffoons of the early theatre.—ED.

POET.

But the piece——

SCARAMUCCIO.

Nonsense! the piece! I am a piece too, and I have a perfect right to say my say. Or do you suppose I have no will of my own? Do you poets labour under the delusion that a gentleman actor is called upon to do just as you say? My dear sir, know you not that the times are changing?

POET.

But the spectators——

SCARAMUCCIO.

And because there are spectators in the world, would you make me unhappy? Nice principles those!

POET.

Friend, you must listen to me.

SCARAMUCCIO.

Very well then, if I must. Here I sit: now talk like a sensible man, if it is in your nature so to do. (*Sits down on the ground.*)

POET.

Most esteemed Sir Scaramuccio! Your Grace has been engaged at this theatre for a special *rôle*—in a word, to express myself briefly, you are the *Scaramuccio*. It is not to be denied that you have reached a degree of excellence in this your speciality, and there is no man in the world more willing than myself to do justice to your talents; but, my dear sir, for all that you are not possessed of the qualities fitting you for a tragedian; for all that you will never be able to play a lofty character.

SCARAMUCCIO.

The impudence of it! By my soul, I'll play you a loftier character than you will be able to write. I take your remark as a personal insult, and I challenge the whole world to out-do me in the high and lofty.

SCAEVOLA (*one of the spectators*).

Oh, Sir Scaramuccio, we'll all take up your challenge.

SCARAMUCCIO.

How so? What now? I confess I am struck dumb by this insolence.

SCAEVOLA.

My dear sir, there is no cause for that. I am here for my money, Sir Scaramuccio, and I can think what I please.

SCARAMUCCIO.

You are free to think as you see best, but you are not allowed to speak here.

SCAEVOLA.

So long as you may speak, I don't see why I shouldn't.

SCARAMUCCIO.

Well, then, what have you done that was so noble?

SCAEVOLA.

The day before yesterday I helped my spendthrift of a nephew out of his debts.

SCARAMUCCIO.

And yesterday I saved the prompter from talking himself hoarse by leaving out a whole scene.

SCAEVOLA.

I was in a merry humour at table one day last week, and gave a whole shilling in charity.

SCARAMUCCIO.

The day before yesterday I quarrelled with my tailor, who came to dun me, and I had the last word.

SCAEVOLA.

A week ago I helped get a tipsy man home.

SCARAMUCCIO.

Sir, I was this tipsy man; but I had been drinking my sovereign's health.

SCAEVOLA.

I confess myself vanquished.

(*Enter Pierrot in a state of excitement.*)

POET.

What's the matter, Pierrot?

PIERROT.

What's the matter? I will not play to-day. On no account will I play.

POET.

Why not?

PIERROT.

Why not? Because it's high time for me to become a spectator. I've been a *mime* long enough.

(*Enter Wagemann, the manager.*)

POET.

You are just in time, Herr Wagemann. There is confusion abroad.

WAGEMANN.

How so?

POET.

Pierrot will not play to-day. He wants to be a spectator, and Scaramuccio insists upon taking the *rôle* of Apollo in my drama.

SCARAMUCCIO.

And am I not right, Herr Wagemann? I have played the fool long enough, and I should like to try my hand at the wise.

WAGEMANN.

You are too severe, Sir Poet. You must give the poor fellows a little more liberty. Let them have it their own way.

POET.

But the requirements of the drama, of art——

WAGEMANN.

Oh, all that will come right enough. Look you, my way of thinking is this—the spectators have paid their money, and with that the most important thing is regulated.

PIERROT.

Adieu, Sir Poet. I go to join the illustrious assembly of spectators. I will venture the bold leap over the footlights, to see if I can be cured of being a fool, and graduate to a spectator. (*Sings.*) Fare-thee-well, thou old love; a new life is dawning for me, and most sensible impulses are moving my heart. No footlight shall affright me, no prompter can hold me. Ah, I would taste the peaceful bliss of being an auditor. Receive me, wild waves; stage, fare-thee-well, my spirit yearns to be drawn beyond thy precincts. (*Jumps into the parterre.*) Where am I? Oh heavens! do I still breathe? Ah! is it possible I stand here below? The rays of the footlights shine over yonder. Ye gods, ye behold me surrounded by people. Who gave me this life, this better life?

THE AUDIENCE.

Monsieur Pierrot is one of us. A hearty welcome to thee, Spectator Pierrot. We greet thee, thou great man!

PIERROT.

Can it be, ye noble ones, that you will count me as your brother? Ah, my gratitude will last as long as there is breath within this bosom.

GRÜNHELM (*one of the spectators*).

Glorious, glorious! By my soul he speaks well! But as for me, I should like to take a part on the stage for a change; it would do my heart good. To be sure I tremble and stammer, and my wit is not of the quickest, but I am never so happy as when I am making a little joke. (*He scrambles up on the stage.*) And so, Sir Scaramuccio, leave your funny *rôle* to me, and then, for all I care, you may play the Apollo.

POET.

And what then is to become of my excellent drama?

AUDIENCE.

Scaramuccio shall play the Apollo. It is a unanimous decision.

POET.

'Tis well. I wash my hands of it. The audience may bear the responsibility. I am deeply miserable. Ah, yes, it is the fate of Art to be misunderstood and travestied, and it is only then that it finds its public. In vengeance for the judgment passed upon Marsyas, Poetry herself is flayed alive to-day. My sorrow is greater than I can endure. Herr Grünhelm, so you undertake to do the joking?

GRÜNHELM.

I do, Sir Poet, and I will hold my own against any rival.

POET.

How will you do it?

GRÜNHELM.

Sir, I have been one of those whose chief business it is to be amused long enough to know what will please. The people down there want to be entertained. At bottom that is the only reason they stand there so quietly and patiently. The good-will of the public is the principal thing, I know

2

that as well as you do. True art is to keep this good-will on the surface.

POET.

Yes, of course, but by what means do you propose——?

GRÜNHELM.

Let that be my care, Sir Poet. (*Sings:*)

"A fowler's trade is mine, heigh-ho," etc.

AUDIENCE.

Bravo! bravo!

GRÜNHELM.

Are you pretty well amused, gentlemen?

AUDIENCE.

Excellently, most excellently!

GRÜNHELM.

Do you feel a longing for anything reasonable?

AUDIENCE.

No, no; but by-and-by we should like to have our feelings worked upon.

GRÜNHELM.

Patience, you can't have all good things in a lump. Do you miss the genuine Apollo?

AUDIENCE.

Not in the least.

GRÜNHELM.

Well, Sir Poet, do you still object to granting the excellent Scaramuccio's request?

POET.

Not in the least. I withdraw all my objections.

AUDIENCE.

But we don't want him to give us nothing but nonsense.

SCARAMUCCIO.

Mercy on us! We would not be guilty of such a sinful thing. What kind of an Apollo were I if I should admit of that? No, gentlemen, there shall be an abundance of serious things—things to think about, things to train one's intellectual faculties.

SCAEVOLA.

Is it to be a tragedy?

PIERROT.

No, gentlemen, we actors have all sworn that we will not die, so it won't be a tragedy, whatever the poet may have in his mind.

SCAEVOLA.

I am relieved to hear it, for I am possessed of a very soft heart.

PIERROT.

Hang it, sir, neither are we made of stone and iron. I have the honour of assuring you that my susceptibilities are uncommonly delicate. The devil take all inelegancies.

SCAEVOLA.

That is what I say. There is nothing above being a spectator. It is the highest thing one can be.

PIERROT.

Ay, that it is. Are we not more than all the emperors and princes that are but acted?

SCARAMUCCIO.

Thunder and lightning! Where, in the hangman's name, is my Parnassus?

GRÜNHELM.

I will go and get it. (*Exit.*)

WAGEMANN.

Now all is in order. Adieu, Sir Scaramuccio.

SCARAMUCCIO.

Your humble servant. Beg you to express my respects to Madam, your wife. (*The manager exit. Three attendants enter, carrying the Parnassus.*) Put it down here,—a trifle further to this side, so that I can hear the prompter. (*He climbs up and takes a seat.*) A pleasant mount this. What revenues does it yield? Can any one tell me? Send for the treasurer.

(*Enter the Treasurer.*)

SCARAMUCCIO.

What does the mount bring me annually?

TREASURER.

Under your predecessor, the only profits derived were those from the Castalian Spring.

SCARAMUCCIO.

What sort of a spring? Was it a mineral spring; a sulphur spring, perhaps? Was there much demand for the waters. What was the price per bottle?

TREASURER.

What little there was wanted was given away. Few people liked the water. Your predecessor, the other Apollo, was fond of it.

SCARAMUCCIO.

I hope there are no mortgages on the mount?

TREASURER.

No, your majesty.

SCARAMUCCIO.

Is it insured?

TREASURER.

Oh, yes.

SCARAMUCCIO.

There is some security in that. I shall have a brewery and a bakery put up at the foot. The common pastures must be otherwise disposed of; Pegasus and the other beasts that belong to me must henceforth be fed in the stable.

TREASURER.

It shall be as you say.

SCARAMUCCIO.

Have the spectators paid for the play?

TREASURER.

Yes, your excellency.

SCARAMUCCIO.

I hereby decree that there shall be no complimentary tickets in future.

TREASURER.

These are innovations not at all in accordance with the institutions of Greece.

SCARAMUCCIO.

Hang Greece! Thank goodness we live in better times. This is an age of enlightenment, and I reign supreme. Send for the Muses. (*Exit the Treasurer.*)

(*Enter the nine Muses, bowing profoundly.*)

SCARAMUCCIO (*lightly nodding to them*).

Pleased to make your acquaintance, Mademoiselles. Hope we shall get on finely together. Henceforth you shall be my tenants on the Parnassus. Should you ever desire to change your residence, quarterly notice is required. What is your name, fair child?

MELPOMENE.

I am Melpomene.

SCARAMUCCIO.

You look so woe-begone.

MELPOMENE.

Oh, Herr Apollo! I am of a very good family. My father had a high position at court, and the thane gave me a matchless education. Ah, how happy I was in my parents' house, and what a dutiful daughter did I strive to be! I also had a lover, but he jilted me, and my parents died of grief. Our family physician, a worthy man, took an interest in me; but he was too poor to marry me, so there was nothing for it but to join the Muses. Have I no right to be sad?

SCARAMUCCIO.

Yes indeed, my child; but I will be as a father to you.

SCAEVOLA (*to another spectator*).

Now see, for heaven's sake, how the tears are flowing from my eyes.

THE OTHER.

Why, neighbour, save them for the fifth act.

SCARAMUCCIO.

And who are you, pretty maid?

THALIA.

Thank you kindly, sir, for asking; I was christened Thalia. I was a servant in the family of this excellent lady, and I could not bring myself to leave her in her distress, and followed her among the Muses.

SCARAMUCCIO.

When the last act comes your faithfulness will surely be rewarded. Where is my groom?

(*Enter the Groom.*)

SCARAMUCCIO.

Saddle my Pegasus. I wish to go riding.

(*Exit the Groom, coming back immediately with a bridled donkey.*)

Help me. (*He gets in the saddle.*)

THE MOUNTING OF PEGASUS.

GROOM.

By what rules of quantity does your Honour choose to take his pleasure to-day?

SCARAMUCCIO.

Oh, fool! I will ride in plain, sensible prose. Do you suppose I wish to be jolted in Alcaic measures, or break my neck in Proceleusmatics? No, I am for sense and order.

GROOM.

Your predecessor was always flying in the air.

SCARAMUCCIO.

Don't talk to me about the fellow. He must have been a very clown, a most eccentric ass. To fly into the air! No, the air has no pillars, I am all for the earth. Adieu, my friends! I am only going to ride a short essay on the value of family portraits. I shall be back presently. (*He rides slowly away.*)

(*The curtain drops.*)

SCAEVOLA.

That was only the introduction.

PIERROT.

The first act is always of great importance for the lucidity of the whole.

THE OTHER TO SCAEVOLA.

There is much morality in the piece.

SCAEVOLA.

Indeed there is; I feel myself growing better already.

PIERROT.

Music!

Ludwig Tieck (1773–1853).

THE UNACCOUNTABLE STRANGER.

(FROM SCENE IV. OF "A TOPSY-TURVY WORLD.")

(*The room of an Inn.*)

INNKEEPER.

Few enough guests put up at my house nowadays. If this goes on I might as well take down my sign. Dear me, those were other times when there was scarce a piece performed but had a tavern and a host in it. I well remember in how many hundreds of pieces the foundations for the finest plots were laid in this very room. Now it was a prince in disguise, who spent his money here; now it was a prime minister, or a wealthy count at the very least, who lay in ambush here for some conspiracy. Yes, even in things that were translated from the English, I always earned an honest penny. Some drawbacks to be sure there were, when I was required to be a disguised member of a band of sharpers, and then be smartly rated by the moral characters; but there was always healthy activity in it. But now!— Now when a wealthy stranger returns from a journey, he goes to stay with his relatives by way of doing something novel and original, and does not drop his disguise until the fifth act; others appear only upon the street, as if there were no respectable house for them to stay at. All this keeps the audience in a marvellous state of curiosity, but it takes the bread out of our mouth.

(*Enter Anne.*)

ANNE.

You seem to be in low spirits, father.

INNKEEPER.

Yes, child, I'm out of sorts about my calling.

ANNE.

Would you like to be something finer?

INNKEEPER.

No, not exactly; but it vexes me more than I can tell you that there is no more demand for my calling.

ANNE.

Surely in time all that will change for the better.

INNKEEPER.

No, dear daughter. The times do not tend that way. Oh, why was I not a Hofrath! You may look at any playbill this day, it always says at the bottom: "The scene is at the house of the Hofrath." If things go on like this I'll study for a gaoler, for prisons, you know, still occur in patriotic and mediæval pieces. But my son must see to it that he gets to be a Hofrath.

ANNE.

Be comforted, dear father, and do not yield to your melancholy.

INNKEEPER.

I've half a mind to turn poet myself, and invent a new art of poetry which shall supersede the Hofrath pieces, and in which the scene shall invariably play in a tavern.

ANNE.

Do so, dear father, and I will attend to the love-scenes.

INNKEEPER.

Hist! There is a diligence pulling up at the door. Indeed it seems to be an express. Kind heavens, where can the unsophisticated person come from who would put up at this house?

(*Enter a Stranger.*)

STRANGER.

Good morrow, mine host.

INNKEEPER.

Your servant, your servant, noble lord. Who in the world are you to travel *incognito*, and put up at my house? Surely you are of the old school, eh? A man of the good old times! Perhaps translated from the English!

STRANGER.

I am neither a noble lord nor do I travel *incognito*. Can I lodge here this day and night?

INNKEEPER.

My whole house is at your disposal. But really, is there no family in the vicinity you wish to make happy? Or do you wish to marry suddenly, or find a sister?

STRANGER.

No, good friend.

INNKEEPER.

So you are only journeying as a simple, ordinary traveller?

STRANGER.

Yes.

INNKEEPER.

Then you will have but little applause.

STRANGER.

The fellow must be crazy.

(*Enter a Postillion.*)

POSTILLION.

Here is your trunk, sir.

STRANGER.

And here is your fee.

POSTILLION.

Oh, that is very little. I drove down the hill so smartly!

STRANGER.

There.

POSTILLION.

Many thanks. (*Exit.*)

STRANGER.

Shall I succeed in finding her? Oh, how all my thoughts turn to my beloved native shore! How can I endure the sight, when once more I view it?—when the past, with all its joys and pains, passes before my inner vision? Ah, thou poor mortal! what callest thou the past? For thee there is no present. Between the times that are flown and the future thou clingest to a little moment, and joys flit past thee, and do not so much as touch thy heart.

INNKEEPER.

If I may be permitted to ask, I take it your grace is from some old worm-eaten drama that some unknown author has modernised a bit?

STRANGER.

What say you?

INNKEEPER.

I greatly doubt that you will have applause! I hope, at any rate, that you have money? Or is it a part of the plot that you should pretend to be poor?

STRANGER.

You are very inquisitive, good friend.

INNKEEPER.

That's part of my trade, sir, as any schoolboy will tell you. Old people must be old; Telephus must be a beggar; the slave must chatter in keeping with his *rôle*. You can look it up in the *Ars poetica*, to which I too am subject in my office as host.

STRANGER.

Thank you for this graceful frenzy; I have not found so rare a curiosity for a long time. Show me to my room.

(*Exeunt.*)

Ludwig Tieck.

VAN DER KABEL'S LAST WILL AND TESTAMENT.

EVER since Haslau was a duke's residence there was no record of anything having been looked forward to with such curiosity—excepting the birth of a hereditary prince—as the opening of Van der Kabel's last will and testament. Van der Kabel might have been called the

Crœsus of Haslan, and his life a comedy of coins. Seven distant relatives of seven deceased distant relatives of Kabel's indulged in some little hope of a place in the testament, the Crœsus having sworn to remember them there; but the hope was a faint one, as he seemed not greatly to be trusted, not only because he was in the habit of managing his affairs in a grimly moral and unselfish manner—in matters of morality the seven relatives were but beginners—but also because he handled things in so cynical a spirit, and with a heart so full of traps and snares that there was no depending upon him. The continuous smile about his temples and thick lips, and his shrill sneering voice, impaired the good impression which his nobly-formed features and a pair of large hands, dropping New Year's gifts and benefits every day, might have made; therefore the swarms of birds declared this man, this living fruit-tree, which furnished them with food and nests, to be a secret snare, and would not see the visible berries for invisible nooses.

Between two strokes of paralysis he had dictated his testament, and entrusted it to the magistrate. When in a half-dying state he handed the receipt of deposit to the seven heirs-presumptive, he said, in his old tone, that he should greatly deplore it if this sign of his approaching decease would strike down sensible men, whom he liked to picture as laughing heirs rather than as weeping ones.

In due time the seven heirs put in an appearance at the Rathhaus with their receipt of deposit. There was the Right Reverend Glanz, the Police-inspector, the Court-agent Neupeter, the Court-attorney Knoll, the Bookseller Pasvogel, the Preacher Flachs, and Flitte from Elsass. They urged the magistrate to produce the *charte* of the deceased Kabel, and open the will with all the formalities of the law. The high executor of the same was the ruling burgomaster in person; the low executors were the town councillors. Without delay the *charte* and testament were fetched out of the private closet and deposited in the court-room, passed around to the senators and heirs, that they might gaze upon the printed town-seal. The directions written upon the outside of the *charte* were read in a loud voice by the town-scribent to the seven heirs, who were therewith informed that the deceased had in truth deposited the said *charte* with the magistrate, and entrusted it to the same *scrinio rei publicae*, and that on the day when he had thus deposited it he had been in his right mind; last, the seven seals which he himself had placed thereon were examined and found intact. After the town-scribent had entered a registry of all these proceedings, the testament was opened in God's name, and read aloud by the ruling burgomaster as follows :—

"I, Van der Kabel, herewith declare my last will and testament this 7th day of May 179—, here in my house in Haslau in the Hundgasse, without many millions of words, though I was once a German Notary Public and a Dutch dominé. But I believe I am still sufficiently conversant with the art of a notary to be enabled to act the part of a testator and bequeather in a proper and becoming manner.

"As for charitable legacies, so far as they are any concern of the lawyer's, I declare that the poor of this town, 3000 in number, shall receive as many light florins, for which they may celebrate the anniversary day of my death next year by pitching a camp upon the public common; make a merry day of it, and then take the tents to make clothes out of them. To all schoolmasters of our dukedom I bequeath a Louis d'or apiece; and to the Jews of the place I bequeath my pew in church. As I desire to have my testament sub-divided into paragraphs, this may be considered as the first.

"*Paragraph* 2.—Declarations of inheritance and dis-inheritance are universally counted among the essentials of a testament. I therefore bequeath to the Right Reverend

Glanz, the Court-attorney Knoll, the Court-agent Peter Neupeter, the Police-inspector Harprecht, the Preacher Flachs, the Bookseller Pasvogel, and Herr Flitte, nothing for the present, not so much because the most distant relatives can lay no claim to a *Trebellianica*, nor because most of them have enough to pass on to future generations as it is, but mainly because I know from their own assurance that they esteem my humble person more than my large fortune, of which I must therefore dispose otherwise."

"SEVEN ELONGATED FACES HERE STARTED UP."

Seven elongated faces here started up. Especially did the Right Reverend Glanz, a young man noted throughout Germany for his spoken and printed sermons, feel himself keenly injured by such sneers. Flitte, from Elsass, permitted a whispered oath to escape his lips; and as for Flachs, the preacher, his chin grew longer and longer, and threatened to grow into a beard. Many a whispered ejaculation was overheard by the magistrate addressing the late Herr Kabel by such appellatives as scoundrel, fool, antichrist. But the ruling burgomaster waved his hand, the court-attorney and the bookseller set all the elastic springs in their faces as in a trap once more, and the former continued reading albeit with affected seriousness.

"*Paragraph* 3.—Excepting my present residence in the Hundgasse, which, according to this third paragraph, I will leave, with all that pertains thereto, to that one of the afore-mentioned seven gentlemen who, in one half-hour (counting from the reading of the paragraph), shall outdo his six rivals by being the first to shed a tear over me, his deceased relative, before an honourable magistrate, who shall register the fact. Should there be a drought at the end of that time, then the property must accrue to my heir-general, whom I shall forthwith name."

Here the burgomaster shut the will, remarking the conditions to be unusual, but not illegal, and in accordance therewith the court would now proceed to award the house to the first that wept: laid his watch, which pointed to half-past eleven, upon the table, and sat down silently to note, together with the lawyers, in his office of chief executor, who would first shed the required tears.

That so long as this world exists there has ever been a sadder and more ruffled assembly than this of seven dry provinces united as it were to weep, cannot fairly be assumed. At first precious moments were lost in dismay and smiling surprise; it was no easy matter to be transported so abruptly from cursing to weeping. Emotion pure and simple was not to be thought of, that was quite evident; but in twenty-six minutes something might be done by way of enforcing an April shower.

The merchant Neupeter asked if that was not a confounded affair and fool's comedy for a respectable man to be concerned in, and would have nothing to do with it; but at the same time the thought that a house might be washed into his purse on the bosom of a tear strangely moved his lachrymal glands.

The Court-attorney Knoll screwed up his face like a poor workman getting shaved and scratched by an apprentice on Saturday night by the light of a murky little lamp; he was greatly enraged at the misuse of testaments, and was not far removed from shedding tears of wrath.

The sly bookseller at once proceeded to apply himself assiduously to the matter in hand, and sent his memory on a stroll through all the sentimental subjects he was publishing or taking on commission; he looked much like a dog slowly licking off the emetic which the Paris doctor Demet had spread on his nose; some time must necessarily elapse before it could take effect.

Flitte, from Elsass, danced about the Session-room, looked at all the mourners with laughing eyes, and swore, though he was not the richest among them, he could not for the whole of Strasburg and Elsass weep when there was such a joke abroad.

At last the Police-inspector Harprecht looked at him very significantly, and remarked that if Monsieur hoped to extract the required drops from the well-known glands by means of laughter, and fraudulently profit thereby, he begged to remind him that he would gain as little as if he were to blow his nose, for it was well known that the *ductus nasalis* caused as many tears to take that direction as flow into a pew under the most affecting funeral sermon. But the Elsassian assured him that he was only laughing for fun without any serious intentions. The inspector on his part tried to bring something appropriate to the occasion into his eyes by opening them very wide and looking fixedly at one spot.

The preacher Flachs looked like a beggar on horseback, whose nag is running away with him; like the sun shining on a dismal day, his heart, which was piled about with the most suitable clouds of hardships at home and in church, might easily have drawn water on the spot, but unfortunately the house swimming in on the high-tide proved too pleasant a sight, and repeatedly served as a dam.

The Right Reverend Glanz, who knew his nature from his experience in New Years' and funeral sermons, and who was quite certain that he would be able to work upon his own feelings if only he were granted an opportunity of addressing himself in touching language to others, now arose and said with dignity that he was sure every one who had read his printed works would feel convinced that he had a heart in his bosom, and that it was rather to be expected of him to suppress such sacred symbols as tears, so as to deprive no human brother, than to extract them by force. "This heart has overflowed ere now, but it was in secret, for Kabel was my friend," he said, and looked about him.

With satisfaction he saw that they were all sitting there as dry as so many sticks. As things stood now, crocodiles, stags, elephants, and witches could have wept more easily than the heirs, irritated and enraged by Glanz as they were. Only Flachs had a turn of good luck. He thought of Kabel's good deeds and of the shabby dresses and grey locks of his congregation at early service, then in haste he gave a thought to Lazarus and his dogs and to his own lengthy coffin, then to all the people who have been beheaded at one time or other, the "Sorrows of Werther," a battle-field; and last he gave a pitiful thought to himself, how young he was, and how he was working and slaving for a miserable paragraph in a testament. Another good heave with his pump-handle and it would fetch him water and a house.

"Oh, Kabel, my Kabel," continued Glanz, almost weeping at the glad prospect of mournful tears, "when on some future day, beside thy precious bosom now covered with dust, my own lies mouldering——"

"I believe, gentlemen," said Flachs, getting up sadly and overflowing with tears, "I am weeping." Thereupon he sat down again and allowed them to run cheerfully down his cheeks; he was high and dry now; he had successfully angled the house away from Glanz, who was very much put out by his efforts, because he had talked away his appetite all to no purpose. Flachs's emotion was duly registered, and the house in the Hundgasse was legally assigned to him. The burgomaster was gratified that the poor devil should have it. It was the first time in the dukedom of Haslau that the tears of a teacher and preacher, like those of the goddess Freya, had changed into gold. Glanz was profuse in his congratulations, and jocosely reminded Flachs that he himself had perhaps been instrumental in bringing about this happy consummation.

"I BELIEVE, GENTLEMEN, I AM WEEPING."

Jean Paul Friedrich Richter (1763--1825).

DIVISION OF LABOUR IN MATTERS SENTIMENTAL.

LOVE is the perihelion of women—ay, it is the transit of such a Venus through the sun of the ideal world. During this time of their highest refinement of soul they love whatever we love, even though it be Science, and the best world of beauty within us; and they despise whatever we despise, even though it be dress and gossip. These nightingales sing up to the date of the summer solstice; their marriage-day is their longest day. The devil does not take it all at once, but piecemeal day by day. The firm bands of wedlock tie up the wings of poesy; to the free play of fancy marriage means imprisonment on bread and water. Many a time I have followed about one of these poor birds of paradise or peacocks or Psyches during their honeymoon, and picked up the moulted feathers that were strewn about; and when later the husband complained that he had taken unto himself a bald and unlovely bird, I would show him the wasted treasure. Why is this? Because marriage erects a crust of reality about the ideal world; it is much the same case as with the sphere we live on, which, according to Descartes, is a sun enveloped in an earthy shell. A woman lacks the power which a man has to protect the inner structures of air and fancy against the encroachments of the rough outside. Where shall she seek refuge? In her natural keeper. A man should ever stand guard with a spoon over the fluid silver of the feminine intellect, to remove the scum as it rises, that the regulus of the ideal may shine the brighter. But there are two kinds of men: the Arcadians or lyric poets of life, who love for ever, like Rousseau when his hair was grey—such are not to be comforted when the gilt-edged feminine anthology of wit shows no gold as they turn the leaves, as is apt to be the case in books bordered with gold; second, there are the boorish shepherds of to-day, the plebeian poetasters and practical men of business, who thank God when their enchantress, like other enchantresses, changes into a growling domestic cat, and keeps the house free from vermin.

No one suffers from greater *ennui* and anxiety than a fat, weighty, slouching, bass-voiced man of business, who, like the Roman elephants of former times, is called upon to dance upon the slender rope of love, and whose amorous pantomimes always remind me of dormice, that seem to be at a loss about their every movement when sudden warmth interrupts their dormant state. Only with widows, who care less to be loved than to be married, can a heavy man of business begin his romance where the novelists end theirs— viz., at the steps of the altar. Such a man, constructed on the crudest style, would have a load off his mind if he could get some one to love his shepherdess in his name until there was nothing more to be done but to have the wedding; the taking upon myself of such crosses and burdens for another is just what I should feel a calling for. I have often thought of advertising it in public papers (had I not feared it might be taken for a joke), that I offer myself to serve as plenipotentiary to any man of business who has no time to properly make love to a girl. Provided only she be tolerable, I should be willing to swear platonic everlasting affection, make the necessary declarations of love, and, in short, substitute myself in the most disinterested manner, or escort her arm-in-arm through the ups and downs of the land of love, until on the border I could make her over to the prospective bridegroom in proper condition to be married. Instead of marriage by proxy we should thus have love by proxy.

Jean Paul Friedrich Richter.

A TENDER-HEARTED CRITIC.

HE composed reviews as others do prayers—only when in straits; it was like the carrying of water of the Athenian so that he might thus be free to devote himself to his favourite studies without hunger. But his satirical sting he would put in the sheath when writing reviews. "Petty authors," he said, "are always bitter, and great ones are worse than their works. Why should I be less severe upon the genius for his moral faults, such as vanity, than upon the dunce? On the contrary. Poverty and ugliness not self-incurred deserve no disdain; but neither do they deserve it *when* self-incurred, though Cicero be against me. For neither a moral fault nor its punishment can be increased by a physical consequence which may follow or may not follow. Is the spendthrift who is impoverished in consequence of his way of living more to be blamed than the spendthrift who goes free? On the contrary."

Applying this to poor writers whose unconquerable self-conceit hides their worthlessness to themselves, upon whose innocent hearts the critic vents his just wrath over their guilty heads, it is certainly permissible to scoff bitterly at the type, but the individual should be more gently dealt with. Methinks it would be the gold-test of a morally immaculate scholar if he were called upon to review a poor but celebrated book.

Jean Paul Friedrich Richter.

THE ACCIDENT OF THE DISTINGUISHED STRANGER.

(From Scene XII. of "Die Deutschen Kleinstädter.")

(*Scene in the Burgomaster's home in a small town. News has just been received of a traveller, whose carriage has met with an accident in a quarry just outside the town.* Frau Staar, *the Burgomaster's mother, is all in a flutter as to the best way of doing honour to the distinguished stranger, and has sent for all of her female relatives, to obtain their advice in this difficult question.*)

Frau Staar. Frau Brendel.

FRAU BRENDEL.

Here I am, most dear Dame Cousin. I ran so, I have no breath left. I was but just drinking my seventh cup of coffee, but I jumped up and left everything, at your message.

FRAU STAAR.

Greatly obliged, most esteemed Dame Cousin. Have you heard——

FRAU BRENDEL.

I know everything! My maid had gone to market, and the butcher told her his neighbour, the linen-draper, had heard how the bailiff had said to his daughter: Mickey, he said, out in the quarry there are a couple of counts lying, who have broken their arms and legs, and will be here in a minute. The watchman will blow a horn from the turret, the children will strew flowers on their path, the magistrate *in corpore* will go to meet them, and the bells will be rung.

FRAU STAAR.

It is only one, Dame Cousin; only one is lying in the quarry, probably a gentleman of quality. He is to be our guest. The Minister of State has written and has asked my son. Now you can fancy, Dame Cousin, the excitement in the house. And everything is on my shoulders! Everything rests upon me!

(*Enter Frau Morgenroth.*)

FRAU MORGENROTH.

Your servant, most esteemed Dame Cousin. Only see how my walk has heated me. I trust I am not too late? With your permission be it said, I had scarce a thing on me, was singing my morning hymn and combing my poodle-dog. At the third stanza your maid came rushing in. My God, I thought the house was on fire! Then and there I jumped up, the poodle-dog dropped from my lap, the hymnal fell in the coals where I was warming my coffee, the coffee was spilled, and two stanzas of the hymn, "Awake, my heart, and sing!" were burned up.

FRAU STAAR.

I regret it, exceedingly, worthy Dame Cousin——

FRAU MORGENROTH.

Oh, it's of no consequence. I know all. Out in the quarry lie three or four princes; one is dead, the other is gasping a bit now and then. The coachman has broken his neck, the horses are lying stiff and stark. I met the Herr Assistant-Bailiff Balg on the street; his cook told him; she knows it from the wife of the Lottery Inspector; her husband's barber told her all the details.

FRAU STAAR.

Tut, tut, it is not quite so bad as all that. A short time ago a peasant came here from Kabendorf——

FRAU BRENDEL.

I know, he got a solid thaler for a tip.

FRAU MORGENROTH.

Far from it, Dame Cousin, a Louis-d'or it was.

FRAU STAAR.

He had run as fast as he could run.

FRAU BRENDEL.

They say it gave him a pain in his side.

FRAU MONGENROTH.

His nose bled too.

FRAU STAAR.

A person of quality met with an accident.

FRAU BRENDEL.

A count——

FRAU MORGENROTH.

Several princes.

FRAU STAAR.

That we do not know. He must be of noble extraction, for he does not lodge in the "Golden Cat," but at our house, at the express desire of his Honour the Minister of

State. Now, as my son, the Burgomaster and Chief Alderman, represents in his person the whole town as it were, you will, of course, understand that he must do honour to his position.

FRAU BRENDEL.

A banquet at the Town Hall——

FRAU MORGENROTH.

A dance at the archers' guild——

FRAU STAAR.

To-morrow, as you know, is the great *fête*.

FRAU BRENDEL.

Oh yes, the woman that stole the cow nine years ago——

FRAU MORGENROTH.

To-morrow she goes to the pillory. I am looking forward to it with a great deal of pleasure.

FRAU BRENDEL.

I have had a brand-new robe made for the occasion.

FRAU STAAR.

There have been many arrangements made to fitly celebrate this event. But to-day the honour of the town is wholly in our hands; to-day *we* must show what we can do, and with the help of God we will. The tables shall bend under His blessings. My worthy cousins are herewith invited.

FRAU BRENDEL.

I look upon it as a great honour.

FRAU MORGENROTH.

Shall not fail.

FRAU STAAR.

Now, you see, I should like to make the distinguished stranger acquainted with our people of quality. So I have sent for you to ask your advice as to the persons to be invited.

FRAU BRENDEL (*meditating*).

Ah, well, I think——

FRAU MORGENROTH.

You might perhaps———

FRAU BRENDEL.

Invite the Herr Convoy-and-Land-Excise-Commissary Kropt——

FRAU STAAR.

No, Dame Cousin, he gave a banquet the other day on his mother's birthday, and did not ask us.

FRAU BRENDEL.

Ah, indeed!

FRAU MORGENROTH.

Perhaps the Herr Board-of-Revenue-Supernumerary-Secretary Wittmann?

FRAU BRENDEL.

No, Dame Cousin; my husband, the late Herr Brendel, had a law-suit with him about his drains.

FRAU MORGENROTH.

That alters the matter.

FRAU STAAR.

I thought of the Herr Post-Luggage-Inspector-General Holbein?

FRAU MORGENROTH.

For heaven's sake, Dame Cousin! he has a most insufferable wife! There's hardly a Sunday passes but she has a new dress, and the way she goes rustling past my pew——

FRAU BRENDEL.

She carries her head higher than need be——

FRAU MORGENROTH.

And we all remember her so well——

FRAU BRENDEL.

Yes, when she wore a grey spencer with a green apron.

FRAU MORGENROTH.

There are strange rumours where she takes it from.

FRAU BRENDEL.

No, I would rather suggest the Herr County-Tavern-Harvest-and-Quarter-Tax-and-Impost-Controller Kunkel.

FRAU STAAR.

Don't mention him, worthy Cousin; he is a rude fellow, who has no manners! Would you believe it, he did not so much as call upon us in a decent and proper manner, the pert addle-head! He left his card, fancy! One might sooner ask the Herr Penal-Raft-Commander Weidenbaum.

FRAU BRENDEL.

No, Dame Cousin, for heaven's sake, no! You remember how the wicked fellow was seen to talk to my brother-in-law's step-daughter three times, and how consequently he intended to marry her? Now he holds himself aloof, and has made the poor girl the talk of the town.

FRAU STAAR.

Goodness me, is there any one we can ask then?

FRAU MORGENROTH.

There comes Cousin Sperling.

(*Enter Sperling, with a large bouquet.*)

SPERLING.

Frau Under-Tax-Receiver, Frau Chief-Raft-and-Fishery Master, Frau Town-Excise-Treasury-Secretary, your humble servant! I was in my garden—the Herr Vice-Church-Superintendent sent for me—I ran like a sunbeam!

Scarce did I take the time to cull these children of the spring.

THE THREE LADIES.

Do you know already?

SPERLING.

I know all. A celebrated professor—carriage smashed up—nose ditto—letter of recommendation from the Minister of State.

FRAU STAAR.

A professor, you say?

FRAU BRENDEL.

Only a professor?

FRAU MORGENROTH.

Oh, my delicious coffee that was spilled in the fire!

FRAU STAAR.

Never believe it, Dame Cousin. All my life I have heard that ministers take little interest in professors. No, no, there is some misunderstanding.

SPERLING.

Nay, but I will stand up for my opinion that the man who has had his nose smashed is a learned professor, on his way from Egypt or Weimar, where he has either been measuring the pillar of Pompey, or else seen Wieland put his head out of the window. In short, there is no time to be lost. Here are the flowers. Now get me some children. Children I must have! Then he may come and see what the town of Krähwinkel can do!

FRAU STAAR.

Gently, gently; they shall be here at once.

(*Exit.*)

(SPERLING *turns aside and mutely practises the pantomimes of reception.*)

FRAU MORGENROTH.

Have you noticed, worthy cousin, what ridiculous airs the old lady is putting on?

FRAU BRENDEL.

Yes, indeed, Dame Cousin; she puffs herself up like dough in the oven.

FRAU MORGENROTH.

Goodness me! Her husband was only *Under*-Tax-Receiver.

FRAU BRENDEL.

When he died he left a debt to the Treasury.

FRAU MORGENROTH.

Dear me, and I wonder what the banquet will be like? Do you remember that joint eight weeks ago? It was horribly burned.

FRAU BRENDEL.

And how she looks! what will she put on?

FRAU MORGENROTH.

Not much choice. She has but three gowns.

FRAU BRENDEL.

To be sure, the brown one——

FRAU MORGENROTH.

And the white one——

FRAU BRENDEL.

And her stuff gown.

FRAU MORGENROTH.

She had that made for the first christening at the burgomaster's.

FRAU BRENDEL.

Begging your pardon, Dame Cousin, it was made when the Vice-Church-Superintendent married his second wife.

FRAU MORGENROTH.

Who was another such fool.

FRAU BRENDEL.

You're right there, quite right there.

(*Enter Frau Staar with two children, the latter eating enormous slices of bread and butter.*)

ENTER FRAU STAAR WITH TWO CHILDREN.

FRAU STAAR.

There are the children.

SPERLING.

Come along then!

FRAU STAAR.

Drop a curtsey to your dear Dame Cousin first, there's a good child! Now shake hands; that's right!

FRAU BRENDEL (*wiping the butter from her fingers*).
Enchanting little creatures. God bless them!

FRAU MORGENROTH.
The very pictures of our dear Dame Cousin.

FRAU BRENDEL.
I trust they have had the pox!

FRAU STAAR.
Not yet. My son wished to have them inoculated, but I will never give my consent. I would not forestall the Almighty.

SPERLING.
Children, lay your bread and butter aside.

CHILDREN.
No, no.

SPERLING.
Well, then, take the flowers in the other hand.
(*Enter Herr Staar and the Burgomaster.*)

HERR STAAR (*hastily*).
They are just driving in through the gate. The street is full of boys. They are running along by the carriage, and yelling at the top of their voice.

BURGOMASTER (*hastily*).
He comes, he comes! The watchman is standing ready with his trumpet.

SPERLING.
Goodness gracious! The children are so awkward——

HERR STAAR.
All you have to do is to strew your flowers and fling them in his face.
(*The blast of a trumpet very much out of tune.*)

BURGOMASTER.

Quick, quick! All go to meet him!

HERR STAAR.

The children lead the way!

SPERLING (*snatches the bread and butter out of their hands and throws it on the table*).

Leave your bread and butter here.

HERR STAAR (*urging the children toward the door*).

Quick, quick!

CHILDREN (*crying*).

I want my bread and butter! My bread and butter!

BURGOMASTER (*following them*).

Will you hold your tongues?

FRAU STAAR.

Frau Chief-Raft-and-Fishery-Master, you will have the kindness to precede me.

FRAU BRENDEL.

Never, Frau Town-Excise-Treasury-Secretary. I most urgently beg you——

FRAU MORGENROTH.

Frau Under-Tax-Receiver, the honour is due to *you*.

FRAU STAAR.

The heavens preserve me! I am at home in this house.

FRAU BRENDEL.

I know my place——

FRAU MORGENROTH.

I will not stir a step.

(*The three begin to bow and curtsey, and all talk at the same time.*)

(THE CURTAIN DROPS.)

August von Kotzebue (1761–1819).

HOW THE VICAR CAME AROUND.

THE Frau Obersteuerrätin was "auntie" to the whole world; and indeed she deserved the name, for she was a motherly friend, counsellor, and helper to all who came within her domain: she was the best and most charitable of women, judging mildly of the weaknesses of others so long as her own little weaknesses were respected. She overlooked the eccentricities of her clerical brother, which he committed in a state of absent-mindedness, and she did not raise any objections to Susie's marvellous *naïveté*, though often enough it caused her bitter dilemmas.

It was a warm May day on which the Vicar entered the room with his usual greeting: "Good morning, Auntie—good morning, Susie."

Auntie nodded pleasantly. Susie, who was sitting by her on the sofa, knitting a white stocking, arose, dropped a little familiar curtsey, and said: "*Votre servante*, Uncle."

"But, Heaven preserve us, what is the matter with you to-day, Vicar?" said Aunt Rosmarin.

"How so?" queried the Vicar, putting his hands in all of his pockets in a vain search for a handkerchief with which to wipe the perspiration from his brow.

"It's very likely you have your wig in your pocket," said Auntie, "for your handkerchief is on your head."

"On my head," exclaimed the Vicar in surprise, and putting his hand there he found it. "I shouldn't be greatly surprised if you were right, Auntie; it's a hot, hot day; the sun was burning, my back was burning; I came from town, so I took off my wig to cool my head, spread my handkerchief over the latter, and lay down in a corn-field."

Again he began to search his pockets, while Susie made room for him on the sofa, and went out to get him a refreshing drink of water and raspberry syrup.

"What are you looking for, Vicar?" asked Auntie.

"If I mistake not, I brought a letter for you from town; but what has become of it is more than I can tell. I think it is from the Burgomaster. Seek and ye shall find."

"But, Vicar, first of all, put on your wig—this is very indecent. It is an insult to your congregation to walk about bald-headed."

"I should hope not. But in that case I trust that there would be bears to obey me, like the prophet Elisha, and devour all bad boys who would make bold to have a laugh at me. But, *ad vocem*, my wig, Auntie; what did you do with it?"

"What did I do with it? You did not entrust it to my keeping. Perhaps you lost it on the way!"

"Heaven preserve us! It was my best wig. You are right, Auntie; it is lying in the grass, together with the Burgomaster's letter, precisely on the spot where I myself lay a quarter of an hour ago, in the shadow of the corn."

Auntie seized her bell. The maid appeared; the Inspector was called, and ordered to send for the wig and the letter—as quick as possible. Auntie was quite as impatient to hide the Vicar's baldness as to read the Burgomaster's letter. The shape of the wig, as well as colour and address of the letter, were explicitly described to the Inspector, and he forthwith sent two grooms, four threshers, and one dairy-boy out upon all roads, footpaths, and byways that run between Nieder-Fahren and Waiblingen. He stationed himself upon the hill by the wind-mill and reconnoitred the field of action through a telescope. Such excellent arrangements could not fail to bring about the desired result. In half-an-hour the seven messengers returned to the house led by the wig, the letter, and the Inspector.

Sure enough the letter was from the Burgomaster. It contained nothing less than a formal invitation to the Frau Obersteuerrätin, together with her brother and Fräulein

Susie and the Inspector Säblein, to the wedding of the Burgomaster's eldest daughter.

Although Auntie felt very much flattered by this attention of the Burgomaster, with whom she was but slightly acquainted, there were some difficulties in the way which must needs be talked over in a family council.

Auntie was very much averse to bringing Susie into contact in any way with the young gentlemen of Waiblingen. First of all, Susie was seventeen years old—a fact which did not seem at all portentous to the child, but all the more so to her cautious aunt. Second, Susie was beautiful as any Susanna, not excepting the one in the Old Testament. Thirdly, she had the prospect of inheriting a considerable fortune, and Auntie had no notion of giving up her darling to the first-comer. Fourthly, Susie was exceedingly inexperienced, though she was not wanting in the usual measure of laudable curiosity.

The young men of Waiblingen were in no way suited to be the companions of such a girl. First, because a great many of them were handsome, which is a very bad thing; and secondly, they were all great lovers of comedies and novels; they kept up an amateur stage; and at Waiblingen two booksellers made their living with circulating libraries —a bad sign of our times! Thirdly, even though one might have forgiven them their sleek faces and romantic tendencies, few of them had a fortune that would weigh in the scales against Aunt Rosmarin's possessions, nor were they of a rank to be compared with the title of Obersteuerrat.

Auntie had pondered this question long since in the silence of her own heart, and she had come to the conclusion that it was best to take defensive measures against the elegant world of Waiblingen. Susie seldom went there, and still seldomer were there any young guests invited to Nieder-Fahren.

After ripe consideration it was decided in the family

council, in which the Inspector also took part, to go to the wedding at the Burgomaster's, but not without the utmost caution.

Auntie undertook to call Susie's attention to the dangers arising out of the affections. The Vicar was to add spiritual admonition, and the Inspector—who had the reputation of having been a good waltzer in his younger years, while now he was unfortunately a bachelor of fifty-six—promised to renew Susie's dancing-lessons. At the wedding all three pledged each other to do their best, and not lose the damsel out of sight.

Hereupon tailors, shoemakers, and milliners were put in a fair way of getting a living. Auntie was desirous of doing whatever was due to her rank, and she also had the pardonable pride of showing off Susie's beauty to the best advantage.

Susie was delighted with the elaborate preparations—all this was a new experience. She put her dancing-master quite out of breath, and her only regret was that his feet being fifty-six years old were not as flexible as hers being seventeen. Joy and nature taught her to dance; but Säblein took it all upon his account. He was nothing loath to practise his noble half-forgotten art, the less so as the family council had decreed that he alone should be Susie's partner at the wedding.

Unfortunately this plan miscarried, and the reason was this. The day before the wedding all the dances were to be reviewed once more under the supervision of the Vicar and Auntie. Before the spectators came, Säblein exerted himself more than was good for him to dance at least no worse than his clever pupil. She floated about like a butterfly, and in her rapture took many a step which was no less graceful for not coming under any rule. Säblein, in an ecstasy of delight, rashly undertook to show her the acme of his art. Years ago he could dance *entrechats*,—

ambition pricked him to make a trial once more. His first attempt was half a failure, his second was a whole one. His lank, thin-whittled legs, which had never been a cause of reproach to him, got so hopelessly and abnormally entangled that, the rest of his body keeping in motion, a disaster was inevitable. The unfortunate dancing-master fell in a most *un*masterly manner upon the floor, and as a falling pine uproots all blooming bushes that surround it, so he pulled down the little sylph that was frolicking about him.

The Vicar, just about to open the door from without, heard the fall which shook the very foundations of the house, and entered hastily. It was partly this haste and partly the Vicar's near-sightedness, which he was wont to forget in his absent-mindedness, which became the cause of a second accident. He stepped upon the dancing-master's leg, which the latter drew back with pardonable abruptness, thereby robbing the Vicar of his equilibrium. Before he had time to beg pardon he lay upon the floor along with the others. While his powdered wig was propelled by the rapid motion far under the sofa, his short legs performed some wonderful antics, and at last turned up their soles toward Heaven, as if imploring its aid.

The whole occurrence was a very short one. The Vicar was the first to gather himself up, and, mistaking Susie's snowy, befrilled cap for his escaped wig, he seized it without more ado, and covered his head therewith because he heard the Obersteuerrätin at the door. Susie was on her feet too before Auntie entered. But Säblein sat upon the floor making horrible faces, for he had hurt his hip.

"Great heavens!" cried Aunt Rosmarin, clapping her hands together, and looking now at the Inspector's painful grimaces, now at her brother's head in a woman's cap. "Are you playing a farce? Are you forgetful of all decency? Do you call this good breeding? and especially you, Vicar?" . . .

"And pray, why is it especially I?" he asked with a touch of sensitiveness, for he did not greatly like his sister's sermons.

Here Susie gained a hearing, and quickly restored peace by giving her perplexed aunt the explanation to this riddle, and laughingly exchanging her cap for the wig.

This apparently unimportant occurrence was the first

THE VICAR HASTENS TO COVER HIS BALDNESS.

cause to all following misfortunes; for Säblein went limping about for many days, and consequently could not dance at the wedding.

. . . . .

Aunt Rosmarin had her suspicions when she saw Susie, now swimming in bliss, now abject and mournful, or when she heard how Susie went walking in the park evening after evening, and when she herself, putting aside her dread of rheumatism, secretly followed her there, but always found Susie alone.

Auntie shook her head, and said to her brother: "I believe, Vicar, our little baroness is in love." She had hit it, but wise Auntie never thought of the baron. "We must keep our eyes on this marvellously mysterious child, for she will confess nothing to me. It is a delicate task, I know, and I myself am too old to run after her in the park every day the Lord makes. And, of course, Vicar, it is not a matter to be entrusted to the domestics; that were contrary to all dignity and order. But at the same time she must be watched, for these constant visits to the park for the last fortnight must have some good reason."

"Trust me, Auntie," said the Vicar—"trust me; I will guard the park like a spy. Murder shall out. This is just the sort of thing that suits me."

The plans were laid with great subtlety. The Vicar looked unconcerned in Susie's presence, and the following day at sunset he started upon his errand.

He was indeed very lucky, for the Baron was really in the park. He was twice lucky, for it so happened that he entered the park from the side where it touched the woods, and where the Baron was wont to enter it. He was in the habit of leaving his horse there, and giving it to the servant to hold.

The servant, finding his task decidedly dull, had to-day tied the Baron's horse to a young birch-tree and gone about his own affairs. The Vicar looked at the elegantly-equipped noble steed from all sides, and nodding his head thoughtfully, unfastened it, saying to himself, "I'll take it home to our stable; the owner will no doubt apply for it, and all the rest will follow. In truth, it's a shrewd plan!"

But there was an unfavourable circumstance. There seemed to be a secret understanding between the horse and his master. He most decidedly objected to being pulled along by the bridle; no amount of patting and caressing had any effect; he planted his fore-legs firmly on the ground and pulled his head back.

"Friend," said the Vicar, "at best you are but a beast, and you have no eyes behind your ears. I'll wager you will go willingly." With that he climbed upon the noble animal's back, which stood as patient as a lamb. To be sure it was thirty years or more since the good Vicar had been on horseback, and, moreover, his legs were about two inches too short for the stirrups; but then it was to be but a few moments' ride, and it was well to show Aunt Rosmarin that he had not forgotten the chivalrous arts over his theology. Over and above all this there was danger in delay.

So he belaboured the horse's shanks with his boots, and the steed, taken aback by such ill-treatment, at once began to canter along the woody path, across the field into the open road, having for weeks past traversed no other way than this with the Baron. The Vicar, in danger of losing his balance, with laudable precaution clasped his fingers in the mane of his Pegasus. Finding himself upon the road, however, instead of parading under Auntie's window, he tried to grasp the bridle. Over this attempt he came very near losing both stirrups. Making sure of these once more, he let the bridle alone. For a while these two purposes warred with each other, and between times he admonished the fiery horse with many caresses to stand still. But it was all in vain; and when in his despair he pulled the line too tight, at the same time clasping the horse's sides firmly with his legs, it forthwith rose upon its hind feet, and, to his inexpressible horror, began to walk about like a human being, and perform tricks which were positively not to the Vicar's taste just at that moment.

He now succumbed to fate and to his horse, clinging to the latter with hands and feet while it sped along at a full gallop till the poor Vicar was deaf and blind with dizziness.

"Out of the depths have I cried unto Thee," he sighed. "If this isn't the very devil himself! Had I but left the beast standing where I was how happy should I be!"

It so happened that right here the road had been barred by peasants in honour of the grazing cattle.

"Te Deum laudamus!" cried the Vicar. "Here surely

"FELT THE WAVES PENETRATE HIS BLACK SILK STOCKINGS."

this rascal of a horse will come to a stand." But the steed leaped over as if he had wings, so that the horseman's hair stood on end, and his hat and wig took flight in horror. "I have learned to ride better than you, for I still hold my seat," said the good Vicar in Christian tranquillity to the truants, not venturing to turn and look after them.

"Whither, in the Lord's name? Twice four-and-twenty hours at this rate and we shall have spanned this terrestrial globe and come out on the other side at Nieder-Fahren." As he was saying this they approached a bridge. The Vicar, in terror lest the horse in its blind rage might miss the bridge and leap into the stream, tugged frantically at the line on the side nearest to the bridge. But he tugged too long; the provoking animal thereupon left the bridge lying at the right, and jumped into the water. The Vicar came very near fainting away when he became aware of floating between heaven and water, and felt the waves penetrate his black silk stockings, and soon after his velvet breeches, until they played about his hips.

The horse, which was a capital swimmer, reached the opposite shore in safety, regained the road, and jauntily continued its journey until it reached Schloss Malzen, where it darted joyfully with the Vicar into the open door of the stable, standing still at last in its own familiar stall.

The servants in the courtyard ran in after him, helped the rider out of the saddle, and anxiously inquired how he had come into possession of the Baron's horse.

An unspeakable sense of blissful security seized the much-tried clergyman as once more he felt *terra-firma* beneath his feet. Deprived of his hat and his wig, to be sure, and the lower half of his body dripping with water, far from home, the approaching night before him, and upon the domain of the arch-enemy of Nieder-Fahren—all these circumstances served to make the situation not altogether agreeable. But what cared he so long as his life was saved?

While the servants were storming the breathless gentleman with questions the Baron's steward appeared upon the scene, and hospitably urged him to come into the house. As upon his request a carriage was promised him to take him back to Nieder-Fahren, he consented to enter and rest before his departure. Meanwhile nearly two hours passed; no carriage appeared, and the Vicar began to wax suspicious lest he was being treated as a prisoner for having run away with the horse, although he had repeatedly affirmed that it was he who had been run away with. He finally decided to take flight. He arose, and was about to open the door, when Baron Pompeius von Malzen entered, having arrived upon his lackey's horse while the despairing lackey was on a search for the Baron's steed through the whole of Ober and Nieder-Fahren.

The Baron, recognising the worthy uncle of his wife—the tale concerning the arrival of the horse with a wigless and decidedly damp clergyman had been related to him in the courtyard—at once escorted him to a better room, ordered dry clothing, and gave the Vicar time to change his garments. His departure was quite out of the question for that night; the Baron would not let the opportunity escape him to heap coals of fire upon the head of one of his adversaries, to entertain him sumptuously, and overwhelm him with courtesies.

Susie's uncle, surprised at the Baron's cordial manner, soon felt very comfortable behind smoking viands and bottles of Burgundy. Still, however soft and firm he sat upon the luxurious cushions of his chair, he could not for the whole evening rid himself of the notion, as he said, of having "the hellish beast" between his legs.

"At the same time I am more grateful to my good horse than I can tell you," said the Baron, "for bringing me the uncle of my beloved wife. I have long wished for the honour of your acquaintance, so that I might beg for your kind intercession. I adore my wife, and a separation is about to be forced upon us. My wife has forgiven me— nay, more, she loves me; she does not desire a separation, and yet——"

"Loves you? Does not desire a separation?" cried the Vicar, shaking his head, which was adorned with the Baron's best cotton night-cap.

"Will you have proofs?" said the Baron. "Ah, I will

be frank with our dear uncle. You shall know all. This hour may decide our life's happiness." He thereupon went and fetched Susie's letters.

And indeed from his niece's letters the Vicar saw that between her and the Baron there was eternal peace, and a great deal more that is eternal.

He seemed greatly touched as he laid the letters down; he stretched out his hand across the table, and said—

"Baron, I for my part will make peace with you. Susie shall be yours, and the law-suit may go to the dogs. But we must handle Aunt Rosmarin carefully. She is a dear, good woman, but she has peculiar ideas about some things. Up to this day I was a raging Saul, henceforth I shall be a gentle Paul, and shall begin at once upon my work of conversion."

The Baron jumped up, embracing and kissing brave Saul in a rapture of delight.

. .

Meanwhile Aunt Rosmarin had heard her brother relate the story of his adventure. When he told her how he found the horse, her eyes sparkled with pleasure at the discovery. The fact of his getting into the saddle she accompanied with the remark: "You don't know how to ride. Every cobbler to his last!" When he came to his aerial flight across the bar, and his swim through the stream, she jumped up, nervously seized her brother's two hands and cried, "For heaven's sake, what dangers were you subject to!" And she did not regain her composure until he halted before the horse's crib. Then, as the Baron came in, her face lengthened; the warmer the Vicar grew in chanting his praises the cooler was Aunt Rosmarin. And when he had the audacity to add, "Susie does not seem to dislike the Baron; seems to me we had better let the law-suit go, and let things take their course," Auntie shook her head, while she gazed at her brother from top to toe with wide open eyes.

"Well, I never!" said she. "I fear me the ride and the fright have done you some injury. If the Baron did not turn you out into the pitch-dark night, giving you lodging and food instead, he did no more than heathens and barbarians would have done. You need not think I'll give him Susie for his roasts and his Burgundy. A weak sort of man you must be to be willing to sacrifice your principles and all the disgrace and sorrow our family has suffered through the Baron for one poor supper."

Then did the Vicar arise in indignation and say, "Why, Aunt Rosmarin, has all Christian charity gone out of you? I wish then that *you* had ridden the Baron's horse in my stead; I wish *you* had been called upon to fly through the air, and to swim through the surging billows, to make the acquaintance of an honourable man Then you would think different."

Aunt Rosmarin thought her brother's remarkable wish very improper, as well as insulting. She thereupon gave him a lecture lasting three hours, and having for its perpetual refrain, "I will not hear another word about the Baron. In future I shall act alone, in strict accordance with my principles."

Heinrich Zschokke (1771–1848).

THE MAN WHO SOLD HIS SHADOW.

WHAT was my horror to see the man in grey come behind with the evident purpose of accosting me. He raised his hat and bowed with a more profound obeisance than I had ever been honoured with. I returned the courtesy, and stood bare-headed in the sun as if rooted to the ground. I stared at him in an agony of terror, like a bird under the spell of a serpent. He seemed greatly embarrassed, did not raise his eyes, bowed repeatedly, approached me, and began to speak in a gentle, wavering voice, with the tone of a mendicant.

"I trust your Honour will have the kindness to pardon my presumption in venturing to address you, being a stranger. I have a very particular request to make. Graciously permit me, sir——"

"For heaven's sake," I cried in terror, "what can I do for a man who——" We both stopped, and, as it seemed to me, we blushed.

After a moment of silence he began again. "During the short time that it was my good fortune to enjoy the presence of your company, I have had occasion more than once to gaze—if you will permit me to say so—with inexpressible admiration upon the well-formed, handsome shadow which, with an air of noble disdain, as if scorning to set any value upon it, you cast behind you. It is a superb shadow you have there lying at your feet. Pardon the temerity of the suggestion; would it be possible to induce you to sell this same shadow to me?"

He ceased speaking, and it seemed as if a wheel were going around in my head. What was I to make of this remarkable proposition? He must be crazy, I thought, and in an altered voice, more suited to the humility of his tone, I replied—

"Go to, good friend; have you not enough with your own shadow?" What you propose is a very strange bargain." He interrupted me with, "I have many a useful thing in my pocket that your Honour might find convenient; for this inestimable shadow there is no price I should deem too high. To show my gratitude to you, sir, I would give you your own choice of all the treasures I carry about with me. I have miraculous wands of the witch-hazel, I have Mercury's cap and potent draughts, the dish-cloth of Roland's page, and a Homunculus, but best of all is the magic purse of Fortunatus." "A magic purse," I interrupted him, and great as was my horror, he had captured my sensibilities with that word. A deathly giddiness came over me, and rows of ducats seemed to twinkle before my eyes.

"Would your Honour have the goodness to examine the purse? He put his hand in his pocket and drew out a medium-sized, strongly-made bag of leather, with heavy leather cords for draw-strings, and handed me the same. I put my hand in and pulled out ten golden coins, and ten more, and ten more, and ten more. I held out my hand to him: "It is a bargain; for the bag I'll give you my shadow." He clasped my hand to seal the bargain, and then quickly knelt down before me, and with marvellous dexterity loosening my shadow from the grass, he lifted it, rolled it up, folded it, and at last put it in his pocket. He arose, bowed once more, and then vanished among the rose bushes. Methought I heard him laugh softly to himself. I held the bag tightly in my hands. Round about me the earth was bright with sunshine, and within me there was as yet no wisdom.

. . . . .

Meanwhile it had grown late, and, unnoticed, the dawn preceding sunrise was brightening the sky. It was a very unpleasant surprise when I looked up and saw the glory of colour unfold in the east. There was no refuge on this open plain that I was traversing from the approaching sun, and that too at an hour when shadows sport their utmost extension! And I was not alone! I glanced at my companion, and once more I trembled. He was no other than the man in grey.

He smiled at my consternation, and continued, without giving me time to speak: "Let us, true to the custom of the world, be united for a while by the reciprocal advantages to be derived from such a union; we have time enough to separate later on. This road which you are taking happens to be my road also. I see you turn pale before the rising sun. I will lend you your shadow for the time of our companionship, and in return I will ask you to tolerate me at your side. You have lost your servant Bendel; I will yield you as good service. You do not look upon me with favour; this I greatly regret. I can be of service to you, nevertheless. The devil is not as black as he is painted. It is true you offended me yesterday; to-day I bear you no ill-will, and I have shortened the way for you so far, as you yourself must confess. Will you not give your shadow a trial?"

The sun had risen, early wayfarers came along the road; however distasteful it might be, I accepted his proposal. Smiling, he allowed my shadow to glide upon the ground. It fell into place on the shadow of my horse, and cheerily trotted along beside me. Strange feelings took possession of me. I rode past a group of country people, who, with uncovered head, respectfully made room for a person of quality. I rode on, and looked with greedy eyes and a beating heart down from my horse upon the shadow that once was mine, and which I had now borrowed from a stranger, ay, from an enemy.

The latter walked unconcernedly beside me, whistling a tune—he on foot, I on horseback! A tremor seized me; the temptation was too great: I suddenly turned my horse's head, gave him the spurs, and off I went in a full canter down a byway; but I did not succeed in bringing the shadow with me; as the horse turned it slipped down, and awaited its lawful master in the road. There was nothing for it but a shamefaced admission of defeat. I rode back, and the man in grey, first finishing the tune he was whistling, laughed at me, pulled my shadow straight again, and informed me that it would not stick to me, and be content to

"OFF I WENT IN A FULL CANTER."

stay with me, until it was once more my lawful property. "I hold you by your shadow," he added; "and you will not escape me. A rich man like you cannot get on without a shadow. You are to be blamed in so far as you did not find that out before."

A. von Chamisso (1781–1838).

THE GHOST OF DR. ASCHER.

THE night I spent at Goslar something very remarkable occurred. Terror seizes me even now as I think back. I am not timid by nature, but I have a mortal terror of ghosts. What is fear? Is it a product of the understanding or of the soul? About this question I had many a discussion with Dr. Saul Ascher in Berlin when we met in the Café Royal, where I used to dine. He would have it that we fear a thing because our reason recognises therein due cause for terror. While I was eating and drinking to my satisfaction he was fond of constantly demonstrating the fine qualities of Reason. Toward the end of his demonstration he would look at his watch, and he always ended with: "Reason is the highest principle!" Reason! When I so much as hear the word I see before me Dr. Ascher with his abstract legs, his tight waistcoat of transcendental grey, and his harsh bitter-cold face, which might have served as a title-vignette to a book on geometry. The man was a straight line personified. In his search after the Positive the poor man had philosophised all grandeur out of life, all sunbeams, all faith, and all flowers, and all that remained to him was a cold, positive grave. He cherished a pet aversion for the Apollo of Belvedere and for Christianity. He even went so far as to write a pamphlet about the latter, proving it to be unreasonable and untenable. Indeed he wrote a host of books, in each of which Reason brags of its own excellence. The poor Doctor was serious enough about it, and in this respect they deserve esteem. But it was just this which was the best joke of all—that he would put on so fatuously serious a mien when he could not understand what every child understands by very reason of its childhood. I called upon this reasonable Doctor in his own house once or twice, and I found beautiful women there, for Reason does not forbid sensuality. Once when I intended to call upon him his servant said: "The Doctor has just died." It did not impress me any more strongly than if he had said: "The Doctor is gone out."

But to return to Goslar. "The highest principle is Reason!" I said consolingly to myself as I got into bed. It did not answer the purpose, however. I had just been reading that horrible story in Varnhagen von Ense's *Deutsche Erzählungen*, which I had brought with me from Clansthal, how a son, whose father intended to murder him, was warned at night by his mother's ghost. The marvellous effectiveness of the story caused me to shiver with horror while reading. Then, too, ghost stories excite the most uncanny sensations when read on a journey, and especially at night in a town, in a house, in a room where one has never been. How many horrible things may have happened upon this very spot where I am now lying? One cannot refrain from conjecturing. Moreover, the moon shone so doubtfully into the room; all sorts of uncalled-for shadows were moving along the wall, and when I raised myself in bed to look closer, I saw——

There is nothing more weird than to come unintentionally upon one's own face in a mirror by the light of the moon. At the same moment a lumbering sleepy clock began to strike, and, moreover, it struck so long and so slowly that after the twelfth stroke I verily believed twelve hours had gone by, and it would have to begin over again and strike twelve once more. Between the last beat and the last but one, another clock struck very rapidly with a rasping shrillness, put out of temper perhaps by the dulness of its kinswoman. When at last both iron tongues subsided and the silence of death reigned in the house, it seemed to me suddenly as if I heard something slur and drag along the passage just outside of my door like the unsteady gait of a man. At last my door was opened, and slowly the late Dr. Saul Ascher walked into my room. A cold chill passed through my bones. I trembled like a leaf, and hardly did I dare to look at the ghost. He looked just the same as ever—the same transcendental grey waistcoat, the same abstract legs, and the same mathematical face: only that the latter was a little yellower than I remembered it, and the mouth, which had always formed two angles of $22\frac{1}{2}$ degrees, was tightly shut, and the circles of his eyes had a longer radius. Wavering and leaning, as had been his custom, upon a slender stick, he approached me, and in his usual lazy dialect said pleasantly, "Do not be afraid, and don't believe me to be a ghost. It is an illusion of the senses if you imagine you see a ghost. What is a ghost? Give me a definition. Deduce the conditions for the possibility of a ghost. In what reasonable relation to your reason would such a phenomenon be! Reason, I say Reason——"

And now the ghost proceeded to analyse Reason, quoting Kant, Part 2, Division 1, Book 2, Proposition 3, "The distinction between phenomena and noumena," constructing the problematic belief in ghosts, piling syllogism upon syllogism with the logical conclusion that there is positively no such thing as a ghost. All the while the perspiration was cold upon my back, my teeth were chattering; in my terror I nodded unqualified assent to every sentence in which the spook-doctor had proved the absurdity of my fears, and the latter was demonstrating so eagerly that in a moment of abstraction, instead of his gold watch he pulled a handful of worms out of his vest pocket, and discovering his error he replaced them with ridiculous nervous haste. "Reason is the highest——" The clock struck one, and the ghost vanished.

Heinrich Heine (1799–1856).

TOURISTS AT THE BROCKEN.

UPON entering the Brocken-house a somewhat unusual romantic mood came over me. After long and lonely wanderings among rocks and hemlocks, one seems suddenly transported to a house in the clouds. I found the house full of guests; and as it becomes a man of wise foresight, I thought of the night and of the discomfort pertaining to a couch of straw. With a dying voice I ordered tea, whereupon the Herr host was so reasonable as to be convinced that an invalid like me must needs have a decent bed. . . . Having refreshed myself, I climbed up to the look-out, and found a diminutive gentleman with two ladies, one young, the other elderly. When I was a boy I thought of nothing but of wondrous fairy-tales, and every pretty woman with ostrich feathers on her head I took to be a fairy-queen. If by good chance the hem of her dress was bedraggled, I took her for a water-nymph. Had I looked upon the fair one with those boyish eyes, had I seen her then upon the Brocken, I should certainly have said to myself, this is the sylph of the mountain, and she has just uttered the charm which makes all below appear so wondrously beautiful. What relation the very lithe gentleman bore to the ladies whom he accompanied I could not ascertain. His was a thin peculiar figure. His little head, sparsely covered with grey hair, which fell over his low forehead nearly to his pale greenish eyes; his clumsy nose far protruding; his mouth and chin timidly drawing back in the direction of his ears. This little face seemed to be modelled out of a certain kind of delicate, yellowish clay, such as sculptors use for their first design; and when his narrow lips were shut tight, a thousand little folds, light and semicircular, covered his cheeks. The little man did not say a word, only now and then, when the elder lady whispered something kind to him, he would smile like a pug with a cold in his head. . . . While we were speaking it began to grow dusk; the air grew chillier, the sun sank lower, and students, travelling journeymen, and a couple of honest bourgeois with their wives and daughters, crowded upon the platform to see the sunset. It is a marvellous sight, tuning the soul to prayer. During a quarter of an hour we all stood in solemn silence, and saw the gorgeous globe of fire slowly sink in the west; our faces reflected the evening glory, our hands were folded involuntarily; it seemed as if we stood a silent congregation in the aisle of a cathedral, and the priest was holding up the body of the Lord, and from the organ sounded Palestrina's immortal anthem.

As I stood thus enwrapped in the fervour of devotion, I heard some one calling out beside me, "How beautiful is nature on the whole!" These words proceeded out of the overflowing breast of my room-mate, the young merchant. I was at once landed thereby in my work-day mood, and was now able to make a great many brilliant remarks to the ladies about the sunset. I escorted them to their room as if nothing had happened. I believe we talked about Angora cats, Etruscan vases, Turkish shawls, macaroni, and Lord Byron, from whose poems the elder lady recalled some sunset passages, which she recited with a pretty lisp and sigh. To the younger lady, who did not know English, and expressed a wish to read these poems, I recommended some excellent translations. Upon this occasion I did not fail to declaim, as it is my custom to do when conversing with young ladies, against Byron's impiety, heartlessness, hopelessness, and heaven knows what all.

It was the coffee's fault that I had forgotten my pretty lady. She was standing outside of the door with her mother and companion, preparing to get into the carriage. There was but just time for me to step up to her briskly and assure her that it was cold. She seemed displeased that I had not come sooner; but I smoothed the pettish frown from her fair brow by bestowing a wonderful flower upon her, which I had picked the day before from a steep precipice at the danger of breaking my neck. Her mother demanded the name of the flower, considering it improper as it were for her daughter to wear a strange, unknown flower upon her bosom. Her taciturn companion unexpectedly opened his mouth, counted the stamens of the flower, and dryly remarked that it belonged to the eighth class. It aggravates me when I see how God's dear flowers are parcelled off into classes as well as we, and indeed, according to a method no less superficial—viz., the difference in the number of stamens. If there must be subdivision, it would be well to follow the suggestion of Theophrast, who would have flowers classified according to their spirit—that is, their fragrance. So far as I am concerned, I have my own system in natural science, and according to it I classify all things—into those that are good to eat, and those that are not.

Heinrich Heine.

MY APPRECIATIVE FRIEND.

HE called my attention to the utility and perfect adaptation of nature. The trees are green, it seems, because green is good for one's eyes. I assented, and added that God has created cattle, because broth is strengthening to men, and that he has created asses that we might have a means of comparison, and that he has created man himself to eat broth and be no ass. My companion was enchanted to have found a congenial spirit; his countenance beamed happiness, and at parting he seemed deeply touched.

Heinrich Heine.

"*MADAM, DO YOU KNOW THE OLD PLAY?*"

"*She was lovable, and he loved her. But he was not lovable, and she did not love him.*"—*Old Play.*

MADAM, do you know the old play? It is quite an extraordinary play, only a little too melancholy. I once played the leading part in it myself, so that all the ladies wept; only one did not weep, not even a single tear, and that was the point of the play, the whole catastrophe.

Oh, that single tear! it still torments my thoughts. When Satan wishes to ruin my soul, he hums in my ear a ballad of that unwept tear, a deadly song with a more deadly tune. Ah, such a tune is only heard in hell!

You can readily form an idea, Madam, of what life is like in heaven, the *more* readily as you are married. There people amuse themselves altogether superbly, every sort of entertainment is provided, and one lives in mere desire and delight. One eats from morning to night, and the cookery is as good as Fagor's; roast geese fly round with gravy-boats in their bills, and feel flattered if any one eats them; tarts gleaming with butter grow wild like sunflowers; everywhere there are brooks of bouillon and champagne, everywhere trees on which napkins flutter, and you eat and wipe your lips and eat again without injury to your stomach; you sing psalms or flirt and joke with the dear, delicate little angels, or take a walk on the green Hallelujah-meadow; and your white flowing garments fit very comfortably; and nothing disturbs the feeling of blessedness; no pain, no vexation—even when one accidentally treads on another's corns and exclaims, "*Excuses,*" he smiles as if enraptured, and assures, "Thy foot, brother, did not hurt in the least; quite *au contraire*—a deeper thrill of heavenly rapture shoots through my heart!"

But of hell, Madam, you have no idea. Of all the devils you know perhaps only the little Amor, the pretty croupier of hell, Beelzebub, and you know him only from Don Juan, and doubtless think that for such a betrayer of innocence hell can never be made hot enough, though our praiseworthy theatre directors spend upon him as much flame, fiery rain, powder, and colophoniam as any Christian could desire in hell. But things in hell look much worse than our theatre directors know, or they would not bring out so many bad plays. For in hell it is infernally hot, and when I was there in the dog-days it was past endurance. Madam, you can have no idea of hell! We have very few official returns from the place. Still, it is rank calumny to say that down there all the poor souls are compelled to read the whole day long all the dull sermons that are printed on earth. Bad as hell is, it has not come to that: Satan will never invent such refinements of torture. On the other hand, Dante's description is too mild on the whole, too poetic. Hell appeared to me like a great kitchen, with an endless long stove, on which stood three rows of iron pots, and in these sat the damned and were cooked. In one row were placed Christian sinners, and, incredible as it may seem, their number was anything but small, and the devils poked the fire up under them with especial good-will. In the next row were Jews, who continually screamed and cried, and were occasionally mocked by the fiends, which sometimes seemed very amusing, as, for instance, when a fat, wheezy, old pawnbroker complained of the heat, and a little devil poured several buckets of cold water on his head, that he might realise what a refreshing benefit baptism was. In the third row sat the heathen, who, like the Jews, could take no part in salvation, and must burn for ever. I heard one of these, as a burly devil put fresh coals under his kettle, cry out from his spot, "Spare me! I was Socrates, the wisest of mortals. I taught Truth and Justice, and sacrificed my life for Virtue." But the stupid, burly devil went on with his work and grumbled, "Oh, shut up there! All heathens must burn, and we cannot make an exception for the sake of a single man." I assure you, Madam, the heat was terrible, with such a screaming, sighing, groaning, quacking, grunting, squealing—and through all these terrible sounds rang distinctly the deadly tune of the song of the unwept tear.

"She was lovable, and he loved her. But he was not lovable, and she did not love him."—*Old Play*.

Madam, that old play is a tragedy, though the hero in it is neither killed nor commits suicide. The eyes of the heroine are beautiful, very beautiful. Madam, do you smell the perfume of violets?—very beautiful, and yet so piercing that they struck like poignards of glass through my heart, and probably came out through my back, and yet I was not killed by those treacherous, murderous eyes. The voice of the heroine was also sweet. Madam, did you hear a nightingale just then?—a soft silken voice, a sweet web of the sunniest tones, and my soul was entangled in it and choked, and tormented itself. I myself—it is the Count of Ganges who now speaks, and the story goes on in Venice—I myself soon had enough of these tortures, and had thoughts of putting an end to the play in the first act, and of shooting myself through the head, fool's cap and all. I went to a fancy shop in the Via Burstah, where I saw a pair of beautiful pistols in a case—I remember them perfectly well. Near them stood many pleasant playthings of mother-of-pearl and gold, steel hearts on gilt chains, porcelain cups with delicate devices, and snuff-boxes with pretty pictures, such as the divine history of Susanna, the Swan Song of Leda, the Rape of the Sabines, Lucretia, a fat, virtuous creature, with naked bosom, in which she was lazily sticking a dagger; the late Bethmann, *la belle Ferronière*—all enrapturing faces—but I bought the pistols without much ado, and then I bought balls, then powder, and then I went to the restaurant of Signor Somebody and ordered oysters and a glass of Hock.

I could eat nothing, and still less could I drink. The warm tears fell in the glass, and in that glass I saw my dear home, the holy, blue Ganges, the ever-gleaming Himalaya, the giant banyan woods, amid whose broad arcades calmly wandered wise elephants and white-robed pilgrims; strange, dream-like flowers gazed on me with meaning glance, wondrous golden birds sang wildly, flashing sun-rays, and the sweet, silly chatter of monkeys pleasantly mocked me; from far pagodas sounded the pious prayers of priests, and amid all rang the melting, wailing voice of the Sultana of Delhi. She ran impetuously around in her carpeted chamber, she tore her silver veil, with her peacock fan she struck the black slave to the ground, she wept, she raged, she cried. I could not, however, hear what she said; the restaurant of Signor Somebody is three thousand miles distant from the harem of Delhi, besides the fair sultana had been dead three thousand years, and I quickly drank up the wine, the clear, joy-giving wine, and yet my soul grew darker and sadder—I was condemned to death.

As I left the restaurant I heard the "bell of poor sinners" ring, a crowd of people swept by me; but I placed myself at the corner of the Strada San Giovanni, and recited the following monologue:—

> In ancient tales they tell of golden castles,
> Where harps are sounding, lovely ladies dance,
> And gay attendants gleam, and jessamine,
> Myrtle, and roses spread their soft perfume—
> And yet a single word of sad enchantment
> Sweeps all the glory of the scene to naught,
> And there remain but ruins old and grey,
> And screaming birds of night and foul morass.
> Even so have I, with but a single word,

> Enchanted Nature's blooming loveliness.
> There lies she now, lifeless, cold, and pale,
> Just like a monarch's corse laid out in state,
> The royal deathly cheeks fresh stained with rouge,
> And in his hand the kingly sceptre laid,
> Yet still his lips are yellow, and most changed,
> For they forgot to dye them, as they should,
> And mice are jumping o'er the monarch's nose,
> And mock the golden sceptre in his grasp.

It is everywhere agreed, Madam, that one should deliver a soliloquy before shooting himself. Most men on such occasions use Hamlet's "To be, or not to be." It is an excellent passage, and I would gladly have quoted it—but charity begins at home, and when a man has written tragedies himself, in which such farewell-to-life speeches occur as, for instance, in my immortal *Almansor*, it is very natural that one should prefer his own words even to Shakespeare's. At any rate, the delivery of such speeches is a very useful custom; one gains at least a little time. And so it came to pass that I remained a rather long time standing at the corner Strada San Giovanni—and as I stood there like a condemned criminal awaiting death, I raised my eyes and suddenly beheld her. She wore her blue silk dress and rose-red hat, and her eyes looked at me so mildly, so death-conqueringly, so life-givingly—Madam, you well know, out of Roman history, that when the vestals in ancient Rome met on their way a malefactor led to death they had the right to pardon him, and the poor rogue lived. With a single glance she saved me from death, and I stood before her revived, and dazzled by the sunbeams of her beauty, and she passed on—and left me alive.

And she left me alive, and I live, which is the main point.

Others may, if they choose, enjoy the good fortune of having their lady-love adorn their grave with garlands, and water them with the tears of fidelity. Oh, women! hate me, laugh at me, jilt me, but let me live! Life is all too laughably sweet, and the world too delightfully bewildered; it is the dream of an intoxicated god, who has taken French leave of the carousing multitude of immortals, and has laid himself down to sleep in a solitary star, and knows not himself that he created all that he dreams—and the dream-images form themselves in such a mad, variegated fashion, and often so harmoniously reasonable—the Iliad, Plato, the battle of Marathon, Moses, Medician Venus, Strasburg Cathedral, the French Revolution, Hegel, the steamboat, etc., etc., are single good thoughts in this divine dream—but it will not last long, and the god awakes, and rubs his sleepy eyes, and smiles—and our world has run to nothing—yes, has never been.

No matter! I live. If I am but a shadowy image in a dream, still this is better than the cold, black, void, annihilation of Death. Life is the greatest good, and death the worst evil. Berlin lieutenants of the guard may sneer and call it cowardice because the Prince of Homburg shudders when he beholds his open grave. Henry Kleist had, however, as much courage as his high-breasted, tightly-laced colleagues, and has, alas! proved it. But all strong men love life. Goethe's Egmont does not part willingly from the "cheerful wont of being and working." Immermann's Edwin clings to life "like a little child to his mother's breast," and though he finds it hard to live by stranger mercy, he still begs for mercy: "For life and breath is still the highest."

When Odysseus in the under-world sees Achilles as the leader of dead heroes, and extols his renown among the living, and his glory even among the dead, Achilles answers—

> "No more discourse of death consolingly, noble Odysseus!
> Rather would I in the field as daily labourer be toiling,
> Slave to the meanest of men, a pauper and lacking possessions,
> Than 'mid the infinite host of long-vanished mortals be ruler."

Yes, when Major Duvent challenged the great Israel Lyon to fight with pistols, and said to him, "If you do not meet me, Mr. Lyon, you are a dog;" the latter replied, "I would rather be a live dog than a dead lion!" and he was right. I have fought often enough, Madam, to dare to say this, God be praised! I live! Red life pulses in my veins; earth yields beneath my feet; in the glow of love I embrace trees and statues, and they live in my embrace. Every woman is to me the gift of a world. I revel in the melody of her countenance, and with a single glance of my eye I can enjoy more than others with their every limb through all their lives. Every instant is to me an eternity. I do not measure time with the ell of Brabant or of Hamburg, and I need no priest to promise me a second life, for I can live enough in this life, when I live backwards in the life of those who have gone before me, and win myself an eternity in the realm of the past.

And I live! The great pulsation of nature beats too in my breast; and when I carol aloud I am answered by a thousand-fold echo. I hear a thousand nightingales. Spring has sent them to awaken earth from her morning slumber, and earth trembles with ecstasy. Her flowers are hymns, which she sings in inspiration to the sun. The sun moves far too slowly. I would fain lash on his steeds that they might advance more rapidly. But when he sinks hissing in the sea, and the night rises with her passionate eyes, oh! then true pleasure first thrills through me, the evening breezes lie like flattering maidens on my wild heart, and the stars wink to me, and I rise and sweep over the little earth and the little thoughts of men.

Madam, I have deceived you. I am not the Count of the Ganges. Never in my life have I seen the holy stream, nor the lotus-flowers which are mirrored in its sacred waves. Never did I lie dreaming under Indian palms, nor in prayer before the Diamond Deity Juggernaut, who with his diamonds might have easily aided me out of my difficulties. I have no more been in Calcutta than the turkey, of which I ate yesterday at dinner, had ever been in the realms of the Grand Turk. Yet my ancestors came from Hindustan, and therefore I feel so much at my ease in the great forest of song of Valmiki. The heroic sorrows of the divine Ramo move my heart like familiar griefs; from the flower lays of Kalidasa the sweetest memories bloom; and when a few years ago a gentle lady in Berlin showed me the beautiful pictures which her father, who had been Governor in India, had brought from thence, the delicately-painted, holy, calm faces seemed as familiar to me as though I were gazing at my own family gallery.

Franz Bopp, Madam—you have of course read his *Nalus* and his system of Sanscrit Conjugations—gave me much information relative to my ancestry, and I now know with certainty that I am descended from Brahma's head, and not from his corns. I have also good reason to believe that the entire Mahabarata, with its two hundred thousand verses, is merely an allegorical love-letter which my first fore-father wrote to my first fore-mother. Oh, they loved dearly; their souls kissed, they kissed with their eyes; they were both but one single kiss.

An enchanted nightingale sits on a red coral bough in the silent sea, and sings a song of the love of my ancestors; the pearls gaze eagerly from their shells, the wonderful water-flowers tremble with sorrow, the cunning sea-snails, bearing on their backs many-coloured porcelain towers, come creeping onwards, the ocean roses blush with shame, the yellow, sharp-pointed starfish and the thousand-hued glassy jelly-fish quiver and stretch, and all swarm and listen.

Unfortunately, Madam, this nightingale song is far too long to be set down here; it is as long as the world itself. Even its dedication to Anangas, the God of Love, is as long

FROM HEINE.

"SIT THE GOOD TOWNSPEOPLE OF A SUMMER EVENING."

as all Scott's novels; and there is a passage referring to it in Aristophanes, which in German reads thus—

"Tiotio, tiotio, tiotinx,
Totototo, totototo, tototinx."

No, I was not born in India. I first beheld the light of the world on the shore of that beautiful stream on whose green hills folly grows and is plucked in autumn, laid away in cellars, poured into barrels, and exported to foreign lands. In fact, only yesterday I heard some one speaking a piece of folly, which in the year 1811 was imprisoned in a bunch of grapes which I myself then saw growing on the Johannisberg. But much folly is also consumed at home, and men are the same there as everywhere; they are born, eat, drink, sleep, laugh, cry, slander each other, are greatly troubled about the propagation of their race, try to seem what they are not, and to do what they cannot; never shave until they have a beard, and often have beards before they get discretion; and when they have at last discretion, they drink it away in white and red folly.

Mon dieu! If I had faith, so that I could remove mountains—the Johannisberg would be just the mountain which I would carry with me everywhere. But as my faith is not strong enough, imagination must aid me, and she quickly sets me by the beautiful Rhine.

Oh, that is a fair land, full of loveliness and sunshine. In the blue stream are mirrored the mountain shores, with their ruined towers and woods and ancient towns. There, before the house-door, sit the good townspeople of a summer evening, and drink out of great cans, and gossip confidentially about how the wine—the Lord be praised!—thrives, and how justice should be free from all secrecy, and how Marie Antoinette's being guillotined is none of our business, and how dear the tobacco tax makes tobacco, and how all mankind are equal, and what a glorious fellow Goerres is.

I have never troubled myself about such conversation, and sat rather with the maidens in the arched window, and laughed at their laughter, and let them throw flowers in my face, and pretended to be ill-natured until they told me their secrets, or some other important stories. Fair Gertrude was half wild with delight when I sat by her. She was a girl like a flaming rose; and once, as she fell on my neck, I thought that she would burn away into perfume in my arms. Fair Katharine flamed into sweet music when she talked with me, and her eyes were of a pure, internal blue, which I have never seen in men or animals, and very seldom in flowers; one gazed so gladly into them, and could then think such sweet things. But the beautiful

Hedwig loved me, for when I came to her she bowed her head till her black curls fell down over her blushing face, and her bright eyes shone like stars from the dark heaven. Her bashful lips spoke not a word, and I too could say nothing to her. I coughed, and she trembled. She often begged me through her sisters not to climb the rocks so rashly, and not to bathe in the Rhine when I was hot with running or drinking wine. Once I overheard her pious prayer before the Virgin Mary, which she had adorned with gold leaf and illuminated with a lamp, and which stood in a corner at the entrance. I plainly heard her pray to the Mother of God to keep him from climbing, drinking, and bathing. I should certainly have been desperately in love with her if she had been indifferent to me; and I was indifferent to her, because I knew that she loved me. Madam, to win my love, I must be treated *en canaille*.

Johanna was the cousin of the three sisters, and I was glad to be with her. She knew the most beautiful old legends, and when she pointed with her white hand through the window out to the mountains where all had happened which she narrated, I became enchanted; the old knights rose visibly from the ruined castles, and hewed away at each other's iron clothes, the Loreley sat again on the mountain summit, singing adown her sweet, seductive song, and the Rhine rippled so reasonably soothing—and yet so mockingly horrible—and the fair Johanna looked at me so strangely, with such enigmatic tenderness, that she seemed herself one with the legend that she told. She was a slender, pale girl, sickly and musing; her eyes were clear as truth itself; her lips piously arched; in her face lay a great story. Was it a love legend? I know not, and I never had the courage to ask. When I looked at her long I grew calm and cheerful; it seemed to me as though it was Sunday in my heart, and the angels held service there.

In such happy hours I told her tales of my childhood,

and she listened earnestly, and strangely, when I could not think of the names, she remembered them. When I then asked her with wonder how she knew the names, she would answer with a smile that she had learned it of the birds that had built a nest on the sill of her window; and she tried to make me believe that these were the same birds which I once bought with my pocket-money from a hard-hearted peasant-boy, and then let fly away. But I believed that she knew everything, because she was so pale, and really soon died. She knew, too, when she would die, and wished that I would leave Adernach the day before. When I bade her farewell she gave me both her hands; they were white, sweet hands, and pure as the frost; and she said, "You are very good, and when you are not, think of the little dead Veronica."

Did the chattering birds also tell her this name? Often in hours of remembrance I had wearied my brain in trying to think of that dear name, but could not.

And now that I have it again, my earliest infancy shall bloom into memory again, and I am again a child, and play with other children in the Castle Court at Düsseldorf, on the Rhine.

Yes, Madam, there was I born, and I am particular in calling attention to the fact, lest after my death seven cities —those of Schilda, Krähwinkel, Polkwitz, Bockum, Dülken, Göttingen, and Schöppenstadt[1] — should contend for the honour of being my birthplace. Düsseldorf is a town on the Rhine, sixteen thousand people live there, and many hundred thousands besides are buried there; and among them are many of whom my mother says it were better if they were still alive—for example, my grandfather and my uncle, the old Herr von Geldern and the young Herr von Geldern, who were both such celebrated doctors, and saved

---

[1] This was a thrust at Göttingen, which town Heine here couples with six others, notorious as the local scenes in comic literature.

the life of so many men, and yet must both die themselves. And pious Ursula, who carried me as a child in her arms, also lies buried there, and a rosebush grows over her grave; she loved rose-perfume so much in her life, and her earth was all rose-perfume and goodness. And the shrewd old Canonicus also lies there buried. Lord, how miserable he looked when I last saw him! He consisted of nothing but soul and plasters, and yet he studied night and day as though he feared lest the warmth might find a few ideas missing in his head. Little William also lies there—and that is my fault. We were schoolmates in the Franciscan cloister, and were one day playing on that side of the building where the Düssel flows between stone walls, and I said, " William, do get the kitten out, which has just fallen in!" and he cheerfully climbed out on the board which stretched over the brook, and pulled the cat out of the water, but fell in himself, and when they took him out he was cold and dead. The kitten lived to a good old age.

The town of Düsseldorf is very beautiful, and if you think of it when in foreign lands, and happen at the same time to have been born there, strange feelings come over the soul. I was born there, and feel as if I must go directly home. And when I say home, I mean the Volkerstrasse, and the house where I was born. This house will be some day very remarkable, and I have sent word to the old lady who owns it that she must not for her life sell it. For the whole house she would now hardly get as much as the present which the green-veiled, distinguished English ladies will give the servant when she shows them the room where I was born, and the hen-house wherein my father generally imprisoned me for stealing grapes, and also the brown door on which my mother taught me to write with chalk. Ah me! should I ever become a famous author, it has cost my poor mother trouble enough.

But my fame still slumbers in the marble quarries of

Carrara; the waste-paper laurel with which they have bedecked my brow has not yet spread its perfume through the wide world, and when the green-veiled, distinguished English ladies visit Düsseldorf, they leave the celebrated house unvisited, and go direct to the Market Place, and there gaze on the colossal black equestrian statue which stands in its midst. This represents the Prince-Elector, Jan Wilhelm. He wears black armour and a long hanging wig. When a boy I was told that the artist who made this statue observed with terror while it was being cast that he had not metal enough, and then all the citizens of the town came running with all their silver spoons, and threw them in to fill the mould; and I often stood for hours before the statue puzzling my head as to how many spoons were sticking in it, and how many apple-tarts all that silver would buy. Apple-tarts were then my passion—now it is love, truth, freedom, and crab-soup—and not far from the statue of the Prince-Elector, at the theatre corner, generally stood a curiously constructed sabre-legged rascal, with a white apron and a basket girt around him full of smoking apple-tarts, which he knew how to praise with an irresistible treble voice. "Apple-tarts! quite fresh, so delicious!" Truly, whenever in my later years the Evil One sought to win me, he always cried in such an enticing treble, and I should certainly have never remained twelve hours by the Signora Guilietta if she had not thrilled me with her sweet, fragrant, apple-tart tones. And, in fact, the apple-tarts would never have so enticed me if the crooked Hermann had not covered them up so mysteriously with his white apron; and it is aprons, you know, which—but I wander from the subject. I was speaking of the equestrian statue which has so many silver spoons in its body and no soup, and which represents the Prince-Elector, Jan Wilhelm.

He must have been a brave gentleman, very fond of art, and skilful himself. He founded the picture-gallery in

Düsseldorf, and in the observatory there they show a very artistic piece of woodwork which he himself had carved in his leisure hours, of which latter he had every day four-and-twenty.

In those days princes were not the persecuted wretches which they now are; the crown grew firmly on their heads, and at night they drew their night-caps over it and slept peacefully, and their people slumbered peacefully at their feet; and when they awoke in the morning they said, "Good morning, father!" and he replied, "Good morning, dear children!"

But there came a sudden change over all this. One morning when we awoke in Düsseldorf and would say, "Good morning, father," the father had travelled away, and in the whole town there was nothing but dumb sorrow. Everywhere there was a funeral-like expression, and people slipped silently to the market and read the long paper on the door of the Town Hall. It was bad weather, yet the lean tailor Kilian stood in his nankeen jacket, which he generally wore only at home, and his blue woollen stockings hung down so that his little bare legs peeped out in a troubled way, and his thin lips quivered as he murmured the placard. An old invalid soldier from the Palatine read it rather louder, and at some words a clear tear ran down his white, honourable old moustache. I stood near him, crying too, and asked why we were crying. And he replied, "The Prince-Elector has abdicated." And then he read further, and at the words, "for the long manifested fidelity of my subjects," "and hereby release you from allegiance," he wept still more. It is a strange sight to see, when an old man, in faded uniform and scarred veteran's face, suddenly bursts into tears. While we read the Prince-Electoral coat-of-arms was being taken down from the Town Hall, and everything began to appear as anxiously dreary as though we were waiting for an eclipse of the sun. The town councillors went about at an abdicating, wearisome gait; even the omnipotent beadle looked as though he had no more commands to give, and stood calmly indifferent, although the crazy Aloysius stood upon one leg and chattered the names of French generals with foolish grimaces, while the tipsy, crooked Gumpertz rolled around in the gutter singing *ça ira! ça ira!*

But I went home crying and lamenting, "The Prince-Elector has abdicated." My mother might do what she would, I knew what I knew, and went crying to bed, and in the night dreamed that the world had come to an end—the fair flower-gardens and green meadows of the world were taken up and rolled away like carpets from the floor; the beadle climbed up on a high ladder and took down the sun, and the tailor Kilian stood by and said to himself, "I must go home and dress myself neatly, for I am dead, and am to be buried this afternoon." And it grew darker and darker—a few stars glimmered on high, and even these fell down like yellow leaves in autumn; men gradually vanished, and I, poor child, wandered in anguish around, until before the willow fence of a deserted farmhouse I saw a man digging up the earth with a spade, and near him an ugly, spiteful-looking woman, who held something in her apron like a human head, but it was the moon, and she laid it carefully in the open grave; and behind me stood the Palatine soldier sobbing and spelling, "The Prince-Elector has abdicated."

When I awoke, the sun shone as usual through the window; there was a sound of drums in the street; and as I entered our sitting-room and wished my father, who sat in his white dressing-gown, good morning, I heard the little light-footed barber, as he made up his hair, narrate very minutely that homage would that morning be offered at the Town Hall to the Archduke Joachim. I heard too that the new ruler was of excellent family, that he had married the sister of the Emperor Napoleon, and was really a very respectable man; that he wore his beautiful black hair in curls; that he would shortly enter the town, and would certainly please all the ladies. Meanwhile the drumming in the streets continued, and I stood before the house-door and looked at the French troops marching—those joyous and famous people who swept over the world—singing and playing, the merry, serious faces of the Grenadiers, the bear-skin shakoes, the tri-coloured cockades, the glittering bayonets, the *voltigeurs* full of vivacity and *point d'honneur*, and the giant-like, silver-laced tambour major, who cast his *baton* with the gilded head as high as the first storey, and his eyes to the second, where pretty girls gazed from the windows. I was so glad that soldiers were to be quartered in our house—my mother was not glad—and I hastened to the Market Place. There everything looked changed; it was as though the world had been new whitewashed. A new coat-of-arms was placed on the Town Hall; its iron balconies were hung with embroidered velvet drapery, French Grenadiers stood as sentinels, the old town councillors had put on new faces and Sunday coats, and looked at each other French fashion, and said, "*Bon jour!*" Ladies peeped from every window, inquisitive citizens and soldiers filled the square, and I, with other boys, climbed on the shining Prince-Elector's great bronze horse, and looked down on the motley crowd.

Neighbour Peter and Long Conrad nearly broke their necks on this occasion, and that would have been well, for the one afterwards ran away from his parents, enlisted as a soldier, deserted, and was finally shot in Mayence; while the other, having made geographical researches in strange pockets, became a working member of a public tread-mill institute. But having broken the iron bands which bound him to his fatherland, he passed safely beyond sea, and eventually died in London, in consequence of wearing a much too long cravat, one end of which happened to be firmly attached to something just as a royal official removed a plank from beneath his feet.

Long Conrad told us that there was no school to-day on account of the homage. We had to wait a long time till this was over. At last the balcony of the Council House was filled with gay gentlemen, flags and trumpets; and our burgomaster, in his celebrated red coat, delivered an oration, which stretched out like india-rubber, or like a nightcap into which one has thrown a stone—only that it was not the stone of wisdom—and I could distinctly understand many of his phrases; for instance, that "We are now to be made happy"—and at the last words the trumpets and drums sounded, and the flags waved, and the people cried hurrah!—and as I, myself, cried hurrah! I held fast to the old Prince-Elector. And that was necessary, for I began to grow giddy; it seemed to me that the people were standing on their heads while the world whizzed round, and the Prince-Elector, with his long wig, nodded and whispered, "Hold fast to me!" and not till the cannon re-echoed along the wall did I become sobered, and climbed slowly down from the great bronze horse.

As I went home I saw crazy Aloysius again dancing on one leg while he chattered the names of French generals, and crooked Gumpertz was rolling in the gutter drunk and growling *ça ira, ça ira*—and I said to my mother that we were all to be made happy, and so there was no school to-day.

The next day the world was again all in order, and we had school as before, and things were got by heart as before — the Roman kings, chronology — the *nomina* in *im*, the *verba irregularia*—Greek, Hebrew, geography, German, mental arithmetic—Lord! my head is still giddy with it! —all must be learnt by heart. And much of it was eventually to my advantage. For had I not learnt the Roman kings by heart it would subsequently have been a matter of perfect indifference to me whether Niebuhr had or had not proved that they never really existed. And had I not learnt chronology how could I ever in later years have found out any one in Berlin, where one house is as like another as drops of water, or as grenadiers, and where it is impossible to find a friend unless you have the number of his house in your head. Therefore I associated with every friend some historical event which had happened in a year corresponding to the number of his house, so that the one recalled the other, and some curious point in history always occurred to me whenever I met an acquaintance. For instance, when I met my tailor I at once thought of the battle of Marathon; if I saw the well-dressed banker, Christian Gumpel, I remembered the destruction of Jerusalem; if a Portuguese friend, deeply in debt, of the flight of Mahomet; if the University Judge, a man whose probity is well known, of the death of Haman; and if Wadzeck, I was at once reminded of Cleopatra. *Ach, lieber Himmel!* the poor creature is dead now; our tears are dry, and we may say of her with Hamlet, "Take her for all in all; she was a hag—we oft shall look upon her like again!" As I said, chronology is necessary. I know men who have nothing in their heads but a few years, yet who knew exactly where to look for the right houses, and are, moreover, regular professors. But oh! the trouble I had at school with dates! —and it went even worse with arithmetic. I understood *subtraction* best, and for this I had a very practical rule— "Four from three won't go, I must borrow one;" but I advise every one, in such a case, to borrow a few extra shillings, for one never knows.

But as for the Latin, Madam, you can really have no idea how muddled it is. The Romans would never have found time to conquer the world if they had been obliged first to learn Latin. Those happy people knew in their cradles the nouns with an accusative in *im*. I, on the contrary, had to learn them by heart in the sweat of my brow; but still it is well that I knew them. For if, for example, when I publicly disputed in Latin, in the College Hall of Göttingen, on the 20th of July 1825—Madam, it was well worth while to hear it—if, I say, I had said *sinapen* instead of *sinapim*, the blunder would have been evident to the Freshmen, and an endless shame for me. *Vis buris, sitis, tussis, cuiumis, amussis, cannabis, sinapis*—these words, which have attracted so much attention in the world, effected this, because they belonged to a determined class, and yet were exceptions; on that account I value them highly, and the fact that I have them ready at my finger's ends when I perhaps need them in a hurry affords me in many dark hours of life much internal tranquillity and consolation. But, Madam, the *verba irregularia*—they are distinguished from the *verbis regularibus* by the fact that in learning them one gets more whippings—are terribly difficult. In the damp arches of the Franciscan cloister, near our schoolroom, there hung a large crucified Christ of grey wood, a dismal image, that even yet at times marches through my dreams, and gazes sorrowfully on me with fixed, bleeding eyes—before this image I often stood and prayed, "Oh, thou poor and equally tormented God, if it be possible for Thee, see that I get by heart the irregular verbs!"

I will say nothing of Greek; I should irritate myself too much. The monks of the Middle Ages were not so very much in the wrong when they asserted that Greek was an invention of the devil. Lord knows what I suffered through it. It went better with Hebrew, for I always had a great predilection for the Jews, although they to this very hour have crucified my good name; but I never could get so far in Hebrew as my watch, which had an intimate intercourse with pawnbrokers, and in consequence acquired many Jewish habits—for instance, it would not go on Saturday—and learned the holy language, and was subsequently occupied with its grammar, for often when sleepless in the night I have to my amazement heard it industriously repeating— *Katal, katalla, katalki; kittel, kittalla, kittalki; pokal, pokadeti; pikat, pik, pik.*

Meanwhile I learned much more German, and that is not such child's-play. For we poor Germans, who have already been sufficiently plagued with soldiers quartered on us, military duties, poll-taxes, and a thousand other exactions, must needs over and above all this torment each other with

"MY SCHOOLFELLOWS FOUGHT WITH ESPECIAL VIGOUR."

accusatives and datives. I learned much German from the old Rector Schallmeyer, a brave clerical gentleman, whose *protégé* I was from childhood. Something of the matter I also learned from Professor Schram, a man who had written a book on Eternal Peace, and in whose class my schoolfellows fought with especial vigour.

And while thus dashing on in a breath, and thinking of everything, I have unexpectedly found myself back among old school stories, and I avail myself of this opportunity to show you, Madam, that it was not my fault if I learned so little geography that later in life I could not make my way in the world. For in those days the French had deranged all boundaries; every day countries were re-coloured—those which were once blue suddenly became green, many even blood-red; the old established rules were so confused and confounded that no devil would recognise them. The products of the country also changed—chickory and beets now grew where only hares and hunters running after them were once to be seen; even the characters of different races changed—the Germans became pliant, the French paid compliments no longer, the English ceased making ducks and drakes of their money, and the Venetians were not subtle enough; there was promotion among princes, old kings obtained new uniforms, new kingdoms were cooked up and sold like hot cakes; many potentates, on the other hand, were chased from house and home, and had to find some new way of earning their bread, while others went at once at a trade, and manufactured, for instance, sealing-wax, or—Madam, this sentence must be brought to an end, or I shall be out of breath—in short, it is impossible in such times to advance far in geography.

I succeeded better in natural history, for there we find fewer changes, and we always have standard engravings of apes, kangaroos, zebras, rhinoceroses, etc. And having many such pictures in my memory, it often happens that at first sight many mortals appear to me like old acquaintances.

I did well in mythology; I took real delight in the mob of gods and goddesses who ruled the world in joyous nakedness. I do not believe that there was a schoolboy in ancient Rome who knew the chief articles of his catechism —that is, the loves of Venus—better than I. To tell the truth, it seems to me that if we must learn all the heathen gods by heart, we might as well have kept them from the first, and we have not perhaps made so much out of our new Roman Trinity, or even our Jewish monotheism. Perhaps that mythology was not in reality so immoral as we imagine, and it was, for example, a very decent thought of Homer's to give the much-loved Venus a husband.

But I succeeded best of all in the French class of the Abbé d'Aulnoi, a French *émigré*, who had written a number of grammars, and wore a red wig, and jumped about very nervously when he recited his *Art poetique* and his *Histoire Allemande*. He was the only man in the whole gymnasium who taught German history. Still French has its difficulties, and to learn it there must be much quartering of troops, much drumming in, much *apprendre par cœur*, and above all, no one should be a *bête allemande*. Thus many bitter words came in. I remember still, as though it happened yesterday, the scrapes I got into through *la religion*. Six times came the question : " Henri, what is the French for 'the faith'?" And six times, ever more tearfully, I replied : " It is called *le crédit*." And at the seventh question, with a deep cherry-red face, my furious examiner cried, " It is called *la religion*," and there was a rain of blows, and all my schoolfellows laughed. Madam, since that day I can never hear the word *religion* but my back turns pale with terror, and my cheeks red with shame. And to speak truly, *le crédit* has during my life stood me in better stead than *la religion*. It occurs to me at this moment that I still owe the landlord of the " Lion," in Bologna, five thalers ; and I pledge you my word of honour that I would give him five thalers more if I could only be certain that I should never again hear that unlucky word *la religion*.

Parbleu, Madam, I have succeeded well in French. I understand not only *patois*, but even aristocratic nurse-maid French. Not long ago, when in noble society, I understood full one-half of the conversation of two German Countesses, each of whom could count at least sixty-four years, and as many ancestors. Yes, in the Café Royal, at Berlin, I once heard Monsieur Hans Michel Martens talking French, and understood every word, though there was no understanding in it. We must know the spirit of a language, and this is best learned by drumming. *Parbleu!* how much do I not owe to the French drummer who was so long quartered in our house, who looked like a devil, and yet had the heart of an angel, and who drummed so excellently?

He was a little nervous figure, with a terrible black moustache, beneath which the red lips turned suddenly outwards, while his fiery eyes glanced around.

I, a youngster, stuck to him like a cur, and helped him to rub his military buttons like mirrors, and to pipe-clay his vest, for Monsieur Le Grand liked to look well; and I followed him to the watch, to the roll-call, to the parade. In those times there was nothing but the gleam of weapons and merriment—*les jours de fête sont passés!* Monsieur Le Grand knew only a little broken German, only the chief expressions—" Bread," " kiss," " honour," but he could make himself very intelligible with his drum. For instance, if I did not know what the word *liberté* meant, he drummed the *Marseillaise*, and I understood him. If I did not understand the word *egalité*, he drummed the march, "*Ça ira . . . les aristocrats a la lanterne!*" and I understood him. If I did not know what *bêtise* meant, he drummed the Dessauer March, which we Germans, as Goethe also declares, have drummed in champagne— and I understood him. He once wanted to explain to me the word *l'Allemagne*, and he drummed the all too simple primeval melody, which on market days is played to dancing dogs—namely, *Dum-dum-dum*. I was vexed, but I understood him.

In the same way he taught me modern history. I did not understand the words, it is true ; but as he constantly drummed while speaking, I knew what he meant. At bottom this is the best method. The history of the storming of the Bastille, of the Tuilleries, and the like, we understand first when we know how the drumming was done. In our school compendiums of history we merely read: "Their excellencies the Baron and Count, with the most noble spouses of the aforesaid, were beheaded. Their highnesses the Dukes and Princes, with the most noble spouses of the aforesaid, were beheaded. His Majesty the King, with his most sublime spouse, the Queen, was beheaded." But when you hear the red guillotine march drummed, you understand it correctly for the first time, and you know the how and the why. Madam, that is indeed a wonderful march! It thrilled through marrow and bone when I first heard it, and I was glad that I forgot it. One forgets so much as one grows older, and a young man has nowadays so much other knowledge to keep in his head—whist, Boston, genealogical tables, parliamentary data, dramaturgy, the liturgy, carving—and yet notwithstanding all jogging up of my brain, I could not for a long time recall that tremendous tune! But only think, Madam, not long ago I sat at table with a whole menagerie of counts, princes, princesses, chamberlains, court marshalesses, seneschals, upper court mistresses, court keepers of the royal plate, court hunters' wives, and whatever else these aristocratic domestics are termed, and their under domestics ran about behind their chairs and shoved full plates before their mouths; but I, who was passed by and neglected, sat without the least occupation for my jaws, and I kneaded little bread-balls, and drummed for *ennui* with my fingers, and to my astonishment I suddenly drummed the red, long-forgotten guillotine march!

"And what happened?" Madam, the good people were not disturbed in their eating, nor did they know that other people, when they have nothing to eat, suddenly begin to drum, and that, too, very queer marches, which people thought long forgotten.

Is drumming, now, an inborn talent, or was it early developed in me? Enough—it lies in my limbs, in my hands, in my feet, and often manifests itself involuntarily. I once sat at Berlin in the lecture-room of the Privy Councillor Schmaltz, a man who had saved the State by his book on the *Red and Black Coat Danger*. You remember, perhaps, Madam, out of Pausanias, that by the braying of an ass an equally dangerous plot was once discovered; and you also know from Livy, or from Becker's *History of the World*, that geese once saved the capital; and you must certainly know from Sallust that a loquacious *putain*, the Lady Livia, brought the terrible conspiracy of Cataline to light. But to return to the mutton aforesaid. I listened to international law in the lecture-room of the Herr Privy Councillor Schmaltz, and it was a sleepy summer afternoon, and I sat on the bench and heard less and less—my head had gone to sleep, when all at once I was wakened by the noise of my own feet, which had stayed awake, and had probably observed that the exact opposite of international law and constitutional tendencies was being preached; and my feet, which, with the little eyes of their corns, had seen more of how things go in the world than the Privy Councillor with his Juno eyes—these poor dumb feet, incapable of expressing their immeasurable meaning by words, strove to make themselves intelligible by drumming, and they drummed so loudly that I thereby nearly came to grief.

Cursed, unreflecting feet! They once played me a similar trick, when I on a time, in Göttingen, sponged without subscribing on the lectures of Professor Saalfeld; and as, with an angular activity, he jumped about here and there in his pulpit, and heated himself in order to curse the Emperor Napoleon in regular set style,—no, my poor feet, I cannot blame you for drumming then; indeed, I would not have blamed you if in your dumb *naïveté* you had expressed yourselves by still more energetic movements,

How could I, the scholar of Le Grand, hear the Emperor cursed? The Emperor, the Emperor, the great Emperor!

The Emperor is dead. On a waste island in the Atlantic Ocean is his grave; and he for whom the world was too narrow lies quietly under a little hillock, where five weeping willows hang their green heads, and a little brook, murmuring sorrowfully, ripples by. There is no inscription on his tomb; but Clio, with a just pen, has written thereon invisible words, which will resound, like spirit tones, through thousands of years.

Britannia! the sea is thine. But the sea has not water enough to wash away the shame with which the death of that mighty one has covered thee. Not thy windy Sir Hudson—no, thou thyself wert the Sicilian bravo with whom perjured kings bargained that they might revenge on the man of the people what he had once inflicted on one of themselves. And he was thy guest, and had seated himself by thy hearth.

Strange! A terrible destiny has already overtaken the three greatest enemies of the Emperor. Londonderry has cut his throat, Louis XVIII. has rotted away on his throne, and Professor Saalfeld is still professor in Göttingen.

Heinrich Heine.

VERSES FROM HEINE.

IT makes a man happy, no doubt,
  But it maketh him weary, i'fegs,
To have three lovely women about him,
And only a couple of legs.

With one I must walk of a morning;
At eve with another I rove;
And a third comes at noontide, and drags me
Right out of my quarters, by Jove!

Farewell, irresistible sirens!
I have but two legs of my own;
Henceforth in some rural seclusion
I'll worship Dame Nature—alone.

THESE fine ladies, understanding
Honour must to poets be,
Bade me to a lordly luncheon—
My great Genius and me.

There was soup, ah! it was stunning;
There was wine no lip would spurn;
There was poultry, simply godlike,
There was hare cooked to a turn.

They talked I remember of poets,
And when I could eat no more,
I rose, and acknowledged the honour,
And bowed till I reached the door.

FRANKLY, this young man I honour,
He exhibits graces rare.
Often he has stood me oysters,
Also Rhine-wine and liqueurs.

And his clothes exactly fit him,
And his tie proclaims the swell;
And he turns up every morning,
And he hopes I'm pretty well,

Talks about my reputation,
And my wit, and grace of style;
And he'd do, if I would let him,
Oh, a thousand things the while!

And at nights, in rooms surrounded
By the fairest of the fair,
He declaims my 'Heavenly' poems
With a soft abstracted air.

Truly, is not this refreshing?
Such young men as him I praise
Are not common; they are growing
Rare and rarer nowadays.

A YOUNG man loves a maiden
Who other hopes has fed,
And her love loves another love,
And to his choice is wed.

The maiden marries straightway
The handiest man to be had,
And this is simple cussedness,
And her young man is mad.

It is an ancient drama,
But any time 'twill fit—
Don't play "first gentleman" unless
You want your heart to split.

LAID on thy snow-white shoulder
   My head is at rest;
And I listen—and know the unquiet
   Desire of thy breast.

The gorgeous hussars have stormed it,
   And entered without strife!
And, to-morrow, a woman will leave me
   That I love as my life.

What tho' in the morning she leave me,
   To-night she is mine—
My head is at rest on her shoulder,
   And her snow-white arms entwine.

Translated by Ernest Radford.

"BUT THOU WENT'ST ON WITH EVEN-STEPPING FEET."

Thou wert a blonde-hair'd maid without a stain,
So neat, so prim, so cool! I stay'd in vain
To see thy bosom's guarded gates unroll,
And Inspiration breathe upon thy soul.

A zeal and ardour for those lofty themes,
By chilly Reason scorn'd for airy dreams,
But wringing from the noble and the good
The toil of hand and heart, and brain and blood.

On hills with vineyards' clambering leafage gay,
Glass'd in the Rhine we roamed one summer day;
Bright was the sun, and from the shining cup
Of every flower a giddy scent flew up.

A kiss of fire, a deep voluptuous blush,
Burn'd on each pink and every rosy bush,
Ideal flames in dandelions glow'd
And lit each sorriest weed that edged our road.

But thou went'st on with even-stepping feet,
Clad in white satin, elegant and neat;
No child of Netcher's brush more trim and nice,
And in thy stays a little heart of ice.

Translated by Richard Garnett.

ABOUT MONEY.

THE world is divided into two kinds of human beings—those that have money and those that have none. But the latter are not human beings at all—they are either devils, viz., poor devils; or angels, viz., angels of patience and renunciation.

Without money, without teeth, and without a wife we come into this world; and without money, without teeth, and without a wife we go out of this world. What then have we accomplished in the world? We have made money, cut teeth, and taken unto ourselves wives! A glorious destiny! There are fevers, pains, convulsions, and sufferings of all kinds attendant upon the getting of teeth and wives, and when one has them they hurt the whole year round, and often the best one can do is to have them extracted. Teeth and wives come to you without your doing, and unless most carefully treated they are liable to decay. But money does not come without your doing, and often a man leaves this world without having had money. It would be interesting to hear the reply of such a person when asked on the other side, "What did you do in the world?"

Who has money? The rich people! That is a misfortune! If the poor people only had money then we should see what poor devils these rich fellows are! It is no art to be rich when one has much money, and it is no merit to be poor when one has none.

What is money? Money is a goodly lump which the Lord God attaches to insignificant people, so as not to lose sight of them in his creation, as a good housekeeper puts a big label on a little key.

What is money? Money is a figure which gains in importance as there is a cipher attached to it.

What is money? Money is a metal heel under the boots of little people to make them appear as tall as others.

What is money? Money is an indemnity which God gives to a certain number of persons on condition that they will not make bold to acquire any such goods as Intellect or Genius.

What is money? Money is the *accent grave* upon a letter which would else be silent.

What is money? Money is the mysterious essence of a being which defines its *ego* in the following words:— " If I were not what I have, I should not have what I am."

But what is no money? No money? No money?

No money is a thing of which all empty pockets are full.

No money is the *alibi* of a being which should testify to our presence in this world.

No money is a disease aggravated by the continuous obstruction of Fortune.

No money is a gentle invitation of nature to incur debts, and a peremptory command not to pay them.

No money is an irresistible inclination to melancholy on the part of our purse caused by hopeless love to an unattainable object.

No money is an *ex*position of no money at all, a *pro*position in abstract philosophy, a fit position for a minister of finance, and a happy *dis*position for platonic love.

No money is a vulgar ballad which common people sing aloud on the streets, but the more refined only hum between their lips within doors.

No money is the watchword of extreme radicalism and the art of making oneself popular at a low price.

Alas, what is man without money? A twice-told anecdote, a song without a tune, a lost poodle-dog without an honest finder, last year's calendar, etc., etc.

Without money no prince can reign, no minister can

minister, no general can make war, no painter can paint, no farmer can till the field; only the bards and poets sing and make verses without money; the poet is true to his muse even though he has no money; indeed he muses more than ever—how to get some.

M. G. Saphir (1795-1858).

A NIGHT IN THE BREMER RATHSKELLER.

IT struck ten o'clock as I descended the broad steps of the Rathskeller. There was a reasonable hope of finding it empty, for a storm was howling without, the weather-cocks were making strange music, and the rain splashed upon the pavement. But the kellerdiener gave me a questioning look when I told him my desire.

"What, so late, and to-night of all nights?" he exclaimed.

"It's never too late for me before twelve," I answered; "and after that it is early enough in the day."

"Are you expecting company?" asked the man.

"I am alone."

"You might have some unasked," he added, looking about timorously at the shadows his lamp cast.

"What do you mean?" I asked in surprise.

"Oh, I was only thinking," answered he, lighting a couple of candles and setting a large beaker before me. "There are all sorts of odd rumours about the 1st of September. Indeed I can't do it, sir! Not to-day, sir!"

I took this to be one of those common tricks wherewith custodians, wardens, and the like work upon a stranger's purse, so I placed a generous coin in his hand, and took him by the arm to make him come with me.

"No, that was not my intention, sir," he said, trying to give it back to me. "I'll tell you frankly what my meaning was—there's nothing in the world would induce me to enter the Apostles' cellar this night, for it's the 1st of September."

"Well, and what of that?"

"In God's name, then, you may think what you please, but it isn't as it should be there to-night, and that's because it is the anniversary day of the *Rose*."[1]

I laughed till the walls rang again. "Well, I have heard many a ghost-story in my life, but never one about a wine-ghost. Aren't you ashamed to talk such nonsense, you with your white hair? But I have the permission of the Senate; I may drink in this cellar to-night, wherever I please, and as long as I please. Therefore, in the name of the Senate, I bid you follow me. Unlock the cellar of Bacchus."

This had the desired effect; unwillingly, but not venturing to remonstrate, he took the candles and beckoned to me. First we traversed one roomy vault, then a smaller one, until we reached a long narrow passage. Our steps reverberated with a hollow sound, and our breath striking against the wall produced what seemed like distant whispering. At last we stood before a door, the keys rattled, with a moan it came yawning open, the light of the candles fell into the cellar, and opposite to me sat Friend Bacchus upon a mighty cask. Refreshing sight! They had not pictured him with delicate grace, those old Bremen artists, not daintily as a Grecian youth; they had not represented him old and drunk, with a disgusting belly, leering eyes, and protruding tongue, as the vulgarised myth profanely portrays him now and then. Outrageous anthropomorphism; blind folly of man! Because some of his priests, grown old in his worship, walk about thus; because their belly swells with satisfaction, their nose takes colour from the burning

---

[1] The name of a gigantic cask of wine of 1624, one of the special sights of the Bremen Rathskeller. It is tapped only on great occasions, and in 1870 the town of Bremen sent a number of bottles of this wine to the Emperor William and Prince Bismarck at Versailles, as a valuable gift of honour.—ED.

reflection of the dark-red flood, their eyes turn up in silent bliss—these things must needs be attributed to the god, while they but adorn his worshippers.

Otherwise did the men of Bremen. How blithely and cheerily does the old boy ride his cask! The round blooming face, the merry little wine-enraptured eyes looking down so knowingly, the broad smiling mouth that has tasted of many a bumper, the short powerful neck, the whole little figure teeming with health and good humour! Is one not tempted to expect that in a gay mood, wine-inspired, he will bend his little round knees, press his calves up close, and stem his heels against the old mother-cask, setting her off at a brisk canter, in which all the Roses, Apostles, and common casks will join with a wild "halloo" through the cellar?

"Lord of Heaven!" cried the custodian, clinging tightly to my arm; "don't you see him roll his eyes and swing his legs?"

"Old fellow, you are crazy!" said I, casting a timid look at the wooden god; "it is the light of the candles flickering about him." At the same time a queer feeling came over me as I followed the old man out of the Bacchus-cellar. Was it really the light of the candles, was it an illusion what I saw? Did he not nod to me with his little round pate, did he not put out one of his chubby legs and shake and writhe with secret laughter? I ran after the old man and walked close behind him.

"Now to the twelve Apostles," I said to him. He did not reply; shaking his head dubiously he walked on. There were two or three steps to ascend from the large cellar into a small one, into the subterranean heavens, the seat of the blessed, where abide the twelve Apostles. What are ye, vaults and sepulchres of royal families, beside these catacombs! Place coffin by coffin, laud upon black marble the merits of the man who sleeps below, employ a garrulous keeper in garments of mourning, let him praise the unspeakable greatness of this dust or of that, let him relate the marvellous virtues of a prince who fell at such and such a battle, the exquisite beauty of a princess upon whose sarcophagus the virgin's myrtle twines with the bursting rosebud—it will remind you of mortality, it may cost you a tear; but can it touch you like this bed-chamber of a century, this resting-place of a glorious race? There they lie in their dark-brown coffins devoid of ornament and frippery. No marble boasts of their silent merits, their inconspicuous virtue, their excellent character; but what man with a heart for virtue of this sort does not feel himself stirred when the old custodian, this keeper of the catacombs, this sexton of the subterranean church, places his candles upon the coffins and lets the light fall upon the illustrious names of the great dead! Like royal heads, these too have no long title and surname; in noble simplicity their names appear upon the brown coffins. There is Andrew, here John, in yonder corner Judas, in this Peter. Who is not touched when he is then told that there lies the noble one of Nierenstein, born 1718; here he of Rüdesheim, born 1726. To the right Paul, to the left James, the good James!

"Good-night, ye old lords of the Rhine; good-night. And if there is anything I can do for you, fiery Judas, or you, gentle Andrew, or you, dear John, come, come to me."

"Lord of Heaven!" the old man interrupted me, slamming the door and turning the key. "Are you intoxicated already by the few drops you had, that you should thus tempt the devil? Don't you know that the wine-spirits arise this night, and visit each other, as they always do on the 1st of September? And should I lose my place thereby, I shall run off and leave you if you speak such words again. It is not yet twelve o'clock, but at any moment one of them might come creeping out of his cask and frighten us to death with a hideous grimace."

"Stop your foolish prattle, old fellow, and be comforted. I will not say another word to wake your wine-spirits. But now take me to the Rose."

We walked on; we entered a vault, the rose-garden of Bremen. There she lay, old Rose, bulky, tremendous, with an air of commanding sovereignty. What an enormous cask! and every bumper worth its weight in gold! 1615! Where are the hands that planted thee? Where are the eyes that revelled in thy bloom. Where are the happy folks that exulted when thou, noble grape, wert cut upon the heights of the Rhinelands, when thou wert pulled and thy golden flood burst into the tub? They are gone, like the waves of the river that bathed the foot of thy vineyard.

"There, and now good-night, Frau Rose!" said the old servant pleasantly. "Now, good-night, and God bless you; here, this way, sir, not around that corner; this is the way out of the cellar. Here, come, do not run against those casks; I will hold the candle."

"No, indeed, old chap," I said; "the joke is only just beginning. All this was but a foretaste. Bring me two or three bottles of your choicest of '22 in the large room yonder."

He stood there with eyes wide open, the poor fool. "Sir," he said solemnly, "put it out of your mind. I will not stay with you for love or money."

"Who told you to stay with me? Put the wine where I tell you, and, in God's name, go along with you."

"But I cannot leave you alone in the cellar," he replied. "I know, begging your pardon, that you wouldn't steal anything, but it is against my orders."

"Well, then, lock the door behind me; put a padlock on, as ponderous as you please, and to-morrow morning at six come and wake me and get your fee."

He tried to remonstrate, but it was in vain. At last he put down three bottles and nine candles before me, wiped

"TWO MEN WITH CEREMONIOUS POLITENESS FELL EXCELLENCE UPON EACH OTHER"

out the beaker, and bade me good-night with a heavy heart as it seemed. He locked the door, and out of tender solicitude for me, as it would seem, more than for the safety of his cellar, hung on a padlock. Just then the clock struck twelve, I heard him mutter a prayer and hasten away. The sound of his steps died away in the vault, and when he shut the outside door of the cellar it reverberated like a peal of thunder through the passages.

So I am alone with thee, my soul, far down in the womb of the earth. Up on the earth they are all asleep and adream, and down here, round about, they slumber in their coffins, the spirits of wine. Do they dream, I wonder, of their short childhood, of the distant hills where they were bred, and of their old father Rhine who murmured a gentle ditty by their cradle?

.   .   .   .

Hark! Was not that the sound of a door? Certainly very queer; if I were not alone down here, if I did not know that men can only walk the earth above, I should be tempted to think that there are steps resounding through the vaults. Ha! here they come, there is something fumbling at the door; it shakes the latch, but the door is locked and bolted; this night no *mortal* will disturb me. Ha! What is that? The door opens. Holy horrors!

Outside the door stood two men with ceremonious politeness urging the precedence upon each other. The one was tall and lean, adorned with a great black wig, a dark-red coat, trimmed with gilt cording and gilt-spun buttons; his legs, of abnormal length and thinness, were attired in knee-breeches of black velvet with gold buckles. His sword, with a heft of porcelain, he had stuck through his trousers-pocket; when bowing he waved a little three-cornered silk hat, while the flowing locks of his wig brushed his shoulders. The man had a pale, sorrowful face, deep-set eyes, and a large nose of fiery red. Quite different was the smaller fellow, who had been specially obsequious in urging the other to pass him at the door. His hair was pasted to his head with the white of an egg, and on either side it was fastened securely in two rolls like the holsters of a pistol; a long pig-tail hung down his back; he wore a little coat of grey faced with red; his lower parts were adorned with large jack-boots, his upper with a richly-embroidered vest of state, which fell over his well-rounded little belly down to his knees; and he was buckled about with an enormous sword. There was an expression of exceeding good-nature in his fleshy face, especially in his little eyes that stood out like those of a lobster. His gestures were carried out with an enormous felt hat turned up boldly on either side.

They hung their hats upon the wall, unbuckled their swords, and sat down silently by the table without looking at me. I was about to take heart and address them, when there was a new sound outside. Steps approached, the door was opened, and four other gentlemen, attired in the same old fashion, entered.

"God greet ye, Lords of the Rhine!" said the tall one of the red coat in a deep bass voice, getting up and bowing. "God greet ye," squeaked the little one; "it's a long time since last we saw you, James!"

"Hallo and good morning, Matthew," replied one of the new-comers; "and good morning to you too, Judas! But what is this? Where are our bumpers, our pipes and tobacco? Has the old knave not yet waked out of his sinner's sleep?"

"The lazy-bones!" cried the little one. "The heavy-eyed rascal! He is still lying over yonder in the graveyard; but, thunder and lightning, I'll wake him up!" With that he seized a large bell that was standing upon the table, ringing it and laughing in a shrill, cutting voice.

As is the case with genuine old drinkers, so among these guests the conversation would not flow without wine. Just then a new personage appeared at the door. It was a little old man, with shaking legs and grey hair; his head looked like a skull over which a thin hide has been drawn, and his eyes shone dimly out of deep hollows; he was tugging at a large basket, and greeted the guests humbly.

"Ah, here's our old kellermeister, Balthasar," called out the guests; "come on, old fellow, put down the beakers and bring our pipes! Why did you tarry so long? It struck twelve long ago."

The old man gaped once or twice rather indecently, and on the whole looked like a person who has overslept. "Came near sleeping through the 1st of September," he grunted; "ever since they have paved the churchyard, I don't hear as well as I did. Where are the other gentlemen?" he proceeded, taking beakers of strange shape and marvellous size out of the basket, and putting them on the table.

"Where are the others? You are only six, and old Rose hasn't come yet."

"Put the bottles down first," exclaimed Judas, "that we may get a drop of something to drink, and then go over yonder—they are still asleep in their casks; tap them with your dry bones and tell them to get up."

But hardly had Judas ended, when there was a rush and boisterous laughter at the door. "Spinster Rose, her health, hurrah, and her sweetheart Bacchus!" The door flew open, the ghostly fellows at the table jumped up and cried: "It is she, it is she, Spinster Rose and Bacchus and the others! Hurrah! Now we're in for a jolly good time!" and with that they touched beakers with a ringing sound and laughed, and the fat one struck his belly, and the pale kellermeister threw his cap skilfully between his legs and up to the ceiling, and joined in with the shouts of the others till my ears rang again. What a sight! The wooden Bacchus, that I had but just seen astride the cask in the cellar, had got down, naked as he was; with his broad, smiling face, with his twinkling eyes, he greeted the group and came walking skittishly into the room; by his hand he led with much ceremony as his betrothed an elderly dame of great height and of goodly roundness. I do not know to this day how it was possible, but then and there it was clear as daylight to me that this dame was no other than old Rose, the enormous cask in the Rose-cellar.

And how gorgeously had she got herself up, the old lady from the Rhine! In her youth she must have been a comely lass, for even now, although the fresh colours of girlhood had left her cheeks, although time had painted some little wrinkles about her brow and her mouth, two centuries could not efface the noble features of her fine face. Her eyebrows had turned grey, and a couple of unseemly grey hairs had sprouted upon her pointed chin, but the hair brushed smoothly over her forehead was brown as nuts, and only intermingled here and there with a little silvery grey. Upon her head she wore a black velvet cap, fitting closely above her ears; then she had on a jerkin of finest black cloth, and the bodice of red velvet showing beneath was fastened with silver hooks and chains. About her throat she wore a broad necklace of glittering garnets, fastened to which was a gold medal; an ample skirt of brown cloth fell about her portly figure, and a little white apron trimmed with white lace added a coquettish touch. On one side there was a large pocket of leather, on the other a bunch of tremendous keys—in short, she was as respectable-looking a dame as ever walked across the street of Cologne or Mayence in 1618.

And behind Dame Rose came six shouting fellows, swinging their three-cornered hats, with their wigs on awry, attired in broad-tailed coats and long embroidered vests.

With ceremonious courtesy did Bacchus lead his lady to

the head of the table, accompanied by the jubilations of his companions. She bowed with becoming gravity, and sat down. At her side the wooden Bacchus took a seat, after Balthasar, the kellermeister, had put a big cushion under him, for he had else seemed pitifully small and low. The others also sat down, and then I saw that they were the twelve Apostles from the Rhine, who at other times lie sleeping in the Apostles' cellar in Bremen.

"So here we are, altogether once more, we young people of 1700," said Peter, after the tumult had somewhat subsided. "Your health, Dame Rose! You don't look a day older; you're as comely and stately as you were fifty years ago. Your health, and your sweetheart's, Bacchus."

"My humble thanks to you, esteemed Apostle," answered Dame Rose, bowing her appreciation. "Are you as much of a tease as ever? I don't know of no sweetheart, and you mustn't say such things to put out a modest lass!" She cast down her eyes as she said it, and emptied a tremendous bumper.

"Love," said Bacchus, looking tenderly out of his little eyes, and taking her hand; "Love, don't put on airs. You know that my heart has inclined to you for two thousand autumns, and that I love you to-day before all others; a fiery kiss upon thy rosy lips shall prove it."

He leaned tenderly towards her. "If only all the young folks were not about," she whispered shamefacedly. But under

"HE TOOK HIS TRIBUTE WITH INTEREST."

the shouts and laughter of the twelve the wine-god took his tribute with interest.

"You are a rogue," he cried, laughing.

"You are a Turk, and make love to many at the same time. Do you suppose I don't know how you pay court to the frivolous Frenchwoman, the Lady of Bordeaux, and to the chalky pale-face of Champagne? Go away; you have a bad character, and are not made for faithful German love."

"The devil, you carry your jealousy too far," he cried snappishly. "I can't break off all of my old connections."

"What is this I see?" said Dame Rose. "You are thirteen at table. Who is that over there in strange garments? Who brought him here?"

Heavens, how I started! They all looked at me with surprise, and did not seem at all pleased at my intrusion. But I took heart, and said: "Your humble servant, gentlemen. I am nothing further than a mortal, graduated to a Doctor of Philosophy."

"But how dare you come here at this hour, mortal?" said Peter very solemnly, shooting lightnings out of his eyes at me.

"Your Excellency," I replied, "there is good reason for that. I am an enamoured friend of noble drink, and by the kindness of your right worthy Senate I have received permission to pay my respects to the twelve Apostles and to Dame Rose."

"And so you like to drink Rhine-wine?" said Bacchus. "Well, that is one good quality, and is the more to be praised at a time when mortals have grown more or less cold toward this golden fountain. I believe the race feels that it is no longer worthy of a noble drop, so they brew some slip-slop stuff of syrup and whisky, call it Chateau-Margaux, Sillery, St. Julien, and all sorts of pompous names, and when they drink it they get red rings about their mouth because the stuff is coloured, and headache the next day because they have had vile gin."

"Ah, it was a different life we led," continued John, "when our blood was young in the years '19 and '26. Nay, as late as '50 there were high times within these noble vaults. Every evening, no matter whether the sun would shine in spring or whether it would rain and snow in winter, every evening these apartments were filled with happy guests. Here, where we are sitting now, sat in state and dignity the Senate of Bremen, splendid wigs upon their heads, weapons at their side, courage in their heart, and a bumper before each."

"Yes, yes, children," said old Rose; "it used to be quite different from now say fifty, or one hundred, or two hundred years ago. Then they brought their wives and daughters with them to the cellar, and the handsome Bremen lasses drank Rhine-wine, or of our neighbours' from the Moselle, and were noted far and near for their blooming cheeks, their crimson lips, and for their lovely, sparkling eyes ; now they drink miserable stuff, tea and the like, which grows far away where the Chinamen live, I am told, and which in my day women drank when they had a little cough or other trouble. Rhine-wine, genuine honest Rhine-wine, doesn't agree with them nowadays; for the land's sake you wouldn't believe it! They put sweet Spanish wine with it to make it taste better; they say it's too sour."

The Apostles burst into a perfect roar of laughter, which I joined involuntarily, and Bacchus laughed so horribly that old Balthasar had to hold him.

"Ah, the good old times!" cried fat Bartholomew. "Our burghers used to drink two measures, and it seemed as if they had drunk water, so sober were they; but now one goblet throws them down. They are out of practice."

There was a terrible bang that made the vault ring again, the door flew open, and upon the threshold stood a tall white figure. With measured, ringing steps, a ponderous sword within his hand, in armour but without a helmet, did this gigantic individual strut into the room. He was of stone, his face was set and without expression. Nevertheless, his stony lips parted and he said—

"God greet ye, beloved vines from the Rhine. I needs must come and visit my fair neighbour on her anniversary-day. God greet you, Dame Rose. May I sit down to your carousal?"

They all turned in surprise upon the giant statue. Spinster Rose broke the silence, clapped her hands together with joy, and exclaimed—

"Goodness me! It's stony Roland, who has stood for many centuries upon the market-place of our dear Bremen town. Oh, it is kind of you to do me the honour, sir knight; lay down your shield and sword and make yourself comfortable; won't you sit here by my side? Gracious me, how pleased I am!"

The Apostles had moved up closer and made room for their guest on a chair by the ancient maiden. He laid his shield and sword in a corner and sat down rather awkwardly upon the little chair; but alas! this had been made for respectable mortals but not for a stony giant; with a crash it broke under him, and he lay full length upon the floor.

"Base generation, which fabricates such stools upon which in my day no delicate maiden could have sat without breaking through the seat!" grumbled the hero, slowly getting up. The kellermeister rolled a cask up to the table, and invited the knight to be seated. A couple of staves cracked as he sat down, but the cask stood the test.

"How tastes the wine to you?" Bacchus asked the new-comer. "It must be long since last you drank any."

"It is good, by my sword! Very good! What growth is it?"

"Red Ingelheimer, august sir!" answered the kellermeister.

The stony eye of the knight took life and fire when he heard this; his chiselled features were softened by a smile, and contentedly he looked into his cup.

"Ingelheim! Thou sweet, familiar name!" he said. "Thou noble castle of my knightly emperor; so thy name has outlasted the centuries, and the vines that Charlemagne planted in his Ingelheim still blossom? Does this new world know aught of Roland and of great Carolus, his master?"

"That you must ask the mortal over yonder," replied Judas; "we have nothing to do with the earth. He is a doctor and magister, and must be able to give an account of his generation."

The giant fixed his eyes inquiringly upon me, and I replied: "Noble Paladin! Humanity has grown cold and depraved; its shallow skull is nailed to the present, and looks neither forward nor backward; but we are not yet so bad that we should forget the glorious heroes that once walked our earth, and threw their shadows into our times."

The spirit of song seemed to have come over the company, for no sooner had Andrew ended than Judas began to sing unasked, and the others followed him. With a resounding bass voice Roland sang a war-hymn of the old Franconians, only a few words of which I understood, and at last, when they had all sung, they looked at me, and Rose nodded encouragingly. So I began—

> "Am Rhein, am Rhein, da wachsen unsere Reben
> Da wächst ein deutscher Wein."

When I had finished, they all came crowding about me to shake my hand, and Andrew breathed a kiss upon my lips.

"Do they sing that?" cried Bacchus. "Now then, Doctor, I'm mighty glad to hear that; your race cannot be so very frail if it sings such clear and cheery songs."

"Ah, sir," I said sadly, "there are many sentimentalists who refuse to give such a song the credit of being poetry, like some pietists who consider the Lord's prayer not mystic enough for devotion."

"There have been fools at all times, sir!" replied Peter. "But talking about your generation, tell us what has happened on earth during the last year?"

"If it would interest the ladies and gentlemen," I replied.

"Go ahead," cried Roland, and the others joining him, I began—

"As regards German literature——'

"Hold on, *manum de tabula!*" cried Paul. "What do we care about your miserable scribbling, about your puerile, disgusting quarrels, about your poetasters and false prophets and——"

I was dumfounded. If our wonderful, magnificent literature had no interest for these people, what could I tell them? I thought a while, and then continued: "It is evident that Joco, so far as the theatre is concerned——"

"Theatre? Go away with you!" interrupted Andrew. "Why should we hear about your puppet-shows and other follies? Do you suppose it is aught to us if one of your comedy-writers is hissed? Have you nothing interesting —no great historical facts to tell us about?"

"Alack-a-day," I cried, "we are quite out of historical facts; in that line there is nothing but the Bundestag at Frankfurt."

The dance the two were performing was according to the mode of two or three centuries ago. Dame Rose had seized her petticoats in both hands, and spread them out so that she looked like an immense cask. She walked trippingly back and forth, bobbing up and down in a succession of curtseys. Much greater vivacity did her partner display, who whirled about her like a top, leaping boldly, snapping his fingers, and shouting ho! and hallo! Odd enough did he look, what with the dainty apron of Mistress Rose, which Balthasar had tied around him, fluttering about in the air; how his little legs jerked, and his round face smiled for heartfelt pleasure and delight!

At last he was tired; he beckoned to Judas and Paul and whispered something to them. They untied his apron, took it by both ends, and pulled and pulled, until suddenly it grew as large as a sheet. "Ah," thought I, "now they will most likely play a joke on old Balthasar. If only the vault were not so low as it is; I fear me he'll break his skull." Then came Judas and Bartholomew and caught hold of me; Balthasar smiled maliciously; I trembled, I resisted, all to no purpose. My senses threatened to leave me as with shouting and laughter they laid me upon the cloth. "Not too high, my honoured patrons," I cried in great trepidation; but they laughed and shouted the louder. Now they began to rock the sheet, Balthasar blowing a tune on a tunnel. Now it began to go up and down, first 3, 4, or 5 feet, then suddenly they gave a jerk, I flew up, and the ceiling opened like a cloud; up, up higher I flew through the roof of the rathhaus, higher than the steeple of the church. "Well," I thought, "it's up with me now! When I fall, I shall break my neck. Farewell, my life and my love!"

I had now reached the highest point of my ascent, and I fell as rapidly. Crash! Right through the roof of the rathhaus, down through the ceiling of the cellar; but I did not fall upon the sheet once more. I lighted on a chair with which I fell over backward upon the floor.

For some time I lay stunned by the fall. A pain in my head and the coolness of the ground woke me at last. At first I could not think whether I had fallen out of bed at home, or what was the matter. At last I remembered, that

I had fallen down from some very high region. With some anxiety I examined my limbs; nothing was broken, only my head pained me from the fall. I was in a cellar, the daylight shone in dimly, the light of a candle was dying out upon the table, there were bottles and glasses about, before every chair a little bottle with a long label about its neck. Ah, now I remembered everything. I was in Bremen, in the rathskeller; I had come in here last night, had been locked in, and then——. Full of horror I looked about me. I ventured to cast shy glances into the corners of the room: it was empty. Or was it possible I could have dreamed it all?

Thoughtfully I walked around the table; the little sample-bottles stood where my strange guests had sat. First Rose, then Judas, James, and John. "No, a dream cannot be so like reality," I said to myself. "All this that I heard and saw did actually occur!" But there was no time for further reflections. I heard keys rattle in the lock, it was slowly opened, and the old rathsdiener entered saying: "It has just struck six."

Wilhelm Hauff (1802–1827).

THE DUEL WITH THE DEVIL.

MEANWHILE something occurred which I[1] must not pass over, as it may serve as a commentary to the customs of this peculiar nation. I had been for some time an ardent visitor at the anatomy-rooms, for I was anxious to make the acquaintance of medical students. It happened one day that I was busying myself about a corpse with several friends, dissecting the organs of the mind, the brain, and heart in order to deduce the absurdity of the belief in immortality.

Suddenly I heard a voice behind me, "The devil, how stifling!"

I quickly turned and saw a young student of theology, who had already excited my wrath in a dogmatic lecture by the ardour and gusto with which he had taken notes of the ridiculous conjectures of the professor on the nature of the diabolical. Hearing him make this remark, which at that moment, and from him, I took as referring wholly to myself, I told him pretty strongly that I objected to such personal and insinuating expressions.

According to the ancient sacred law called "Comment," this was an insult which could only be obliterated with blood. The theologian, a famous bravo, sent me his challenge the next day. This was just such a lark as I had been hoping for. Whoever cared for the good opinion of his fellow-students was expected to have a duel on record, although all of my friends admitted the custom to be utterly irrational and unnatural. I had prevailed upon my opponent to have the affair come off at a public resort, a couple of miles outside the town, and both parties put in an appearance at the designated place and time.

[1] The Devil is the speaker.

Solemnly each arrival was conducted into a room, where his coat was removed and replaced by the "paukwichs," a sort of armour in which the duel was to be fought. This "paukwichs," or armour, consisted in a hat with a broad brim sufficiently protecting the face; an enormously broad bandage made of leather, wadded and decorated with the colours of the society, to be strapped over the abdomen; an immense cravat standing stiffly about the neck, and affording protection to the chin, throat, part of the shoulders, and the upper portion of the chest. The arms were covered from the hands to the elbows with gloves made of old silk stockings. It must be confessed a figure in this unique armour looked funny enough. However, there was great safety in it, for only a part of the face, the upper half of the arm, and a part of the chest were at the mercy of the opponent's rapier.

"A FIGURE IN THIS UNIQUE ARMOUR."

A strong impulse to laugh came over me as I examined myself in the mirror. "The devil, in such attire, and about to enter the lists on behalf of the odour in the anatomy-room!"

My companions took my hilarity as an expression of courage and valour. Thinking, therefore, the right moment had now come, they conducted me into a large hall where the position of the enemy had been marked on the floor with chalk. A freshman considered it a high honour to be permitted to carry my rapier, as sword and sceptre were carried before the ancient emperors. It was a well-made weapon of finest steel, with a large hilt offering at the same time a protection for the hand.

At last we stood facing each other. The student of theology put on a fierce expression and looked upon me with an air of disdain, which strengthened me in my purpose of setting a right handsome mark upon him.

We put ourselves into the traditional posture, the blades were crossed, the seconds yelled "Ready!" and our rapiers whizzed through the air, and fell clinking upon the hilts. I confined myself to parrying the really masterly and artistic cuts of my opponent. I knew that my glory would be the greater if I merely defended myself at first and then gave him his deserts in the fourth or fifth round.

Applause followed each pass. Never had there been such bold and decisive attacks, never such dignified and cold-blooded self-defence. My skill in fencing was lifted up into the seventh heaven by old hands, and there was much curiosity and conjecture as to my tactics of retaliation. No one dared urge me to the onset.

Four rounds had passed without one thrust that had drawn blood. Before stepping forth for the fifth, I pointed out to my comrades the spot on my theologian's right cheek where I intended to hit him. He seemed to get wind of my purpose, put himself under cover as much as possible, and carefully abstained from venturing an attack on his part. I began with a superb feint, which was received with an admiring "Ah!" made a couple of regular thrusts, and with a clap my rapier was in his cheek.

The honest theologian was very much taken aback. My second and witness rushed up to him with a tape-measure, examined the wound, and said in a solemn voice, "It is more than an inch, and it gaps horribly, so 'Abfuhr!'" Which is as much as to say, the poor boy having a hole in his face an inch long, his honour has been vindicated.

Now my friends crowded about me; the elder grasped my hands, the younger gazed with veneration upon the weapon with which the deed, surpassing anything in history, had been done. For who could boast of first having designated the spot he intended to hit, and then hitting it with such marvellous precision?

With a serious mien my opponent's second stepped up to me, and in the name of the former offered me amity. I approached the invalid, whose wound was just being attended to with needle and thread, and made friends.

"I am greatly indebted to you," he said, "for having marked me thus. I have been forced to study theology against my will. My father is a country parson, my mother is a pious lady, who would like above all things to see her son in a surplice. But your decisive stroke has altered matters; with a scar reaching from my ear to my mouth there is no church that would have me."[1]

The companions of the brave theologian looked upon him sympathisingly. Who could measure his sad regrets at the thought of the old parson's grief, the pious mamma's despair, when the news of this disaster should reach them? But to me it seemed like a great piece of good luck for the youth to be given back to the world by so short an operation. I asked him to what studies he would now devote himself, and he frankly confessed that the calling of a cuirassier

---

[1] Even at the present day persons conspicuously marked in a student's fray are not allowed to enter the theological profession, unless there is a fair prospect that the scar may be hidden under a prospective beard.

or of an actor had always seemed chiefly attractive to him.

I felt like embracing him for this happy thought, for it is in these very professions that I have most of my friends and adherents. I advised him urgently to follow the bend of nature, and promised to supply him with the best recommendations to distinguished generals and to the most notable stages.

As for all the persons in any way connected with this remarkable duel, I gave them an excellent dinner, in which of course I included my opponent and his followers. I then privately paid the debts of the quondam theologian, and when he had recovered I supplied him with money and letters, which opened a right jolly and brilliant career to him.

Neither the elegant conclusion of the duel nor my unobtrusive charity remained a secret. I was now looked upon as a being of a higher order, and I know many a young lady who shed tears over my generous sentiments.

The students of medicine sent a deputation presenting me with a superb rapier, because, as they thought, I had fought on behalf of the faultless odour of their anatomy-room.

Wilhelm Hauff.

EDITORIAL CO-OPERATION.

"AS our paper must needs be very universal," I said, "and as there should be something in the title to express this tendency, how would it do to call it 'Literary Provender'?"

"That would not be bad; there might be a vignette representing the public as a bevy of fowls clustering about the Muse, who is cutting up food for them; but it will not do. Some might take offence at Provender; it might seem as if only the leavings from the great dinner-table of literature were to be served to the public. It won't do!"

"Well, then,—'Evening-Bells.'"

"'Evening-Bells?' Ah, indeed. That is an idea! There is something so soft and soothing about the word. I'll make a note of the suggestion. But we should have to have a critical supplement. I have been thinking we might call it 'The Distiller.'"

"It is very expressive," I replied; "it is quite customary in these times to subject books to a chemical process of review or criticism; the distillation is carried on until the spirit sought for has evaporated, or until the learned chemist can announce to the world what all the different elements were that combined in the decoction he analysed. But with such a name the paper might appear to smell of the gin-shop. How would it strike you to call it 'The Critical Chimney-Sweep'?"

The publisher gazed at me in silence for a moment, and then embraced me with emotion. "An idea," he cried; "a remarkable idea! What a volume of meaning there is in the word! German literature is the chimney, our reviewers are the sweepers: they scrape down the literary soot, to preserve the house from fire. It must be an extremely radical paper; it must be striking, that is the first thing. 'The Critical Chimney-Sweep!' And we will bring the art critiques under the promising title, 'The Artistic Night-Watch.'" Hastily putting down the names, he continued: "Sir, my guardian-angel has brought you to my door; when I sit by my table writing my mind seems blocked up, but I have often noticed that when I once begin to speak, my thoughts flow like a stream. So when you were speaking of Walter Scott and his influence a glorious idea arose within me. I will make a German Walter Scott."

"How so? Are you too going to write a novel?"

"I? Dear me, no; I have something better to do; and one? no, twenty! If I only had my thoughts all ordered. I am going to procure a great Unknown, and this mysterious personage is to consist of a party of novel-writers; do you understand?"

"It is not quite clear to me, I confess. How will you—— ?"

"There is nothing that cannot be accomplished with money; I shall address myself to, say, six or eight clever men who have already made their mark in writing novels, invite them here, and offer the proposal that they should join to produce this Walter Scott. They choose the historical subjects and characters, discuss the secondary figures to be introduced, and then——."

"Ah, now I understand your glorious plan; then you will erect a factory like the one at Scheeran. You will send for cuts of all the most romantic scenery in Germany; the costumes of old times can be procured at Berlin; legends and songs can be found in the *Boys' Wonderhorn*, and other collections. You engage two or three dozen of aspiring young men; your sexavirat, the great Unknown, gives the general plot of the novels, here and there he models and corrects an important character; the twenty-four or thirty-six others write the dialogue, picture towns, scenes, buildings, after nature——"

"And," he interrupted me gleefully, "as the one has more talent for the delineation of scenery, the other for costumes, the third for conversation, the fourth or fifth for comedy, others for the tragic——"

"Ah, I see: so the young poets will be divided into painters of scenery, tailors of costume, leaders of conversation, comedians, and tragedians, and the novel passes through the hands of each, like the pictures at Campe's in Nuremberg, where one draws the sky, the other the earth, this one roofs, and that one soldiers, where one paints green, the other blue, the third red, the fourth yellow."

"And in this way harmony and uniformity would be reached, just as they are in Walter Scott, where all characters have a striking family resemblance. And we'll have a pocket-edition as cheap as possible; we can count on forty thousand."

"And the title shall be: 'The History of Germany, from Hermann the Cheruskian to 1830, in one hundred historical novels!'"

Herr Salzer shed tears of emotion. Having recovered, he seized my hand. "Well, am I not as enterprising as anybody?" he said. "Think of the talk it will make. But to you, most excellent friend, I am indebted for aid in bringing forth this giant thought. Pick out the handsomest book in my shop, and in token of my gratitude I name you to be—one of the twenty-four!"

Wilhelm Hauff.

"HE PUT THE ORANGE ON THE TABLE BEFORE HIM."

MOZART'S JOURNEY TO PRAGUE.

IT was in the autumn of the year 1787 that Mozart, accompanied by his wife, undertook the journey to Prague to supervise the performance of *Don Juan*.

"The waggon drawn by three horses," writes the Baroness von T. to her friend, "a stately chaise of reddish yellow, was the property of a certain old Frau Generalin Volkstett.

who was fond of setting her relations to the Mozart family, and the kindnesses she bestowed upon the same in the right light." This hasty description of the vehicle in question can easily be enlarged upon by any connoisseur of the taste of those days. The reddish-yellow chaise was decorated on each side with bouquets of flowers in their natural colours; the edges of the doors bore narrow gilt mouldings; the whole could not by any means boast the glassy varnish of to-day's Vienna mode; the body was not fully rounded, though drawn in below with a bold, coquettish curve; then there was a high top with stiff leather curtains, which, for the time being, were pushed back.

Regarding the attire of the two passengers there is this to be said. With wise economy Frau Constanze had packed her spouse's new and splendid garments of state and chosen modest ones for the occasion; with an embroidered vest of somewhat faded blue there was his common brown coat with a row of large buttons, so fashioned that there was a layer of reddish gold-leaf glimmering through a starry surface, black silk trousers and stockings, and gilt buckles on his shoes. For the last half-hour he has abandoned his coat on account of the unusual heat, and sits gaily talking bare-headed, and in shirt-sleeves. Madam Mozart wears a comfortable travelling-dress, light green and white striped; a wealth of light-brown curls, but loosely fastened, fall over her neck and shoulders; as long as she lived they were never disfigured by powder; her husband's thick cue was also more scantily supplied than usual owing to the ceremonial freedom of travel.

The horses had just walked slowly up a gently sloping hill between ripe fields that interrupted the long stretches of woodland here and there, and now they had reached the edge of the woods.

"Through how many miles of woods have we passed to-day and yesterday and the day before," said Mozart, "and thought nothing of it, it never so much as occurring to me to set my foot within them. Let us get down now, darling mine, and get some of those dainty blue-bells over there in the shade. Your poor beasts, postillion, will be glad of a rest."

As they both arose a little mishap came to light, which brought upon the Meister something of a scolding. Through his carelessness a flask of fragrant essence had come open, and had poured its contents unobserved over their garments and over the cushioned interior of the chaise. "I might have known it," lamented Frau Constanze; "there was such a sweet odour all the time! Alack-a-day, a whole flask of pure *Rosée d'aurore* quite empty! I was so chary of it." "Ah, little miser," he comforted her, "take thought, and consider that thus, and thus only, could your divine smelling-whisky do us any good. At first we sat as in an oven, for all your fanning, and then suddenly there was a cool and refreshing atmosphere. You attributed it to the drop or two I poured on my jabot; we were revived, and conversation was once more animated and gay, whereas before our heads had hung low like those of sheep on the butcher's cart; and this benefit will stay with us for all the rest of the way. But now let us put our Vienna noses into the green wilderness here."

Arm-in-arm they scrambled through the trench by the side of the road and entered the dusky shade of the fir-trees. The spicy freshness, the sudden change from the sunny glow without, might have proved disastrous to the reckless man but for the prudence of his companion. She had some trouble in urging his discarded garment upon him. "Ah, the glory of it," he cried, gazing up the tall trunks; "it is like being in church! Seems to me I never was in the woods before, and it is only now that I can see what

"ARM-IN-ARM THEY ENTERED THE DUSKY SHADE OF THE FIR-TREES."

this means, this assembly of trees! No man's hands planted them, they all came of themselves, and stand so only just because it is jolly to live and labour together. Fancy, when I was young I passed this way and that through Europe; I saw the Alps and the ocean, the most beautiful and most sublime things that were ever created; and now here stands the fool in an ordinary forest of firs on the boundary-line of Bohemia, astonished and enraptured that such things should be, that it's not just *una finzione di poeti*, like the nymphs and fauns and all that, and no stage-forest; no, it's a genuine one, grown out of the earth, nourished by its moisture and by the warm light of the sun."

"To hear you talk," said his wife, "one would think you had never gone twenty steps into our Vienna *Prater*, which surely can boast of similar wonders and rarities."

"The *Prater?* Thunder and lightning! How dare you name the word here! What with their carriages, and state uniforms, and toilets and fans, and music, and all horrors under the sun, there's nothing to be seen beyond. And even the trees, though they are big enough to be sure, I don't know how it is—beech-nuts and acorns lying on the ground can't for the life of them help looking like brothers and sisters to the hosts of worn-out corks among them. For miles it smells of waiters and sauces."

"Was there ever such ingratitude!" cried she; "and all this from a man who is deaf to all other delights when he can dine on baked chickens at the *Prater!*"

When they were both seated in the chaise once more, and the road, after running through a flat stretch, began to fall again to where a laughing landscape unfolded, losing itself in the distant hill-lands, the Meister began again after a span of silence: "This world is truly beautiful, and no one is to be blamed for wishing to stay here as long as possible. Thank God, I feel as strong and hale as ever, and there are a thousand things I should like to be up to as soon as ever my new *opus* is done and on the stage. How much there is out in the world and how much there is at home,—things remarkable and things beautiful, that I do not even know of, wonder-works of nature, science, art, and useful trades! The black collier-boy yonder knows just about as much as I do about some things, by my soul. I should like for the life of me to take a look into this, that, and the other thing, that doesn't come within the narrow limits of my trade."

"The other day," she answered, "I came across an old pocket calendar of yours; it was of '85; there are three or four memoranda in it. One of them, under-scored, is: *Professor Gattner, to visit him.* Who is he?"

"Yes, yes, I know—the kind old gentleman at the observatory, who has invited me there from time to time. I have always wished you and I could take a look at the moon and the man in it. They have a tremendous telescope up there now; they say it seems as if you could touch the mountains and valleys and rifts, and on the side where the sun doesn't shine the shadows that the mountains cast. It's two years now that I've wanted to see it, and I don't manage to get around to it, ridiculous and shameful though it seems!"

"Ah, well," said she, "the moon won't run away. There are many things we'll make up for later. I have a presentiment."

"Out with it!"

"I heard a little bird twitter that ere long the King of Prussia would need a *Capellmeister.*"

"Oho!"

"General Musical Director, I would say. Let me spin a dream! It is a weakness I have from my mother."

"Go ahead! the wilder the better!"

"No, quite natural. First then take the time, a year from date——"

"When the Pope marries Kate——"

"Hush, you clown! I say a year from to-day there must be no such person as an Imperial composer named Wolf Mozart to be found within the walls of Vienna."

"Thank you kindly for that!"

"I hear our old friends talking about us and our fortunes."

"Give us an example."

"Well, say one morning, shortly after nine, our exubriant old neighbour, Frau Volkstett, strutting straight across the cabbage market. She had been absent for three months; her great journey to visit her brother-in-law—her constant theme since we knew her—had at last become a reality; and now she has come back, and her full heart—bubbling over with the joy of travel and the impatience of friendship, and all sorts of delightful news—draws her irresistibly to the Frau Oberst. Upstairs she goes, taps at the door, and, without waiting to be bidden, walks in; you can imagine the delight and the embracements from both sides! 'Now, dearest, best Frau Oberst,' she begins, after some preliminaries, taking a fresh breath, 'I bring you a bagful of messages! Can you guess from whom?' 'What? is it possible—did you pass through Berlin? Did you see the Mozarts? Ah, dear, sweet friend, relieve my impatience! How are our good friends? Do they like it as well as they did at first?' 'Yes, indeed! This summer the king sent him to Karlsbad. When would his beloved majesty, Emperor Joseph, have thought of doing such a thing? They had both but just come back when I was there. He is beaming with health and life, is growing stout and roundish, and is as lively as Mercury.'"

And now the little woman proceeded to elaborate everything in her assumed *rôle* in the most glowing colours. Of their home *Unter den Linden*, of their garden and country-house, of the brilliant effectiveness of his appearance in public, and of the exclusive little gatherings at court, where he accompanied the queen's song on the piano, her descrip-

tion taking life as she went on. Entire conversations, the
most charming anecdotes, she seemed to shake out of her
sleeve. At the same time she was roguish enough to supply
the person of our hero with a number of brand-new homely
virtues, which had sprouted out of the solid ground of
Prussian existence, and among which the said Frau
Volkstett had noted as the highest phenomenon and proof
of the marvellous potence of new surroundings the wee begin-
nings of a most praiseworthy little trait of parsimony, which
proved a most graceful acquisition. "Yes, and only think,
he has three thousand thalers secure, and all that for what?
For leading a concert once a week and the opera twice.
Ah, I saw him, our dear, little precious Mozart, in the
midst of his *kapelle*. I sat with his wife in her box right
across from their majesties. And what did the handbill
say? Here it is; I brought it for you,—I wrapped it about
a little present I brought you from myself and the Mozarts;
here it is in plain letters!

"Heaven help us! *Tarar!* Ah, dear friend! To think
that I should live to see it! Two years ago, when Mozart
was writing his *Don Juan*, and that confounded villainous
Salieri was also making preparations to repeat the triumph
his piece brought him in Paris upon his own territory, and
when he and his boon-companions thought they had plucked
the *Don Juan* as they had *Figaro*, leaving it neither dead
nor alive to put it upon the stage, don't you remember, I
then and there took a vow not to go and see the infamous
piece, and I kept my word. When everybody rushed to
the show—you too, dear Frau Oberst--I sat down quietly
by my stove and took my cat upon my lap to spend the
evening. But now, think of it! *Tarar* on the Berlin stage,
the work of his bitterest enemy, directed by Mozart! 'You
must come,' he said to me, 'though it were only to tell them
in Vienna that I do not hurt a hair of his head. I wish he
were here himself, the envious knave, to see that there is no

need for *me* to murder another fellow's thing to remain what I am!'"

"Brava! bravissima!" exclaimed Mozart with roaring delight. He took his little wife by the ears, kissing and tickling her, until this bright soap-bubble game of a dreamy future—which, alas! never approximated this happy culmination—ended in mirth and boisterous laughter.

Meanwhile they had reached the valley, and were approaching a village which they had noticed from the hill-top, and behind which a pleasant country-house in modern style, the residence of the Count von Schinzberg, became visible. It was their intention to rest and dine in the place. The inn where they stopped was quite at the end of the village, and close beside it a by-road planted with a row of poplars led to the garden of the Count.

Mozart left the ordering of dinner to his wife, merely signifying his intention of having a glass of wine in the common room below, while she asked for a drink of water and for a quiet spot in which to enjoy a peaceful hour's sleep. She was shown up a flight of stairs, her husband following, humming and whistling a tune as he went. In a newly whitewashed room, just aired, there was, among other old-fashioned furniture of noble origin,—which had, no doubt, wandered hither out of the possessions of the Count,—a neat, airy bed, with a painted canopy resting on slender green posts, the silk curtains of which had long ago been replaced by some more common fabric. Constanze exacted a promise from her husband to be waked in time, and bolted the door behind him, he seeking amusement in the common tap-room. There was not a soul there, however, except the host; and, finding the conversation of the latter as little to his taste as the wine, he thought to fill out the time before dinner with a walk to the Count's park. He was told that respectable strangers were allowed to enter, and, moreover, the family had gone out for a drive.

He went, and ere long he had reached the open gate, and was walking slowly along under the stately limes until he had the schloss in view. It was built in the Italian style, light in colour, with a generous flight of steps lying broadly to the front; the slate roof was decorated with statues in the usual manner, gods and goddesses, and a balustrade.

Turning away from the *parterres* of blooming flowers, the Meister bent his steps toward the shrubbery, passing groups of beautiful pines, and gradually approaching sunnier spots once more, attracted by the merry sound of a splashing fountain which he soon reached.

The large oval basin was set round with orange trees in tubs, intermingled with laurels and oleanders; there was a small arbour at one side, and a soft path of sand led around to it. The arbour seemed a most attractive spot for a rest; there was a seat and small table in it, and Mozart sat down near the entrance.

Inclining his ear indolently to the gentle plash of the water, his eyes resting upon an orange tree of medium size standing apart from the others close by his side and covered with exquisite fruit, our friend, under the influence of these reminiscences of the South, fell to musing on a graceful episode of his boyish travels. Smiling thoughtfully, he put out his hand to touch the fruit and feel its delicious juicy coolness in his hollow hand. In connection with the youthful scene arising before him there was a half-forgotten musical memory the uncertain trail of which he was dreamily following. Now his eyes begin to shine, they wander restlessly here and there; a thought had seized him, and he is eagerly following it. Absent-mindedly he takes hold of the orange once more: it breaks from the branch, and he holds it in his hand. He does not see it; so far is he absorbed in his artistic preoccupation that he turns and twirls the fragrant fruit under his nose, moving his lips inaudibly to some newly-caught melody. At last, without knowing what he does, he takes a small enamelled case out of a pocket of his coat, pulls out a silver-handled knife, and slowly cuts the golden ball in two. Perhaps he was led by a vague feeling of thirst, but the delicious fragrance seemed to satisfy his stimulated senses. For moments he gazed fixedly at the two inner surfaces, then gently put them together, very gently separated, and joined them once more.

Suddenly he heard steps approaching; he started, and the consciousness of where he was and of what he had done dawned upon him. He was about to hide the orange, but desisted immediately, impelled by pride or by the knowledge that it was too late. A tall, broad-shouldered man in a livery, the Count's gardener, stood before him. He had evidently seen the last suspicious motion, and looked at him dubiously. Mozart was silent also, and felt as if he were nailed to his seat; he glanced up with a half-laugh and a visible blush, but at the same time there was a look of undaunted frankness in his large blue eyes; then with a petulant air of courageous audacity, which would have been absurdly funny to an unconcerned looker-on, he put the orange, apparently uninjured, in the middle of the table before him.

"Begging your pardon," said the gardener, now repressing his indignation, after having inspected the unpromising garb of the stranger, "I do not know with whom I have the honour——"

"Kapellmeister Mozart from Vienna."

"Doubtless you are an acquaintance of the Count?"

"I am a stranger here, passing through the village merely. Is the Count at home?"

"No."

"The Countess?"

"Is occupied, and it is unlikely she will see any one."

Mozart arose and seemed about to go.

"I beg your pardon, sir,—by what right did you help yourself in this garden?"

"What?" cried Mozart; "help myself? The devil! do you believe I wanted to steal and eat that thing here?"

"Sir, I believe what I see. These fruits are counted, and I am responsible. This tree is designed by the Count to figure at an entertainment: just now it was to be carried away. I cannot let you go before having made mention of this affair, and before you explain how this happened."

"Well, then, I will wait here. You may depend upon it."

The gardener looked around doubtfully, and Mozart, thinking he might be manœuvring for a fee, put his hand in his pocket, but there was not a coin in it.

Two lads came up now, lifted the tree upon a barrow, and carried it away. Meanwhile our Meister had pulled out his note-book, and while the gardener did not leave his side, he wrote—

"GNÄDIGSTE FRAU,—Here I sit, a poor unfortunate, in your paradise, like Adam after having tasted the apple. The evil is done, and I cannot even seek refuge by throwing the guilt upon the shoulders of gentle Eve, for the latter is sleeping the sleep of innocence at the inn guarded by the Graces and Cupids of a four-post bed. You have but to command, and I will personally give your Grace an account of my incomprehensible offence. In sincere contrition, your most obedient servant,

"W. A. MOZART (on the way to Prague)."

. . . . . .

While this was passing in the schloss, our prisoner, not greatly concerned about the final result, had occupied himself with waiting. But as no one appeared, he began to walk up and down uneasily; then there came an urgent message from the inn to tell him dinner was ready, and would he please come at once, the postillion was anxious to get started. He picked up his things, and was about to leave without further ceremony, when the two gentlemen appeared before the arbour.

The Count greeted him as he would an old acquaintance, with a ringing, sonorous voice, did not listen to his apologies, but at once expressed his desire to have the couple for his guests. "You are, my dear *maistro*, no stranger to us; indeed I may say that the name of Mozart is heard nowhere more frequently and with greater fervour. My niece plays and sings, spends nearly the whole day at her piano, knows your works by heart, and has the greatest desire to approach you personally, as she could not do in your concerts last winter. As we are going to Vienna for a few weeks, her relatives had promised her an invitation from Prince Gallizin, where you are often to be found. But it seems you are going to Prague, and there is no knowing when you will come back. Rest with us for a day or two! We will send your carriage back, and you will have the kindness to permit me to see to the continuation of your journey."

The composer, who was always willing to bring friendship or pleasure any sacrifice ten times as great as was here demanded, gladly complied for this half-day, at the same time setting his departure most definitely for the next morning. Count Max asked to be permitted to escort Frau Mozart from the inn, and to give the necessary orders there. . . .

Edward Mörike (1804–1875).

A RAPID PHILOSOPHER.

AT last I fell asleep, but it was only to be awakened at dawn by resounding footsteps passing to and fro in the adjoining room, intermingled with sounds from which I judged that there was an impatient searching of drawers or tables, and in every corner of the apartment. The hurrying and rummaging grew more violent, a soliloquy which at first softly accompanied the movements grew louder and louder, and gradually passed into exclamations of rage, and at last into a volley of oaths, which was not exactly in a Christian spirit, and which was accompanied by a savage stamping and bellowing. It seemed to me the man had gone mad. I dressed myself hastily, knocked at the door, and in my excitement, forgetting all form, I entered the room without awaiting his call. With flashing eyes the occupant darted at me as if about to seize me by my throat; suddenly he controlled himself, stood stock-still before me, gave me a penetrating glance, and said with quiet severity, "Sir, an unconscious thirst for knowledge has brought you to this room." My conscience reproaching me for my breach of good manners, I was disarmed, and merely said "Yes," in a dejected tone. I then asked him what for heaven's sake was the matter with him. A. E.—for brevity's sake I will henceforth call my fellow-traveller so—falling back into his fit of violence, cried in a voice of thunder, "My spectacles, my spectacles! They've seen fit to go and hide themselves—to say nothing at present of the key, the little devil!"

"So you are merely looking for your spectacles? Is this an object worthy of such rage? Don't you know what it is to be patient?"

He was about to fly at me again, but, controlling himself

once more, he merely looked at me and said: "Screw-drivers? cork-screws?"

"What do you mean by that?"

"I dreamed I had a wife—horrible to relate. I laughed at her for reading papers without cutting the leaves, and for putting up for years with a drawer that would not go. Thereupon she gave me a sermon on patience, and required me to exercise myself in that virtue by wearing screws and screw-drivers on my coat instead of buttons and button-holes, suggesting that they might be quite ornamental if made out of oxidised metal; or she said I might have corks, which I would be obliged to remove by means of a cork-screw every time I wished to unbutton my coat. Ah, pshaw! a woman is quite capable of putting a cover upon a dressing-case in such a manner that it will catch every time the upper drawer is opened and shut. Sir, a woman has *time* for the struggle with the villain called matter; she lives in this struggle, it is her element; a man has no business to have time for this, he needs his patience for things that are *worthy* of patience. It is an imposition to expect him to waste either for what is worthless, an imposition against which he may, can, and must rage! You must know that. You must know that these unworthy objects, these hooks and crooks of matter, never get entangled with your destiny except when you are in most desperate haste to complete something which is necessary and reasonable! Miserable gimcrack, worthless button or ball of twine, or string to my eye-glasses that gets twisted about one of the buttons of my vest just at the very moment when it is necessary to look over a time-table in small type at the railway station, I have no time, no time for ye! And if I were to set a thousand leeches on eternity, they would not draw out a single moment of time for ye!"

"But what is the use of all this bluster?"

"Oh, insipid! Was it of no use to Luther—if you are going to talk about use—to rail at the devil? Don't you know what it is to disburden your poor soul? Have you never heard of the precious balm that lies in a good round oath?"

"I TOOK THE EXASPERATED MAN AND POINTED SILENTLY TO THE SPOT."

The evil spirit took possession of him anew; he rushed about the room in another paroxysm of rage pouring out a volley of abuse upon his poor innocent spectacles. Meanwhile I looked about the floor; I picked up a couple of shirts that were clean, but terribly messed, and my eyes fell upon a mouse-hole in the boards. It seemed to me I saw something glitter there; I looked closer, and the discovery was made. I took the exasperated man by his arm and pointed silently to the spot. He gazed at it, recognised his missing glasses, and remarked: "Look at them well! Do you notice the sneer, the demoniac triumph in that evil glassy leer? Out with the entrapped monster!"

It was not easy to pull the spectacles out of the hole; the trouble was really out of proportion to the value of the object. At last we succeeded; he held them out at arm's-length, dropped them from there, cried in a solemn voice, "Sentence of death! *Supplicium!*" raised his foot, and crushed them with his heel, shivering them to bits.

"That's all very well," I said, after a pause of astonishment; "but now you have no spectacles."

"No matter. At any rate this imp has met with a just retribution after years of indescribable malignity. Look you!" He pulled out his watch; it was a very common one—in fact, one of the lowest products of the horological industry. "In place of this honest, faithful creature," he continued, "I once had a gold repeater, which, I may truly say, cost a deal of money. It requited this sacrifice for years and years with untold malice; it never would go right; it made a point of falling down and hiding; the crystals broke constantly, thereby nearly reducing me to pauperism; at last the monster conspired with the hook of my gold watch-chain, and the two together entered into an intrigue against me. As for the hook, sir, there is much that might be said on that subject. The insidiousness of objects in general—I should like to talk to you about that, sir, but I fear I should discourse at some length—the insidiousness, I say, is expressed so visibly in the villainous physiognomy of hooks that one cannot be too much on one's guard in having anything to do with these fiendish features. One is apt to think: 'I know you, the wicked crookedness of your outer form betrays you, you shall not get the better of me;' and then this very sense of security misleads one into being unwary. It is quite the reverse with other objects. Who, for instance, would suspect a simple button of any evil design?"

I begged him to finish the tragic story about his watch and hook.

"Ah, yes! Well, one night the hook crept softly across the small table, upon which I had carefully laid my watch, and artfully entwined itself into the seam of my pillow-case. I did not want the pillow. I lifted it suddenly and flung it to the foot-end of the bed, the watch of course going with it. In a noble arch it went flying through the air, struck the wall, and fell to the ground with a broken crystal. This was the last straw. I crushed it in cold blood like these criminal spectacles; the imp gave forth a sound, a hiss like a persecuted mouse; I swear to you that it was a sound quite outside the realm of physical nature. I then went and bought this modest timepiece for an absurdly low sum. Look at this faithful creature; note the expression of honesty in these homely features; for twenty years it has served me with steadfast fidelity; yes, I may say it has never given me any cause for complaint. The gold watch-chain I gave to my footman, the hook was condemned to die a shameful death in the sewer, and I wear my faithful turnip on this gentle silken cord."

During this detailed account he had grown quite tranquil, and now placidly continued—

"Now for the story of this black hour! Look at this key" —he pulled out a small key, probably belonging to his valise- "and then at this candlestick!"—he held up the metal candlestick upside down close before my eyes, so that I could see a hollow place in the foot—"what do you think, what do you suppose, what do you say?"

"How am I to know?"

"For the space of a good half-hour I have looked for that key this morning. I nearly lost my senses; at last I found it, like this, do you see?"

He laid the key upon the little stand by his bed, and set the candlestick down upon it; the key just fitted the place under the foot.

"Now tell me who would suspect this, who would be capable of such superhuman circumspection as to foresee and avoid such infernal tricks on the part of the object! And is this what I live for? Am I to waste the precious bit of time I have in such a slavish search for a bagatelle? To search and search, and to search again! One should never say A. or B. has lived for such and such a time,— not lived, but searched! And I am very, very punctual, believe me!"

"Ah, yes, life is a perpetual search," I said, with a sigh which might be taken to refer to the trials of life, while in truth it was called forth by the *ennui* which this detailed occupation with the bagatelle had caused. This accounted for my flat remark, the sole object of which was to change the subject at all hazards.

I little knew to whom I was talking. "What, sir, symbolic?" he said. "And I suppose you think that is deeper! Ah, oh!"

"Well, what now?"

"You see, my dear sir, to search in a symbolical sense, to think that all of life is but a searching, that is not what I complain of, that is not what you should sigh about. The ethical goes without saying. An honest fellow will search and yearn and never complain, but be happy in the midst of this misery of an ever-rising and never-terminating line. That is our upper storey. But what we have to take along with it, the vexation and bother we must put up with in the lower storey of life, that is what I am talking of. There, for instance, is the necessity of searching, which makes you mad, nervous, insane. And, what is more, it strands you in Atheism. The dear God sitting on high and counting the hairs on our head, who sees me searching for my spectacles for hours at a time, he sees the spectacles too, knows just where they are,—can you bear it, the thought of how he must laugh? A kind, omnipotent Being! Do you think such a one would permit the curse of colds in your head? Alas, we are born to search, to undo knots, to sneeze and cough and spit! Man, with a proud world within his arched brows, with his beaming eyes, his spirit dipping into the depth and breadth of infinitude, with his soul rising on silver wings into the heavens, with his imagination pouring streams of golden fire over hill and vale and transforming the image of mortality to God, with his will, the flashing sword within his hand to adjust, to judge, to conquer, with pious patience to plant, to cherish, and watch over the tree of life that it may grow and flourish and bear heavenly fruit of noble culture, Man with the angelic image of the divine and beautiful within his longing, yearning bosom,—yes, this same Man, changed to a mollusc, his throat a grating-iron, a nest of devils, tickling the larynx with finest needles for nights and nights, his eyes dim, his brain heavy, dull, perturbed, his nerves poisoned, and, with all that, not considered ill; and you say that God——!"

Here our denier of the existence of God was seized with so deplorable a fit of sneezing and coughing that I repressed a remark I had upon my tongue.

. . . . . .

Upon entering I noticed that he cast an uneasy glance all about the floor of the dining-hall; he seemed much relieved when in one corner he noticed a small object which may be of service to coughing persons. In a tone of supreme content he remarked, "This room is really very well furnished;"

and from that time he seemed to be in tolerably good humour. As is common at the Swiss hotels, breakfast had been placed upon the table awaiting whoever should come to partake of it, and A. E., having pushed the butter and honey aside with some violence, helped himself freely. We were alone in the room, but soon another tourist entered. He was a middle-aged man, attired in a duster of unbleached linen, with a short cape hanging over his shoulders, and carrying a knapsack of some weight on his back. There were drops of perspiration visible upon his brow; it appeared evident that he had walked for some hours that morning. He laid down his burden, put his bulky umbrella in a corner, sat down at the other end of the table, pulled his chair up, took out his glasses, carefully looked at everything that had been set upon the table, seemed to quite approve of the completeness of things that go to make up an English breakfast, and then, with all the appearance of a soul conscious that the body belonging thereto had severely earned its breakfast, began the enjoyable task of cutting and spreading some slices of bread. It was easy to see that the man belonged to the class of scholars, and his pale complexion led me to judge that he was one of those tourists who strive to make up by pedestrian exertions for the harm they have done their bodies throughout the year by sedentary habits.

A. E., who had meanwhile appeased his appetite, seemed to be in no special haste to depart. He lit a cigar, and said to me, "You admit, then, that physics is at bottom synonymous with metaphysics, the science of the spiritual. That is, I take for granted that you admit it, although I have not yet proved it to you philosophically, for you have surely recognised the universal insidiousness, ay, animosity of matter, what physical science has heretofore insipidly named the law of gravity, statics, etc., while it is in truth to be explained merely as demoniacal possession."

Meanwhile the stranger had split a long roll lengthwise with dexterity and precision, and was occupied in spreading on the butter with great regard to perfect smoothness and evenness; he made a moment's pause at the last words, casting a peculiar glance from under his bushy eyebrows over to our end of the table, and then thoughtfully continued his plastic occupation, wagging his head now and then with an expression of ironical surprise. The thought came to me that A. E. had designs upon the stranger. But I concluded that it was not the case. He had given him but a cursory glance as he entered, though it was a glance which might be supposed to grasp the personality before him, for his eye was wont to seize what it looked upon as if there were a strong hand within it; at the same time there was no sign of his paying any attention to the unknown.

"Friend," he continued, "have you noticed how a piece of falling paper will mock us? Are they not graceful, the sneering motions with which it flutters back and forth? Does not every turn tell you with elegant, voluptuous nonchalance that you are beaten? Oh, matter lies ever in waiting. I sit down cheerfully after breakfast to begin my work, never suspecting the enemy. I dip in my pen, there's a hair in it; that is the way it begins. The fiend will not come out; I get ink on my fingers, the paper gets stained. I look for another sheet, then for a book, and so on; in short, my blessed morning is gone. From early dawn until late at night, so long as there is a human being about, matter is on the alert to play him a trick. The only way to do is to treat it as the lion-tamer does the beast whose cage he has ventured to enter—he meets its gaze and the beast meets his. To talk about the moral power of a human being is all nonsense, a mere fairy tale; no, the steady gaze only tells the brute that the man is on his guard, and gaze against gaze the monster lurks to see if for one single moment he will forget himself. So lurks all matter, lead-pencils, pens, inkstand, paper, cigar, glass, lamp all, all for the moment when you are not watching. But, ye saints! who can ever do it? Who has time? And like the tiger that leaps upon its unfortunate victim the moment he knows himself to be unnoticed, so does matter, drat it! sometimes clumsily, sometimes subtly, as the case may be. Diabolically subtle, for instance, was the bit of iron filing that landed in my eye the morning I was about to start out on my tour. Oh, believe me, when a respectable person is going a-travelling all the devils hold an œcumenical council to defeat him. But one of the favourite tricks dear to the heart of all objects is to creep stealthily to the edge, and drop down from a height to slip out of your hand—you forget yourself but a single moment and there goes——"

At this moment we heard a slight sound at the end where the other man was sitting; we saw him dodge hastily under the table, and then emerge with an object in his hand, which he looked upon in evident distress, and then with deep dejection. It was his roll, spread first with butter and then with honey in the most accurate and approved manner, and, "of course," as A. E. would say, it had fallen upon the buttered side.

It was with a great effort that I overcame a strong desire to laugh, for it seemed exactly as if there had been a mystic primordial relation between his words and the disaster. A. E. glanced across the table with perfect gravity, and gently nodded his head without a vestige of irony; nay, rather, with an expression of sympathy, as much as to say: we poor mortals know all about it. The stranger shot not only one but a whole battery of venomous glances over to our side, and sullenly set to work to produce a fit successor to the incurable roll.

A. E. continued quietly: "Then too I don't like that business about that *thing*, or rather the two things, that Kant called the pure form of *à priori* perception."

"Space and time?"

"That's it. What is space but an impertinent arrangement by means of which I am forced to remove A before putting B here" (he illustrated it with cups, dishes, and bottles, which were rather closely set upon the table), "and

"WE SAW HIM EMERGE WITH AN OBJECT IN HIS HAND."

to make room for A put C somewhere else, and so on *ad infinitum*——? And time? That is what you never have for anything. For, ye gods and little fishes! is that what we live for to have need of ten motions for things that are not worthy of one!"

The stranger now shook his head with more violence, laughing petulantly, and a vague unrest seemed to take possession of his legs.

A. E. rambled on. "At other times," he continued, "the reverse action takes place. Things go together that don't belong together. Do you know one of the most pestiferous forms of going along? When a precious sheet belonging to manuscript A manages to become attached to manuscript B, and slips into the wrong drawer, and declines to be found for days and weeks and years, while you are searching for it in rage and despair and impotent frenzy. Compared to that such a thing as the well-known slipping under your chair of a lady's dress is but a little playful pleasantry on the part of the devil-ridden object, albeit it is interesting as a fact sufficient to defeat our nonsensical science of physics, for who could ever explain such a thing mechanically?"

Here the stranger jumped up with the exclamation, "This is too much!" came upon us with heavy strides, planted himself firmly before A. E., and cried in a voice of thunder, "Sir, I would have you to know that I am a Professor of Physics! And, moreover, you have, so to speak, knocked my roll out of my hand!"

A. E. gave the man a long, contemplative look and was silent. Who could tell how this was coming out? Suddenly a crimson flush came into his face, his eyes sparkled, he jumped up, and I, not knowing my man very well as yet, was beginning to fear for the peace, when he with enormous strides, ay, with leaps like a panther, rushed straight across the room towards the corner which held the article before delicately referred to, and now followed a fit of coughing and sneezing intermingled with strange, wild, gurgling sounds, a perfect storm of rasping, rumbling, rattling, snarling, groaning, and barking tones; it was like a chorus of infernal spirits. It took considerable time for this terrific natural phenomenon to pass over; then the sufferer feebly raised his head, seized his hat, bag, and cane, and said to me in a pitiful, broken treble, "Will you have the goodness to appease the gentleman? Good morning to you both."

Friedrich Theodor Vischer (1807–1889).

HIS SERENITY WILL BUILD A PALACE.

"HIS HIGHNESS ADOLF FRIEDRICH IV. TREMBLED FROM TOP TO TOE."

IT was in the year 1700 and something or other, on a pleasant May day about bed-time, that his Serene Highness the Duke of Mecklenberg-Strelitz, Adolf Friedrich, fourth of the name, and his dear sister, the Princess Christel, were sitting side by side in their palace telling each other true ghost stories, thrilling yarns that nobody under the sun would have believed if they hadn't really happened; and they both sat shivering, more especially his Serenity Adolf Friedrich.

Suddenly through the still summer evening there came a sound across the lake, a most uncanny sound, a sound that none but the most masculine ghost would be guilty of to frighten a poor mortal out of his seven wits. With a hollow cadence long drawn out did it pass over the whole of Neu-Strelitz, and the princely pair could not for the life of them say whether it came from up in the air or from underneath the earth. It was all the same anyhow, it was gruesome enough either way. His Highness Adolf Friedrich IV. trembled from top to toe, and Princess Christel, who was confoundedly resolute for a woman, had just enough presence of mind left to catch hold of a silver bell and ring and storm with might and main. Why she did it she couldn't have told you, but at any rate it brought human aid to the spot. Rand, the *valet de chambre*, and Von Knüppelsdörp, the gentleman of the bed-chamber, came rushing in to ask the why and wherefor. Princess Christel was just able to motion the two to a chair, and so the four of them sat staring at each other in dead silence, and none of them knew what was the matter except that they saw his Serenity had the shivers. All at once the sound came again, and as it was dying away over Neu-Strelitz in its hollow weirdness Adolf Friedrich IV. clapped his hands over his most serene ears and cried, "There it is again!" Von Knüppelsdörp, gentleman of the bed-chamber, took the words out of the mouth of Rand, the *valet*, on the strength of the Mecklenborgian regulations concerning rank, and remarked, "Your Highness, it's the bittern." And the Princess Christel had just enough presence of mind to ask what new kind of spook that might be. And the gentleman of the bed-chamber said it was no spook at all, it was only a bird that took a devilish sort of delight in frightening honest folk by putting his beak in the swampy ground and then bellowing like a good one. I'm sure I don't know whether he was right, but he ought to have known, for he was also page of the hunt. But his Serenity did not take much stock in what he said, and after having meditated a bit he remarked, "All good spirits praise the Lord; and as for you, Rand, I want you to sleep with me this coming night." With that he left the room.

Princess Christel sat a bit longer with the gentleman of the bed-chamber, discussing the question what potent charms she should employ to banish the ghost for the coming night, and who should sleep with her, for her lady-in-waiting, Caroline Soltmanns, was an old superstitious chatterer, and at last she came to the conclusion that it would be by far the best thing she could do to invite the scrubbing-maid Wendula Steinhagens for the night. Wendula was a d—d plucky person, who was not afraid of the devil nor of his Serenity the Duke, for she had been known to say, "Hallo there, your Highness; get out of the way, will you!" And had flourished her broom in his face.

So the princely pair had passed the night safely under the tender care of Rand and Wendula, and were sitting at the breakfast table next morning drinking chocolate. Then did his Serenity come forth with his deep thoughts and remark, "Sister Christel, you are a woman, and you know I don't think much of 'em; but you are a member of our most serene house, and for this reason, and on this account, I will make known to you the measures of my government. Would you know the news? I'll build me a new palace on some pleasant spot in my domains."

"That's right, your Grace," said she. "You are lord of the whole; but how will the money hold out?"

"Oh, I've thought of all that," said his Serenity; "but what have I got my bailiffs for? They must help me out of the lurch, and the workmen can wait awhile for their pay; for it is scandalous that Serenissimus Streliziensis should have to endure a spook under his very nose. To be sure, that fool Knüppelsdörp says it's a bittern,—but what is a bittern? I'll believe anything, but to believe an explanation like that is more than can be expected of me in my quality as sovereign lord."

"Rand," he said to his *valet de chambre*, "tell Jochen Boenhas to hitch up the gilt coach, three footmen on behind, and the two runners to run ahead; the coachman and the footmen to put on their best livery with the gilt tassels, and the two runners shall wear their new flowered hats from Paris—*à la Pompadour*," he added aside to his sister—"for I am going on a journey through my estates."

"Dear me, your Honour," said Rand, "I'm afraid that won't do, for our old mare that goes as the off-horse has the spavin, and can't set one foot before the other."

"Confound the mare!" exclaimed his Serene Highness in a burst of displeasure. "If the mare can't go, all you have to do is to go to our Burgher Sachtleben and borrow one of his horses."

"Dear me, your Honour, he won't let us have it. This is just the busiest time for carting manure, and it's no wonder he can't spare his team."

"Do as I bid you, Rand; we are sovereign lord."

And Rand went, and Sachtleben gave him his old stiff bay horse to harness on the resplendent state chariot.

Jochen Boenhas pulled up before the door with his gilt coach, three lackeys jumped up behind one after the other, the two runners floated along the street; Rand sat on the box, and his Serene Highness and sister Christel sat inside the coach.

"Where to?" asked Jochen Boenhas.

"Straight ahead," said Rand; "over beyond Stargard, up

HIS SERENITY WILL BUILD A PALACE. 163

to our boundary-line; but don't for the life of you drive over the line, for we are only going to travel through our own domain."

And Jochen Boenhas drove through Stargard and through Frieland up to the Prussian line, and pulled up his horses: "Whoa, whoa I say! Here we are at the end!"

"SACHTLEBEN GAVE HIM HIS OLD STIFF BAY HORSE."

And his Serene Highness gave orders to drive to the east over Woldegk; and when they had passed Woldegk and reached Wolfshagen, Jochen Coachman turned around once more on his old horse and said, "Rand, here's the end again, we can't go any further."

And Princess Christel, who had overheard it, said: "Your Grace, this is the first time I have travelled through our estates; I'd never have thought it was such a short way."

"Christel," said his Serene Highness, "you're a woman, and you don't know much. What do you suppose? There's a good lot more toward noon. Feldberg and Mirow and Fürstenberg, all that is in my domain, and then beyond Mirow there's quite a lengthy bit stretching into our neighbour Schwerin's possessions that makes a good show."

"Nay, your Highness," said Rand, who had overheard, "it doesn't make much of a show, for the sand just pours into a person's eyes, as *I* ought to know, for I was born and bred there."

His Serene Highness very nearly lost his temper at Rand's foolish twaddle. He leaned far out of the gilt coach, and called out: "Jochen Boenhas, we'll go home now! And to-morrow we'll take the Fürstenberg hemlock grove and Mirow."

And it was done exactly as his Serene Highness had said, for he was a high-spirited prince, and when he had once said, "I say!" then sure enough he *had* said it.

So the next day they went beyond Fürstenberg to the hemlock grove, and when Rand turned to look into the carriage and say, "Your Grace, here we are at the end again," then his Serenity looked sinister, and shouted "Wesenbarg!" to console himself; but in spite of Wesenbarg, he came back to Neu-Strelitz in an utterly discontented spirit, and Rand and sister Christel stood in the hall together, shaking their heads and saying, "Where will this end?"

And the evening and the morning were the third day, and his Highness did not reign during that night, for he slept. The bitterns kept silent, and all the ghosts that had of late taken to haunting the palace at Neu-Strelitz had their off-night.

The next morning the *valet de chambre* came down to the princess and said: "Thank goodness! we have slept in peace for one night, and reigned right along without let or hindrance, and to-day we are going to travel westward, toward Neu-Bradenburg, and that finishes up the whole business."

And Princess Christel said, "The Lord be praised! Then he will have peace; he is too ambitious a prince." And three hours later they passed the inn near Neu-Brandenburg, and Sachtleben's old bay horse, having got to the end of his rope, one of the innkeeper's horses was hitched up, and his Serene Highness walked up and down before the door, and looked across the sunny lake over to the woods of Broda, and said to his sister Christel in High German—for the innkeeper's wife stood near, and he must needs show her his Serenity at its finest--

"What say you, Princess? Shall we build our Belvedere on the other side of this pleasant lake?"

Princess Christel was about to reply, but Rand intercepted her and said—

"Your Highness is always right; of course we'll have a Bellmandur! All people of degree have a Bellmandur except us!"

And his Serene Highness said: "Rand is right." And so they drove into Neu-Brandenburg.

Having reached this pearl of his possessions, and coming up in fine style on the market-place, he called out of the gilt carriage: "Rand, tell Jochen Boenhas to stop!" And with that he and his sister Christel descended from the coach, and Rand from the box, and the three lackeys from their seat, and the two runners stood panting.

And then said his Serene Highness Adolf Friedrich IV.: "This suits us right well, and here we will build our palace!"

Her Highness Sister Christel opened her mouth to say something, but his Highness the liege lord took the words out of her mouth and said: "Princess Christel, what more would your Grace have? Are you still critical? Look yonder." For the time being he was surrounded by a circle of his most devoted subjects, and though these were mostly small street urchins, he felt constrained thereby to speak High German to his sister. "Look, yonder, by the side of the mansion-house, we'll put it up."

And Princess Christel said: "*Cela me convient!* And I hope your Highness will have a couple of wings put on, and I will go and live in one of them."

"That's just what you won't do, Sister Christel," said his most Serene Highness, turning on his heel. "Don't make plans, and then they won't miscarry! I don't want any womankind with their chit-chat and nonsense in this new palace. I've had a deal too much of that at Neu-Strelitz. Rand!" he called; "go and find the two Burgomasters; and you," he said to two of the footmen, "go and cite the aldermen; tell them *I* wish to consult them, *I*, their liege lord. You are to stay here," he said to the third lackey; "it will not do to strip ourselves entirely of attendance."

And thereupon he walked up and down with his sister, and did not so much as notice that she made a wry face and protruded her nether-lip; and the lackey trotted behind them.

Fritz Reuter (1810-1874).

HIS SERENITY AND THE THUNDER-STORM.

ON his way to school the Konrektor felt so cheery and good-natured that his pupils might have expected to have a good day. As he stepped into the schoolroom he had the pleasant surprise of seeing a complete Roman battle before him, which his precious boys were carrying out in honour of Livy, and probably to give him an unexpected pleasure, and the noise they made was as natural as if the room were full of genuine Roman soldiers and genuine horses.

It was all very well for the boys, but it was not quite befitting the quiet which is supposed to reign in a schoolroom; nor was it the best means of allaying the flushed spirits of a schoolmaster who had his own private troubles to contend with. The Herr Konrektor sat down on his platform, opened his Homer, and when the noise had somewhat subsided, he gave vent to his ire: "Now listen, you dunces; first learn something, then you'll be better able to play heroes! Last time we stopped just before the splendid passage where Hector said good-bye to his dear wife Andromache, and she exhorts him—

"Δαιμόνιε, says she; φθίσει σε τὸ σὸν μένος, οὐδ' ἐλεαίρεις, says she; but it's hardly worth while to read anything so fine to you scatterbrained dolts. παῖδά τε νηπίαχον, says she; καὶ ἔμ' ἄμμορον, ἢ τάχα χήρη, says she. Karl Wendt, confound you, if you don't stop talking I'll stand you up by my platform, and then it'll be *my* turn to have a talk with you. σεῦ ἔσομαι, says she, τάχα γάρ σε κατακτανέουσιν Ἀχαιοὶ πάντες ἐρορμηθέντες, says she; ἐμοὶ δέ κε κέρδιον εἴη σεῦ ἀραμαρτούσῃ, and so on, says she.—Langnickel, you begin."

And Langnickel cleared his throat once or twice and nudged his neighbours right and left with his elbows, as much as to say: " Fellows, help me; I'm in an awful fix."

"Well," said the Konrektor, "how long before you're ready? Δαιμόνιε—what does that mean?"

"*Oh, thou monster!*" said Langwickel, looking at the Herr Konrektor very doubtfully to see what he would say.

"It's more likely you are a monster. The next, go on," said the Konrektor, pointing to Karl Siemsen. "Well, Karl! Eh? the word's not easy; how do we call a fellow that can do more than ordinary folks?"

"A Tausendsasa," said Karl.

"Well, I never! We may say that for a joke, but do you suppose Hector's wife felt much like joking just then? Nay, she is scolding him. You madcap you, says she, bridle your pluck! says she. Have you no pity for your little boy—she means her little Astyanax that she has on her arm,—and for poor luckless me, says she, who will soon enough be a widow? For how long will it be? says she, before the Archæans pitch in on you and kill you, and what is left to me but sorrow when I sit here without you? says she. Well, here I am translating the whole of Homer for you. Go ahead, Karl Siemsen!" he exclaimed, then the door was opened, and one of his Serene Highness's lackeys came in.

"Herr Konrektor, his Highness wants to know if you think we'll get a thunder-storm to-day?"

Now this was the last straw for the Konrektor's patience. He turned upon the fellow in a mad choler and shouted, "Yes! Go and tell his Highness we'll get seven."

"Seven?" asked the lackey, looking blank and walking toward the door, and the Konrektor called after him: "Yes, seven! Tell him we'll get seven!"

The first lesson was over and the second had begun; it was Latin, and there was Virgil's *Bucolica* to translate.

HIS SERENITY AND THE THUNDER-STORM. 169

The Herr Konrektor had in the meantime taken a look at the weather, and now he was quite sure there was a storm coming up; his pupils had taken a look at his face, and they also knew for sure that there was a storm brewing; they were only doubtful where the lightning would strike. This question was about to be solved in a drastic manner when his Serenity sent the lackey once more:

"Herr Konrektor, his Highness wants you to come to him at once. The storm is coming mighty fast."

"Tell his Highness," cried the Konrektor in a rage, and was about to add, "to remember me to his grandmother," but he recalled himself and said: "First I must be through school, then I'll come."

At the palace things had gone on queerly enough for a while; his most Serene Highness walked up and down in his apartments with pale cheeks, as if he were the walking ghost of the deceased Henry of the Three Oaks; the footmen stood in the corners and along the walls silent and fearful like the stage mimes when Dame Macbeth walks about washing her hands; the gentleman of the bedchamber, Von Knüppelsdörp, carefully bolted all the windows and doors, and looked as if he were gagged.

"Rand," called his Highness in an undertone, "smoke is a good conductor. Are all the fires put out?"

"Yes, your Highness, all except the kitchen—you know the dinner has to be cooked."

"We shall not dine to-day. Tell them to throw water on the fire."

"Dear me, your Highness," Rand began, for fast-days were not much to his taste, not even when there was a thunder-storm.

"Do you hear what I say?" cried his Highness with such alacrity that he frightened himself.

"And there shall be no bells pulled; the sound is a good conductor," he added in a lower tone.

"The sound, your Highness?"

"Confound you, fool! I -I say! It *might* draw, you know!" whispered his Highness snappishly.

"Humph," said Rand to himself, looking out of the window with one eye, "we can afford to be cross; the storm isn't high yet; later on we'll be more polite."

"Goodness me," said his Highness nervously, "why doesn't the Konrektor come?"

"Good gracious! what good is the Konrektor? He's no more able to——"

"He *must* be able to, he *must!* Here, get these buckles off from my shoes; metal is a good conductor. Is all in order in my cabinet?"

"Yes," growled Rand, looking at the floor while trying to take the buckles off, "we've put up all the mummery, and the carpenter says it looks for all the world like a bird-cage."

"Gracious goodness! Did you hear that? Did you hear it, I say? It's here already! Where can the Konrektor be? I am going into my cabinet. Send for the Konrektor. Don't go so fast! Don't go so fast! The lightning will catch. Oh, goodness me!" he said quite tremulously; "and here I am calling so loud!"

The lackey met the Konrektor on the market-place, the door was opened, just a trifle, according to the Duke's orders, so that there should be no draught, and the Konrektor crowded in with his fox-tail and the rest of it. He now entered his Highness's cabinet, and the sight he saw put him at first quite out of countenance. For a moment he stood bewildered in the door, and stared into the cabinet open-mouthed, then all at once he broke into a perfect roar of laughter.

"What the devil have we here? Begging your Grace's pardon! But what in the name of goodness can this mean?"

"HE BROKE INTO A PERFECT ROAR OF LAUGHTER."

And Rand laughed too, and said, "Ay, you may well say so!"

I don't know but what I should have forgotten the dutiful respect I owed his most Serene Highness if I had been called upon to behold what the Konrektor beheld. Right in the middle of the room there was a small platform resting on the necks of bottles, on top of that a sort of pavilion made of glass that came down to the floor, and roofed over with a light-blue silk tent, that looked like a parasol for fifteen persons, and in this remarkable affair sat his Highness in his innocent terror, clothed in a yellow silk dressing-gown, with a green silk nightcap on his head, and with a pair of shoes on his feet varnished with red sealing-wax. He looked for all the world like a handsome canary with a green top-knot, that had been put in a cage to sing a sweet song; and he might have begun singing at any moment if only he had felt less down at the mouth.

In his quality as sovereign lord he would doubtless have sung a right testy little song at the Konrektor for laughing, the more so as he had a crow to pick with him anyway for his matrimonial intentions,[1] had not a sudden stroke of lightning interrupted his Highness's sing-song. "What nonsense are you———?" and now came the lightning, and he clapped his silk handkerchief over his eyes—"Mercy on us!" and he peeped out from behind the handkerchief, listening for the thunder, and when it came he stopped up his ears and exclaimed again, "Mercy on us!"

The Konrektor had stopped laughing by this time, and examined the cage from before and behind, and his Highness looked at him in an uncertain way, and asked at last—

"Well, what do you say? Will it do? Glass, silk, and"—here he raised one of his legs—"here is sealing-wax; and I have had everything taken out that's made of metal."

"Ay," said the Konrektor, "I dare say it's all right, your Highness; what man can do has been done; but, begging your pardon, the gold ducal crown that's up on top of the throne you are sitting on you've forgotten."

"Didn't I tell you so? Didn't I tell you so? That ass, Rand. Oh, mercy on us!" for it lightened again.

"Sheep-headed fool, you! bring another chair! I don't

---

[1] The Duke was a pronounced woman-hater, and objected most vehemently to the contraction of marriages by persons in any way connected with his little court. The Konrektor intended to profit by this interview as a means of influencing the Duke in favour of a young runner who had been imprisoned for the crime of making love.

want any ducal honours. When there's such a storm as this I'm no more than another man—mercy on us!" and he held his hands over his ears. "Eh, Konrektor?"

The Konrektor said he believed it; but the throne with the crown on it might stay there; they could wrap up the crown in a silk handkerchief.

After that his Highness ordered Rand to go out and take a look at the weather. Rand did it, and came back: "The storm is over, but there's another one all ready to burst, and it looks mighty grim."

"Rand, bring another chair in my weather-temple for the Konrektor."

"Oh, your Highness," said the Konrektor, "I don't need to come in."

"Ay, but *I* need you in here; but you can't come in like that; you'll drag in the lightning. Rand, another silk dressing-gown and nightcap, and the red-waxed shoes!"

Resistance was useless, he had to give in; and in a short time he stood there in a black nightcap and a bright orange bed-gown and red shoes; and he stood like a sorcerer in olden times, who might be supposed to have changed an unfortunate prince into a canary-bird, and put him into a glass-box, where it was likely he would have to stay for ever, for naught but the sweet kiss of a beauteous fairy upon his beak could ransom him, and his Highness was possessed of a holy horror of kissing, and there was no beauteous fairy near, for Rand, who was the only other person about, could not possibly figure as such.

When the old sorcerer sat beside his enchanted victim, his Highness ordered Rand out, because the exhalations of so many persons might draw the lightning, but told him to put his head in at the door from time to time and give the news concerning the weather; and Rand was quite willing, for now he could run over to the baker's wife and have some talk.

"What say you, Konrektor? Is it safe now?" asked his Highness.

"Ay, so far as I can see."

"But is it *quite* safe?"

"Well, your Highness, what man can do has been done; but what are mortal measures against the will of our Lord God?"

"That's what I say," exclaimed his Highness; "that fool the carpenter was to have made it round, and he made it square. Corners always draw lightning."

"What good would that do? If our Lord God sees best He can blow away the whole of Neu-Brandenburg in a moment. Think of Sodom and Gomorrah."

"Goodness gracious! Yes, I know it, I——" Just here Rand put his head in at the door: "There's another one coming, and the baker's wife says——"

"Fool, I don't want to know what that impertinent woman says."

Rand retired. "That woman has a lot to say; she says too—goodness gracious! she says you are going to get married, Konrektor. But I forbid you. I'll never set eyes on you again. I'd banish you from court."

"I esteem your Highness as my liege lord," said the Konrektor, quietly getting up, "but whether I marry or don't marry ought to be all the same to you, and I wont brook interference from any man. If you want to banish me from court you can do it, that's in your power; but I can also go of my own free will, that's in my power. I have the honour of bidding you farewell."

"Mercy on us! Do stay here; you're the only comfort I have. Oh, goodness gracious!"

Here Rand put his head in at the door.

"Your Highness, this one is going to be pretty bad; the storm can't come across the lake, and the baker's wife says——"

"You hare-brained dolt, I don't want to know what she says. Shut the door and bolt it on the outside, so that he can't get out."

"Well, your Highness," said the Konrektor, taking off his sorcerer's habit and donning his own honest coat, "you can hold me by force—that was a terrific clap!"

"Mercy on us!—yes, that it was. Do come in here again."

"Nay, your Highness, I'm not afraid of lightning," said the staunch old fellow, and gave his liege lord a quiet look. "I fear God, my judge, when I stand before Him as a miserable sinner, but I do not fear God, my father, for He knows what is good for me, and if He calls me to Himself by a stroke of lightning and without any suffering, then I know that it was an act of mercy, and I thank Him for it."

There was another awful clap, lightning and thunder falling almost simultaneously, and his Serene Highness screamed aloud.

"Konrektor, I'll grant ye a favour. What shall it be?"

"I need only God's favour; I don't need any man's favour, for all he may be a prince. Princely favour is the crutch that lame justice leans on, and when princes are gracious they are either trying to make up for past injustice and reap thanks for it, or they are about to commit some new injustice."

"You're growing mighty bold. I'll show you what princely disfavour is!" shouted his Highness in sore ire, for there had been no thunder for some time. "I'll show you——"

Then Rand put in his head. "Your Highness, the lightning struck a poplar on the embankment, the baker's wife says, and there's another storm coming up."

"Konrektor, do think up something that will help us!"

"How can *I* think up anything, your Highness. At such times when our Lord God is nearer than at others it is best to examine ourselves closely, and think of all the wrong one has done, and firmly resolve to undo it—that will give us courage and comfort."

"There is no man I have ever wronged," exclaimed his Highness hastily; but the storm was drawing nigh, and he covered his face with his handkerchief once more, and cried, "Goodness gracious!"

"Well, your Highness, I imagine it's much the same with you as it is with the rest of us; or is that no wrong when you imprison your courier Halsband for no fault of his?"

"My courier? He is my servant; how can a prince—mercy on us!—how can a prince be in the wrong against his own servant?" And again there was a flash of lightning, and his Highness disappeared behind his handkerchief. "Mercy on us! Let him go! Let the fellow go!"

"Ay, your Highness, that's all very good; but you must take the disgrace off from his shoulders as well."

"Mercy on us!" cried his Highness, stopping his ears because of the thunder. "I'm to ask his pardon, am I? No, no! The fellow——"

Rand appeared. "This will be a good one."

"Run and let Halsband out of prison," said his Highness.

"And," said the Konrektor, "give me pen and ink, and some paper."

"Here is paper and pen; but our ink is dried up. We're not much given to writing, except when the cashier is here."

"That's a fact," said his Highness. "Mercy on us! Go and buy some ink immediately." The ink came, and the Konrektor wrote.

"Good gracious," said his Highness to himself, "how can the fellow write in this storm!"

The Konrektor got him to sign it.

"Don't you feel a vast deal better," he said, "after this good deed?"

"Not a bit of it," said his Highness; "first the storm must be over."

The sky was clearing. Rand's head appeared again. "Now it's all over; the baker's wife says we had seven storms."

His Highness took breath once more, and said to himself, "Seven storms! And he knew it before, the insolent old fellow, with his confounded speeches! What becomes of the deference due to the prince from his subject, I'd like to know? But I can't do without him; he's too well posted about the weather."

Fritz Reuter.

THE LIEUTENANT'S DINNER.

COMING home to his bachelor quarters one day, Lieutenant Karfunkelstein found a note of invitation upon his library table. As he took it up and examined it, his chagrin was almost too great for his dignified self-possession. Frau von Diamant was known all over the town for her good dinners, and he, poor fellow, had orders to march in an hour. Moreover, to aggravate matters, the widow was the lady of his heart. He would have liked nothing better than to spend an hour or two in her company, and have the added gratification of dining most sumptuously. But there was no help for it. Love and hunger must both be set aside as a malignant fate had decreed. He must march, and no amount of railing at destiny would improve matters, however it might ease his much-enduring temper. So he called his man Joching, and entrusted to him his painful message of regrets to the widow. "And Joching, are you sure you understand?" "To be sure I do, sir!" replied good Joching dutifully, departing therewith on his errand. It occurred to the lieutenant then that before his march he might partake of a meal to be sent from his hotel. Opening the window hastily, he called after the departing Joching, "When you come back bring my dinner with you."

And Joching reached the lady's house. "Well, Joching, what have you to tell me?" "Best compliments from my master to your gracious ladyship. And as for the Herr Lieutenant, he cannot come to dine to-day, for in little more than an hour the troop must march to Woldegk."

"Ah, what a shame. I'm sorely grieved!"

And Joching still did not move from the spot; he stood twisting his cap and wringing it between his knuckles. The lady asks him why he does not go. "The dinner," says he; "I was to take it with me." Well, she was a right jolly woman who did not take a joke amiss, and quickly said, "Stay, in a minute you shall have it." And in less time than it takes to tell it, she had a portly basket filled and placed on Joching Pacsel's arm. He trotted off therewith, nothing loath. The Herr Lieutenant was waiting for him, and sat down with a surly look. "Well," he said, "now for it. The everlasting pork and mutton, I suppose. Ah, to be invited to dine most exquisitely with a superb woman, and then to be condemned to eat hotel stuff!" But soon his humour took another turn. The dinner truly was not bad, what with meats and pastry, ices and dainties, not to mention a bottle of champagne. It was a dinner fit for any man, and most especially for a man about to march and meet pale Death. With vain surmises did he try to solve the riddle of this unlooked-for excellence, and turning to his servant, asked if there were a wedding or a christening at his wonted eating-house. "Nay," says good Joching, "that's from her." "Where did you say you got it?" asked the Herr Lieutenant. "I got it from Frau von Diamant, sir, as you bade me do." It was worth something to hear the Herr Lieutenant then; to hear him rave and tear, and swear that honest Joching was the greatest ass that ever walked upon two legs. As time goes on, however, even a lieutenant's rage blows over, and he, being quite cooled down by this time, drew his purse, and taking three thalers therefrom, spoke thus to Joching, "Here are three thalers; do you see them, lout? Take the money and go at once to the nearest pastry-cook's. Do you understand me, fool?" "Yes, Herr Lieutenant," said honest Joching. "And there you buy a tart, the finest that the shop holds,

"SHE HAD A PORTLY BASKET FILLED."

and then you go and take it to the house where I was asked to dine. Tell Madam Diamant that you are noted for a fool, and would she kindly overlook your error; and if the tart but taste one-half as good to her as did her roast and confects to me, 'twill give me pleasure more than I can tell. Now, do you understand it, stupid fellow?"

"Ay, sir," said Joching Pacsel.

And Joching went and brought the tart to the lady. "Best compliments from the Herr Lieutenant to the gracious Frau von Diamant——"

"What is it you bring me now?"

"And says he's long been noted for a fool———"

"Tut, tut," the lady said, "we know all that."

"So please forgive him then, and here's a tart, and eating it will give you pleasure more than you can tell."

Madam, after recovering from a hearty laugh, then said: "Well, tell your master we will talk about that at some future time, and here is for your trouble."

She laid a thaler in his hand, and hoped that now he would leave her in peace. But no, Joching stood quite still, and held his hand up to his face, and gave a furtive peep at it again and again, as if this were the first and only thaler he had ever seen.

"Why do you stand there? What is it you are waiting for?" the lady asked, at last struck by his manner. "Your difficulties are all straightened now."

"Nay," said good Joching doubtfully, "this is but one; the tart alone cost three."

Fritz Reuter.

THE HIGHER ALTRUISM.

"GOOD morning to you, apothecary. Tell me now, do you know of aught that's good for headache day?"

"My lad, it is a sore complaint that; one of the worst of

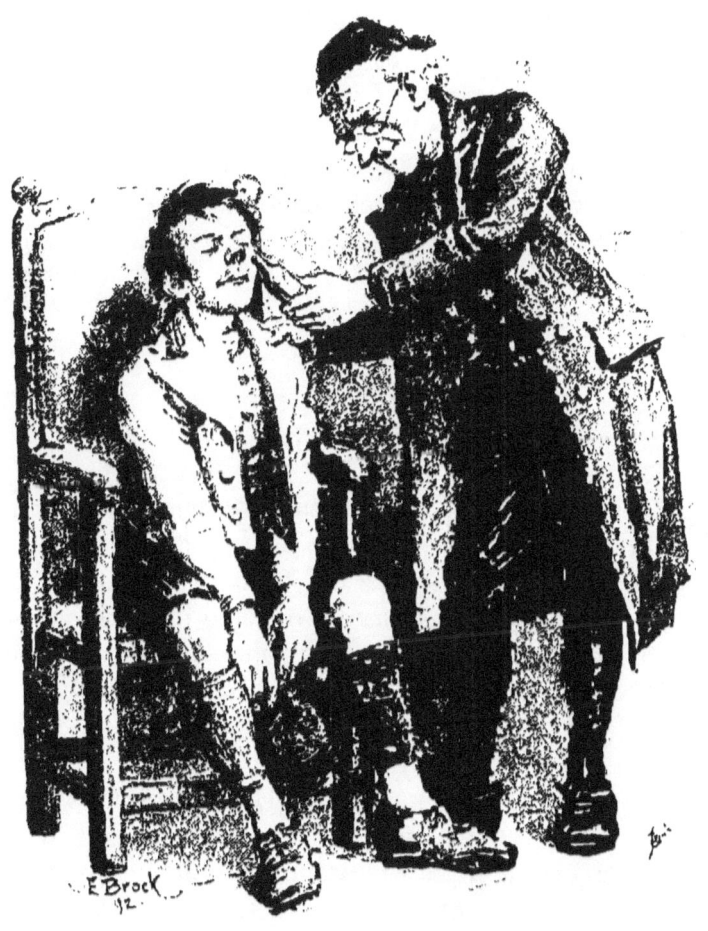

ills that flesh is heir to. Well, sit you down a bit. Are you from the manor?"

"Yes, sir; I'm one of the farm-servants there."

"And do the headache days come often?"

"Well, no, but when they do they come bad."

"We'll soon manage them, my lad. Come here now, and first shut both your eyes. There, that is right. Now, quick; smell of this bottle as hard as e'er you can."

The fellow did precisely as he said. First shut his eyes and smelled right heartily of what was in the bottle; and with a heavy thud he fell from off his chair. And as he was beginning to come to, says the apothecary, "Now, my lad, tell me is your headache day now gone?"

"Oh, sir, it's not of me that I was talking. It's our young lady has her headache day."

Fritz Reuter.

MY PICTURES.[1]

SO I took to painting, and particularly to making portraits. My old friend G—— was the first to have his turn. I sketched him from the right and from the left, from the front and from the back, in lead-pencil and in black crayon, and then in colours, once with a sky-blue background, once with clouds wrapped about him, and once in a lovely pink light, as if the sun were setting. That piece made me a lot of trouble, and when it was done it didn't look like it.

When G. was used up it was the Herr Inspector's turn. The likeness was to be for his betrothed, so I had to idealise him a bit, and put a pleasant and winning expression on him. It was hard enough, but I fetched it at last. As

---

[1] Reuter and his companions were at this time political prisoners at the fort of Dömitz, in Mecklenburg, his sentence of death having been converted into one of thirty years' imprisonment.

good luck would have it, he had a long nose, which is always a piece of luck for a beginner. I seized him by that, and when I had it, all the rest had to come after whether it would or no. But how about the pleasantness and the winning expression? I managed that beautifully; I screwed up his eyes a bit, puffed out his cheeks in one place, pulled up the corners of his mouth a quarter of an inch, and made a couple of regular little folds there, so that it looked like a button-hole that a careful tailor has fastened well at the right and left.

"AS GOOD LUCK WOULD HAVE IT, HE HAD A LONG NOSE."

The portrait brought me much honour. In the delight of his heart the Inspector showed it to my comrades, and now they all wanted to be painted. With all sorts of devices we wheedled the Inspector into letting one or two of my friends come in to me. My painter's work-shop was as good as any other; the light came from above, and it was the coolest north-light a painter could wish to have. Besides, I had an advantage over and above my colleagues in the art: the people that sat to me were used to sitting still, and could stand it for any length of time, and when I shoved my table up close upon them, and G. moved his chair to within half a foot of theirs, they sat as in a vice, and there was no escaping; they had to bear it.

Here I'll have to confess that during this time I sinned more than once against the image of God; I painted faces that never were, and never could be, and I painted them with colours that don't occur anywhere else in life. The black-headed ones I managed to do to my satisfaction, but when a flaxen-head happened along then it was pretty bad. I had got the habit—more's the pity—of shading flaxen hair with green, and as I was given to working over the face pretty freely with sienna, my flaxen-haired portraits seen at a little distance looked for all the world like a pine-apple, especially when it so happened that there was a green coat below.

My pictures were mostly sent to old fathers and mothers, or sisters and brothers, for their birthday or for Christmas; and if any of these good folks should be alive now, I will take this opportunity of asking their forgiveness if I gave them a fright for the holidays about the looks of their relatives. I know that my old father wrote me, when I sent him my own portrait, which was very like, that it gave him a heart-sinking to see how horribly I had changed.

Be that as it may, it gave us the opportunity of visiting each other, and though D. did not take kindly to this innovation, and threw a wet blanket over our enterprise whenever he could, he always relented a little after a fresh pound of tobacco; and when I caught him helping himself from the box of cigars that a good friend in Lübeck had sent to my friend G., and when the Major in person wanted to be painted by me, then his severity disappeared, and he walked up and down the long corridor like a cherubim that has put his flaming sword into the sheath for fear he might scorch his wing-feathers.

Painting the portrait of the Major was the crown of my artistic activity at M. I was invited to leave my cell and betake myself to the Inspector's room, for here the great feat was to be accomplished. I came with all of my artistic belongings. I had mounted a sheet that had a remarkably fine greenish tint, and all my pastels were sharp; but as I stepped into the room I stood aghast, for my fine skylight that I had grown accustomed to was missing—the room had a large natural window. I began by taking the Major around into all the corners to find the right light, but it was all wrong until we tied the blanket from off the Inspector's bed to the lower part of the window.

Unfortunately the Major had flaxen hair and no eyebrows, and I, poor fellow, had a way of always beginning with the eyebrows. What now? At other times I would daub in a pair of eyebrows first and then hitch on the nose, long or short, as it might happen to be. But what now? He had no eyebrows, and I had nothing to begin on, and his nose was, from an artist's point of view, but so so at best. I had measured all the proportions, but there seemed to be no way of getting out of my difficulty. I must needs begin, and I must needs have something *hairy* to begin on. I was too completely wedded to the habit, so I began with the moustache.

I never regretted it; and if one of my colleagues in the trade should ever find himself in a similar fix he may confidently follow my example, for it was not long before the Inspector, who was looking over my shoulder all the time, said that it was going to be very like, and the man was something of a connoisseur, and had trustworthy opinions on the subject, for he had often watched me, and had been educated up to the point by my pictures.

In a short time the face was all done, very handsome too, only with a peculiar green light, but it may be that was in the paper. Now came the uniform, blue with a red collar, and then the gilt epaulets and the bright buttons. Any one who has never tried his hand at that will find it no easy job, I can tell him. That was the way I felt. I had French blue and chrome yellow in my box, and I was in for it. Having read somewhere or other, "The accessories of a portrait should be treated with a certain sketchy cleverness," I acted accordingly. Sketchy enough it was, but as far as the cleverness was concerned I got stuck; for when I was through with it they both said, the Inspector and the Major, that it was no good. The French blue for the coat might possibly do, but the epaulets and the buttons looked as if they hadn't been polished up for seven years; and as for the collar, they said it was no major's collar, but an ordinary Prussian postmaster's collar. I was dreadfully put out, of course, but it was true; it did look sort of yellowish. I must have been cheated with the vermilion; it was unadulterated red lead, and I had been at the shadows again with that confounded sienna.

But I had learned enough of the art not to let them snub me, and so I said I would take the picture with me, and in a day or two we would talk about it again. And then I tried one kind of light after another, and polished up the Herr Major's epaulets and buttons until G. was moved to pity and told me they were bright enough. But that collar! To this hour, when I see one of those collars of the Prussian infantry, I remember my sins. It wasn't right, and it wouldn't come right! At last an accident put me on the right track; G.'s canary spattered a drop of his water down upon the collar, and on the spot where it fell it immediately turned a bright scarlet. If I could get a kind of varnish over it to make it look like that, I said to myself. But no, varnish is too oily; it might make it look like a grease spot. How would gum arabic do? But I didn't happen to have any handy. I mused and mused, and at last I hit upon sugar. That might do. I melted a couple of lumps of sugar in a little water, and began cautiously testing it along the edges. Beautiful! I struck out boldly, and it wasn't long before the collar would have passed muster for a first-rate Prussian soldier's collar.

G. said, to be sure, that the collar was too bright for the rest of the picture, but what did G. know about painting? I stood my major on the table, went to bed, and lay looking and looking at him until it struck nine and the sentinel shouted, "Lights out!" I shouldn't wonder if Raphael looked at his Madonna for a long time when she was done, but I don't believe that he was as much in love with her as I was with the Herr Major. I lay awake for ever so long. I couldn't sleep for delight. A Prussian officer in full uniform; that is something to be proud of, gentlemen! At last I fell asleep, and slept far into the next day.

And when I woke up—ye gods, what did I see! G. had not acted as a friend by me. He might have hindered it. Thousands of flies were eating up the Herr Major's collar, and there were little black specks in my highest lights.

That's what I call a misfortune. And what now? There was nothing for it but to varnish it up again and keep off the flies so long as I had it on my hands. I got rid of it as soon as I could. But what the Herr Major's gracious lady said about the likeness, and whether the Herr Major hung it up in his room to remember me by, I have not heard to this day. So much I know, I was in his and the Inspector's good graces after this, and that was a good thing not only for me but for all of us.

Fritz Reuter.

LISZT EXPECTED AT AN EVENING PARTY.

IT is enough to say that Liszt had come. The whole town spoke of him and of nothing else. . . . Not only was it considered an inevitable requisite for a person of culture to have heard at least one of his concerts, but for those of musical proclivity it was a question of life and death to have seen the *virtuoso* at their own house. A *salon* was greatly in danger of losing its painfully acquired reputation if Liszt had not honoured it with a visit. Much higher than the musical treat, which was easily attainable for two thalers, stood the consciousness of being able to say at the proper moment, with apparent nonchalance, but with the blessed assurance of crushing a less fortunate rival: "Do you know, my dear, Liszt was with us on Thursday? We had only a few friends to meet him. He played the Erlkönig!" Thereupon your rival would go home, lie down on the sofa, and have ice and cologne applied to her throbbing forehead.

When the excitement in town had reached its height I found, one evening after coming home exhausted by a round of lessons to untalented beginners, an invitation from Frau Medicinalräthin Pfeffermünze. She asked me to put in an appearance at her *salon* that very evening at eight o'clock; something very unusual must have occurred. Her instrumental and vocal clients were in the habit of assembling on a Saturday, once a fortnight; this was evidently an extra under difficulties. We had never before been asked so late.

The note bore signs of haste; Frederick the Great and Napoleon had granted themselves more time to sign the orders of cabinet than had the Frau Medicinalräthin. I pitched into my dress-coat head over heels, for there was not a moment to spare, and hastened to the Charlotten Strasse.

The first storey was illuminated with an unreasonable

profusion of oil and wax. A gentle shiver passed over my back; in the little reception-room, the inviolable sanctuary of the Medicinalrath in the eyes of young and giddy musicians, glittered the lights of a chandelier. The hall door stood wide open with that philosophically resigned hospitality which in general confines itself to funerals with four horses. At such supreme moments the lesser laws of life become void, and each sympathetic soul, who would never be asked to a place at the family table, is made welcome.

"Heavens!" I exclaimed in a whispered monologue, "it cannot be that the Medicinalrath has died an unexpected death!" The absurdity of the supposition immediately became apparent, for, passing through the reception-room, the head of the house appeared before me in person, at the right of the gilded mirror, surrounded by satellites, and saluted me graciously with a mild wave of his hand. As long as we could remember he had not condescended to receive any ordinary musicians, such as we were personally, for we were never invited to the higher esoteric *fêtes*. To make his presence more emphatically imposing, he had adorned himself with three or four little badges of honour instead of wearing merely the ribbons belonging thereto.

What had occurred? What was about to occur?

The Medicinalrath was to me an unapproachable entity. I dared not ask him. Etiquette demanded that I should confine myself to replying if he should address me. His lady might be looked upon as more condescending, but to-day I should have to forego any polite advances. Like the vestal High Priestess in Spontini's opera, she stood in the centre of a group of maidens festively arrayed. Man, at any other time a much-sought-for article, had evidently fallen in price. The young gentlemen, even the boldest lions of society, stood close together, and did not venture above a whisper.

What had occurred? What was about to occur?

My vague forebodings became certainty as I heard a pale and criminally lean gentleman, one notorious for his festive odes, say to his neighbour: "He is coming! You will see the godlike youth face to face." The person addressed like the contrite Brahmin stared at the tip of his nose, and preserved a worshipful silence. "I breakfasted with him yesterday. A most delightful companion! The very picture of unpretentious simplicity," continued the other. Ah, could he but breakfast with him every day, life had looked brighter to him!

Among the bards near by a wild state of excitement made itself felt. Their leader distributed printed leaflets among them, and the poet stepped nearer to designate a certain passage in the third stanza which required a decided crescendo. Just then the Frau Medicinalräthin came rustling into the circle.

"Would it not be better," she said, smiling benignly, but struggling with a nervous tremor, "if the chorus were to retire into the adjoining room, so as to have the music come from a greater distance?"

"Frau Medicinalräthin is right," exclaimed the poet encouragingly, urging the youths of Berlin into the next room. "The chant should impress him as coming from another, purer world. Then in the third and last stanzas the angels descend and greet the genius here below as a brother. Carry out my suggestions, gentlemen, and go into the other room."

The chorus would greatly have preferred to be present from beginning to end, after the fashion of its antique prototypes in Sophocles and Euripides, but there was nothing for it but to yield. It took a covered position, attentively re-read the melodious lyric made to fit a well-known tune, and cleared its throat.

The clock on the mantel struck nine; the Medicinalrath

still stood sentinel at the right of the mirror, conversing with the aristocratic element. In the background preparations for a sacrificial offering of tea seemed to be going on, but no one ventured to begin the solemn ceremony. My conjecture was that the hostess feared thereby to offend the august spirit of the expected genius.

It struck a quarter, it struck half-past—still no Liszt!—

The Medicinalrath and his æsthetic wife moved nearer to the windows, and convulsively started every time a carriage passed near enough to give one reason to suspect it of an intention of stopping. The assembled guests had said everything they had to say, and the need of an impetus, physical or psychical, was making itself sadly felt.

"We certainly cannot have tea served now. He may come at any moment. The effect would be quite lost!" whispered the Frau Medicinalräthin as her husband approached her, reminding her of the bodily needs of her guests.

A general restlessness took possession of those assembled. "Punctuality is the politeness of kings, but not of geniuses!" a young lawyer, who was at other times the Aristophanes of these receptions, ventured to remark with some bitterness.

"Liszt did not name the hour, I should say by way of vindication; he merely promised to come. You know that his time is tasked to the utmost. A king may seclude himself from his worshippers, but a *virtuoso* has not an hour of the day to call his own," said the Medicinalrath, soothingly.

A carriage came rattling wildly up to the door and stopped. "It is he!" cried an academic youth, whom the master of the house had stationed as a sentry at the first window.

The moment was overwhelming. As fast as circumstances would permit the guests grouped picturesquely. The Medicinalrath took the centre at the right of the mirror;

his lady, our gracious patroness, seized the white silk ribbons on which the ode had been printed in gilt letters. The chorus of priestesses arranged itself artistically about her; the chorus of Berlin youths began to sing in the adjoining room; we mutes sent greedy eyeshots to meet the expected.

A nimble young man put his small, coal-black head through the door, and seemed undecided to whom to turn.

"Pfeffermünze," whispered an old gentleman to the Medicinalrath, "that is not Liszt!"

"That is not the blond head of our Samson. Avaunt, venal slave!" muttered the manufacturer of festive odes. The black-headed little fellow was actually one of the secretaries of the genius sent out to calm the assembly on account of his late arrival; perhaps, also, if I rightly judge the much-enduring *virtuoso*, to ward off the boisterous ovations in store for him. The inhabitants of dangerously-situated Alpine villages erect plough-shaped stone walls as a security against avalanches; the mass of snow is disrupted, and falls powerless on either side.

There was a universal disappointment; the chorus of youths was hushed with difficulty, the gilt-illumined ode was laid aside, the secretary was surrounded, and by way of reward for his good news that his master was following, he was made much of. The commotion was so turbulent that no one noticed the entrance of a slender young man, stooping perceptibly, with lank arms and long yellow hair, who had been peeled out of a magnificent sable greatcoat in the reception-room by a servant. But he did not escape the eagle eye of our patroness.

"Mein Gott, Liszt!" she exclaimed in a broken voice, and then she sank into the arms of two robust alto singers, who, always on the alert for such unaccountable tricks of destiny, were ever at her side. There was a sympathetic movement among the guests, only the one most nearly

concerned, the Medicinalrath, retaining a posture of stoic
composure. The master of tone also did not seem quite
inexperienced in the treatment of such misadventures. He
rapidly approached the invalid, seized the right hand of the
lady overcome by the magnitude of her feelings, ordered
"things strengthening and refreshing," like Mozart's Don
Ottavia, and raised her spirits with marvellous speed.

So Liszt was come; but all the effects arranged for his
reception had failed. But his tortured soul was not
spared the ode. He was compelled to sit down between
two ladies and listen to the song. Then the artistic hostess
presented the silk ribbon. It was entwined about a fresh
laurel wreath.

During this offering of gratitude I had been making some
remarks of condolence to the secretary. Since nightfall his
liege lord had been visiting five families of distinction.
The Erlkönig had been wrung from him at four places.
The burden of pianoforte fame weighs heavy; at the
thought the trials of teaching dwindled. Was the genius to
escape the Erlkönig here? From out of the music-room
the concert-grand loomed forth majestically like the heavy
cannons in forts that are used to practise recruits.

The illustrious one bore all of the trials inflicted upon
him with rare firmness; he deported himself somewhat as a
prince humouring a company of persons of little estate,
permitted aspiring instrumentalists and singers, profes-
sionals and amateurs, to be presented, said something
apt and encouraging to each, jested with the ladies in a
courtly manner, and endured the aged with a philosophic resignation rare in one of his years. He escaped
from tea, it probably having been urged upon him five
times already. The whole company was intoxicated by
the charm of his manner. More than twenty album-leaves
had been clandestinely introduced by the ladies, and he
wrote his name on each without a groan. I feared in

secret that one of the fair Delilas might stealthily draw a pair of scissors out of her pocket and clutch the lion's mane as a signal for the lurking envy which began to show signs of being abroad. But the god of the muses watched over his precious head; he kept his locks and his titanic strength, and he permitted himself to be persuaded to play. Counting by the programmes of previous concerts, and the

"HIS APPRECIATIVE HOST AND HOSTESS EXERTED THEMSELVES TO GET HIM INTO HIS SALLT GREATCOAT."

receipts consequent upon the high price of admission, the magnanimous fellow played, at a modest estimate, for 375 thalers.

The Frau Medicinalräthin would have given a great deal to induce him to finish the fourth hundred, and she did her very best to force the poor unfortunate to give her the Chromatic Gallop. It was not possible. Inexorable fate still had a *souper* in store with which the genius was to finish the day's task. It became necessary to dismiss him.

As he went all the guests escorted him to the antechamber, his appreciative host and hostess personally exerted themselves to get him into his sable greatcoat. Deep sorrow shone in the eyes of the Frau Medicinalräthin, perhaps at her inability to be able to induce the vocal youths of Berlin to prostrate themselves before him by way of a musical carpet to the master's carriage.

The reputation of her *salon* had been established for one generation.

E. Kossak (1814-1880).

A PRINCE IN DISGUISE.

"IN SHORT, IT WAS A LIVELY INNINGS."

ON a dismal November day a poor devil of a tailor was walking along the country-road to Goldach, a little wealthy town but a few miles from Seldwyla. The tailor carried nothing in his pocket but his thimble, which in lieu of coin he was incessantly twirling between his fingers; it was so cold that he was obliged to keep his hands in the pockets of his trousers, and his fingers began to ache smartly, what with this eternal twirling and twisting. He had lost his pay and his work at the same time, because some head-tailor at Seldwyla had failed, and there was nothing for it but to take to the road. A couple of snow-flakes that had blown into his mouth were the only breakfast he had had, and there was as little prospect for any dinner. Begging was made difficult, ay, seemed quite out of the question; because over his black Sunday suit, which was the only one he had, he wore an ample dark grey mantle faced with black velvet, which gave its wearer a noble and romantic exterior, the more so as his long black hair and little moustache were well cared for, and he was the happy possessor of pale, regular features.

Attire of the sort described had become a necessity to him, and he indulged in it with no evil or deceitful purpose; he was quite contented when he was not interfered with and left in peace to do his work, but he would sooner have starved than give up his mantle and Polish fur-cap, which he managed to wear with an inimitable grace.

For this reason he could work only in good-sized towns, where he did not become too conspicuous; when on the road and without savings he was in a sorry enough plight. Did he approach a house, he was looked at with surprise and curiosity, and there was nothing farther from the thoughts of the inhabitants than that he would beg; so the words died on his lips, the more so as he was not a possessor of many words, and he became in truth a martyr of his mantle, and suffered hunger as dark and dismal as the latter's velvet lining.

As he was wearily ascending a rise of ground he came upon a new and comfortable carriage, which a gentleman's coachman had fetched from Basle for his master, a foreign count who was awaiting it somewhere in Switzerland on an old estate he had bought or leased. The carriage was designed for travelling, and had all sorts of arrangements to hold luggage, so that it seemed to be heavily loaded, although it was empty. The coachman was walking by his horses on account of the steepness of the road. When he reached the top of the hill he got up on the box again, and asked the tailor if he would not have a ride; for it was beginning to rain, and he saw at a glance that the poor fellow was faintly and sorrowfully trudging along.

He gratefully and humbly accepted the offer, whereupon the carriage took him at a rapid pace over the rest of the road, so that in one short hour they passed, with a hollow, thundering sound, through the town gate of Goldach. Before the best hotel, called Zur Wage, the elegant turn-out stopped, and at once the groom pulled the bell violently, so that the wire nearly broke. Down came the host and his people and pulled open the carriage door; the children and neighbours came crowding about the splendid carriage, full of curiosity to see what kernel could be contained in this marvellous shell, and when the dumfounded tailor came forth in his mantle, pale and handsome, gazing pensively upon the ground, he seemed to them to be a mysterious prince or count at the very least. The space between the carriage and the door of the hotel was narrow, and the rest of the pavement pretty well blocked by the curious crowd. It may have been due to a certain lack of presence of mind, or possibly of courage, that he did not break through the rabble and simply go on his way; he did not, but weakly allowed himself to be escorted into the house and upstairs, and did not become fully conscious of his new and remarkable position until he found himself in a comfortable dining-room, and his portentous mantle was being officiously removed.

"The gentleman wishes to dine?" said a voice. "Dinner will be served at once; it is nearly ready."

Without waiting for a reply the host rushed for the kitchen, and cried: "In the name of three devils! now we have nothing but beef and a mutton joint! I dare not cut the partridge-pie, because that was ordered for the gentlemen coming this evening. *Isn't* this a shame? The only day when we don't expect any such person, and when there is nothing in the house, so fine a gentleman must turn up! And the coachman has a coat-of-arms on his buttons, and the carriage is good enough for a duke! And the young man is so grand that he doesn't so much as open his mouth!"

And the phlegmatic cook said: "Well, there is nothing to grumble about, sir. Of course he shall have the partridge-pie; he won't eat it up! We'll serve it on small plates for the gentlemen this evening. We can get out six platefuls!"

"Six platefuls? You must forget that the gentlemen are accustomed to eat their fill at *my* hotel!" answered the host; but the cook looked unmoved, and continued: "And so they shall! We must send for half-a-dozen of cutlets; we need them for the stranger as it is; and what he leaves I'll cut up into little squares and mix it in the pie. Just leave all that to me!"

But the honest host said, with a serious mien, "Cook, I have told you before that such things cannot be in this town and in this house! I wish to be respectable and honourable, and can afford to be so."

"Ye saints!" cried the cook, at last getting somewhat excited, "if there is no help for it, one must do the best one can! Here are two snipes that I have bought from the hunter this minute; I'll put them in the pie. A partridge pie adulterated with snipe will be good enough for your gluttons! And then there are some trout; the biggest I threw into the water as that remarkable carriage came to the door; and there is some soup in that little pan. So then we have fish, beef, cutlets with vegetables, the joint, and the pie. Just give me the keys now, so that I can get out the sweetmeats and the dessert! And, by the way, you might do me the honour, sir, to entrust the key to me once for all, so that I wouldn't have to run after you for it and get into awful straits."

"Good woman, you must not bear me a grudge for that. I promised my wife on her deathbed never to give the key out of my hands, so it's a matter of principle, not of mistrust. Here are the cucumbers, and here are the cherries; here are the pears, and here the apricots; but this old, stale pastry cannot be used. Quick! send Lise to the pastry-cook's to get fresh cakes, three dishes full, and if he has a good tart he may send it also."

"Dear me, sir! you can't put all that on one gentleman's bill. It will cost you more than it is worth!"

"Never mind that. It's all for the honour! It won't kill me, and when a grand swell like that passes through our town he shall be able to say he dined well, though he was not expected, and it was in winter! I won't have it said of me as they say of the hosts of Seldwyla, that they eat everything good themselves and leave the bones for their customers. Go ahead, then, all of you, and do your best!"

. . . .

Without further delay he was asked to table, a chair was placed for him, and as the fragrant odour of the savoury soup, the like of which he had not smelled for many a day, robbed him completely of his will, he sat down in God's name and at once dipped his heavy spoon into the golden brown liquid. In deep silence did he refresh his wearied spirits, and he was waited upon in respectfully hushed awe.

When he had emptied his plate, and the host saw how he had relished it, he encouraged him politely to have another spoonful; it would do him good, the weather being so inclement. Now the trout was served adorned with greens, and the host helped him to a generous piece. But the tailor, tormented by anxiety, did not venture in his shyness to boldly use his knife, but coyly and shamefacedly dabbed at it with his fork. The cook, who was watching behind the door to see the grand gentleman, noticed it, and she said to her subordinates, "Praised be our Lord Jesus Christ! There is one who knows how to eat a fine fish, as he should; he does not saw the delicate thing with his knife as if he were butchering a calf. That is a person of quality. I'd swear to that if it were not wicked! And how handsome and sad he is! There isn't a doubt of it, he is in love with some grand lady whom they won't let him have. Ah yes, grand people have their troubles as well as others!"

Meanwhile, the host seeing that his guest left his glass untouched, said deferentially, "My table wine is not to your honour's taste. Permit me to bring you a glass of good Bordeaux, which I can greatly recommend."

And then and there did the tailor commit his first spontaneous fault by obediently saying yes instead of no; and thereupon did the landlord of the "Woge" betake himself in person to his cellar to pick out a choice bottle; for he was greatly concerned to have it said that there was something first-class to be had in the place. When his guest, suffering under the torments of an evil conscience, ventured only to sip faint-heartedly of the contents of his glass, the host ran exulting into the kitchen, smacked his tongue, and cried: "The devil take me, there's one to the manner born; there's a judge of good wine for you. He takes it on his tongue as one would lay a ducat on the gold scales!"

So dinner took its course, very slowly indeed, for the poor tailor ate and drank very coyly and undecidedly; and the host, to give him time, left everything on the table for longer than ordinary. For all that, what the guest had eaten up to this time was not worth speaking of; but now his hunger, which was constantly being tempted in so dangerous a manner, began to conquer his terror, and when the partridge-pie appeared the mood of the tailor suddenly changed, and one fixed thought began to master him. "Things are as they are," he said to himself, warmed and incited by a new glass of wine. "I were a fool now if I should bear the brunt of the coming shame and persecution without having eaten my fill for it! So look to it while it is time. This is likely to be the last dish; I will devote myself to this, come what may! What I once have in my stomach no king can rob me of!"

No sooner said than done. With the boldness of despair he attacked the savoury pie, with no thought of stopping, so that in less than five minutes it was half gone, and the cause of the gentlemen who had ordered it was sadly in want of support. Meat, mushrooms, balls, crust, and top he swallowed without distinction, only anxious to bag it all before a cruel destiny should overtake him. He drank his wine in a hearty draught, and put enormous bits of bread into his mouth; in short, it was a lively innings, as when before a storm the hay from the near meadow is cast into the barn with a pitch-fork. Again the host ran to the kitchen and cried: "Look, he is eating up the pie, while he scarcely touched the roast! And the Bordeaux he drinks by glassfuls!"

"Let him," said the cook. "He knows a partridge when he sees it! If he were a common fellow, he would have gorged on the roast!"

"That's what I say," remarked the host; "it doesn't look very genteel; but I have often seen generals and the high clergy eat so!"

Meanwhile the coachman had had his horses fed, had eaten a substantial meal himself in the servants' room, and as he was in haste, he had ordered his horses to be harnessed again. The menials could not resist asking him, before it was too late, who his master was and what was his name. The coachman, a jolly and sly fellow, said, "Has he not told you himself?"

"No," they said; and he replied, "It is no wonder. He doesn't have much to say from morning till night. Well, he is Count Strapinsky! He is going to stay here all day,—perhaps longer, for he told me to take the carriage home."

He perpetrated this vicious joke to take revenge on the tailor, who had, as he thought, without giving him a word of thanks for his kindness, gone into the hotel to play the false *rôle* of a gentleman. Carrying his waggishness still further, he got up on his box without so much as asking what there was to pay for himself and his horses, cracked his whip, and drove out of town, no one interfering, for it was all put down on the bill of our friend the tailor.

Gottfried Keller (1815–1887).

A DISREPUTABLE SAINT.

ABOUT the beginning of the eighth century there lived at Alexandria an eccentric monk called Vitalis, who had set himself the special task of luring away the lost souls of women from the path of sin, and restoring them to virtue. But his methods were so singular, and the infatuation with which he untiringly followed his aim was mixed with such remarkable self-renunciation and hypocrisy, that the world has scarcely seen his like again.

In his cap he carried about with him a small silver case containing a parchment scroll with the names of those to be converted. This he took out again and again to add some new-discovered suspicious name to the list, or to count over those he already had, and to decide which one of their owners should be the next to be regenerated.

As a matter of fact, his reputation was of the worst. For

while in secret he touched the heart of many a lost one with his burning words of exhortation and the sweet whisperings of his fervid prayers, and was the means of leading them into virtuous ways, in public he gave himself the air of being a lascivious, sinful monk, gaily paddling in the pool of the world, and making his cowl a flag of shame.

Finding himself at dusk of evening in respectable company, he would suddenly exclaim, "Ah, what am I thinking of? I had well-nigh forgotten that brown-eyed Doris. My little friend is awaiting me! The deuce! I must begone at once, lest she should pout!"

Returning at dawn to his cell, he would cast himself down before the Mother of God, to whose honour and glory alone he undertook these adventures and bore the world's reproaches; and if he had been successful in leading back one lamb that had gone astray, and placing it safe in the same holy monastery, he thought himself more blessed in the sight of the heavenly queen than if he had converted a thousand heathens. For this was pre-eminently to his taste, to bear the martyrdom of appearing before the world as a libertine, while our purest Lady in Heaven well knew that he had not so much as touched a woman's hand, and that he wore an invisible crown of white roses upon his reviled head.

Once he heard of a particularly alluring young person, whose beauty and unusual charms had wrought much mischief and even bloodshed, as a noble and ferocious warrior kept guard at her door, making short work of any one who made bold to enter into dispute with him. Vitalis resolved to attack this hell and to conquer it. He walked straight to the disreputable house, and at the door encountered the soldier attired in bright scarlet, and walking haughtily up and down, spear in hand.

"Get thee gone, holy father!" he cried scornfully at the

sight of pious Vitalis. "How canst thou venture to crawl about my lion's den? Heaven is for thee, the world is for us!"

"Heaven and earth and all that is therein," cried Vitalis, "belong to the Lord and to his jolly servants! Begone, thou gaudy fool, and let me go where it pleases me!"

"THE MONK PARRIED THE BLOW."

Enraged, the warrior raised the shaft of his spear to bring it down upon the monk's head, but the latter pulled out an olive branch from beneath his habit, parried the blow, and hit the ruffian's forehead with such force as nearly to rob him of his senses, whereupon the valiant ecclesiastic gave him some smart raps under his nose until the soldier, wrathful and cursing, made room for him.

Vitalis entered the house as a conqueror. At the head of a narrow staircase stood a woman holding a lamp, and listening to the noise and shouting. She was above the ordinary height, and firmly built, with handsome though insolent features, surrounded by rich wild waves of reddish hair, like a lion's mane.

Scornfully she looked down upon the approaching monk, and said, "Where are you going?" "To see you, my dove!" he replied. " Have you never heard of the amorous monk Vitalis?" But she answered brusquely, barricading the staircase, "Have you any money, monk?" Taken aback, he replied, "Monks do not carry money!" "Then begone," she cried, "or I will have you flogged out of the house with firebrands!"

Vitalis scratched his head at this new dilemma; the creatures he had converted hitherto had of course not thought of demanding the wages of sin, and the unconverted were content to punish him for wasted time with venomous words. But here he was excluded from the field on which to begin his pious deed; and still there was a fascination in taming this reddish-golden daughter of Satan, because large and beautiful specimens of humanity again and again betray the senses into imputing a higher human value to them than they possess. Feeling about his habit, he came across the little silver case, which was decorated with an amethyst of some value. "I have nothing but this," he said. She took the case, examined it closely, and then allowed him to enter. True to his custom, he went into a corner of her room and prayed in a loud voice.

The woman, thinking he was about to begin his worldly enterprise with a Christian introduction of prayer, burst into uproarious laughter, and sat down to look at him, being vastly amused by his gesticulations. Soon, however, she tired of the sport, and walking up to him she put her strong white arms about him, and pressed his tonsured head so vigorously against her bosom, that he was in danger of choking, and began to blow and sputter as if he were in purgatory. He beat about him like a young horse at the blacksmith's until he had freed himself from the hellish embrace. He then took the long rope that was tied about his body, and seized the woman to tie her hands upon her back. It was a hard struggle before he bound her and threw her down with a heavy thud, returning thereupon to his corner and continuing his prayers as if nothing had happened.

The fettered lioness threw herself about angrily and uttered a hundred curses; then she grew more quiet, while the monk did not cease praying, preaching, and exhorting, and toward morning sighs became audible, followed by a sound of bitter sobbing. In short, when the sun rose she lay as a penitent Magdalene at his feet, and bathed the hem of his garment with tears. With serene benignity Vitalis laid his hand upon her head, and promised to return the following night to tell her in which monastery her contrite soul might find refuge.

What was his horror, coming back at the appointed hour, to find the door fast locked, and the woman looking out of the window in gay and stately attire.

"What wilt thou, priest?" she called down, and greatly surprised, he replied in an undertone, "What means this, my lamb? Remove this sinful frippery and let me in, that I may prepare thee for repentance!" "Thou would'st come in to me, wicked monk?" she said smiling, as if she had misunderstood him. "Have you money, or money's worth, with you?" Vitalis gazed at her open-mouthed, then he shook the door despairingly, but it remained locked, and the woman was gone from the window.

The jibes and sneers of the passers-by drove the apparently corrupt and shameless monk away from the house; but his one thought was to conquer the Evil One, who had taken possession of this woman by every means within his power.

Occupied by this thought he entered a church, and instead of praying, he pondered ways and means of accomplishing his purpose. His eyes fell upon a chest containing gifts of charity, and no sooner was the church empty than he knocked it open with his powerful fist, and gathering up his gown, threw the contents of the chest, consisting of a quantity of small silver coins, into it, and with more than a lover's speed, hastened to the house of the sinner.

He threw the stolen money upon the table and said, "Sufficeth it for this night?" Silently she counted it over, and saying, "It suffices!" she put it aside.

The two stood facing each other with peculiar sensations. Repressing a laugh, she looked as if she knew of nothing, and the monk measured her with uncertain and sorrowful glances, not knowing how to call her to account. But as she was about to put her hand in his lustrous black beard, the storm of his spiritual indignation broke forth. Angrily he struck her hand, then threw her down with a mighty effort, and kneeling upon her and holding her hands, untouched by her charms, he began to plead with her soul until her stubbornness seemed to melt.

The storm of his eloquent indignation changed to a soft and transcendent compassion, and his words flowed soothingly, like a mild spring-breath over the broken ice of this heart.

With a lighter heart than the sweetest of earthly happiness could have brought him he hastened away, not to get an hour's sleep upon his hard couch, but to pray for the poor repentant soul at the altar of the virgin far into the early dawn; for he vowed not to close his eyes in sleep until the stray lamb was safe behind the protecting walls of a monastery.

As the morning advanced he set out once more for her

house; at the same time he saw the ferocious warrior advancing upon him from the other end of the street. He was half intoxicated, and after a night of dissipation was on his way to win the harlot once more.

Vitalis was nearer to the fatal door, and he dexterously leaped to reach it, when the soldier threw his spear at him, which, in the twinkling of an eye, was lodged with quivering shaft in the door, close by the monk's head. But ere it ceased to quiver the monk wrenched it out of the wood with all his might, turning it against the warrior, who was advancing with his sword drawn, and quick as lightning he pierced his breast; the man dropped down dead, and at the same moment Vitalis was arrested by a troop of spearmen returning from a night-watch, who bound him and led him away to prison.

For many days he was kept there, but at the end of his trial he was dismissed free of punishment, because he had killed the man in self-defence. At the same time there was the stain of manslaughter upon him, and every one exclaimed that it was high time to deprive him of his religious orders. But Bishop John, who was at that time the ecclesiastical head of Alexandria, must have had an inkling of the true facts of the case; certain it is he refused to expel the ill-reputed monk, and gave orders to let him go his own eccentric way for a while.

Without delay he sped to his converted sinner, who in the meantime had again vacillated, and did not give the sorrowful Vitalis entrance until he had again possessed himself of some valuable and brought it to her. She repented and suffered herself to be converted for the third time, and soon after for the fourth and fifth times, as she found these conversions more profitable than anything else, and, moreover, the evil spirit within her took a fiendish delight in hoodwinking the poor priest with changing arts and inventions.

The latter was now a martyr in a deeper sense. The more he was deceived, the more firmly did he cling to his aim, and it seemed to him as if his own salvation depended upon the conversion of this particular person. He was now a murderer, church-robber, and thief; but he would not for the world have given up one iota of his shameful reputation, and if at times this weighed heavy upon his heart he devoted himself with renewed ardour to keep up this discreditable exterior with ribald words. For this specialty of martyrdom was his free choice. He grew pale and thin over it, and began to creep about like a shadow on the wall, but always with laughing lips.

Opposite the house of trial lived a wealthy Greek merchant, who had an only daughter named Jole. Being at liberty to do whatever she pleased, she was often at a loss how to spend her day. Her father read Plato, and when he was tired of that, composed neat xenia about the antique cameos, of which he had collected a great number. Jole, when she had laid aside her lyre, knew no outlet for her vivid thoughts, and restlessly gazed into the heavens, and into the distance, wherever there was an opening.

So she discovered the doings of the monk upon the street, and through her slave, who was on confidential terms with the slave of the wicked courtesan, she heard the truth about him. She meditated for a while, growing more and more dissatisfied, while her sympathy for the monk increased, though it was intermingled with an odd feeling of indignation.

Suddenly she resolved that if the Virgin Mary had not enough common sense to lead the wandering one back upon a respectable road, she herself would undertake to do so. She thereupon went to her father, complained bitterly about the improper neighbourhood, and begged him to remove the objectionable person.

A certain sum being offered for the house, the courtesan

left it that very hour, while the old Greek returned to his Plato and gave the matter no second thought.

Not so did Jole. She had everything removed from the little house which bore any relation to its former occupant, and when it had been swept and cleaned it was perfumed with incense, and clouds of fragrant smoke poured from the windows.

Then she had the empty room furnished with nought but a rug, a potted rose-bush, and a lamp, and when her father, who was wont to retire at sunset, had gone to sleep, she went over there herself, with a wreath of roses on her head, and sat down on the rug, while two trusty servants guarded the outside door.

They concealed themselves as Vitalis approached, and allowed him to enter. What was his surprise as he stepped into the room to find it emptied of all the tawdry finery of the red lioness, and instead of the latter a slender and graceful little person sitting upon the rug, with the little rose-bush opposite!

"Where is the lost one that dwelt here?" he cried, looking about him, and then fixing his eyes upon the lovely apparition before him.

"She has gone into the desert," replied Jole, without looking up, "where she will lead a hermit's life, and do penance."

"Praised be the Lord and His gracious Mother!" cried Vitalis, folding his hands with pious cheerfulness, while it seemed as if a stone rolled from his heart; at the same time he gave a curious glance at the girl and her wreath of roses, and said—

"And who art thou? From whence comest thou, and what is thy purpose?"

Sweet Jole lowered her dark eyes still more, while deep blushes covered her face, for she was greatly ashamed of the wicked things she was about to say to this man.

"I am an orphan," she said, "and this rug, this lamp, and this rose-bush is all that is left me of my possessions. So I have resolved to begin life where the other woman left it who was here before me!"

"The deuce you will!" cried the monk, beating his hands together. "Alack-a-day, how busy Satan is! And this harmless little creature tells me the thing as dryly as if I were not the monk Vitalis! Well, tell me again, pussy, what is it you will do?"

"I will give my life to love and serve men so long as this rose blooms!" she said, pointing lightly to the bush; but she could scarcely speak the words for shame, and cowered down low upon the floor, and this natural shame served the rogue very well to convince the monk that here he had to do with an innocent child possessed of the devil. He stroked his beard with pleasure at having appeared upon the scene just at the nick of time, and said slowly, and with a twinkle of fun—

"And then later, my dove?"

"Then my poor soul will go to Hell, where beautiful Madam Venus is; or perhaps if I find a good preacher, I will go into a monastery and do penance!"

"Better and better," he cried. "As regards the preacher, he is here already, and stands before you, you black-eyed child of Hell! And the monastery is awaiting you like a mouse-trap, and I will see to it that you walk in there before sinning, do you hear? Before sinning, except for the laudable purpose which shall serve you to do penance on. And now," he added in a serious tone, "down with the roses and listen to me!"

"No," said Jule, growing bolder, "I will listen first, and then see about taking down the roses. Having once overcome my feminine modesty, words do not suffice to hold me back before knowing sin, and without sin I shall know no repentance."

Now Vitalis began the most beautiful sermon he had ever preached. The girl listened with a charming raptness, which in its turn influenced the choice of his words, the beauty and grace of the object to be converted imperceptibly calling forth a higher eloquence. But as she was not at all serious in the frivolous speeches she had made to him, she could not be very deeply impressed by his words; a sweet smile floated about her lips, and when he had finished, Jole said, "I am but half touched by your words, and cannot give up my project; I am too curious to know the joys of this world!"

It was the first time that his art of conversion had met with so complete a failure. With contemplative sighs he walked back and forth in the

"NOW VITALIS BEGAN THE MOST BEAUTIFUL SERMON HE HAD EVER PREACHED."

room, and then glanced at the little candidate for perdition. The power of the Devil seemed to have made a strange compact here with the power of innocence.

"I will not leave this room," he cried at last, "until you repent!"

"That would but make me more stubborn," replied Jole. "I will ponder your words, and the coming night I will hear you again!"

"So be it then!" cried Vitalis; whereupon he left her, and Jole slipped quietly back into her father's house.

She slept but a short time, and awaited the evening with impatience. She had seen what an ecstatic fire beamed within the eyes of the monk; she had seen how manly were his motions in spite of his ecclesiastical dress. When she thought of his self-renunciation, of the steadfastness with which he followed his chosen aim, she could not but wish that these good qualities might serve her own use and pleasure, in the shape of a loving and faithful husband. Hence it seemed her mission to make a good martyr into a better husband.

The following night Vitalis was at his post betimes, and with undiminished ardour continued his exertions for her virtue. He was obliged to stand, except when he was kneeling in prayer. Jole, however, took her ease; she lay down upon the rug, folded her arms under her head, and watched the monk with eyes half-closed. Whenever she quite closed them Vitalis touched her with his foot to awake her. But this rough measure was always more gentle in the end than he intended, for no sooner did his foot approach the slender figure of the girl than it involuntarily slackened speed, and but softly touched her side, and, at the same time, a most wonderful sensation passed up the whole length of the tall monk—a sensation the remotest approach to which he had never experienced near any of the fair sinners he had had to do with.

Toward morning an angelic smile flitted across her face, and she said: "I have listened attentively, and I now hate sin; the more so, because it is so hateful to you, and nothing can henceforth please me that displeases you!"

"Is it true?" he said rapturously. "Have my efforts been crowned with success? Now, to make sure of you, come quick to the monastery!"

"You misunderstand me," replied Jole with a blush, fixing her eyes upon the ground; "I am in love with you. Now you must convert me of this new evil, and banish it; and I hope you will succeed!"

Vitalis, without a word, turned and rushed out of the house. He ran out into the silvery grey morning, and considered whether he should leave this suspicious young person to her fate, or try to rid her of this last whim, which was the most fatal one of all, and, perhaps, not without danger to himself. An angry flush rose in his face at the latter thought; but then he remembered that the devil might have set this trap for him, and now was the time to flee. But supposing the poor little creature really meant well, and by a few vigorous words might be cured of this last unhealthy fancy? In short, Vitalis could arrive at no decision; the less so, because deep within his heart great waves had arisen and set his little ship of reason all a-rocking.

He slipped into a church by the wayside, where a fine old marble statue of Juno, supplied with a gilt halo, had been made to do service as the Virgin Mary. Before this Mary he threw himself down, and ardently unfolded all his doubts, and begged his mistress to give him a sign. If she nodded her head he would finish the conversion; if she shook it, he would desist.

The statue, however, left him in a state of cruel uncertainty and did neither the one nor the other. But as the pink glory of a passing cloud flitted across the marble, the face appeared to smile most benignantly, perhaps it was that the ancient goddess, the protectress of married love and faith, declared her presence, or else that the new Queen of Heaven felt constrained to laugh at the plight in which her worshipper found himself.

At the same time Jole's father was walking under the cedars of his garden. He was lost in the contemplation of some new stones he had acquired. One was a beauteous amethyst, upon which Luna was pictured driving her chariot through the heavens, unaware that Cupid was catching a ride behind her, while little love-sprites flitting about her shouted out in Greek, "There's a chap on behind!" A magnificent onyx had Minerva engraved upon it, with Cupid in her lap, polishing her breast-plate with his hand to see his image therein.

These scenes tempted the old man to write some verses about them, and while he was choosing which to begin on, his little daughter Jole came into the garden. He showed her his treasures and explained them to her.

She sighed deeply, and said: "Ah, if all these great Powers, Chastity, Wisdom, and Religion, cannot war with Love, how shall I?"

These words took the old gentleman by surprise. "What is this I hear?" he said; "has the arrow of the all-powerful Eros touched you?"

"It has pierced me," she replied, "and if within another day I am not in the possession of the man I love, I shall die!"

"Shall I then," cried the old man, "take upon myself that most wretched of parental duties — shall I go and find the chosen one, the man, and bring him back by main force to the most precious of my possessions, and courteously ask him to take it for his own? Here is a pretty little woman, dear sir; I beg that you will not despise her! I should greatly prefer to box your ears, but my daughter would die, and I must be polite!"

"We are spared all that," said Jole, "for if I have your permission I hope to get him to come and ask for my hand."

"And what if, not knowing him at all, he should prove to be a rascal and a good-for-nothing?"

"Then you may turn him from your door! But he is a saint!"

"Go, then, and leave me alone with the Muses!" said the good old man.

Another Vitalis came up the steps that evening than had come down the morning before, though he himself least understood the change. The notorious monk and girl-converter did not even know the difference between the smile of a courtesan and that of an honest woman.

As he entered the room it was richly decorated, and bore a homelike aspect. The delicate breath of flowers filling it was quite in keeping with a certain respectable worldliness; upon a snowy couch, the silk of which showed not a fold, sat Jole like a meditating angel. The folds of her dress were turbulent as a storm in a cup of milk, and though her beautiful white arms gleamed as she crossed them over her bosom, all those charms had an air of lawfulness which silenced the monk's wonted eloquence.

"You are surprised to find all this pomp and show here," began Jole. "Know, then, that this is my farewell to the world and to the love which I have unfortunately conceived for you. You must help me to put it from me as far as lies in your power, and in the manner which I shall designate. When you speak to me in your present attire and in your clerical function I am unmoved, for a priest cannot convince me, who am of this world. A monk cannot cure me of love, as he knows not the passion, and is ignorant of that of which he speaks. If, then, it is your earnest wish to give me peace and turn my heart toward heaven, go into yonder chamber, where worldly attire is awaiting you. Exchange your monkish cowl for the garb of a worldly man, and then return and partake of a small repast with me, during which you may bring all your wits and mental force into play to turn my heart away from you and set it toward heaven!"

Vitalis considered for a moment; then he decided to parry the devil of this world with his own weapons, and concede to Jole's proposal.

He betook himself into the adjoining chamber, where servants were awaiting him with gorgeous apparel of linen and purple. No sooner had he donned them than he appeared to be a head taller, and with a noble bearing he walked back to Jole, who clapped her hands for joy.

A miracle occurred then and there, for no sooner did he sit in worldly pomp by the side of this sweet woman than his immediate past seemed wafted away out of his brain, and he quite forgot his purpose. Instead of saying a single word he listened eagerly to Jole's prattle, who had seized his hand and was now telling him her true story—viz., who she was and where she lived, and how it was her most ardent wish to make him abandon his eccentric mode of life and ask her father for her hand, and become a good and God-fearing husband. She said many other marvellous things in well-set words about a happy and virtuous love, adding with a sigh that she well knew how vain was her longing, and how she hoped he would convince her of the folly of it all as soon as he had refreshed himself at her table.

Thereupon Jole mingled some wine in a bowl for the silent monk, and lovingly fed him with sweets, so that his mind wandered back to his childhood to the time when his mother tenderly cared for the little lad. He ate and drank, and then it seemed to him that he must needs rest as after

"THEY DROVE HIM OUT OF THE MONASTERY."

a time of sore distress, and thereupon his head fell toward the side where Jole sat, and he fell asleep.

When he awoke he was alone. He jumped up hastily, terrified at the sight of his gorgeous attire. He sped through the house from top to floor to find his cowl, but there was no vestige of it to be seen, until he noticed a small courtyard, with a heap of coal and ashes, upon which lay a half-burned sleeve of his priestly garment.

He put his head out into the street once or twice, and drew it back as soon as he saw any one approaching. At last he threw himself down upon the silken couch with as negligent an air as if he had never lain upon the hard bed of a monastery; then he jumped up, suddenly tore open the outside door, and with dignity stepped out into the open air.

He did not look to the right nor to the left, but went straightway to his monastery, where it so happened that all the monks together with their prior had just decided to expel him out of their midst, because the measure of his sins was full, and he was a disgrace to the church. When they saw him approach in his pompous worldly attire that seemed the last straw to break the back of their Christian charity; they poured water on him and hooted him, and with crucifixes, brooms, forks, and soup ladles they drove him out of the monastery.

Such infamous treatment would at another time have been the greatest triumph of his martyrdom. Now too he laughed silently, but it was in a different sense. Once more he walked about the wall of the town, his red coat fluttering in the wind; a glorious breeze blew across the glittering sea from Holy Land, but the monk's heart was growing more and more worldly, and involuntarily he turned his steps back to the noisy streets of the town, sought out the house where Jole lived, and did her will.

He now grew to be as excellent and complete a man of

the world and husband as he had been a martyr. The church, hearing the true facts of the case, was inconsolable to have lost such a saint, and did all within her power to win the truant back to her bosom. But Jole held him fast, and said she thought he was well enough where he was.

Gottfried Keller.

MILITARY INSPECTION.

THE officers stood about the right wing of the battalion, two young lieutenants and—yes, it was he—my friend and patron in former times, the Premier-Lieutenant von Schwenkenberg. There was no mistaking him, he was quite the same; the endless stretch of neck, which made the low collar of his uniform look quite childish, the tall and lank figure with the formidable-looking sword at the hip, which almost grazed the ground, and was in constant collision with his heels. Now he went to meet the sergeant a few steps. Oh, I should have known him among thousands by his gait! He leaned forward a trifle, and swung from side to side as he stepped.

"Be—sure—you—don't—forget—Sergeant Möller," said Lieutenant von Schwenkenberg, "that—we—are—to—have—an—artillery-drill—on—the—bastion—this—afternoon. Pick—out—the—weakest—of—the—men; a—bit—of—exercise—will—be—just—the—thing—for—them. Lieutenant Schwarz—will—have—the—goodness—to—take—charge—of—this matter."

Lieutenant Schwarz was a young second-lieutenant, whom, of course, I did not know. It was evident that he was fresh from the artillery school. His face still retained that indescribable expression of supreme astonishment with which young officers just entering practical military life are wont to regard things. Everything about him was new—his uniform, his epaulettes, his way of dressing his hair, his beard; while Lieutenant von Schwenkenberg looked as if he had just passed through a hazardous winter campaign.

Shyly I walked about the battalion and looked at the Captain, who was standing by a fine horse fully equipped for battle, which one of the soldiers was holding. The Captain's was a short but very agile figure, never keeping the same position for two seconds at a time. Now he went tripping from the right side of the horse to the left, then darting behind it for a more thorough inspection.

"The parade doesn't agree with him," he exclaimed, "doesn't agree with him at all. But there's no help for it. Misdemeanour must be followed up by punishment. Sergeant Möller, how often has Cæsar been to parade? If I am not mistaken, it was eight times. I want him to come four more times. Let's have the dozen full, by all means. Confound him! We'll teach him better manners than to get up on his hind legs and caper. All I could do to keep him from falling. Did I tell you all the details of the story, Lieutenant von Schwenkenberg?"

"I—had—the—good—fortune—to—be—an—eye-witness," leisurely remarked the lieutenant.

"Ah, presence of mind, presence of mind, there's nothing like having presence of mind in an emergency. The deuce! the very last thing we'd want on the battle-field would be a nag that stumbles and falls.—Keep right on, Sergeant Möller," he added, turning to the latter, who had stopped calling the roll to listen to the Captain's speech, and looked up to his superior with unbounded reverence. "Keep right on; never mind me. I always take this time to examine not only the battalion within and without, but the barracks as well—yes, the barracks." Saying these words, he had twice pranced round about the battalion, casting many a glance into an open door which, as the emerging smoke would indicate, marked the entrance to the regimental kitchen.

"What is the story about the horse?" the young lieutenant asked his superior.

The latter shrugged his shoulders gently to and fro, and then replied, "The—horse—behaved—rather—badly,—the —Herr—Captain—thought—best—to—chastise—him,— and when—the—horse—took—it—ill,—they—parted company,—you—see. As—a—well-deserved—punishment— Cæsar—is—to—come—to—parade—for—twelve—consecutive—days—saddled—and packed with—the—full—equipment—for—battle."

"Seems to me that is harder on the groom than it is on the horse."

"Does—it—strike—you—so?" remarked Lieutenant von Schwenkenberg with imperturbable tranquillity.

Now the voice of the Captain was heard again. "Lieutenant Schwarz, will you have the goodness to look at this man of your column." He had ordered a man in the left wing to turn around, and was standing close before him. "I have told you, no doubt, that it takes a practised eye; look closely at the man, will you? Well? What is it? What do you see that's wrong about him?"

The young officer inspected him carefully from all sides, but he was bound to confess, with a shrug of his shoulders, that he saw nothing unusual.

The Captain smiled with evident satisfaction. Then he said in a gratified tone, "Ah yes, a practised eye is not a thing to be acquired in a day or two. Just look at the buttons on his jacket."

"They are not polished as brightly as they might be," the young officer remarked timidly.

"It's not that, Lieutenant Schwarz. Ye saints, it's not that," replied the Captain, raising his left hand like a mason holding a plumb-line. "Imagine a line drawn from the hook of his collar to the middle seam of his trousers. Do you discover nothing? Nothing whatever? Well, my dear Herr Lieutenant, it would really be expecting too much, altogether too much. All that will come to you in good time, no doubt. I have not served in the army for twenty-five years for nothing. Well now, I'll tell you. The fourth button counting from the top is about half a line too far to the left. You think it is the tailor's fault, do you? No, sir; I never make the tailor responsible for such things in my regiment. Saints preserve us! I always test them with a plumb-line. Tell that fellow to unbutton his jacket, and if you don't find a *manœuvre de force* at the fourth button then I'm very much mistaken."

The cannoneer unbuttoned his jacket, and sure enough it was just as the Captain had said. Instead of being sewed on, the fourth button was fastened with a small stick, which set it slightly awry, and brought its owner under the ban of the penal code.

F. W. Hackländer (1816–1877).

THE KING OF MACCAROONIA.

"WITH HORROR HE SEIZED THE STOCKING."

THE King of Maccaroonia, who was just in the prime of life, and in fact had been there for some time past, arose one morning and sat himself down in his night attire upon a chair by the side of his bed. His Minister of State stood before him holding his stockings, one of which had a large hole in the heel. Although he carefully turned the stocking in such a way that the king should not perceive the hole, and although it was much more in the king's line to have an eye for dainty boots than for well-mended stockings, the hole had not escaped his royal penetration. With horror he seized the stocking, put his fore-finger through the hole up to his knuckles, and then remarked with a sigh—

"What good is there in being a king, so long as I have no queen! What think you of the project of taking a wife?"

"That, your Majesty, is indeed a sublime idea," replied the Minister; "an idea which I am confident I, your humble subject, should have made bold to conceive, had I not felt that your Majesty himself would deign to utter it this very day."

"Very well then!" answered the king; "but do you think it will be an easy matter for me to find just the right kind of a wife?"

"Pooh!" said the Minister, "you'll find a dozen!"

"Do not forget that I am very fastidious. To please me, a princess must be beautiful and clever. And then there is another point that I would lay special stress on. You know how fond I am of ginger-nuts. In my whole kingdom there is not a person who knows how to bake them—that is, to bake them as they should be baked, not too hard and not too soft, but just nice and crisp. She must *partout* know how to bake ginger-nuts."

When the Minister heard this his heart fell. But he soon recovered, and replied: "A king like your Majesty will, without doubt, be able to find a princess who can bake ginger-nuts."

"Well then, we will look about us!" said the king; and that same day he set out accompanied by his Minister on a journey to such of his neighbours as had princesses to dispose of. But it so happened that only three princesses were discovered whose beauty and cleverness were sufficient to satisfy the king, and none of the three could bake ginger-nuts.

"I am sorry to say I can't bake ginger-nuts," said the first princess, in answer to the king's question, "but I can bake delicious little almond-cakes. Wouldn't those do?"

"No!" replied the king, "nothing short of ginger-nuts will do!"

The second princess snapped her fingers when he asked her, and said pettishly, "Go away with your nonsense! There is no such thing as a princess who can bake ginger-nuts."

But the king fared worse than this even with the third, who was, alas! the fairest and cleverest. She gave him no opportunity to ask his question; before he could do so, she confronted him with a query on her part asking him if he knew how to play on the Jew's-harp. When he answered in the negative she rejected him, politely expressing her regrets. She liked him well enough, she said; but she had a particular fancy for the Jew's-harp, and it was her firm intention to marry no man unable to play upon that instrument.

So the king and his minister drove home again, and as he was getting down from the carriage he said quite dejectedly, "So this was a wild-goose chase!"

But a king must needs have a queen, and some time later he sent for the minister once more, and informed him that he had given up finding a wife who could bake ginger-nuts, and resolved to marry the princess they had visited first. "It is the one who knows how to bake little almond-cakes," he added. "Go and ask her if she will be my wife."

The next day the minister came back, and narrated to him how the princess was quite out of the reach of such offers, having married the king of the land where capers grow.

"Well, then, go to the second princess!" But this time too the minister came home again without having accomplished his errand. The old king, he said, regretted exceedingly that it was quite out of his power to gratify him, his daughter having unfortunately died.

The king was very thoughtful for a while, but being quite determined to have a queen, he ordered his minister to go once more to the third princess, as there was no knowing but she too might have changed her mind. And the minister yielded to his orders, although his own inclination was quite averse to the project, and although his wife told him it would be quite useless. The king awaited his return in some trepidation. He was thinking of the question concerning the Jew's-harp, and the recollection was no agreeable one.

But the third princess received the minister very graciously, and told him that once she had been quite determined to have only such a husband as could play on the Jew's-harp; but that now, after all, she had come to the conclusion that dreams are flighty, especially the dreams of youth. She saw now, she said, that the realisation of her wish was quite out of the question, and as she had taken a fancy to the king she was willing to have him.

Then the minister drove home as fast as his horses would go, and the king embraced him, and gave him a tremendous medal to wear about his neck. Bright flags decorated the town, garlands were hung from house to house across the streets, and altogether the wedding was such a splendid affair that nothing else was talked of for the next fortnight.

The king and the young queen lived in a state of bliss and rapture for the space of an entire year. The king never thought of ginger-nuts, and that little matter of the Jew's-harp had quite slipped out of the queen's mind.

But one morning the king got up with his wrong leg first, and everything went wrong. It rained the whole day long;

"WITHOUT ANOTHER WORD THEY BOTH WALKED AWAY."

the imperial globe fell down, and the little cross on top of it
broke off; then the court painter came and brought the new
map of the kingdom, and when the king looked at it he
found that the land was painted red instead of blue, as he
had ordered it; and besides all this, the queen had a
headache.

So it happened that the couple had their first quarrel;
what it was all about they themselves did not know next
morning, or if they did know it they did not want to say.
In short, the king grumbled and the queen pouted and
would always have the last word. After they had wrangled
for some time, the queen shrugged her shoulders contemptuously and said—

"It seems to me you might be silent, and stop finding
fault with everything you set your eyes on, when you yourself
don't even know how to play on the Jew's-harp."

But no sooner were the words out of her mouth than the
king petulantly interrupted her with the words, "And you
cannot so much as bake ginger-nuts!"

Thereupon the queen for the first time had no repartee
upon her tongue's end, and succumbed into silence, and
without another word they both walked away. The queen
sat down in a corner of her sofa in her own room, weeping
bitterly, and thinking, "What a foolish woman I am!
Where did I have my senses? That was the silliest
thing I could have done!"

The king walked up and down in his room, gleefully
rubbing his hands, and saying, "What a piece of good
fortune it is that my wife doesn't know how to bake ginger-
nuts! If she did, I should have been sadly put to for an
answer when she reproached me for being unable to play on
the Jew's-harp!"

After he had repeated this three or four times his mood
brightened visibly. He began to whistle a favourite tune,
then he went and looked at a large likeness of the queen

hanging on the wall. He got up on a chair and took out his handkerchief to brush off a cobweb hanging down straight over the queen's nose, and at last he said—

"She must have been very much put out, the dear little woman! I will go and see what she is doing!"

With that he went out into the hall, into which all the rooms opened. But this being a day on which everything went wrong, the valet had forgotten to light the lamps, although it was already eight o'clock, and moreover pitch dark.

So the king put out his hands before him so as not to bump his royal head, and cautiously felt his way along the wall. Suddenly he came upon something. "Who is there?" he asked.

"It is I," answered the queen.

"What are you looking for, my love?"

"I was coming to ask your forgiveness," replied the queen, "because I hurt your feelings."

"You needn't do that!" said the king, putting his arms about her neck. "The fault was more mine than yours, and I don't give it another thought. But I'll tell you one thing: two words shall be forbidden on pain of death in our kingdom, Jew's-harp and———"

"And ginger-nuts," the queen interrupted him, laughing and secretly wiping a tear from the corner of her eye; and that is the end of the story.

Professor Volkmann (1830–1891).

THE SAD TALE OF SEVEN KISSES.

IT is quite a while ago, I think, since one day the dear God called the angel Gabriel to him, as he often does, and said, "Thou Gabriel, go and open the slide and look down! Methinks I hear some crying!" Gabriel went and did as the dear God said, put his hand up to his eyes because the sunlight dazzled him, looked all around, and finally said, "Down there is a long green meadow; at one end sits Barbelie pasturing her geese, at the other sits Christoph pasturing his pigs, and both of them are weeping to melt a heart of stone."

"Indeed!" said the dear God; "go away, you tall fellow, and let me see."

When he had looked he found it was just as Gabriel had said.

And this was how it came that Christoph and Barbelie were weeping so pitifully. Christoph and Barbelie loved each other dearly; one of them took care of the geese and the other took care of the pigs, and so it was a very suitable match, there being no disparity of rank. They made up their minds to be married, and they thought being fond of each other was a good enough reason. But here their employers differed from them. So they were obliged to be content with a betrothal. Now, as it is well to be methodical in all things, and as kissing plays an important part in betrothals, they had come to an agreement to the effect that seven kisses in the morning and seven kisses in the evening would be quite the proper thing. For a while all went well, the seven kisses being duly given and received at the appointed time. But on the morning of the day when this story occurred it came about that, just as the seventh kiss was coming around, Barbelie's pet goose and Christoph's pet pig had a falling-out over their breakfast, threatening to end in a serious *melée*. To settle this difficulty it was necessary for the two to stop short of the proper number. Later, when they were sitting lonely and far apart by the edge of the meadow, it occurred to them how very bad a thing this was, and they both began to weep, and were still weeping when the dear God looked down.

The dear God thought at first that in the course of time their sorrow would subside of itself; but when the sound of weeping waxed louder and louder, and Christoph's pet pig and Barbelie's pet goose began to grow sad for sympathy, and to make woe-begone faces, he said, " I will help them ! Whatever they wish for this day shall come true."

But as it was the two had but one thought; as each looked in the direction where the other one sat, and neither could see the other, for the meadow was long and there was a bush in the middle, Christoph thought, " If I were but over where the geese are ! " and Barbelie sighed, " Oh, could I but be near the pigs ! "

All at once Christoph found himself sitting by the geese, and Barbelie was with the pigs ; but for all that they were not together, and there was still no possibility of correcting that wrong number.

Then thought Christoph : " Barbelie very likely wanted to make me a little visit ; " and Barbelie thought, " No doubt Christoph has gone around to see me ! " " Oh, if I could but be with my geese ! " " Oh, if I could but be with my pigs ! "

So Barbelie sat once more beside her geese, and Christoph sat beside his pigs, and so it went turn and turn about all day, because they always wished past each other. And so to this day they are short of that seventh morning kiss. Christoph, to be sure, was all for making it up that same evening when they both came home tired to death with wishing, but Barbelie assured him it wouldn't do a bit of good, and that there was no possibility of getting things straightened out again.

And when the dear God saw how the two had been wishing themselves away from each other, he said : "Well, this is a nice kettle of fish. But what I have once said I *have* said! There is no help for it!" He made up his mind then and there never to grant lovers' wishes rashly in future, before having made careful inquiries as to what it was they wanted. Later, I am told, he once told Gabriel confidentially that it was really a great pity that their wishes were so very rarely of a kind that he could grant them; and a long long time ago, when I applied to him in a similar affair, he did not so much as give me a hearing. Later Gabriel told me this story, and then I ceased to wonder.

Professor Volkmann.

A COUNTRY COMEDY.

IN the open door of the house the dark figure of a woman stood out distinctly against the brilliant snow—it was Eva Barbara. Without a word she seized his hand and drew him after her; he felt her pulses beat, and her quick breath betrayed her excitement. At a rapid pace she drew him along the silent streets, retarding her steps only as she approached her father's farmyard, where she dropped his hand, and with a shiver wrapped herself closer in her little shawl.

Suddenly the girl raised her head as if listening, and with a sob she said, "I am the most unhappy lass on God's earth!" Then with a sudden start: "Hark! they are coming. I am yours, Paul, whatever may come. Sure you can depend on me. Don't you hear them? For God's sake, Paul, don't stay here. It would be death to me to think you might fall into the hands of the Rottenstein lads! Be quick and away—why do you stand and look at me? If you care for me, go! God knows what a hard time I shall have of it with the old folks, without having to tremble for your safety!"

"Eva Barbara—my own Eva Barbara! I *will* turn over a new leaf; I——"

"Oh, my God, don't you hear how they are surrounding the house? Away with you, before it is too late!"

Paul turned to fly—it was too late! Logs of wood came crashing into the farmyard, and were shivered into bits against the house. With a leap Martin, who was far ahead of his comrades, came bounding around the corner, and with a cry of rage he threw himself upon his hated rival. But in the face of danger Paul had regained his self-possession; cleverly evading the attack, he seized Martin and threw him down. Then he felt his hand seized, he dipped into deep darkness, a door was thrown to—at the same time there was a fearful crash upon the threshold, making the silent house resound. Eva Barbara quickly fastened the bolts and hooks, and for the time being Paul was safe.

For the time being!

A thrill of suppressed rage passed through the lad standing in the dark, icy-cold entry beside the weeping girl, while his enemies raged about without the house, now shaking the doors, now demanding admission. What an ill-fated, miserable sort of scrape was this he was in! He felt like a grain of wheat between two mill-stones. He dared not go out; his life, or at least his future bodily welfare, was at stake. But if he stayed, and the farmer found him in his house—and there was not the slightest doubt that the peasant would soon find him, what with the unearthly din without—what would await him then he faintly divined!

Again there were heavy thumps against the door, and Martin's voice was heard crying, " Open it quick! Open it, peasant, or by the devil we'll smash the door! Open it —Paul Schülzle is in your house—deliver him over, or we'll open fight!"

"My God, my God! how shall this end?" moaned the trembling girl. " Hark! Don't you hear anything? Sure enough—— Oh, goodness me, father is awake! Come upstairs. I can't let you into the barn because the door creaks, and you can't stay here by the stairs. Come, find a hiding-place upstairs, in the hall or in the kitchen— come quick! Oh, blessed Saviour, turn this misfortune! Come! father will be here with a candle in a minute; if he finds us together—you know what his temper is!"

Paul's hand was seized again, and he was drawn upstairs;

fortunately the resounding blows against the door smothered his stumbling steps. In the sitting-room the peasant was swearing about the matches that would not catch fire; the girl trembled. "Straight ahead you'll find the kitchen-door! God be with you; I can help you no further. If father finds me here all is lost."

A ray of light falling through the key-hole frightened the girl away. Paul was alone. Cautiously he felt his way in the direction she had indicated, but he found no door; in fact, he did not have much time left to feel for it, for just then the sitting-room door was opened. Paul bounded into the shade and then behind the door, which the farmer in his excitement forgot to shut. Again Paul was safe for the moment, although he feared the beating of his heart might betray him.

A new attack upon the door put the peasant beside himself; he put his candle on the floor, then pulled open the hall window, and a very excited interview took place between him and the men without. Hot words fell between the peasant and Martin, until finally Martin declared that if the peasant did not deliver over Paul at once he would storm the house in good earnest; whereupon the peasant replied he certainly would not have that rogue of a trumpeter in his house for a minute, but as for doing a thing because Martin said so, there was nothing further from his mind, and if there was one more blow upon the door he would not be slow to reply.

The lads actually stepped back, and the peasant shut the window. He approached the door—Paul bit his lip; if he moved it, it would bring him face to face with the old man!

But the peasant paid no attention to the door—he merely called into the room, "Wife, they say that scamp of a musician is in the house! Get up! strike a light, and help me wake the servants; the fellow shall not go unpunished!"

"AN EXCITED INTERVIEW TOOK PLACE."

"I've been up this long while," replied a faint woman's voice trembling with cold; "but there's no finding those matches!"

"I don't wonder! I was so flurried I threw them in the wash-bowl," replied the peasant. "Strike a light in the kitchen, and hurry up."

The peasant disappeared with his candle in the narrow passage-way which passed through the entire depth of the house; in the dusk a figure flitted past Paul; he heard a rustling sound beside him, and then a ray of faint bluish light streamed through a half-open door. So that was the kitchen! If the woman came out now the light would first fall into that nook between the wall and the door which harboured him—discovery was inevitable. He could not stay where he was—but whither should he turn? The approaching steps of the farmer's wife startled him. He must away —just then there was only one exit possible—with one bound he was in the sitting-room behind the stove.

Again he was safe for the moment—but he was more securely than ever in the trap. Where should he go when the farmer came back with his servants?

The woman shut the door of the room and walked away along the passage to the back of the house. Paul stepped up to one of the frost-painted windows, thawing it with his breath, and looked out.

A leap into the garden was hazardous, but it was not impossible. By the pale light of the moon he saw how the men from Rottenstein were surrounding the house. This cut off all possibility of escape for the present.

He heard steps approaching; he heard the peasant's wife talk soothingly to his weeping sweetheart, Eva Barbara, the maid-servants also endeavouring to comfort her. So then he might expect all the feminine inmates of the house to enter the room at any moment—where should he find refuge?

Other sounds became audible throughout the house. He heard the farmer rail, the men-servants laugh and swear—whither, oh whither? In the room there was no nook, no hiding-place.

Nearer and nearer came the women; desperately, with a curse between his lips, he ran out into the bed-chamber of the worthy couple. It was a narrow room, a so-called *rafenetle;* two thin panels of wood, about six feet high, connected with the ceiling above by carved lattice-work, just enclosed two broad beds, leaving merely a passage between them. The panelled walls were closely hung with wearing apparel, under which Paul quickly crept, squeezing himself tightly into a corner and resigning himself with a sigh to his fate.

It was a tragic situation! How could he ever hope to leave this prison unnoticed? The only window was barred, and there was no other exit except through the room and across the hall! It was horrible! More than once did Paul scratch his head. As a measure of precaution he began to take off his boots, and, together with his trumpet, he hung them across his shoulders in order to have his arms and hands free in case of need.

His situation was the more painful for the proximity of his beloved; he saw her shadow on the wall and ceiling, he heard her pitiful sobs, which showed him how helpless were the words of her mother and of the maids to comfort her—he knew only too well why Eva Barbara would not be comforted. How despicable he seemed to himself, crouching in his corner!

Meanwhile the uproar in the house continued; by the zeal with which all nooks and corners were searched he could judge what store the farmer set upon his discovery, and at the same time how hot a reception was awaiting him if he were found. Time seemed endless until the peasant came back into the room shivering with cold, and declared—to Paul's infinite relief, "Those Rottenstein fellows shall pay dearly for this hubbub! Thunder and lightning! Those fools! It's clear as day that Paul Schülzle is not in this house. Like as not he got away from them while they were thumping on the door for dear life! He can't crawl into a rat's hole, I take it, and he's not invisible—we should have found him sure as pop if he were in the house. Every corner has been searched—every room except the *rafenetle*, and there he can't — humph, the devil! There is no knowing! Never say die!"

Terror took Paul's breath away—whither, oh whither? He heard the old man's wife say fretfully, "Go along with you! Have you lost your senses? How could anybody get into this room, not to mention the *rafenetle?*"

But he did not wait to hear the result of this intervention, and with an alacrity worthy of a better cause he crawled under the bed nearest him. This was no easy thing to do; first his boots and his trumpet hindered him, and then he found under the bed a collection of band-boxes, jars, and baskets filled with eggs, which he cautiously pushed aside, arranging them in such fashion that in case of need they might serve as a barrier to screen him from view. One round basket of eggs he very nearly knocked over; the eggs were still rolling and rumbling about in their receptacle as the farmer entered the *rafenetle* saying, "That's all very well, but there is no knowing!"

The farmer examined the clothing hanging along the panels, then, sure enough, he put his candle on the floor and looked under the beds—but for the boxes and baskets the poor devil had been lost. So the farmer went back into the sitting-room grumbling, and Paul heard him say, "There's nothing to be seen of him! Now I'll have a word to say to those Rottenstein lads!"

Thereupon a heated debate took place in the hall and in the courtyard, which Paul could not understand. At last the farmer clapped the window to, sent the servants to bed, and came back into the room panting with ire.

"So there!" he roared, "we are well rid of the musician, and of that fellow Martin as well! It is well—quite well so! About Martin I am rather sorry, but you never cared for him much, Eva Barbara, so let him go—there'll be no lack of suitors. And now, stop crying, child! Go to bed and sleep! But there's one thing you must promise me, Eva Barbara: be sure you don't so much as look at that trumpeter again,—that's all over, d'ye hear me? Eh, will you promise me that?"

"Now hush, don't say another word, and leave the poor lass in peace!" interrupted his wife. "Have you forgotten that this whole business is your fault? Now go to bed, dear child. Don't you be troubled; I'll let no harm come to ye! Go now, the Lord will turn it all to a blessing!"

To lose no word of this conversation, which made Paul's heart beat faster, he had kept quite still, and now it was too late to leave his uncomfortable place under the bed. The maids left the room and the old people hastened to get into bed.

Shame, rage, fear, and contrition joined to raise Paul's bitter indignation against himself. So this was what his stubbornness had brought him—to lie in fear and trembling, shaking with cold, under the bed of the man whose son he might have been! To hide like a thief, to be so disgracefully situated that he dared not stir for fear of discovery. Paul ground his teeth. Suppose to-night's adventures should become known! Holy Virgin! to think of the laughter and the scoffs!

The peasant threw himself from side to side in a restless manner, greatly to the discomfort of his guest, who was vastly alarmed every time the bedstead creaked. And when his wife on the other side began to sigh audibly, the farmer said, "I say, old woman, I can't sleep. I can't for the life of me get that vile affair out of my head!"

"It's just the same with me!" was the troubled answer.

"A most provoking piece of business it is, confound it!"

"Swearing don't make it any better! Don't be foolish! The lass likes him better than Martin; there's no denyin' it! It's not so very dreadful that he walked home with her!"

"That's not what I mean!" growled the peasant. "The lass will not be willing to let Paul slip; and, to tell the truth, for all I'm so enraged with the fellow, I like him better now than all the other lads. *That's* where the trouble lies!"

"Good gracious! If that is what you mean——"

"I might have known what was coming!" interrupted the farmer angrily. "There's no such thing as talking sensible to you women-folks. It's all over between the lass and Paul Schülzle, now and forever, I tell you. Don't you say another word about that, whatever you do!"

Except the sighs of the woman and the creaking of the peasant's bedstead, it was now quiet in the chamber. Paul did not stir. Although the frost was shaking him, and he was biting his fur-cap so that the chattering of his teeth might not betray him, there was a fire raging within him. He was very unhappy under the bed!

In feverish excitement he waited for the couple to fall asleep. After a while the sighs died away, the bedstead ceased to creak, but it was in vain he waited for the reassuring sound of healthy snoring. At Paul's slightest movement the peasant would lift his head and ask, "Old woman, don't you hear anything?"

"Be quiet, it's only mice a-chattering!" was the answer every time; but Paul was obliged to resign himself to keeping very quiet, so as to raise no suspicions.

He suffered the pangs of hell under that bed. It was

not only that he was growing stiff and stark with cold—every limb pained him from his uncomfortable position. Now and then he would consider the question of leaving his hiding-place, even at the risk of a fight, and so escaping by main force. What was there to fear? To overpower the old man was child's-play to him, and before the servants could be roused he would be well out of the way. He would do it—yes, he would! When he had reached this point a tremor seized him. Should he lay hands on a man who had never harmed him, in his own house—ay, in his own bed-chamber? Paul cursed and raved, then he set his teeth more firmly in his fur-cap, and stayed where he was.

His only hope was that in the morning the peasant and his wife would leave the chamber to wake the servants. This movement should serve him to leave his undignified retreat, and seek a transient hiding-place in the hall or kitchen, from whence to slip out of the house later on, when the farm-work had begun.

This hope also was made futile by no less a person than Eva Barbara! Anxiety for Paul had robbed the poor child of sleep; his mysterious disappearance filled her mind with horrible fancies. What if he had come to grief by a fall! Or perhaps in his distressed search for a hiding-place he had wedged himself into some tight place which would not let him escape! There was no doubt to her that he was still in the house; she had seen only too well how the Rottenstein men had surrounded the house; an attempt at flight would have caused a great tumult at the least. Where could he have hidden? She wept bitterly, and each passing hour laid a new burden upon her soul. At last the deep, unbroken stillness in the house grew unendurable to her. How could she rest while he was in danger, suffering pain and distress perhaps? Softly she arose, and walked stealthily through the house, wringing her hands, and whispering his name. There was no reply; everywhere the same deep and fearful silence. Without, the Rottenstein men were still guarding the house. Where could he be? Overpowered by grief and despair, she fell upon her knees.

But there was no help or satisfaction in that. If Paul was still in the house, he was in need of aid and succour. Above all she must master the situation, and gain a free hand to act in his favour. Rousing herself, she hastened to her parents' bedroom, asked them to remain in bed to make up for the night's rest they had lost, and saying that she would wake the servants and look after the household.

Had she but known in what a despairing rage her lover close beside her was biting his cap and clenching his fists!

The old people were greatly touched by this tender filial attention after the storms of the previous night; they praised the girl, and gladly assented to her proposal. The house now grew lively; a shrill whistle in the courtyard told Paul that his opponents had given up their plan and were about to disperse. Holy Virgin!—and he was still under the bed! Every moment lessened the chances of escape. How should this end?

At last the family sat about the breakfast-table, on which an enormous dish of sourkraut was steaming. Eva Barbara came in, and without ceremony turned out a large potful of boiled potatoes directly on the table-cloth round about the sourkraut-dish. While the men and maids eagerly seized the potatoes, blowing them, and often shaking their burned fingers, the farmer shook his head thoughtfully, and said, "Lass, lass, if I but knew what's the matter with ye! You look like a ghost, and there's still water in your eyes! Do be sensible! Come, wipe off your tears and eat. Sit down; my breakfast swells in my mouth when I see you so woful!"

"I cannot eat, not the least bit. There's nothing the

matter. I'll be all right again, ere long!" replied Eva Barbara softly. The mother shook her head, the father growled; but they let the girl have her own way, and Eva Barbara walked slowly away to make up the beds in the *refenetle*.

"A PALE FACE EMERGED."

Suddenly something began to stir in the clothing on the wall, a pale face emerged, and a pair of lips, trembling with cold, whispered, "Eva Barbara, help me!" With a scream the girl retreated.

The face disappeared, and immediately the good mother put her head through the door, and cried, "For the Lord Christ's sake—what is it?"

Eva Barbara began to grow dizzy; rapture to find Paul still living, terror to find him so dangerously near discovery, nearly robbed her of her senses. Covering her face with her apron, she stammered, "Oh, dear—I don't know—I shouldn't wonder if it was a mouse!"

"How you did frighten me, you silly girl. I am trembling in every limb!" cried the mother indignantly. "Is that all? The mice made a deal of noise the whole night long. I'll tell you what, you'd better take out the old straw, and fill the ticks with new at once."

Eva Barbara was unable to reply; she only nodded her head. When her mother was gone, she whispered, "Keep quiet, I'll help you!" and she hastened away. Before long she returned with a huge basket, removed the bedding, and began to fill in the straw.

Eva Barbara was an uneducated girl; she had never heard of the women of Weinsberg, but in the simplicity of her heart she hit upon the same expedient. It was a difficult piece of work that she undertook; while she was panting under her load it seemed as if her heart would break, for she was deeply conscious of the fact that she was now bearing away her life's happiness on her back.

Hanehret, one of the servants, thoughtfully remarked, "It's queer how that basket creaks, and how hard it seems for Eva Barbara to carry it, and there's naught but straw in it!"

Eva Barbara started, and tried to walk faster, when there was a sudden crash! All of a sudden her load grew horribly light, and there was a muffled thud behind her! She did not dare to look about her; with a cry of despair, "God have mercy upon us!" she rushed out of the room.

The heap of straw in the middle of the room began to

stir, a dark figure arose—slowly Paul emerged out of the cloud of dust, and sitting down with the resignation of despair upon the bench behind the stove, he put his hand under his fur-cap, scratching his head, and saying dejectedly, "Good-morning to you all! Here I am—do what you will with me."

Heinrich Schaumberger (1843-1874).

"SHE GAVE THE FELLOW A RESOUNDING BOX ON THE EAR."

HOW BLINDSCHLEICHER WENT COURTING.

BLINDSCHLEICHER was a handsome lad, but dull-witted. One would think therefore that he must have been a great favourite with the women. But the village lasses of Zesendorf were not that sort. They would not "put up with a fellow whom nature had but half-finished," as one of their spokeswomen had it.

"But nature did not leave me half-finished!" said Blindschleicher.

"She did," exclaimed the girl, "because she did not put a head on you."

He immediately seized that member in both of his hands, thereby proving the truth of what she had said.

The fact was corroborated later by the military commission. He was nearly six feet high, but they dismissed him with the verdict, "too short by a head."

But there was one thing Blindschleicher knew—viz., that women-folks are to be prevailed upon mainly by flattery; and that a good head is not a necessary equipment for flattery and courtship is a well-known fact. But the handsome gardener's apprentice had nothing that was at all available in his curly pate, and it must be admitted that nothing at all is too little. He was sweet as a fig-pudding. When he went out most of his button-holes were decked out with roses and rosebuds. If it looks pretty to wear one rose, as others do, he would argue, it must improve the effect to wear a number. His hair was made smooth and shiny with lard, and above each ear he would plaster it on each temple in a delicate crescent, like a Vienna dandy. He always chose bright and striking colours for his neckties, and tied them into knots, with long ends gracefully flowing. This as an indication of originality, and to attract the girls. But instead of the girls, the turkeys ran at him, and chased him with cackling vindictiveness through the village.

In associating with men, he was rather helpless, and he avoided them as much as might be, because they either chaffed him or ignored him, according as their mood was frolicsome or serious. Toward women he put on his most gracious mien, and oftentimes he would secretly sigh, "Ah, if I had a wife! if I only could get a wife!" For a long time he could not make out the reason for his desire, but at last his feeling consolidated into a point, and then it grew into a thought, and he gradually became conscious why it was that he wanted a wife. He could then say to his tormentors, "You may laugh as much as you please. Here is one who will have me!" And there was one in particular before whose countenance he would melt like butter in the sun.

That was Liese, the farm-maid. She was the most blooming lass in the valley, and he set a wistful eye upon her.

And Blindschleicher confided his troubles to his friend the watchman, as they walked through the silent village one night. "Man," he lamented, "never was there such ill luck as mine. You wouldn't believe it. I'm head over ears in love with the lass, and there's no help for it."

"Why don't you take her, then?" said the watchman.

"Take her, fool! when she won't so much as look at you!"

"She needn't look at *me*. My old woman is firmly yoked to me."

"But it is at *me* that she might look," said Blindschleicher. "When I think of all the trouble I go to to make myself agreeable! And as for her—when I say to her, 'Liese, good morning, Liese!' she turns on her heel; and when I say, 'How bonny you are, Liese!' she says, 'How clever you are, lad!'"

"Well, don't that please you?" said the watchman.

"How can it please me, when she goes on to say 'she will only take a fool.' She's a vixen, is Liese! And when I give her a rose, and say, 'You look just like it, you are as pink, and you are as sweet, and you are as thorny!' she takes the pretty blossom out of my hand, and gives it to the goat to eat."

"Blindschleicher," said the watchman in a low tone, "you're on the wrong track to get a wife."

"I am sick at heart," said the gardener's apprentice, and he looked it and hung his head. "Time and time again have I said to her, 'Precious Liese, darling Liese, you are like butter and honey; I could eat you up for love. I will kiss your feet, and you may tread upon me. There is nothing you could do that would hurt me,' I said. 'You may put your arms tight around my neck, and smother me with your cheek; it would not hurt me. You are like a heavenly paradise to me. I can do a great deal of fine talking when I once get started. Think of the ardour of my youthful blood,' I said."

"And what did she reply?"

"'Go to the barber and get bled,' she answered. "Oh, she is a stone, man; she is a stone."

"Be comforted, lad," said the watchman, who was a kind and experienced man. "If she is a stone, we will manage her. Stones cannot be raised by whining and pining, good friend. When there is a stone on the ground you must loosen it first by a sharp knock, then you can lift it. Do you understand?"

"What do you mean? Shall I run into her to shake her loose?"

"Not so fast, my lad. There is such a thing as a simile you must know. Supposing, for instance, I say you are an ass, you must not take it in dead earnest, but merely as a means of comparison."

"Yes, yes," said Blindschleicher. "When I hear you talk like that I understand you well. You are not rude like the others, and you are my best friend. But if I could but have Liese!"

"Women," said the watchman with an air of superior knowledge, standing still and leaning upon his long staff, "women are the most peculiar among God's creatures. The first human being did sorry credit to his creator, as is apt to be the case when you're a new hand at making things. It turned out a plain wooden man. But the second human being—the second, you see, was much more of a success. It turned out to be something very different from the man, much finer, so much finer. The truth is, man is the job of an apprentice; woman shows the touch of a master. I understand women; ah, I understand them! An old watchman like me, who has his eyes open every hour of the night, knows a thing or two, good friend. If you cannot win them with dainties and fine manners, remember that it isn't every bird that can be caught with sugar. Try some other way; do something to offend her. Not in any faint-hearted, playful way, but seriously and thoroughly; do something to her that will make her think of you, and that will give her pain when she thinks of you. Soon she will stop teasing you and looking upon you with disdainful indifference. Perhaps she will hate you; but, my friend, you must know that hatred is a good deal nearer to love than indifference is. There is many a tale I could tell you of how love began with anger and pain. That's what I meant about loosening the stone. There is nothing like the harsh, reckless deed of a man to make an impression. Try it; you can't lose anything."

Blindschleicher went his way and made extensive preparations to think out this new idea. For hours he walked by the side of the brook, but how can we catch hold of an idea when the water is making so much noise! He stole across the fields, but there the crickets disturbed him, or a dark, mysterious figure would rise up in front of him which, for all he knew, might be a ghost. To be sure the schoolmaster had said to him, "Blindschleicher, I pledge you my word, you are safe from ghosts!" But then, who knows! It seems wicked enough to be thinking out something in the silent night wherewith to offend one's beloved. "Wicked or not wicked, if I could but make her have me!"

It was not until he was pulling off his boots in his own room that various more or less attractive devices occurred to him by means of which he might offend her. When he was in bed he discarded them one by one. He thought he could hurt her most deeply by going up to her and saying, "Liese, you do not love me; farewell for ever, I go to die!"

He was quite stupefied by the power of this thought. It gave the poor fellow a headache, and the next morning when he got up, and the sun shone brightly upon the flowers of the garden, he felt that this would not do, and he said to himself, "Best say nothing about dying."

This selfsame day was a Sunday, so he donned his tight grey pantaloons, a yellow flowered vest, with the ends of a cherry-coloured necktie fluttering over it, put rosebuds in all of the button-holes of his blue jacket, arranged the two little greased crescents of hair neatly upon his cheeks, bestowed due care upon his sprouting moustache, and a look in the mirror convincing him that he was irresistible, his heart swelled with happy forebodings.

It was with solemn feelings that he walked through the shady alley to church; this very afternoon he would try to meet Liese, and would carry out his purpose of mortally offending her. She would weep, she would pout; he would ask her forgiveness, and then their relation would appear altogether in a new light. Should these extremest measures prove unsuccessful, then he would put her out of his mind and offend some other girl. If that was all that was required, why love was easy play.

"There goes the girl-hunter!" called out a giggling urchin as Blindschleicher was passing a group of lads with a mien half haughty and half self-conscious.

As he reached the church the bells were just ringing for High Mass, and the people were crowding through the door, and he joined them like a good Christian as he was. Turning once to see who it was that was in such a mighty hurry behind him, whom should he discover quite near his side but Liese. She was giggling with some lads, who pressed close about her. Blindschleicher saw the vessel for holy water wherein each dipped his fingers in passing. At that moment the gardener's apprentice was seized with a sudden impulse. Dipping his hollow hand in the water, and crying, "Here is one whose devil I would expel!" he threw the entire handful into fair Liese's face.

Liese caught her breath, said loud and distinctly, "He is out already!" and gave the fellow a resounding box on his ear.

And that is how Blindschleicher went courting, and what it brought him.

P. K. Rosegger.

"*WHOM FIRST WE LOVE.*"

May 1.—I love him! Only thou, my journal, shalt know it, thou silent confidant of all my sorrows and my hopes. Without it is spring-time, and the nightingales warble and the lilacs are in bloom. What a lovely time for one's first love!

May 2.—All night I lay awake and thought of him, and made poetry. It seems like the bitterest irony of fate that I must go to school to-day, as if I were a child!

May 3.—He is perfectly heavenly, handsome, ravenlocked, with dark, glowing eyes, and a pale Roman face; his moustache is simply enchanting. There is certainly something demoniacal about him. I adore demoniacal men. They are so exciting and interesting. He looks marvellously like Lord Byron. Perhaps he is a poet, or a Polish prince in exile. He looks so melancholy and aristocratic. I imagine Max Piccolomini looked like that as Mortimer in *Mary Stuart*.

May 4.—How he looked at me as he passed me on the way to school to-day! I put that provoking school-bag behind my back. I trust he did not see it.

May 6.—I have confided my secret to Lina. She is my most intimate friend; our hearts are joined for now and eternity. We wept together for hours. Lina understands me perfectly. She too has loved and has suffered unspeakably, poor girl! He was an officer of the Dragoons, I believe, and came to their house a great deal; at last he came nearly every day. Lina expected his declaration from hour to hour, but he went and proposed to her elder sister. Lina thought her heart was broken. I should never have survived such perfidy. Men are very wicked and false. Lina has read *Faust*. He reminds her of Faust a little, she says. I must try to get the book. Lina raves over it, although she says it is very immoral.

May 7.—I have seen him again, and am in a state of unbounded felicity. Lina and I were sitting in the park, eating candy and talking of him, of course, when he came walking up the path. I pinched Lina's arm; I could not speak, but she understood me. Oh, heavens! he sat down on the seat beside us! I felt my blood rush to my heart. Lina blushed too, which was very silly of her. I studied his noble profile; he was rapt in thought, and did not move. Lina talked and laughed quite loud; she is really very much of a flirt. Of course he paid no attention to her.

May 8, *Sunday*.—The whole afternoon I read in the "Book of Songs." Heinrich Heine is simply sweet. What a pity it is he wrote so many things they won't let me read! Mamma does not like him at all, but then mamma is so very matter-of-fact. I wonder if I could ever grow to be so prosaic? At *his* side surely not.

May 9.—No one knows him here. I have made some cautious inquiries. He is probably spending some time here *incognito*. I feel pretty sure he is a political exile from Russia perhaps, or Siberia. Perhaps he is a revolutionary hero like Lafayette, or Brutus, or Kosciusko. Maybe he has killed somebody in a duel—he always looks so sad and unhappy; or he is the captain of a band of robbers, like Carl Moor, awfully noble and gallant of course. Heavens! what if his pursuers should come upon him! But I love him all the same; it is not a matter of choice or volition. "Man cannot loose what heaven binds," says Schiller. I think that is quite well put. We went through the "Bride of Messina" to-day. I find a great deal in it that applies to me nowadays. I think Dr. Strempel saw me blush once or twice.

May 10.—I have taken him for my hero. All the girls in the class have a hero. Alexander the Great, or Nikolaus Lenau. Before this I had Count Adolar, in "The Pearl of Venice." I call him Lohengrin, that sounds so poetic and unusual; and I too do not know where he comes from, like Elsa von Brabant.

May 11.—Mamma looks at me so queerly sometimes. She does not want me to sit in my room alone so much instead of taking a share in her household cares. It is very sad to think that parents so often have little sympathy with the deepest emotions of their children's hearts.

May 13.—All is over. My ideals are broken, my faith in humanity is gone for ever. Would I could die or enter a convent! I can write no more to-day—I have naught but tears and sighs to record. I only ate two apple-dumplings for dinner; they all noticed it.

May 14.—No one knows what I suffer. This terrible secret of my poisoned youth shall follow me to my grave. Lohengrin! How absurd the name sounds now, like a cruel irony of Fate.

What would the girls at school say if they knew that Lohengrin, my interesting exiled Count, my Knight of the Swan—oh, horrors!—is nothing but a waiter?

May 16.—Did ever maiden's heart suffer like mine? Ophelia or Margaret? Hamlet was at least a prince, and Faust had his college-degree, entitling him to social distinction. Ah, if he were but a shepherd or a hunter! There are such pretty poems about such with princesses and noble ladies—but a waiter? It is too horrible!

It was on the 12th of May, the most tragic day of my life. Can I ever be happy again, can I ever forget it? Aunt Hedwig was visiting us, and in the evening papa and I went with her to the winter garden of the Victoria Hotel. Papa and auntie were talking together, and I sat quite still, —I have grown very quiet of late,—and as I was sipping my iced lemonade my thoughts hovered tenderly about my beloved. A mysterious power suddenly constrained me to look up. Near me, leaning against the trunk of a palm-tree, stood Lohengrin. How distinguished and elegant he looked! His dress-coat fitted him like a glove, the one softly-curled lock of hair falling over his brow gave him an air of classic grace. A heavy ring of gold gleamed on his slender hand. Thank God, it was no wedding ring!

"Waiter!" called papa—I heard it as in a dream. His eyes grew larger and more lustrous, a beam of light seemed to flit across his countenance. My heart almost stood still. He approached our table. Does he not see papa and Aunt Hedwig? Does he not see all the people about us? He bows, he says: "Do you require anything, sir?"

"A bottle of Médoc," says papa. I hear his voice as if it came from a great distance. I felt as if something within me had snapped asunder at that moment.

"What a nice-looking fellow!" remarked Aunt Hedwig.

"A Pole," said my father. "He looks like the veriest fashion plate. Dear me, little girl, how pale you are! The wine will do you good, and you must order your iron pills again to-morrow. Here waiter, the rest is for you!"

Lohengrin, my Lohengrin, and twopence for his tip! Even now it is a mystery to me that I did not faint away.

Three days later.—I have scratched out the last nine pages of my journal word for word. The occupation did me good. This episode is wiped out from the pages of my

"HOW DISTINGUISHED AND ELEGANT HE LOOKED."

life. Lohengrin is dead to me. There is one thing that comforts me—I now have an unhappy love. I always envied Lina a little for hers, she put on such airs about it. Unhappy loves are so very interesting and poetic.

P.S.—In future I shall fall in love only with gentlemen in uniforms. You have something you can depend on then, and the world is so false and deceitful nowadays.

H. von Kahlenberg.

"PLANTED HIMSELF SQUARELY BEFORE THE SCRIBENT, AND STARED AT HIM IN SILENCE."

WOOING THE GALLOWS.

IN the year 1594 the town-scribent of Nördlingen had an extraordinary visitor. A herculean lad of about twenty, unkempt and ragged, came to the court-room one morning, planted himself squarely before the scribent, and stared at him in silence.

Unto the gruffly put question, "What do you want?" he answered no less gruffly, "A rope!"

The town-scribent told him he had come to the wrong door, the rope-maker lived around the corner. But the fellow replied to the effect that he did not need the rope-maker, but the hangman; he wanted to be hanged. The town-scribent shivered, for he thought the stranger was crazy. He therefore called a vigorous servant before entering further into this extraordinary conversation.

The stranger now confessed himself to be a homeless tramp, called by his companions Jörg Muckenhuber, and his language being pieced together out of as many rags of dialect as his coat was of rags of cloth, there was no further certificate required to make it evident that he was at home everywhere and nowhere.

He then proceeded to relate briefly and coldly how several weeks ago he had murdered a travelling pedlar upon the precincts of Nördlingen, and also between Augsburg and Kaufbeuern a foreign Jew. Both the Jew and the pedlar gave him no peace at night, so he wanted to be hanged, and as the last murder had been perpetrated on the ground of Nördlingen, so the senate of that town could not refuse to hang him on the Nördlingen gallows.

The town-scribent swore furiously, and said it wasn't every fool could have that for the asking, the town of Nördlingen had built its gallows for its own citizens and not for villainous vagrants; at the same time Muckenhuber was taken into custody, and the scribent presented the affair to the senate.

The senators put their heads together without coming to any definite conclusion as to whether the lad was a fool or a desperate villain. As it was customary, however, in those days to cast the insane into the same dungeon as thieves and murderers, Jörg Muckenhuber was put in safe keeping in the tower, and the business was getting under way in a most correct manner, whatever further details might be brought to light.

The executioner, the parson, and the barber, who went in turn to visit the prisoner and sound him each in his own way, declared with one voice that the fellow was rough and uncared for, but that his mind was very clear, and that there was no gainsaying him in his confession.

Meanwhile the news was scattered through town, and the good citizens had lively quarrels as to whether a person could be hanged upon the strength of his mere confession and urgent demand, even though there was no further proof of the deed of which he accused himself; for nowhere was there to be found a trace of the travelling pedlar and the murder perpetrated on him.

And when Muckenhuber was taken out, well guarded and followed by a curious crowd, to show them the exact spot where he had murdered the pedlar and buried his corpse, he managed to confuse and puzzle his judges by fine-spun evasions and equivocations, but there was no actual evidence of the crime to be found. The prisoner, however, clung with tenacity to his previous declaration, that he had murdered the pedlar upon the precincts of Nördlingen, and must therefore be hanged on the Nördlingen gallows.

Although German burghers of provincial towns were as well accustomed to highly-spiced criminal dramas in those days as they were to their daily bread, the sensation about this unusual case grew from day to day; especially was the reply of the Augsburg and Kaufbeuern magistrate anxiously looked forward to, to whom the acts had been submitted with a neighbourly request to have inquiries made concerning the murder said to have been perpetrated between those two towns upon a foreign Jew. But here too there was not a vestige of a Jew or a murder to be found.

But in the scrupulous proceedings of the sixteenth century, confession of crime was considered a proof by far superior to any other, and so the judges refused to be satisfied, the more so as the prisoner continued to bring forth reasons to explain the absence of all testimony.

It was deemed best to fall back upon that most unrelenting test of truth, the rack. How often had people who objected to being criminals been tortured into a confession; why should it not be possible to reverse the method and torture a man, who had set his mind on being a criminal, into a confession of his innocence?

But in the torturing-chamber the senate of Nördlingen got out of the frying-pan into the fire. For when the thumb-screws were applied Jörg Muckenhuber persisted in piping his old song, and when the effect was heightened by forcing him into the Spanish boots, he proceeded at once to add to his original offence by confessing a list of robberies, each of which alone would have brought him to the gallows. The inquisitor had also a ride upon the sharp-edged ass upon his programme, but fearing lest the invincible Jörg should add two or three cases of arson into the bargain he did not press the point, and the triumphant rogue was conducted back into his dungeon, while the senate was writhing in an agony of impotent rage.

To the more sagacious it became more and more evident that Jörg Muckenhuber was making game of the town authorities, but at the same time a joke of such ghastly grimness was unprecedented. Then too, no one could hit upon a possible motive why the churlish fellow should subject his neck to the rope and his limbs to the rack with an amount of courage and power of will that was worthy of a better cause. This seemed too much for the most vicious facetiousness. Moreover, not only the acknowledged crime but the whole person of this Muckenhuber seemed to have sprung up out of the ground over-night as it were. For his sudden appearance in Nördlingen was surrounded with as much mystery as his crime. There were some who confidentially affirmed that he was the devil, who was out for a lark and had chosen this method of twitting the whole of Nördlingen by the nose.

However, this did not help solve the difficult question of what was to be done with the vagabond.

Public opinion in those days generally inclined to the assumption that where the case was doubtful it was better to hang three innocent men than let one guilty one get away. And, moreover, Jörg Muckenhuber was guilty any way you might look at it. For if he had committed the murder in question then he deserved the gallows, and if he had not committed it, then he deserved the gallows more than ever, because by reason of his iniquity the senate of the town had made a confounded fool of itself. But as there was no unanimity in court in which of these two ways he had deserved the gallows, he was left for the present quietly in the dungeon.

It was not exactly attractive there. The cell was half above ground and half below, in a small tower, which upon three sides faced a swampy bog; there was no surplus of light, but a narrow little window let in a bit of chiaroscuro, which would have enabled one to distinguish a chair from a table on a sunny noon-day—that is, if there had been any such objects of luxury at hand. There was more pleasure to be derived from outside. Under the window the frogs sang in a varied and full chorus. At one side there was another dungeon, occupied by an old hag, who obstinately refused to confess to being a witch. Her so-called window also faced the bog, and when the two neighbours looked out of the window they could converse with facility, although it was without seeing each other, and no one excepting the frogs overheard their conferences.

Jörg had received the first intimation of his neighbour's presence by hearing her pray aloud one day. It was no soft, humble prayer; it was passionate, almost as if the old woman were storming the Almighty with commands rather than petitions. Jörg had never learned to pray, and at first the devotions of the old woman struck him as very odd; gradually it came to look very grand to him that an old hag should venture to address herself to God with such vehemence, and he came to the conclusion she must be a giant in strength and able to hold her own against ten men.

He did not open the conversation, but waited until his neighbour should discover his proximity and address him. Even heroic women like to talk. Soon an intimacy sprang up between these two comrades in distress who had never seen each other. At first Jörg often interrupted his neighbour's kind words with many a scornful and dogged remark, but she always answered him so mildly, and at the same time with so much quiet superiority, that Jörg's insolence was soon tamed.

In the course of a few days Jörg knew the history of his neighbour by heart, but he obstinately kept silence about his own.

The old woman was the well-to-do, childless widow of an innkeeper. In her sixtieth year she had the misfortune to be accused of witchcraft. A wealthy witch is a rarity. But it so happened that during the last five years all ugly poor women had been burned up in Nördlingen, and as every witch was called upon to name accomplices, and as the zeal of the judges increased with each execution, at last it came to be the turn of young, handsome, and rich women as well. There were enough of these unfortunate women, but none was so unfortunate, and at the same time so heroic, as Maria Hollin. She had been in the rack fifty-eight times, and had confessed nothing. She was indeed, as Jörg had rightly judged from her prayer, able to hold her own against ten men. The judges were in despair; it was out of the question to acquit a person who had been tortured fifty-eight times, and it was equally so to condemn her without a confession.

Moreover, the rumour of her firmness had gone among

the populace, and there was much sympathy with her, and a threatening murmur of displeasure against the much-feared judges. Up to now everything had gone smoothly and comfortably. Thirty-two women had been accused, put on the rack, convicted, and burned; not one of them had made any trouble. At the worst, the one or the other had to be left hanging with weights on her feet until the judges had had some refreshments. But when they came back from lunch the fullest confession had always rewarded them. And now, through the obstinacy of this woman, the smooth course of events had been most aggravatingly interrupted.

And then, too, there was that provoking affair with Muckenhuber.

The one would not confess her guilt, while they were hankering to condemn her; the other they would have been only too happy to let go, but even the rack was powerless to extract the confession of his innocence. The town-scribent thought if Jörg Muckenhuber were only a woman, then by a bold strategy he might be burned, as it were by mistake, instead of Maria Hollin, and she might be dismissed in his stead, so that each should have his heart's desire, and the court should preserve its authority.

But the worst of all for the senate was the prospect of a diplomatic storm that was brewing at the horizon in the direction of Regensburg. Maria Hollin had well-to-do relatives at Ulm, and the magistrate of that town, convinced of her innocence, had applied for her release. But that did her little good. The town-scribent thought it would endanger the reputation of a court to put a person on the rack for fifty-eight times and then not even to have the satisfaction of singeing her a little, not to speak of burning. But the burghers of Ulm would not be silenced. At Regensburg there was an important Reichstag that year, and the Emperor, Rudolph II., was present in person. The ambassador from Ulm received orders from his town to intercede for the accused, and as he was not given a hearing he threatened to set the Emperor and the Reich against the law-court of Nördlingen.

The history of Maria Hollin made a deep impression upon Jörg Muckenhuber. Until now he had looked upon himself as a hero before his judges, but by the side of this true heroine he appeared to himself to be playing the part of a bad boy. Out of stubbornness and pride he had kept silent about his true history before his judges; before this woman he kept silent for shame. But finally he could not resist the firm, sympathetic voice of his invisible companion.

So he was tame at last, and began to confess his tale to the old woman. At first he asked her if she had ever seen a pair of fighting dogs that had locked teeth, and so held each other as in a vice, for all the cuffs they got to make them let go. He and his judge, he said, were like such dogs. From a child he had led a bold vagabond life; he had enjoyed all the pleasures of a restless, adventurous rover, and had suffered all the deprivations and distress and shame of such. He had never murdered or robbed, only taken along what he needed. He was tired of the whole business. Life was a burden to him, but to take his own life, and be found later in the water or in the woods like a beast, was not to his taste.

He had often heard death on the gallows lauded as the best, and when his companions spoke of their "heroes," it was always of such persons as had reached the highest point of their career on the upper round of the ladder leading to the gallows.

To put a showy end to life, which had lost its attraction for him, Jörg went to Nördlingen, a town which was then notorious for its hasty justice.

Dame Hollin thereupon gave Jörg a most terrific lecture. To judge by the tone of her voice, he thought of her as standing in her dark cell like the angel with the flaming sword. For all that her sermon did not touch him specially. He was much more deeply contrite when in the silent night he compared her heroic courage and disdain of death with his own sorry tale, making his invincible obstinacy look like the caricature of her bravery. He admitted the justice of everything she said when with a firm hand she shook his conscience; but he did not admit the justice of what the others said. And when Dame Hollin condemned him it frightened him as much as damnation at the last judgment might; but before that day came he was determined to play his joke upon the senate of Nördlingen, and hang on their gallows.

Months passed. The two neighbours grew to be more and more to each other. The hardened witch succeeded in implanting a little bit of Christianity upon him, at least as much as could be crowded through the narrow-barred window. Jörg accepted her dogmas willingly enough, but would not let go of his own dogma, that he must be hanged on Nördlingen ground.

Jörg had locked teeth with the senate, but the senators had also locked teeth with each other because of this same Jörg.

Two parties formed and quarrelled so heartily that they quite forgot the object of their quarrel. One side, as before mentioned, wished to hang him because he had committed murder; the other, because he had not committed murder. Only the town-scribent constituted, in silence and all by himself, a third party of mediation. He wanted to let Jörg get away. For, he said to himself, if he had been put on the rack the first day, the truth would most likely have come to light; now it is too late. If we wait until both parties agree as to which offence Muckenhuber shall be hanged for, he may meanwhile die of old age in the tower. This would be a clear loss to the town, which supplies the vagabond with food and lodging all for nothing. The town-scribent further concluding with subtle psychological insight that Jörg would probably by this time be mellow and tired of the poor fare of prison, it seemed to him to be the best plan to leave the door open by accident, so that the fellow could run away.

So he gave orders to have the door of his cell left unbolted from time to time. Jörg noticed it, but did not stir; he was determined to be hanged on Nördlingen ground.

But when he told his neighbour of the growing carelessness of his gaoler, things took a new turn. With the knowledge of the open door, though it was not that of her cell, the mighty love of freedom awoke in Dame Hollin. 'If I could get out!' she cried, "it would not be to escape; I should but go to come back—go to tell my friends at Ulm of the disgrace I have suffered, and come back with witnesses and testimonials of my innocence. I do not want freedom; I want my honour and reputation——!" She did not finish what she wanted to say, but Jörg understood her.

For some time he had been at work breaking through the thin partition between the two cells. His only tool was a small piece of iron, and the work progressed but slowly. After these words of Dame Hollin he worked day and night with the utmost exertion of his strength, and in the third night he could manage to crawl through the small hole.

There was no time to be lost. This same night Jörg's door was left unbolted again, so there were a few hasty words of farewell spoken. Dame Hollin crept through into her neighbour's cell. Thus Jörg, trembling from head to foot, threw his arms about the old woman's knees, and, as if he wanted to throw the fulness of his obedience and gratitude into one word, he cried, "Mother!" and she passed her hands gently over his face, feeling his features in the darkness, and crying, "My poor, unhappy son!"

Dame Hollin hid in the house of a faithful friend, to escape to Ulm the next day. Jörg slipped over into the deserted cell, and when his gaoler came to the door in the morning to push in a dish of humble fare, he crouched down in a corner, wrapped in the cloak of the old woman, and when the man passed on to his cell, he slipped nimbly through the hole in the wall, and in the garb of Jörg Muckenhuber received his own ration. He kept this up for about a week with much skill and secret delight, if sorrow for the loss of his faithful comrade had not choked his pleasure.

But one day the door was opened wide enough to admit the town-scribent, together with the gaoler, the former ordering Dame Hollin to follow him to the court-room. Jörg played his *rôle* as long as he could, crouched down in terror in the darkest corners, and repelled his tormentors with silent gestures. But when the town-scribent cried reassuringly, "Woman, come boldly forth; I lead thee not to the rack, but to freedom," then Muckenhuber forgot his mask, threw his cloak from his shoulders in impotent rage, started up indignantly and cried, with his clenched hands in his side, "You will do no such thing; I want to be hanged, and I won't let you off!"

The town-scribent tore his hair in despair and rage when he perceived that the witch was gone and the vagabond was left. He had intended to conduct Dame Hollin to freedom, but it was to have been freedom under weighty conditions; and now she had disappeared without any conditions whatsoever. Jörg, however, who was to have disappeared and no questions asked, sat once more firmly upon the neck of the senate. "Fellow, there's no putting an end to you!" cried the town-scribent, foaming at the mouth. But Muckenhuber replied coldly, "It is this I complain of, that you won't even try!"

The senators poured bitter reproaches upon each other,

at first in a low tone, then louder, until the storm grew, and there was a wild confusion of voices. Then the townscribent silenced them all with his deep bass, and united the disputants with a word. He cried, "The cause of all this trouble is only Jörg Muckenhuber. Hang him at once if he does not recant his old confessions!" Jörg replied, "I do *not* recant!" and when the town-scribent asked him for the second time, "Now, I certainly shan't recant," and the third time . . .

There stood old Dame Hollin as if she had grown out of the ground, conducted by two of the most respectable burghers of Nördlingen and Ulm. She looked sharply at Muckenhuber, and said in a firm tone, "Jörg, you will recant your false confession!" The voice struck the insolent fellow like a peal of thunder. He was silent and lowered his eyes. There was no sound, one could hear the laboured breathings; then he spoke, "No other power on earth could have made me recant, but I cannot lie in the face of this woman;—I recant!"

Meanwhile the tumult of the populace without was increasing. The air was filled with wild threats, and with demands for the immediate release of Dame Hollin. The gentlemen saw that there was danger in delay. After a short, whispered debate the town-scribent read aloud the writ the old woman was to swear to. But Dame Hollin replied that she did not want mercy but demanded her right. The gentlemen of the senate made very wry faces and began to try persuasion, but they had learned ere this that there was little to be gained in that way with Dame Hollin.

After a moment's thought, she said to her judges, "You have tried to make a bargain with me. Having done so, you are no longer my judges, and cannot give me my right. Well then, I too am ready to offer you a bargain. Release that wicked lad yonder, I will adopt him in child's stead, and take him to Ulm with me, and see if I can do better by him than you have done. My property has lain dead while you kept me in the tower. You should refund the usury I have lost; instead of that give me this wicked lad. On this condition will I sign your writ."

Already the populace clamoured outside the door. The senate would have had no choice, even though she had demanded much more than this.

As she signed the writ, she found a bill appendixed for her fare during the time of her custody. She returned the leaf with a courteous smile to the town-scribent, and as the rabble was knocking at the door he plucked the interesting supplement into bits as fast as possible, and strewed the pieces under the table.

Meanwhile the chains had been removed from Jörg; he looked about him as in a dream. Dame Hollin took his hand, and went to the door with him, where both were received by the gratified shouts of the shuffling crowd.

. . . .

The old woman kept her word. In her house Jörg became an honest, valiant man, who in the Thirty Years' War did great service to Ulm, the town of his adoption, and his name was never spoken but in honour and gratitude. But the witch's counsel was forced to resign office, and after those five years of terror followed a better decade, during which law and justice reigned once more in the old Reichstadt.

W. H. Riehl.

ELECTIVE AFFINITIES.

1.

HIGHLY-ESTEEMED MADAM,—I venture to write these lines to you in the firm belief that you, like all women of mental distinction, love the unusual, and hate to the utmost the commonplaces of ordinary conventionality. . . .

Having left the company, and wending my lonely way through the streets of Berlin, I felt myself to be in a state of lively excitement. The events of the evening passed once more before me, and ere long I was in that incomprehensible mystical mood, which comes so suddenly we know not how or whence. I was quite capable of calling to the spirits that seemed to float about me: "Answer me, if ye hear me!" when the sound of a passing carriage called me back to reality, and my gaze turned from the stars of heaven to a pair of star-like earthly orbs whose mild light shone for a passing moment with full radiance into my soul.

These starry eyes belonged to a young lady who was seated by your side in the carriage. At that moment I was seized with the purpose I am now carrying out.

I herewith enclose an unsealed letter to the lovely possessor of those gleaming stars, and I leave it to your never-erring tact to decide, after having read the letter, whether you will hand it to the young lady, who is doubtless one of your intimate circle of acquaintances, or consign it to the atoning flames of your grate.—Yours most sincerely,

VON SCH.

II.

HIGHLY-ESTEEMED MISS,—If Frau von B. should decide to give these lines into your hands, I shall consider it as a mark of confidence in me which encourages me in a measure to express to you a very singular request, as I am about to do. Perhaps you would have the goodness to look upon this mark of confidence on the part of so admirable a lady as a sort of pledge of my character, on the strength of which you will kindly permit me to conceal my name and social functions. At the same time I shall endeavour, dear Fraulein, to remain in complete ignorance so far as you are concerned.

After these preliminaries touching the scenic arrangement, permit me to come to the point.

I am sure you, as well as most persons possessing a lively imagination, have had occasion in life to observe the following occurrence. We stroll through the crowd of a large town thinking of nothing in particular, and indifferently passing a thousand faces that meet ours with the same indifference. . . .

And in the midst of this placid, colourless mood we are suddenly surprised and fascinated by a pair of eyes that unexpectedly emerge out of the senseless crowd to meet ours for a second and then to disappear again. But what a wealth of experience lies in that passing moment! We know for certain that never in our past life has that face crossed our path, but the sight has touched us with an electric thrill. And as our soul rises into our eyes to greet that other soul, a hundred questions and answers fly back and forth with the rapidity of lightning.

"Who art thou? I have so much to say to thee. Secrets I scarce dare whisper to myself, I would entrust to thee. I feel that there is an invisible band between us."

"Ah, I feel it too! It would bind us closer than all other human bands."

And then comes the fear of making oneself ridiculous, and all the tame considerations that hamper every pure and fresh impulse. And all this, dear Fraulein, you and I have experienced. Our souls have met and recognised each other. This is a mighty fact, which you felt as well as I three days ago as your carriage crossed the Kurfürsten Bridge. If we were to meet now in society, the ordinary conventional preliminaries of getting acquainted would take away our naïve impression, we should be bereft of that elemental undeviating conviction which constituted the mysterious charm of our meeting. Let us then remain strangers to each other outwardly, trusting only to these first glowing intuitions.

Let us exchange a few letters, freely and without a thought to conventionality. Their contents shall bind us to nothing in real life, and should we meet by some strange accident, they shall be but a memory.

Do not, I beg of you, listen to the faint-hearted criticism of reason, but follow the first hearty impulse of your soul. It will lead you aright.

With warm sympathy,

THE UNKNOWN OF THE KURFÜRSTEN BRIDGE.

III.

DEAR SIR,—I have decided to answer your interesting letter. Frau von B. is to read all letters that pass between us, so that I can enter upon this correspondence with a happy sense of freedom from responsibility.

I am weary of the dryness of ordinary intercourse, and there is nothing I should like better than to talk to a man for once without reserve. I drop my worsted-work as the prisoner drops his chains, and dip my pen into the ink with the thrilling rapture of dawning freedom.

Do you know what it is to do worsted-work? Have you ever thought about this last reminiscence of mediæval times, this glaring anachronism in a time of steam and electricity and enlightenment? . . .

Liberty flows and surges about us, and life brings forth thousands of rich blossoms, and we sit imprisoned and—do worsted-work, or drum on the piano, murdering Chopin, or if we are very clever, sing Schumann's songs with the pathos of dilettantism.

When I met you on the Kurfürsten Bridge, Frau von B. and I were just coming home from a ladies' party, to which all the guests had brought their worsted-work. I had really suffered under the unendurable weight of conversation on topics of the utmost indifference, under a hypocritical interest in things which cannot possibly interest anybody. My heart was full of bitterness, and on the way home I was considering the question whether such a life was worth living, whether it would not be wiser to run away, to adopt the garb of a man, and try one's powers boldly in the stream of life.

At that moment I saw you, and I felt all that you speak of in your letter. In that short second in which our eyes met, pictures clearly defined and wondrously bright arose before me.

Dressed as a youth, I seemed to descend from my carriage and seize your hand, and you knew all. Silently we walked through the streets, hand in hand, until we reached your house. There, I told you everything about my lonely childhood, my joyless youth, and the world of dreams and ideals within me. You spoke earnest words of duty and work, called me your friend, and said we would go along part of the way side by side. . . .

After a winter of severe work came bright, sunny days of spring, and I felt at last that in the arms of nature, at her pure altar, I had received a "purer life, and the glad courage of hopeful youth."

I hope you will return my frankness in full. When we end our correspondence, and return after this bold aside into the track of everyday life, perhaps we shall bring back some new, fresh courage, and the graceful memory of having been for once in our lives as foolish as we pleased.

Kind greetings from your

UNKNOWN.

IV.

HIGHLY-ESTEEMED UNKNOWN FRIEND,—Your amiable letter made me supremely happy. Now I know without a doubt that the mysterious quality of reading the soul of a being akin in spirit is no empty illusion. In that deeply mystical moment I recognised your charming self just as you describe it with winning simplicity. What you write me in many pages I have read word for word out of your eyes. And now that I know how near you are to me in sympathy and in intuitive understanding, now I have so much to say to you, so much to receive from you, that it were a crime not to tear down the paper barriers between us and to replace the dead letter by the living word.

I only await your permission. I promise myself a great deal from this meeting, perhaps a friendship for life, and I warmly beg you to look upon the unusual beginning as an earnest of a happy end.

Hoping impatiently for a gracious reply, I am, your truly devoted,

UNKNOWN.

V.

DEAR FRIEND,—Allow me to tell you that, in spite of your somewhat too lively imagination, I have always looked upon you as a person of much sense, and that there is nothing that moves me more to pity than to see a sensible man attacked by a fashionable craze like spiritualism. I am always seized by the desire to heal the patient, which seems the more difficult the absurder—forgive the word, but I know no better—the cause of the attack.

I hope you will laugh heartily over the following story,

"THE UNUTTERABLE EXPRESSION IT PRODUCED UPON MY VISAGE."

and have a healthful feeling of convalescence when you have bravely conquered the first bitter taste of the medicine.

A young widow, living in great seclusion, allows an old friend of her husband's to persuade her to make a concession to him and to the carnival, and visit a masked ball at his house, in company of her brother, a comely school-boy.

The latter, dressed as a young lady looks charming, makes countless conquests at the ball, and rides home at night in an open carriage with his sister, wrapped in a charming evening-cloak of hers, flushed with champagne, and with the triumphs of the evening.

And lo and behold, upon the Kurfürsten Bridge the glowing eyes of the lad make, as it seems, a deep and lasting impression!

A few days later the widow receives a very remarkable letter from a friend, which tempts her irresistibly to give him a lesson, which I am sure he will have the kindness to take in good part.

She put herself as far as possible in the mood of her ecstatic friend, rummaged among her youthful reminiscences, and composed an answer which puts her friend quite beside himself, and convinces him that there is such a thing as mysterious sympathy of soul, electric glances, mystic bands, spirit kisses, etc., etc.

And now—what do you say?

In a gay carnival-humour, your old friend,

ALEXANDRA VON B.

VI.

DISPATCH.

Frau Alexandra von B——, H—— St.

Had a photograph taken immediately upon receipt of your letter, to preserve the unutterable expression it produced upon my visage.

Shall take the liberty of presenting you with a specimen ere long. Acceptance to be looked upon as an act of penal justice. In abject humility at having made an everlasting fool of himself, your friend,

VON SCH.

Franz von Schönthan.

HOT PUNCH.

THERE is one thing that is beginning to strike me as very odd in life. It is how you make experiences without knowing it, and time goes on, and suddenly it dawns upon you that such and such an event was an experience. For instance, you spend an evening out of doors, because the weather is inviting, and you don't in the least suspect the gentle breeze that is caressing you of any evil design, and then the next day, when the rheumatism sets in, or a toothache, or a stiff neck, or something or other of a surgical nature, which is best met by an application of spirits of camphor, then you know for certain that you were in a draught, and you are the wiser for the experience. You promise yourself solemnly that you will not be caught that way again, but the next time maybe it is not the draught, but sour milk, or beer that was too cold, and instead of a swollen cheek you find yourself in possession of the native semicolon bacillus, which luckily is unable to exist in hot punch, as they have discovered at the Imperial Health Office. This is a great thing, for when Frenchmen raise diseases in their undrained seaport towns, we in Berlin don't have to confine ourselves to drinking carbolic lemonade, as we once feared, when we had lent Dr. Koch to France, and the papers were so full of cholera that one hated to touch them.

Hot punch is a scientific discovery, which is efficient against the very fear of the disease, as I had occasion to observe in the case of Frau Postlieutenant, who was so moved by reading the papers that she was once affected in a peculiar manner, and could not find her pulse when she felt for it, which put her in an indescribable state of mind; for when the pulse is gone the last stage is approaching, and it is time to give a thought to one's funeral. A glass or two of hot punch allayed the symptoms immediately, and before fifteen minutes were gone Frau Postlieutenant could feel her pulse all over. She assured us that it was hammering in her toes quite as strongly as in her temples. She was saved.

"Frau Buchholz," said she, "if you had not happened to come in just now, who knows but the black omnibus would have had to be harnessed for me by this time?"

"It did look bad enough," I replied, "but not so bad as all that. It was enough, though, to frighten a person out of her seven wits."

"I shan't read another paper until the fruit season is over," said the Frau Postlieutenant.

"There you are right," said I. "A juicy pear in one hand, and in the other thrilling accounts of the cholera would be more than Goliath could stand."

So this was an experience once more, to the effect that not everything that the papers bring is good for people, and that there is no better thing to bring one's pulse back than a glass of punch, provided it is good and hot.

The Frau Postlieutenant does not belong to that class of persons who try to give themselves an air by being ungrateful; who, when they have visited anywhere, talk about the discomfort of the beds, and, when they have been asked out, run to tell their neighbour the next day that it is quite beyond them to understand how any one can venture to offer such poor refreshments. No, she is not that sort, for when she had quite recovered she sent around to invite me to take a ride with her to the Grunewald, and drink coffee at Paulsborn, and then back again by way of Schildhorn. She had hired a very swell turn-out for the afternoon, first-class, with a coachman in livery, whose coat-tails, gorgeous with buttons, hung down from the box like a yard and a half of starry sky.

It is not to be denied that the further end of the Kurfürstendamm, where there are no more houses, is pretty sandy, and the dust is given to flying about at a great rate; but as I had on my potato-coloured dress, trimmed with light brown satin, I did not suffer perceptibly, but the Frau Postlieutenant, in her black gown all covered with fine braiding, soon looked as if she had been done up in packing paper. Every vigorous breath of air brought some of the landscape between our teeth, where it gave a horribly rasping sound, but we bore up bravely, knowing that in Paulsborn the coffee-pot was awaiting us with its soothing contents.

Our conversation was of a very refined strain, chiefly about the lack of really cultured society, which naturally led us to talk about the Bergfeldts. Frau Postlieutenant admitted that Frau Bergfeldt might have many excellent qualities, but she for her part should certainly never be willing to ride through the Grunewald with her in an open carriage.

"Do you see, Betty," I said, "what delicate distinctions the Frau Postlieutenant makes? This afternoon will be one of our proudest memories."

Mila also said that the weather was exquisite, and there were so few common people on the road. They never went anywhere on Sundays, she said, because the company was so promiscuous.

Betty, who had been reading a good deal lately about human rights and the equality of the classes, was going to reply, but fortunately the carriage stopped just then before the lodge at Paulsborn. I am sure there is no class or rank that I despise, and I respect everybody that gets an honest living; but for all the books in the world, and all the talk about equality, I don't feel in the least inclined to give a *thé dansant* to the milkman and the chimney-sweep.

Julius Stinde.

WOMAN.

IN his relation to women man is always more or less of a fool, whether he be their husband, lover, counsellor, or friend. He explains the same thing to them over and over again; he declares, he demonstrates with a will; he would have it thus and so, because only in this wise, and at such a time, will it fulfil his purpose; he points the argument and he grounds it with such explicitness that a very sign-post would strike root at listening to him; he accents the *casus quæstionis* with all possible pantomime, and with all logical emphasis. For a moment the lady fears the threatening storm; but as for the mental effect, the effect which the argument should make as such, which truth should make as truth,—for that her ladyship has no respect; indeed she does not even respect law and justice with all her heart, but only under compulsion, and driven thereto by despair.

Man may talk as much as he pleases; the spoken word exerts no potent influence over a genuine woman. So long as her emotions are strongly affected, the whole line of argumentation to which the word gives expression seems to her but a piece of academical man-invented pedantry— the learned twaddle of the schools. She inclineth not her ear to *reasons;* she considers them an intolerable imposition, an encroachment upon the realm of her sentiment and the supremacy of her feminine intuition. Her logic is passion;

she feels but her mood, her interest; she sees things and relations but as they regard her personally. Whether there is an injustice to others implied, and what is the true import of things *per se*, all that is rarely comprehended and retained by a woman where her interest or her antipathy comes into play. In the entire course of the clearest and concisest exposition the fair listener is occupied only with her excitement and opposition, and never with the subject in question and its importance. The spoken word, as soon as she is required to acknowledge its office as bearer and representative of spirit, to value its absolute potency, is to her but empty sound. At the last she yields to pathos— to emphasis, to oratory, as she might do in a play. The dialectics affect her possibly by their eloquence, diction, and plastic qualities, rarely by the force of conviction. When all his arguments are exhausted, and the speaker looks forward to the effect for the sake of which he has marshalled all his rhetorical art and logic, and taken his eloquence into both hands as it were, Madam comes back to the same fatal point, to the same nonsense from whence she started; and all the forces of rhetoric, all the concentrated reasoning goes for nothing.

Now the man's temper rises, and he waxes indignant; a piece of copper is finally persuaded by the hammer to become a tea-kettle; words can be engraved on stone and steel, why not upon the *tabula rasa*, the blank daguerreo-type-plate of a woman's mind?

The quietest, most serene of men must despair when there is no appealing to human reason. But Madam *shall* be convinced. He counts again the serried syllogisms on trembling fingers, with flashing eyes and tremulous lips, with a voice half suppressed by rage; every word is accentuated as if it were to conjure up spirits and wake the dead. Arguments are applied like thumb-screws, the entire demonstration is held up menacingly like a pistol with trigger drawn; she is accused of reason, and in the next moment it is demanded of her, as one demands the evidence of his five senses from a person suspicious of insanity. Madam is asked to declare, brief and plain, whether she had understood; she is not to say what she will do or not do; the matter under discussion and its fulfilment is to remain secondary; the man wants naught but the satisfaction of an acknowledgment that he is right, that his better-half possesses and respects human reason. All material interest is to be set aside; her ladyship shall have quite her own way; it is only demanded that there be a declaration in the interest of truth, of logic, of human dignity; but of this the fair sufferer in the cause of Reason is not capable, it is asking too much of her feminine nature, it breaks her heart. She feels herself ill-treated; in her excitement she has heard nothing but words, and like a tragedy-queen, she has been occupied only with her grief. She comprehends naught but her boundless misery, and the axiomatic barbarity of the genus man. And the tears she has long repressed burst forth, washing away demonstrations, syllogisms, and all; *that is a woman's logic.* Nature will not be forced, and least of all woman-nature. Dosed with argumentation and logic, it loses appetite, fulness, wit, complexion, grace, amiability, and vivacity. A platonic friend of the ladies is, as a rule, an unmanly creature; that is, quite as unreasonable and weakly constructed as the female to whom he feels sympathetically drawn. Manly differences and manly reconciliations are quite out of the question in so unnatural a relation. Especially is there one case which calls for commiseration—viz., when a genuine man is called upon to be the dependant, the counsellor, and the gallant friend of a vain old hag abandoned of all graces; when, for instance, a son-in-law is condemned to manage the affairs of madam his mother-in-law. Either the lady is ungently set to rights, or else his unbounded respect for old age brings the son-in-law to an untimely grave. With the most uncongenial male one can discuss a question, and there is a possibility of arriving at an understanding or compromise; with every man some manœuvre will catch, but never with a woman who thinks her interest and the authority of her wilfulness endangered. In this desperate case she is destitute of reason and character, without method and consistency, without understanding and common justice, an enemy of all business principles and all promptness, ay, even without conscience and pity.

She would like to make a bargain but not risk anything; yes, she will risk but not lose anything; yes, she will lose but it must not cost her anything. All old ladies are parsimonious; they have a passion for playing cards, but there is always the one condition that their cavalier, with dutiful politeness, lets them win his money. Dull are all old ladies, and hard to entertain if they cannot indulge in weather-worn flirtations, or if they do not perceive themselves to be the objects of devotion and attention. Ignorant of affairs are all ladies, the old and the young; but the old never to their disadvantage where money plays a part. Suspicious are they all by unalterable right, and curious because they are suspicious, if for no other reason. In some cases they are compassionate—*i.e.*, in cases of illness, of which they have more innate knowledge and power of subtle diagnosis than an experienced physician gets to his dying day; but toward their creditors they are worse than barbaric, they persecute them without sense or reason.

Women are always mixing up the most insignificant things with the most important; the details with the principal points, the person, and the cause.

Neither an old barrister nor a young lawyer can bring them to see the *punctum juris*, for they have as little sense of right and justice as a Hottentot, or an Englishman making a bargain.

Of two evils women cannot choose the lesser until the greater is hard upon them.

They want to build a large house, for instance, but are unwilling to lay a deep foundation; it is to have three storeys, but without the inconvenience of stairs, and there must be a cellar in each storey; else what is the use of having an architect for your lover, or indulgent husband, or friend? They want to go a-travelling, but at the same time things must be more comfortable and cheaper than at home; there is to be no luggage-waggon, but of course they must have twelve trunks and a half, and by dint of much coaxing they will spare you the half. Their goal is toward the north, but they wish to drive in a south-westerly direction, because it blows into the carriage from the other side.

A woman has leased her farm, and is afterwards indignant at the good harvest which she might have had instead of her tenant. At last she has sold the estate, and has the money safe in her pocket, but she is quite taken by surprise at the thought of moving and giving up the old homestead. A woman is always greatly disconcerted to hear that she cannot sell things and keep them at the same time.

Bogumil Golz (1801–1870).

A CHRISTMAS TALE.

IT is a most charming thing to compose fairy-tales at Christmas-time. But there are difficulties to contend with, take my word for it, dear reader. I am an honest sort of fellow, who never makes a murderer's den of his heart, as the proverb says. So I will confess that I have a strong aversion to telling any particularly preposterous lies to the good people who may chance to read this, by relating wonderful, supernatural tales, and calling forth an impression as if I had elves to black my boots every day of my life. Ah no! sooner than do that I will give up the whole secret as to how the following story came to me, and at best I cannot swear that it is a pretty one. I said to myself, "Good friend, you must cultivate a certain mood; conjure up the breath of the woodlands about you, and all the rest will follow." This was not so very difficult. I bought a little fir-tree, and set it up among the folios of the oaken table in my study.

It was a nice little tree, and I pictured to myself the spot in the forest where it came from : a snow-covered opening, enclosed by tall dark pines, the edges thickly set with various young evergreens which must needs be thinned out. I smelled of the tree until my nose burned under its prickly needles. Ah, how sweetly aromatic! Like shades out of the lap of eternity, the Christmas-eves of long ago rose up before me, with many sweet memories interesting only to myself, with hosts of fairy-tales which Grimm and Ludwig Bechstein have long since put into charming books. But soon I perceived that the breath of the fir-tree would not suffice for my purpose, and that my mood required to be worked upon by means of other aids. I thereupon pulled down the blinds, although it was noon, and lit my large lamp, thinking of a well-known Vienna novelist, who is in the habit of putting himself into the bloodthirsty and terrible train of thought which serves his purpose by means of a piece of black cloth and four burning tapers, upon which he gazes in the pauses between his work. My large lamp sings, moreover, which is a quality that cannot be prized too highly, for oil-lamps do not as a general thing feel called upon to yield sweet music. As the lamp burned and hummed, I took great pains to start up a rousing fire. It roared and sputtered with a will, for the wood was somewhat damp. But this was all the better, for a good, noisy fire plays a great part in literary difficulties. Hereupon I made myself some tea in my little tea-urn, which puffs and spits like a furious cat, and lit my cigar. The scene now comprised—

    A fragrant fir-tree.
    A burning and singing lamp.
    A roaring and sputtering fire.
    A puffing and spitting tea-urn.
    A glowing and smoking cigar.
    A meditating poet.

I will not deny the fact that at this point I addressed some words of stern exhortation to myself.

"Carl Pfründner," I said, "if you don't catch hold of a brilliant idea now, you never will. Such a comfortable state as you are in would inspire a chimney-sweep to write poetry. Suppose you get up something about an "Enchanted Sparrow," or a "Bewitched Harlequin," or a "Noodle in Luck"? As I was still pondering, my eye-lids grew heavy, and I fell asleep. I scorn to make use of the threadbare artifice of telling you that a brilliant thought came to me in my sleep. On the contrary, my nap was dreamless, and I awoke only strengthened in my dearth of ideas. The fir-tree was as fragrant as ever, the lamp and the fire still burned, and all the other aids to my imagination were still there. I now lit a second lamp, placing it upon the antique desk, and gazed thoughtfully into the hollow space between the drawers of the upper part, which can be shut off by a little sliding door. Thousands of times before had my eyes rested on that very spot, as if all possible subjects were contained therein, and my pen had but to choose before transferring them to paper. But never before had I looked with such particular interest at the small carved bar running across the partition.

This bar is removed about a hand's-breadth from the back of the ancient desk, which came down to me from the last century. I had always taken it to be nothing but an ornament to hide the rough board at the back. This time I suppose I held my head a little lower than usual, for I suddenly beheld a bolt behind the carved bar, which, when pushed back, fitted exactly into a groove cut into the upper edge of the bar. It was this circumstance which drew my attention to the said bar. I pushed the bolt back and forth, but it was back so far in the dark that I could not see how it influenced the bar. A couple of matches, used with great caution near the rotten wood, only showed me that the position of the bar remained unchanged. While I was pondering the object of the bolt, I made a second discovery. Far back behind the bar there was a narrow slit in the wood, like those which one sees on children's earthen savings-banks. This was the more curious as the edges of the slit, as I approached it with a candle, appeared to be whetted off as if, in times past, they had frequently come in contact with hard objects. The resemblance to the slit of a savings-bank tempted me to drop in a coin. Of course I sacrificed only a kreuzer to this experiment, pushing it slowly through the hole, and then letting it drop.

Heavens! what was that? The kreuzer fell first upon wood, judging by the sound, then it seemed to roll down some distance, and fell with a metallic sound. There was no doubt then that the desk contained a secret drawer, the existence of which I had never even suspected; and over and above this, it was evident that this secret drawer was designed especially to harbour coins, as the opening was not suited to paper-money or documents. The metallic ring gave good reason to suppose that the kreuzer had not fallen into an empty wooden drawer, but had joined the society of other coins filling the secret partition up to a certain height.

I beg the reader to put himself in my position. Here I have a desk dating from the last century, my rightful property, and containing a secret drawer, which harbours, in all probability, a treasure of gold coins. I had often wondered at the tremendous weight of the old desk, and sometimes the motion of writing at it seemed to call forth a softly ringing sound. And now in this prosaic age my hand was destined to come upon a hoarded treasure, a treasure of gold and mayhap some other rare valuables! I trembled with excitement, and would have knocked down any one who in this supreme moment had asked me to think of that confounded fairy tale, not to mention writing it. My one thought was how to open the secret drawer.

At first I tested the carved bar. It was immovable. I threw in another kreuzer, and, aided by the sense of hearing, tried to locate the secret drawer. Plainly I heard the metallic ring once more. It seemed to come from behind the carved bar, but the latter would not budge.

I will not tire the reader, as I did myself, with my labours of research. For two hours I worked in the sweat of my brow, taking the old desk to pieces, so far as that was possible, without coming any nearer to the solution of the mystery. Furious at last, I ran out to get a hatchet, and swung it with might to crush all obstacles, when once more my eyes fell upon the left-hand set of drawers that I had put upon the floor during my search, and I laid the axe aside. Both of the drawers showed grooves along the sides, which were evidently there for some purpose, probably in order that they might be fastened from the side, frustrating any attempt to draw them out. Mastering my excitement, I put the drawers back in place, and saw now that the carved bar exactly corresponded to the position of the grooves. I tried to push it to the left, a thing I had of course not thought of before—it moved, and fitted as snugly as need be. Now, treasure, your last hour is come; that's what I call a

Christmas present worth having! Two seconds later the drawers were out, I pushed the carved bar around further, and behold, two small, dust-stained drawers were revealed. I put out my trembling hand——

I would say here that there must have been infamous rascals in the past century, who, not content with wantonly causing great excitement to honest people of these modern times, steal away their time, which they might have spent in writing a tolerable fairy-tale. Is there any one that can tell me why in the world one of those ancient fellows should have put the key of his street-door into a secret drawer? I wish it were the key to paradise which he had forgotten! The vicious old sinner might roast in purgatory so long as I lived, for of course I left the rusty key, together with my two kreuzers in the secret drawer, adding my curse.

Every sympathetic Christian soul will understand that after this heavy disappointment I was not in the mood to spin out the graceful fairy-tale I promised. Indeed the holidays were quite spoiled for me that year!

Eduard Pötzl.

THE CASE OF MINCKWITZ.

IN the course of the past month I have been called upon to bear the most acute sorrow, dear friend, of which a fine-strung soul like mine is capable. Indeed, my friend, terrible things have occurred! I am *misunderstood!* And misunderstood by whom? You will scarce believe me when I tell you, but it is even so: misunderstood by Professor Johannes Minckwitz,[1] of Leipsic, the great epic

[1] In a previous number of the *Salon* Lindau had published a keenly satirical article on Professor Minckwitz's writings, culminating in a parody on his style, entitled, "The Death of a Youthful Hero," and purporting to be an extract from the professor's epic poem.

poet and literary connoisseur, for whom I feel the deepest reverence and the most tender affection.

Hear the sad news. One morning as I was innocently turning the leaves of my "Neuhochdeutschen Parnass,"[1] my thoughts naturally enough wandering somewhat, my faithful maid-of-all-work stepped over the threshold of my door with weeping eyes.

"What in the world has happened to you?" I asked in great consternation. "Has your lover proved faithless, Thrine?"

"I shall have to leave this place, sir," sobbed the honest creature.

"I don't understand you, Thrine; express yourself more explicitly."

"You are dishonoured! And sooner will I starve than serve a dishonoured master, for folks do say that 'a servant is no better than his master,' and I am a respectable woman. Here is the paper, you'd better read and see for yourself!" Thrine sobbed bitterly, and handed me a number of the Leipsic local paper, containing an article heavily marked with a red pencil, and thereby recommending itself specially to my attention.

No sooner had I glanced over the first lines of the terrible article than I grew dizzy, and therewith began to tremble convulsively. Thrine fainted away. Picture the scene to yourself, dear friend. Without raged the storm. Ah, the situation was dramatic. From the paper I gathered that Professor Johannes Minckwitz, in just indignation over the last of my harmless letters, had sued the editor of the *Salon* for misuse of his name, and for literary forgery, and had entrusted Dr. Coccius, a lawyer in Leipsic, with the impeachment.

"Thrine," I began, after an effective pause, "I begin to understand that we must part! You knew me in happy

---

[1] A modern German Literature written by Professor Minckwitz.

"I GLANCED OVER THE FIRST LINES OF THE TERRIBLE ARTICLE."

days of yore, do not forget me now when sorrow is breaking in upon me. One service I would ask of you before parting, it is the last. Do me the favour to accept the "Neuhochdeutschen Parnass" as a token of remembrance from me. You always need paper to clean the windows, I know. Fare-thee-well, Thrine!"

I was left alone with my anguish. Dishonoured, I cried, dishonoured! Misunderstood, indicted! How different was it, oh *Kleinstädter*, when you glided innocently through the pages of the *Salon* in the company of better wits than Minckwitz! Johannes turns from me, and

> "Wo ich ihn nicht gab,
> Ist mir das Grab."

So "The Death of a Youthful Hero" did not flow from the pen of the great poet! Never was I more surprised than over this discovery. I am to stand before the jury; I shall be condemned to dishonourable penalties—in a word, like the knapsack of the lieutenant, I am *perdu*.

The *Kleinstädter* before the jury? Since I have heard that in the "Lawyer Hamlet" the jury are brought upon the stage to do nothing at all, I have a very clear impression of this horrible situation. In this "Lawyer Hamlet," which, by the way, has been very scantily advertised (indeed scarce thirty papers devoted more than five columns to a detailed account of the piece), there is a certain Baron von Sonne who defends all poor people, and takes this opportunity of speechifying on various topics. This Baron von Sonne is the man for me; I shall turn to him in my extremity. And as I need not fear that the unknown author of "Lawyer Hamlet" will impeach me for misuse of his name—a guilt which he himself has been careful to avoid—I will herewith give the last act of the play, that is to say, the last act as it would have read if the accused had been the *Kleinstädter* instead of Stella.

Here goes then—

LAWYER HAMLET.

Fourth Act.

(The court-room. At the left the benches of the jury. In the middle a table for the judge. At the right two small tables for the Crown solicitor and for the defendant. To the front a bench for the accused. As the curtain rises the judges are seen to enter. The jurymen take the seats appointed. The Kleinstädter, with his hands and feet securely fettered, is dragged into the room by gens d'armes. The defendant, Lawyer Hamlet, exchanges some words with the accused. The court solicitor breathes revenge.)

First and Last Scene.

Chairman Lehmann. I request the audience to remain quiet; at the first signs of applause or displeasure all persons occupying the gallery will be turned out. The accused will rise from his seat. (*The Kleinstädter rises, his chains clash, the audience shudders.*) What is your name? (*The Kleinstädter looks perplexed, and does not reply.*) Do you hear what I say? I asked you what your name is?

The Accused (*greatly embarrassed*). Oh, Mr. Chairman——

Chairman. Well now, go ahead! What is your name?

The Accused. My name's *Lehmann* too.

Chairman. You are accused of having published a poem in the *Salon* under the name of our honoured and esteemed Professor Johannes Minckwitz, and so to have passed off your own production for his. What have you to say for yourself?

Accused. Nix.[1]

---

[1] Vulgar for Nichto, nothing.

Lawyer Hamlet. Gentlemen of the jury, I beg that you will note this "nix"; it is of the greatest importance.

Chairman. I must request the defendant not to interrupt the proceedings. Prisoner, no doubt you are aware of the fact that it is culpable to assign to Professor Minckwitz the name of poet—that is, of course I mean poet of verses which he did not make.

Accused. I did not know it, Mr. Chairman; I am innocent.

Lawyer Hamlet. Gentlemen of the jury, I beg that you will note these words; they are of the utmost importance to the following transactions.

Chairman. I wish to ask whether the accused has ever read the poems of Professor Minckwitz.

The Accused (*in violent excitement*). Never, Mr. Chairman, never! My record is spotless.

Chairman. Why did you not read the poems?

The Accused. All my efforts to obtain the volume were fruitless. I called upon three of my friends who possess a well-equipped library; two of them threatened to impeach me for libel, the third kicked me down stairs.

Chairman. You may sit down. (*To the jury.*) A number of witnesses have been summoned before the court whose names the *Kleinstädter* is also charged with having forged. It seems indeed that forgery of names has been systematically indulged in by the prisoner. (*To the bailiff.*) Bid the witnesses enter.

(*General tumult. Chairman's bell.*)

Chairman (*to first witness*). What is your name?

Witness. Dr. Max Hirsch.

Chairman. Not related to the accused? Not in his service?

Witness. No.

Chairman. In the *Kleinstädter's* second letter a speech is quoted which purports to have been delivered by you in

Parliament, beginning, "In England . . . Sheffield . . . partnership . . . etc." Is that correct?

Witness. No. (*Sits down.*)

Chairman. Second witness: His Majesty the Emperor of Siam. In his fourth letter the *Kleinstädter* relates how your most serene Highness said to your Highness' servant among other things, "Ra-phra, how could my predecessor condemn a man of your integrity?" Is that true?

Witness. Never a word of it, by Jove. (*Sits down.*)

Chairman. Third witness: His Excellency the Imperial Chancellor Freiherr von Beust.

Lawyer Hamlet. I protest against the examination of this witness. Mr. Chairman and Judges, without venturing to impute motives not strictly impersonal to the witness, I feel it my duty to call attention to the fact that the relations between the accused and the witness are too close to assure an unbiassed testimony. Both are countrymen, both are great men; in the name of my client I move that this witness should not be cross-examined.

(*The judges put their heads together. After some time the Chairman announces that the court rejects the arguments of the defence as irrelevant, and demands the cross-examination of the witness.*)

Chairman. Freiherr von Beust! Not related to the accused?

Witness. No.

Chairman. Not in his service?

Witness. No.

Chairman. In his fifth letter the *Kleinstädter* quoted a long telegram with the signature of your Excellency, which your Excellency was said to have addressed to the diplomatic representatives at the *Journalistentag*. Will your Excellency have the kindness to inform us as to the precise facts?

Witness. Well, now, good friend, I'm afraid I'll not be able to help you. I have sent a good many telegrams in my day.

Chairman. Thank you. (*Witness leaves the stand. Chairman addresses the jury.*) Provided the gentlemen of the jury have no objections to offer, I will cross-examine the other witnesses all together. Fourth, fifth, and sixth witnesses: Victor Hugo, public writer on the Isle of Guernsey; Richard Wagner, musician *in spe*, and just now in Switzerland; and third, the man who wrote the prize novel! Gentlemen! in the letters of the *Kleinstädter* he quotes, or pretends to quote, from your writings; from you, Victor Hugo, a chapter from an unprinted novel about Barbara Ubryk, entitled, "*La nonne qui ne rit pas—mais pas du tout.*" The chapter to be headed, "Naxos, nix, nox, nux," and beginning, "Night. Deep night, gloomy, dark. Upon the ground rotten straw. Husks and stems without fruit. In a word, straw." From you, Mr. Wagner, he quoted verses from *Rheingold*—

> "Winselnde Winde
> Wagalaweia!
> Oh Eselinde,
> Oh Eseleia!"

From you, prize-crowned poet, the novel, *The Bloody Tragedy at the Churchyard.* Are these quotations authentic—are you the authors of the same?

Witnesses (*in concert*). No. (*They sit down.*)

Chairman. Has the accused anything to say for himself?

The Accused. Nix.

Chairman. The list of witnesses is exhausted; the representative of the plaintiff, the Crown Solicitor, has the floor.

Crown Solicitor. Never, gentlemen of the jury, did I fulfil the serious and difficult function of my office with a more quiet conscience or a lighter heart. There is not the faintest doubt stirring within me, no shadow of uneasiness falls upon me; the guilt of the accused is clear as day! We have here before us a hardened villain, a sinner of the deepest dye. What has occurred? A well-known magazine brings out a poem under the name of "Minckwitz." The poem is not by Minckwitz; the forgery is evident. Taken alone, the fact of choosing this form of criticism would not be criminal; but, gentlemen, when this misuse of a writer's name has the result of lowering him in public opinion it is decidedly culpable. And here this is the case. If Minckwitz were a poet of distinction, criticism would do him no harm; but as the *Kleinstädter's* criticism is just in all points, it *does* harm Herr Professor Minckwitz, and lowers him in public opinion. The defendant might perhaps say that there is no penal law in the world which forbids criticism of a poet, and that the satire in question did not attack Minckwitz the man, but Minckwitz the poet. Do not permit yourself to be influenced by such sophistry. It is impossible to attack the *poet* Minckwitz, because there is no such person; whoever attacks Minckwitz attacks the man. I would be the last to restrain the freedom of speech. I admit the value and the necessity of criticism. But the chosen subject must be worthy of criticism. If Minckwitz takes pleasure in tripping up the great ones of literature with the utmost nonchalance in his "Neuhochdeutschen Parnass," there is no reason why he should not indulge himself; but to criticise Minckwitz in his quality of poet is quite another matter; such a gross misuse of the function of criticism should be interfered with by a court of justice in the interest of the public.

There is another argument which the defence will doubtless bring, to which I should like to reply right here. You will be told, gentlemen of the jury, that the degradation of an author in public opinion can be effective only if the verses published in the *Salon*, under the name of Minckwitz, are poorer than his authentic ones, and that this is decidedly not the case. Well, it strikes me that the contrary is true! It is just because the verses in the *Salon*—as I must gladly admit—are much better than any Minckwitz verses; it is for this very reason that public opinion is unfavourably influenced. For, gentlemen, when Minckwitz brings his epos before the public, all the world will say, "The verses in the *Salon* were much more amusing," and it seems to me this will not have the effect of heightening the author's reputation. I have done, gentlemen of the jury. I believe I have proved to your satisfaction that the accused is guilty of the crime with which he was charged, and in consideration of the frequent repetition of literary forgery, as shown by the witnesses, I move that sentence be pronounced for the most severe penalty of the law—viz., confinement in intellectual pursuits to the works of Professor Minckwitz.

(*Sensation. Chairman's bell.*)

Chairman. The defendant has the floor.

Lawyer Hamlet. Gentlemen of the jury! We do not come before you with witnesses from the most distant confines of this globe, we do not come with ringing words; no, we are simple, harmless, plain, and true. We need no witnesses; the facts speak for us. Gentlemen of the jury, cast a glance upon the accused, look well at his stolid face, his fixed eyes, his enervated lips; and this innocent creature you would declare guilty of the heinous crime charged to him? Never, if I can help it! The representative of the Crown has told you that literary forgery in a legal sense is only possible where public reputation is endangered. I admit that in a merely human sense the name of Minckwitz was forged, but certainly not in the sense of the law. It strikes me that Professor Minckwitz would do well to get down on his knees and thank the

Kleinstädter for occupying himself so minutely with his small person; by means of the article in question Professor Minckwitz is not only not lowered in public opinion, on the contrary he is given more honour than he deserves. Granting, however, that the *Kleinstädter* could be convicted of forgery, would this be sufficient cause to pronounce sentence upon him? No, gentlemen of the jury, a thousand times no! I asked you just now to note my client's physiognomy; I repeat my request. In these flaccid muscles, in these dim eyeballs, lurks idiocy. Far be it from us to avenge where we should pity. Yes, gentlemen, this *Kleinstädter* is an idiot, his physiognomy shows it, and still more evident does it become when you look back upon his conduct during these proceedings—when you remember the imbecility of that perpetual "nix," and, most of all, by the deed of which he stands accused. There might be some sense in misusing the name of Goethe, Schiller, Heine, Geibel, Heyse, Lenau; I can understand that, though I would not condone it; but to misuse the name of Minckwitz as a poet, that, gentlemen of the jury, cannot be accounted for otherwise than by presupposing complete paralysis of the intellectual functions on the part of the accused. My client is a poor, irresponsible creature; his mental condition annuls his penalty. Gentlemen of the jury, I appeal to your heart. You all have children, rosy-cheeked, blooming, happy; imagine what would be your grief if one of your children should suddenly lose his reason; would you punish that child? No, you would not do so, you could not do it, and you will prove it now by fully acquitting my unfortunate client!

(*Sensation and weeping. Bell.*)

Chairman. Prisoner, is there anything you have to say for yourself?

The Accused. Nix.

Chairman (*recapitulates the proceedings and closes*). There are these questions then to be submitted to your judgment —

First: Is the accused guilty of having with malice aforethought forged the name of Minckwitz in such manner as to thereby injure Professor Minckwitz's public reputation?

Second: Is the accused sane?

> (*The jury retire. After a short time they return, and their foreman declares in a strong voice that the jury answered both questions unanimously in the affirmative. Great excitement. The court solicitor repeats his proposition; the defendant does the same. After a half-hour's debate the bell of the Chairman is heard.*)

Chairman. Considering that the accused has been convicted of the penal offence with which he had been charged, considering further that the mental condition of the accused gives cause for leniency, the Court sentences the accused to the penalty of finding Minckwitz's poetry excellent reading.

Paul Lindau.

STUDENTS' SONGS.

OLD ASSYRIAN-JONAH.

IN the Black Whale at Ascalon
   A man drank day by day,
Till, stiff as any broom-handle
   Upon the floor he lay.

In the Black Whale at Ascalon
   The landlord said: "I say,
He's drinking of my date-juice wine
   Much more than he can pay!"

In the Black Whale at Ascalon
  The waiters brought the bill,
In arrow-heads on six broad tiles,
  To him who thus did swill.

In the Black Whale at Ascalon
  The guest cried out: "O woe!
I spent in the Lamb at Nineveh
  My money long ago!"

In the Black Whale at Ascalon
  The clock struck half-past four,
When the Nubian porter he did pitch
  The stranger from the door.

In the Black Whale at Ascalon
  No prophet hath renown;
And he who there would drink in peace
  Must pay his money down.
            Joseph Victor Scheffel.

HEINZ VON STEIN.

OUT rode from his wild, dark castle,
  The terrible Heinz von Stein;
He came to the door of a tavern
  And gazed at the swinging sign.

He sat himself down at a table,
  And growled for a bottle of wine;
Up came, with a flask and a corkscrew,
  A maiden of beauty divine.

Then, seized with a deep love-longing,
  He uttered, "Oh, damosell mine,
Suppose you just give a few kisses
  To the valorous Rotter von Stein."

"IN A SWAMP HE FELL—HOW SHOCKING!"

THE TEUTOBURGER BATTLE.

When the Romans, rashly roving,
Into Germany were roving,
First of all—to flourish, partial—
Rode 'mid trumps the great field-martial,
Sir Quintilius Varus.

But in the Teutoburgian forest
How the north wind blew and chor-rused;
Ravens flying through the air,
And there was a perfume there
As of blood and corpses.

Missing Page

Missing Page

All at once, in sock and buskins,
Out came rushing the Cheruskins
Howling, " Gott and Vaterland !"
They went in with sword in hand
Against the Roman legions.

Ah, it was an awful slaughter,
And the cohorts ran like water ;
But of all the foe that day
The horsemen only got away,
Because they were on horseback !

O Quintilius ! wretched general,
Knowest thou not that such our men are all ?
In a swamp he fell—how shocking !
Lost two boots, a left-hand stocking,
And, besides, was smothered.

Then, with his temper growing wusser,
Said to Centurion Titiusser,
"Pull your sword out —never mind,
And bore me through with it behind,
Since the game is busted."

Scaevolo, of law a student,
Fine young fellow—but imprudent
As a youth of tender years,
Served among the volunteers—
He was also captured.

E'en his hoped-for death was baffled,
For ere they got him to the scaffold
He was stabbed quite unaware,
And nailed fast *en derrière*
To his Corpus Juris.

When this forest fight was over,
Herman rubbed his hands in clover;
And to do the thing up right,
The Cheruscian did invite
To a first-rate breakfast.

But in Rome the wretched varmints
Went to purchase mourning garments;
Just as they had tapped a puncheon,
And Augustus sat at luncheon,
Came the mournful story.

And the tidings so provoked him,
That a peacock leg half choked him,
And he cried—beyond control—
"Varus, Varus! d—n your soul!
Redde legiones!"

His German slave, Hans Schmidt be-christened,
Who in the corner stood and listened,
Remarked, "Der Teufel take me wenn
He efer kits dose droops acain,
For teat men ish not lifin."

Now, in honour of the story,
A monument they'll raise for glory.
As for pedestal—they've done it;
But who'll pay for a statue on it
Heaven alone can tell us.

J. V. Scheffel.

"OLD CLO',—TAKE THEM, THEY ARE THINE!"

THE LAST PAIR OF BREECHES.

Air—"'Tis the last Rose of Summer."

'Tis my la-a-st pair of bre-e-eches
    Le-e-ft sa-a-dly a-lone;
Ah—and she too with her riches,
    With another hence has gone.

Oh, they seemed in one piece knitted,
    Such a pair is seldom matched;
Winter buckskin, how they fitted!
    Large plaid pattern, never patched!

Strutting proudly as a turkey,
    With those breeks I first sailed in;
In my pocket to the door-key
    Rang such lots of lovely tin.

Ah, we fall as we have risen—
    Soon no specie showed its face;
And the Heidelberg town-prison
    Is a dark and silent place.

Soon I pawned all things worth pawning,—
    Dress-coat, frock, and mantle light.
You too, now, ere morrow's dawning,
    My last trousers, good—good-night!

Day of trial, with what sorrow
    Do I feel thy pain at last;
Nothing earthly bides the morrow,
    And the pledge-laws travel fast.

All must go, though strictly hoarded,
    Oh, last trousers, last of mine!
Elkan Levi, gloomy, sordid,
    Old clo',—take them, they are thine!

Boots!—of all my friends the truest,
    Come and prop my suffering head;
But one pint, and that of newest,
    May'st thou bring—enough is said!

Then abed, from this sad hour,
    I'll not rise, though all should ring,
Till a heavy golden shower
    Through the roof comes pattering.

Then begone, for we must sever;
   Greet thy fellows in their cell.
Ah! my legs already shiver;
   My last breeches,—fare ye well!

J. V. Scheffel.

ENDERLE VON KETSCH.

[This ballad is founded on an incident narrated in the description of the Palatinate by Merian (1645), where, speaking of the village Ketsch, he tells us that "The Counte Palatine Otto Heinrich, afterwards Kurfürst, sailed in the yeere 1530 to the Holie Lande and to Jerusalem. Returning thence, hee came over the greate open sea, where a shipp from Norwaie mett him, and from it there came this cry: 'Flye, flye, for ye fatt Enderle von Ketsch cometh!' Now the Counte Palatine and his Chancellor Mückenhäuser knew a godless wretche of this name who dwelt at Ketsch, and therefore whenn they returned home they inquired of ye fatt Enderle and of the tyme of his deathe, and observed that itt agreed with the tyme whenn they did heare the crye upon ye sea, as whilom a professor of Heidelberg hath narrated in divers wrytings which hee left behinde."]

Chorus.

"Away—along! Away—along!
   With trembling, your jaws on the stretch.
Away—along! We sing the song
   Of Enderle von Ketsch!"

Solo.

Old Heinrich, the Pfalzgrave of Rhine—oh!
   Spoke out of a morning, "Kem blem!
I'm tired of the sour Hock wine—oh!
   I'm off for Jerusalem.

"Far lovelier, neater, and nicer
   Are the maids there who give you the cup;
Oh, Chancellor! oh, Mückenhäuser,
   Five thousand gold ducats pack up."

And as before Joppa they anchored,
    The Chancellor held up his hand:
"Now drain to the dregs your last tankard,
    For the ducats are come to an end."

Old Heinrich said, "Well, and no wonder;
    Rem blem! what remains to be seen!
We'll paddle for Cyprus out yonder,
    And make a small raise on the Queen."

But just as the galley was dancing
    By Cyprus, in beautiful night,
A storm o'er the billows came prancing,
    With thunder and flashes of light.

In a ghastly wild glare, by the landing,
    A black ship came rushing along;
There a ghost in his shirt-sleeves was standing,
    And howling a horrible song.

Chorus.

"Away—along! Away—along!
    With trembling, your jaws on the stretch.
Away—along! I sing the song
    Of Enderle von Ketsch!"

Solo.

The thunder grew calmer and wiser,
    Like oil lay the water below;
But oh, the old brave Mückenhäuser
    The Chancellor felt sorrow and woe.

The Pfalzgrave stood up by the rudder,
    And gazed on the billowy foam;
"Rem blem! all my soul's in a shudder,
    Oh, Cyprus—I travel for home!

"THERE A GHOST IN HIS SHIRT-SLEEVES WAS STANDING,
AND HOWLING A HORRIBLE SONG."

"God spare me such terrible menace—
    I'm wiser through trial and pain;
Back, back on our course to old Venice—
    I'll never borrow money again.

"And he who 'mid heathens at table
    His cash to the devil has slammed,
Let him hook it in peace while he's able,—
    It sounds like all hell and be damned!"

J. V. Scheffel.

GOD AND THE LOVER.

Then full of longing hieing,
Straight I sought the Father, sighing:
O may I, may I, may I,
May I love the girl?
"You blackguard!" he outswore,
"If you want your back beat sore,
Then you may love the girl."

Then full of longing hieing,
Straight I sought the good Priest, sighing:
O may I, may I, may I,
May I love the girl?
"My dear son, by my soul,
If you seek for Hell's deep hole,
Then you may love the girl."

Then full of longing hieing,
Straight I sought the Lord God, sighing:
O may I, may I, may I,
May I love the girl?
"My boy," laughed he, "go take her:
Why the devil did I make her?—
Faith, you may love the girl!"

Old German.

UNINTENTIONAL WITTICISMS OF THE ABSENT-MINDED GERMAN PROFESSOR.

IN the day of Achilles the Greeks had no books except Homer.

A panic seized the Persians at Marathon, and crying, "Lord Jesus, there are the Athenasians," they rushed for the sea.

Alexander would undoubtedly have subjugated the whole of Asia, but he will soon die.

Alexander was poisoned twenty-one years before his death.

The death of Alexander was felt by all Asia, but not until after his death.

Demetrius was the son of his father, and had an army of 100,000 Reichsthalers.

Charilaus was born very young.

This is a common incident in Roman history, which, however, does not occur often.

Servius came to Rome and was born there.

At the battle of Cannæ the Roman army consisted of 30,000 men, 20,000 were made prisoners, 40,000 fell, and 120,000 escaped.

If Cæsar had not crossed the Rubicon there is no knowing where he would have gone.

Brutus and Cassius murdered Cæsar in a manner very detrimental to his health.

His brother, whom he had caused to be murdered, he at last proscribed.

Varus was the only Roman general who succeeded in being conquered by the Germans.

Gallus was murdered in the presence of the populace, and he met the same fate once more at the hands of an assassin.

Julianus first killed himself, then his father, and then himself.

Tacitus says the ancient Germans were as tall as our Gardes du Corps.

The Cimbers and Teutons are descended from each other.

Alfons was two years old when he was born.

So did King Alfons surrender the eastern part of his career.

Returning from Spain, the roads were so poor that it was necessary to take eight waggons to one horse.

Richard III. murdered all his successors.

After the execution of Mary Stuart, Elizabeth appeared in Parliament, in one hand a handkerchief, in the other a tear.

It is unnecessary to say anything about Newton except that he died.

Danton was not executed until he had cut his own throat.

To be sure Marat was murdered, but he died first of a disease so virulent as to rob him of life.

Maximilian I. had hopes of seeing the throne upon his head.

After the battle of Leipsic there were a large number of horses that had lost three or four or more legs running about without a master.

Gustavus Adolphus, King of Sweden, lived until shortly before his death.

Stanislaus was not yet in existence when his father was born.

Suwarow marched at so rapid a pace with his army that neither the infantry, nor cavalry, nor artillery could keep up with him.

The Polish army was beaten by Suwarow because it ran away and fled.

A bitter war ensued on page 94.

The earth like all bodies has parallel circles, which intersect, and this is mathematical geography.

UNINTENTIONAL WITTICISMS.   319

He drew his sword and shot him.

Gotha is not much farther from Erfurt than Erfurt is from Gotha.

I am unable to give you the titles of books about Africa just now. I have them in my head, but not on paper.

Among the most excellent products of Egypt the climate must be counted.

The sources of the Nile are much farther south than where Bruce discovered them.

The eye-sight of the Hottentots is so well developed that they can hear the tramp of a horse at an incredible distance.

The walls of Babylon were so broad that four waggons could go on top of each other.

North America consists of a great number of large and small islands, very few of which are surrounded by water.

When Humboldt ascended Mount Chimborazo he found the air so thin that he could not read without glasses.

There is so much coal-smoke in London that even when the sun does not shine you cannot see the sky.

There would be far less leather produced by the English if they tanned only their own hides.

There are many propositions in mathematics that can only be proved by beginning over again.

The theory of parallel lines explains itself, for it tends toward infinity.

Professor: "That impertinent fellow, Sustorf, must be reported." *Pupil:* "Herr Professor, his name is not Sustorf; it is Thomas." *Professor:* "Well, then, we will not report him."

It must strike four soon, for it struck a quarter-to half-an-hour ago.

I see a great many pupils who are absent.

If any of you would like to read up this subject, you will find something to the point in a book the title of which I have forgotten. It is in the forty-second chapter.

"WITH A SINGLE TOUCH IT WAS LOCKED THE DOOR."

THE INCARCERATION OF THE HERR PROFESSOR.

WHEN he got to the hall before the door of the schoolroom, the Herr Director heard a tremendous uproar. Forty boyish voices were shouting "Encore," and "Da capo!"

INCARCERATION OF THE HERR PROFESSOR. 321

Professor Samuel Heinzerling began to frown.

Now there was a lull in the wild chorus, and a clear, penetrating voice was heard in a tone of absurd magniloquence—

"That will do faw to-day, Heppenheimer. It ith vewy evident you've come to clath unprepared. I'm vewy much put out by thuch conduct. Thit down!"

Thundering applause.

The professor seemed turned to a stone.

By all the gods of Greece, that was his voice, his manner, and no mistake. To be sure, there was an exaggeration of caricature, but the likeness was so evident that none but a connoisseur would be able to distinguish the slight shade of difference. It was little short of sacrilege. To think that one of his pupils should have the audacity to ridicule him, the sovereign authority over all school matters; him, the author of "A Latin Grammar for use in schools, specially adapted to the higher classes;" him, the renowned follower of Kant, from the hallowed heights of his own platform! *Proh pudor! Honos sit auribus!* This was a prank such as none but the soul of the arch-rogue Wilhelm Rumpf could bring forth.

"Will you take a pathage, Möwicke," the voice of the godless pupil continued. "What, you are indithpothed? Deaw me, when I heaw young men of your age thay they are indithpothed that lookth ill, it lookth vewy ill indeed. Knebel, put down in the clath-book: Möwicke, being called upon to tranthlate, wath indithpothed."

The professor was unable to control his temper longer.

With a sudden movement he opened the door, and stepped in among the startled boys.

His intuition had been correct.

It was indeed Wilhelm Rumpf, the greatest good-for-nothing the class could boast of, who had committed the unpardonable offence against the majesty of his person.

For four weeks only this lad had been one of Samuel Heinzerling's pupils, and already there was no scamp in class from first to last who did not own his superiority. His collar drawn up high in front, an immense pair of paper spectacles upon his nose, in his left hand a book, in his right the traditional tiny lead-pencil, there he stood upon the platform, just about to commit himself further when the indignant professor crossed the threshold.

"Wumpf!" said Samuel with dignity, "Wumpf! you will go to the *carcer*[1] faw two dayth. Knebel, put down in the clath-book: Wumpf, condemned to two dayth in the *carcer* faw childith and unworthy conduct. Heppenheimer, call the *pedell!*"

"Why, Herr Professor,—I did not—I only——" stammered Rumpf, putting the paper spectacles in his pocket, and walking back to his seat.

" Not another word!"

" I thought——"

" Be thtill, I tell you!"

" But won't you permit me——"

" Knebel, put down: Wumpf hath one day added to the owiginal penalty faw obthtinathy. I am tiwed of fighting it out with you. You ought to be athamed to the vewy depth of your thoul!"

"*Audiatur et altera pars*, Herr Professor. This is a precept to which you have always called our attention!"

"Vewy good! You thall not thay that I am untrue to my printhipleth. What have you to thay faw yourthelf?"

" I can only assure you, sir, that it was not my intention to do anything disrespectful. I was only exercising myself in the art of mimicry."

" It would have been better to exerthithe yourthelf in Latin thtyle and in Greek compothithion."

---

[1] *Carcer*, a place of imprisonment common to German gymnasiums and universities.

"I do that also, Herr Professor. But aside from those branches of knowledge, art also has her privileges."

"Thertainly, I have never denied that. Do you pretend to call your nonthenthe, art? It ith an art that you will never be able to live on."

"There's no knowing, Herr Professor!"

"Be thtill, I tell you! If you go on at this wate you will be shipwecked soonaw or lataw in life. Knipke, go and see why Heppenheimer doeth not come back with the *pedell*."

"Oh, just this once, Herr Professor," whispered Rumpf coaxingly. "You might let me off just this once."

"No indeed! You go to *cawcer*. But we will not let thith dithagreeable affair intewupt our work. Hutzler, begin the wepetition."

"Herr Professor, I was ill when we translated this. Here is my certificate."

"Indeed! So you were ill, ath uthual. Do you know, Hutzler, it stwikes me that you are oftener ill than well."

"Unfortunately, Herr Professor, my delicate constitution——"

"Delicate? Eh, delicate? You don't thay tho, Hutzler! I with every man under the sun were ath delicate ath you are. Lathy, that's what you are, but not delicate——"

"Lazy? When I have a high fever you don't expect me to——"

"I know all that! Dare thay you dwank too much beer. You twanthlate, Gildemeister."

"Absent!" cried a number of voices at once.

Samuel shook his head sadly.

"Doeth nobody know what ith the matter with Gildemeister?"

"He has a cold!" replied one of the lads.

"Cold! When I wath hith age I never had a cold. But why don't Knipke and Heppenheimer come back? Schwarz, you go and thee if you can't find them, but mind you come wight back!"

Schwarz went, and returned after ten minutes with the *pedell* and the others.

"Herr Inaddler was occupied with papering his wall," said Heppenheimer in a respectful tone; "he had to change his coat."

"Ah, indeed! And doeth it take you half-an-hour to do that? Inaddlaw, theemth to me you are beginning to neglect your offith!"

"I beg your pardon, Herr Professor; the young gentleman came to my door just two minutes ago."

"Oh!" cried three indignant voices.

"Well, it theemth witheth to let thith matter wetht! Here, take Wumpf to the *cawcer*. Wumpf, you will behave yourself and not be continually calling the *pedell* ath you did the latht time you were there. Inaddlaw, don't let anything induthe you to let him come out into the hall."

"Very good, Herr Professor."

Wilhelm Rumpf bit his lip, turned to go, and disappeared with Inaddler in the dim twilight of the hall.

"What is it you did, Herr Rumpf?" asked the *pedell* sympathetically, as they were passing upstairs.

"Nothing."

"Oh, but, begging your pardon, you must have done *something?*"

"I only did what the professor does all the time."

"You don't say so! How is that?"

"Well, you just listen to me. Don't you thee, dear Inaddlaw, this fellow Wumpf is a pawfect scapegwace, and there ith no penalty severe enough faw him."

"Good gracious!" stammered the *pedell*, clasping his hands above his head. "To think that such things are possible! It's positively uncanny, Herr Rumpf, that it is! Heaven knows if I didn't see you right here before me with my own eyes I'd swear that it's the Herr Professor in person whose voice I hear this minute. You'll make your fortune with such a gift as that some day, sir. Why, once when I was drinking my beer over at Lotze's there was a magician who'd imitate anything you wanted him to, twittering birds and neighing horses, barking dogs and ranting priests. But it didn't come up to your performance!"

"Yeth, yeth, dear Inaddlaw! I dare thay you're wight!" replied Rumpf, still continuing in the voice and tone of the professor.

"You don't mean to say you kept this thing up in his presence? Well, I must say, Herr Rumpf, there's a time for everything. No wonder the Herr Professor was very much put out."

"Now weally! Do you think tho?"

"I shall have to ask you to stop this now. You see, it's not compatible with the dignity of my office. Will you please walk into this room?"

"Thertainly——"

"Herr Rumpf, I shall tell the Herr Professor that your punishment is altogether too lenient."

"What bithiness ith that of yours, you abthurd old fellow? I can do what I pleathe."

"That you cannot do."

"You will thee that I can. I can talk ath it thuits me, and whoever doeth not like it can thtop up hith ears."

"You wait and see."

"Wait for what?"

"I shall inform the Herr Professor."

"Give him my compliments."

Inaddler turned the key and slowly walked away.

. . . . . .

Inaddler, having done what was incumbent upon him, devoted himself lustily to his interrupted occupation. He dipped his brush into the tremendous pot of paste and supplied strip after strip of wall paper with the faintly fragrant liquid.

Wilhelm Rumpf sat yawning upon the seat of his prison, and assured himself in a soliloquy that he was heartily sick of the gymnasium and of the uncalled-for restrictions of school life.

Herr Samuel Heinzerling scratched his head, pushed his large round-eyed spectacles up high on his nose and shook his pedagogical head three or four times.

"A mithewable boy, thith fellow Wumpf," he murmured, "but I half believe I could win him by gentler methodth more weadily than I can by severity. I will make one more attempt to appeal to hith conscienthe. It ith a pity to let him go on like thith. He ith one of my motht gifted pupilth!"

He touched the bell.

After two minutes Annie appeared, Inaddler's daughter. She was evidently about to go out, for a tiny hat surmounted by feathers was perched jauntily upon her curly head.

"What can I do for you, Herr Professor?" she asked with a dainty curtsey.

"Where is your father?" whispered Samuel, with a remarkably pure pronunciation for him.

"He is papering. Is there anything you wish him to do, Herr Professor?"

"Ah, he ith papawing. Well, then, I will not dithturb him. It ith of no consequenth, Annie; I dare thay the key is on the *anwer?*"

"I will run and ask, Herr Professor."

She ran down the stairs like a deer, and was back in a few seconds.

"Yes, sir; the keys are on the hall door as well as on the cell. Is there anything else?"

"No; I thank you."

Annie turned to go, while Samuel looked after her with a

smile. He passed his hand once or twice over his closely-shaved chin, then he took his hat from the table and ascended the stairs to the *carcer*.

Wilhelm Rumpf was greatly surprised when after so short a time of imprisonment the door turned on its hinges. His astonishment reached its climax when he recognised Professor Samuel Heinzerling.

"Well, Wumpf?" said that philosopher with dignity.

"What do you wish, Herr Professor?" responded the pupil in a tone of resolute obstinacy.

"I have come to athk if you are not beginning to thee that thuch puerilenetheth are out of plathe altogether in a gymnathium, and that——"

"I am not at all aware of having done——"

"What, Wumpf? I did not expect to find you tho thtubborn! I wish you would put yourthelf in my plathe. I am sure you would be much more thevere with thith unmanageable Wilhelm Wumpf than I have been, eh?"

"Herr Professor——"

"Surely thuch childish conduct ith not what one would expect of a young man of good family. You'd betht be on your guard, for the next time I catch you in a thewape I shall expel you!"

"Expel me?"

"Yes, Wumpf, expel you. So you would do well to turn over a new leaf, and let your dithgratheful nonthenthe go. I wepeat it, put yourself in my place!"

Wilhelm Rumpf lowered his head. He felt that his expulsion was only a matter of time. Suddenly a diabolical thought took possession of his brain.

"If I must get expelled," he said to himself, "it shall be with flying colours."

He smiled like the villainous hero of a sensational novel after some dark deed, and said in a tone of simulated humility—

"You say, sir, I should put myself in your place?"

"Yes, Wumpf, that ith what I thay."

"Well then, seeing you will have it so,—I wish you much pleasure!"

And with a single bound he was outside the door, turned the key, and left the poor professor to his deplorable fate.

"Wumpf! what ith thith you are up to? I'll exthpel you thith vewy day! Open the door at onthe! At onthe, I thay!"

"I give you two hours' *caweer*," replied Rumpf with dignity. "You told me to put mythelf in your plathe!"

"Wumpf! you will thee what will happen! Open the door; I inthitht upon it!"

"You have no wight to talk to me in that tone. Jutht at pwethent *I* am the Herr Profeththor! You are merely the pupil Wilhelm Wumpf. Be thtill! I will not bwook oppothition!"

"Dear Wumpf! I will fawgive you thith onthe. Pleathe open the door like a good fellow. Your penalty shall be a vewy slight one. I give you my word faw it, you shall not be exthpelled. Do you hear what I thay?"

Dear Rumpf did not hear. He had crept stealthily along the hall and was now hastening downstairs to complete his escape.

As he was passing the *pedell's* door a tempting idea took possession of him.

He put his eye to the keyhole. Inaddler was standing upon a ladder, his back to the door, and was just attempting to put a heavily-pasted strip of paper in place. Wilhelm Rumpf just lifted the latch, and called out with the purest Heinzerling accent of which he was capable—

"I am going now, Inaddlaw. Keep an eye on that fellow Wumpf. The lad is cawying on at a gweat wate. He ith thtill keeping up hith impertinent nonthenthe. You keep wight on with your work. All I want to thay ith that you are not to open the door faw him on any conthideration. The fellow ith quite capable of knocking you down and wunning away. Do you hear what I thay, Inaddlaw?"

"Very good, Herr Professor. Excuse me for not getting down——"

"Thtay wight where you are, I thay, and finish your papawing. Good mawning."

"Your servant, Herr Professor."

Wilhelm Rumpf went upstairs again, and once more entered the hallowed precincts of the *carcer*. Samuel Heinzerling was raging terribly. Now he seemed to have discovered the bell, for just as Rumpf sought refuge behind an enormous linen chest belonging to the Inaddler family, it resounded shrilly through the hall like the yell of indignant demons.

"Help!" moaned the professor. "Help! Inaddlaw; you will lothe your plathe thith very day, if you don't come up thith minute! Help! Fire! fire! Murder! Wobbers! Help!"

The *pedell*, recalled to his duty by the uninterrupted sound of the bell, left his private occupation and put in an appearance before the door of the prison. Deceitful Wilhelm Rumpf crept deeper into his hiding-place. Samuel Heinzerling, utterly exhausted from calling and crying, threw himself down upon his seat. His bosom was palpitating; his nostrils worked like a pair of good bellows.

"Herr Rumpf," said Inaddler, giving a warning knock on the door, "look out, I'm making a note of all your doings!"

"The Lord be praithed that you are here, Inaddlaw! Open the door, I thay! Thith mithewable thcoundwel hath locked me in. Thuch conduct ith unheard of!"

"Let me tell you, Herr Rumpf, you'd better stop your joking. You may be quite sure I'll tell the Herr Professor how you called him a miserable scoundrel!"

"Have you lotht your wits, Inaddlaw?" shouted Samuel in

a tone of supreme indignation "The devil! don't you hear me thay how Wumpf, the knave, hath locked me in here when I came to thee him, and talk like a father to him! I thay, don't keep me waiting! Open the door at onthe!"

"You must take me to be very stupid, Herr Rumpf. The professor was at my door this moment, and has my word for it that I won't let you out. And now I advise you to behave yourself, and stop ringing that bell, else I'll take it down, sure as fate!"

"Inaddlaw, I'll thee to it that you are thent to gaol for depriving me of my freedom!"

"Now just you listen to me, will you? It's positively childish this everlasting imitating of the Herr Professor. There is no denying that the professor lisps a bit, and pronounces his r's in a funny way, but never so long as I knew him was he guilty of such a silly twaddle as you are indulging in. And now then, for the last time, all I can say is, be quiet, and conduct yourself like a gentleman——"

"But I wepeat to you, upon my honour, that confounded scoundwel turned the key behind me, before I knew what he wath about! Inaddlaw! Knave, ass! You must know me! Have the goodneth to considaw!"

"What? You call me an ass? You call me a knave? I'd have you to know it's a question who is the greatest ass or the greatest knave, you or I! Well I never in all my born days! The impudence! A green boy like you calling an honest old man an ass! You are an ass yourself! Do you understand! But you'll get your deserts!"

"You are an ass and a fool!" moaned Heinzerling in despair. "So you wefuse to open the door?"

"I'd never think of doing such a thing."

"Good, vewy good!" groaned the philosopher with a dying voice. "Vewy good! I'll stay wight here in the *cawew* then! Do you hear, Inaddlaw? Wight here in the *cawew!*"

"I am glad to hear you are beginning to come around to

common sense. And now I hope you'll let me alone. I've no more time to listen to your farce!"

"Inaddlaw!" cried Samuel, getting enraged once more. "Hour by hour I'll thit here, do you understand? Hour by hour. Like a thcamp of a thchoolboy I'll bear the dithgwace of it! Do you hear me, Inaddlaw?"

"I'm going now. You'd better do your translation."

"Holy heavens, I'm lothing my weason! Am I cwathy? Man, won't you look through the keyhole. Then at leatht you might thee——"

"You don't catch me. I haven't forgotten how you blew in my eyes the other day!"

"Well, then, go to the devil by all meanths. There's no wawing with such pawverse thtupidity. Just wait till I come out of thith. You won't have thith plathe of *pedell* much longer, I'll pwomithe you that!"

Inaddler felt his way downstairs in a very ill humour. This lad Rumpf was surely the most impertinent fellow he had ever come across. An ass did he call him? Thunder and lightning! Ever since the decease of Mrs. Inaddler the like had not occurred to him——!

These miserable schoolboys!

Meanwhile Samuel Heinzerling passed up and down his cell with long steps. His whole appearance bore a certain resemblance to an African lion condemned to imprisonment by human sagacity without losing thereby any of the original pride and strength of his noble nature. His hands crossed on his back, his head with its grey mane inclined wofully toward one shoulder, his lips tightly shut—so he walked back and forth, back and forth, the darkest and most misanthropic thoughts in his bosom.

Suddenly a broad smile flitted across his features.

"Most abthurd thith ith!" he muttered to himself. "Weally, though thith ith a very disagweeable affair for me to be in, there ith no denying the humour of the thituation——"

He stood still.

"Ith there weally any dithgwace in being outwitted by a thchoolboy? Go to, Thamuel! Did not a thelebrated king hold the ladder faw a thief to thteal his watch? Wath not even Pwince Bithmarck locked in by wuthless hands? Not to name a hundred other cases. And thtill hithtory treath thith king with rethpect. And thtill Bithmarck hath lotht none of hith reputation ath the betht diplomatitht in Europe. No, no, Thamuel! Your dignity ath thchoolmathter, ath thitizen, ath philothopher, need not thuffer by thith mortifying thituation. Retht assured, Thamuel——"

He continued his walk in a self-satisfied mood; but soon he interrupted himself anew.

"But thothe boyth!" he stammered, turning pale. "When thothe boyth hear how I wath impwithoned at the *cawcer!* Fearful thought! I might ath well give up my authowity ath a teacher at onthe. And they *will* hear it. There ith no help faw it! Ye godth, ye godth, why do ye thmite me thus?"

"Herr Professor," whispered a familiar voice at the door of the cell, "you are not yet dishonoured. Your authority is as unassailable as ever——"

"Wumpf!" muttered Samuel; "you godleth fellow you! Open that door, I thay, thith minute! Conthider your earth boxed! Conthider yourthelf expelled!"

"Herr Professor, I've come to save you! Do not insult me!"

"To thave me? What impertinenthe! Open the door, or I'll——"

"Will you hear me speak, Herr Professor? I assure you all will end well."

Samuel considered.

"Vewy well," he said at last; "I'll condethend to hear you. Thpeak———"

"I only wanted to show you that my art is not quite

without practical import. Forgive me if in doing so I have seemingly left out of consideration the very high esteem and respect in which I am happily conscious of always having held you!"

"You are a wogue, Wumpf!"

"Herr Professor! suppose you dispense me from the *carcer* penalty, withdraw your threat regarding expulsion, and permit me to guard the most complete silence over what has passed!"

"It would never do, Wumpf. You mutht hold out your time——."

"Yes? Well, then, good-bye to you, Herr Professor! Don't ring the bell too often!"

"Wumpf! hear what I thay to you! Wumpf!"

"Well——?"

"You are in many wespects an extwaawdinawy lad, Wumpf; and tho I am quite willing to make an extheption in your favour,—open the door!"

"Will you dispense me from *carcer*?"

"Yeth."

"Do you intend to expel me?"

"No, in the devil'th name."

"Give me your word of honour, Herr Professor!"

"Wumpf, how dare you?"

"Your word of honour, Herr Professor!"

"Vewy good, you have it!"

"Jupiter Ultor is witness."

"What?"

"I call upon the gods for witnesses."

"Open the door, I thay!"

"Presently, Herr Professor. You are sure you bear me no grudge?"

"No, no, no! *Will* you open that door?"

"You give me full absolution?"

"Yes, under the condition that you tell nobody a word

of your guilty conduct. I have told you that I take you to be an extwaawdinawy lad, Wumpf——"

"Thank you for your good opinion. My word of honour then that so long as you are in your present position at the town gymnasium no word shall pass my lips!"

With that he turned the key and opened the door.

Like the king in Uhland's ballad did Samuel Heinzerling step out into the pure air of heaven. He took a deep breath; then, brushing his hair from his brow as if trying to remember something, he said—

"Wumpf, I can take a joke ath well ath any man; but I wish you would do me the favour not to mimic me in future. You—you weally do it too well!"

"Your wish is my law!"

"Vewy good! And now you'd betht hathten down to the clath-woom. It'th not yet a quarter to—you'll be just in time!"

"But how can I do that, Herr Professor? They all know that you have given me three days!"

"Vewy good! I'll go with you."

They quickly walked downstairs.

"Inaddlaw!" called the professor into the basement door.

The *pedell* appeared at once and officiously asked what was his behest.

"I have dithpenthed Wumpf fwom his penalty faw sevewal weasons," said Samuel.

"Ah! that is what you came back for. Well, all I wish to say is that Herr Rumpf was not at all quiet in his cell. It's none of my business, I suppose, but he shouted and swore like a good 'un——"

"Well, never mind, Inaddlaw; I have thpecial motiveth faw dealing leniently with him thith time. You may wemove the key to the *cawcer*."

Ernest Eckstein.

OUR WAR-CORRESPONDENT.

THE natural and justifiable mistrust which the reading public brings to bear upon published reports from military headquarters has caused us to send our extra special correspondent, Herr Wippchen, whose presence has already graced several official festivities at the porter brewery, as well as two general assemblies of the architects' club, to be an eye-witness upon the field occupied just now by the oriental question.

No sooner was our intention made public than four managers of the most renowned life insurance companies applied to us, declaring their willingness to insure the life of our Wippchen against all the dangers of war upon the most reasonable conditions.

Yesterday, at eleven o'clock in the forenoon, Herr Wippchen set out on his journey, favoured by the most glorious weather. In the evening we had his first report from Bernau,[1] which we here publish:—

BERNAU, *May* 3, 1877.

After travelling for two hours I arrived here, and in this friendly little town I found rooms far from the deafening noise of the railway, where I can devote myself with leisure to my task. It is my purpose to give you a battle of some dimensions every day. Certain it is that the position of Bernau is decidedly favourable to my enterprise, for not only is it possible to take the train for the battle-field twice a day, but also to write to Berlin much more frequently.

On the train it was the opinion of many that the die had fallen, and that the temple of Janus would not be sheathed

---

[1] A small town near Berlin.

again for weeks to come. Indeed, at the "Kaiserhof," the night before we left, we were quite unanimous about that.

I am sorry to say that I am not supplied with the necessary maps. The geography I had when I went to school is rather old, and the map of Turkey is partly torn out.

It was a capital idea to send me here. There is no denying the fact that a war-correspondent should not be constantly seen in the streets of the town where his reports are printed.

The most important thing to-day seems to me to be the fact that this oriental war is not the first in history. There is no denying that there have been several others, none of which have ended with the annihilation of Russia or Turkey. Both arose again like Aphrodite out of the ashes.

To be sure, Russia says the beard of the prophet must be shaved from the earth, because Turkey persecutes and torments Christianity. But how if Turkey should suddenly turn and say that in Russia too the Christians sigh under the bed of Procrustes, and that the lash of civilisation must be applied to the Russians! What then?

And as for England, there is no denying that England will never look on and permit the aggrandisement of Russia from without. But with all its Armada it will never be able to hinder its aggrandisement within.

Where is Ariadne's thread to guide us out of the Scylla of this Augean stable?

I enclose my first letter from the battle-field, and at the same time I would ask you to send me a couple of those new gold 5-mark pieces, which the inhabitants of Bernau are curious to see.

LEOWA, *April* 24.

Rosy-fingered Eos had but just struck five when I arose from the naked earth and betook myself to the Pruth to see the Russian troops cross it. There is no denying that there may have been about 13,000 men; Tschetschentians, Svanetians, Zaporopian Kossaks, Lesghians, mostly adults, were all marching towards Glatz. They sang a song which I should like to call "The Watch on the Pruth." When General Strobelew saw me he declared me to be a spy, and condemned me to the knout for life. At that, of course, I turned my back upon him; but even as I did it, I lay upon the bench, and two Kossaks raised the knout of Damocles above me to execute the stroke of death, when the general declared I should be let off this once with a black eye. One of the Kossaks proceeded to strike me one, and the general shook my hand heartily, assuring me that soon no Christian should sigh at the hands of the Turk. I saluted him by laying two fingers of my right hand upon my injured eye, and the general turned to continue his way.

The Roumanians who had hastened to the spot to witness the passage of the Pruth cursed with ringing hurrahs, and waved their hats with clenched fists.

I hastened to Kars, where there is a skirmish going on.

BATUM, *April* 26.

The Russians and Turks had pitched into each other near Batum. I stood upon a pile of corpses where I had a good view. The Turks struck to the right and left with such vehemence that all their crooked swords were soon fully straightened out. The Russians did not wait to be told twice, and knew no mercy. The thunder of the cannons was terrible. Boom! boom! only a good deal louder. Ill-luck would have it that I came to stand right between a Russian and a Turk, and they both shot at me at the same moment. I stooped down quickly, and both fell down lifeless, each having been pierced by the other's ball. It was a marvellous escape. The scythe of Charon spared me by a miracle, as it were.

For hours the battle raged. Finally it was left undecided. The Russians, as well as the Turks, were victorious.

Exhausted with hardships, and with the display of courage, I at last fell asleep upon a drum, and did not awake until a Russian beat the retreat upon me. *C'est la guerre!*

Soon there will be more or less more.

To Herr Wippchen at Bernau.

Since the 3rd you have not sent us a single skirmish, for we presume you do not expect us to look upon your request for a further remittance, with which we unfortunately complied, in the light of a war report. You seem to take the oriental complication as an opportunity to live in the country at our expense. Do you think this is acting like our own correspondent? If so, you mistake. If we do not receive one of the bloodiest battles by return post, we shall look about for another war-correspondent. It was only yesterday that one of the profession offered his services, declaring his readiness to furnish us with war at 5-pfennige a line. We wish to bring this to your notice, saluting you in the firm expectation of a desperate conflict.

Yours cordially,
The Editor.

Paris, *May* 14, 1878.

Here I sit in my cosy *pro doma*, which I have rented with my hard-earned savings on the bulwarks of the temple (*Boulevard du Temple*). It was so hot at the exhibition that it seemed as if Helios had poured out all the tropics upon it, and when at last I turned to leave I found that all the cabs were filled with weary visitors.

The soirée at Minister Waddington's was a very brilliant affair. The entire aristocracy and plebeocracy of Paris was present. Especially the Prince of Wales. He looks for all the world exactly like his mother. When I was presented to him, he at once got entangled in a lengthy toast. It is well known that the prince is a connoisseur in delicately done slices of bread. He closed with the words, "In this sense I seize the empty glass and fill it to the alliance between Germany and England." I answered with, "God save the Queen," in which I joined with fervour. I then added, "In this toast every German will join so long as he calls his soul his own upon this terrestrial globe."

"To be, or not to be," replied the prince, and thereupon he toasted on the alliance between England and the terrestrial globe. I recommended the prince to the favour of heaven, whereupon he toasted the alliance between England and heaven. He then joined other groups, and toasted every one of them. Presently he left the soirée, not without having favoured the footman in the ante-chamber, who helped him on with his overcoat, with a toast. When he was in his carriage, he was overheard to pronounce several toasts to the Paris vehicles, the driver, the moon and stars, and the institution of street-gas.

No wonder the prince is very popular in Paris society!

Yesterday His Serenity the Shah left. A few hours before his departure I saw him at the exhibition standing before a piece of soap (*savon*). "How much is this letter-weight?" he inquired, and thereupon bought it.

Julius Stettenheim.

SCHNORPS' SWALLOW-TAIL.

HE played the bass viol in the orchestra of the theatre.

The bass viol had come to be the hereditary instrument for all the male members of the Schnorps family, who were invariably musical, and I remember an anecdote from the life of Aegidius Schnorps, the grandfather of my hero, which well deserves to be handed down to posterity.

Of course Aegidius played the hereditary instrument.

But he did not play it at the Royal Theatre; he had not yet arrived at such distinction. Instead of that he was a member of a rather obscure band which used to gather its laurels at country dances on Sundays and special holidays. The leader was supposed to furnish the bass viol, but the Schnorpses had always had their own instrument, and prided themselves not a little upon this family possession. Although the peasants were not at all particular about any involuntary variations that might perchance find their way into the tune, for 'tis easy to pipe to those that want to dance, it so happened that one day Father Aegidius produced tones of such singular impurity that the leader, whose week-day occupation was that of an honest shoemaker, called out, greatly enraged, "Confound you, Aegedi, why don't you play right?" "Hold your tongue, shoemaker!" replied the indignant Schnorps. "I can play as I please; this bass belongs to me."

Ah yes, they were always very self-sufficient, were the Schnorpses, and had little respect for the rest of the world. They were always trying to force their square heads through thick and thin.

After Aegidius came Sebastian Schnorps, who of course also devoted himself to the grumbling bass, and who was gathered unto his fathers in the very midst of his professional activity, inasmuch as he and his instrument fell down together from a high ladder, by means of which he had intended to reach a place in a barn which should furnish him the necessary acoustic conditions for evolving seraphic tones, and properly affecting the crowd of dancing peasants beneath him.

Peace be unto his ashes!

After him came Gottlieb Schnorps, the man who is to occupy our attention to-day. It were really needless to say that the hereditary proclivity had come down to him, if it were not incumbent upon me to do justice to him by mentioning the fact that he was a musician of a better sort than his ancestors. He had worked his way up from a country fiddler, had studied a little, and though in his general manner and bearing he had remained true to the family traditions of the Schnorpses, he had struck out a new path in going to see something of the world, and one day he came back with the contract of a court engagement in his pocket, and with a wife whom the dear God must have created for his special convenience, so well were her characteristics adapted to his.

. . . .

They arranged their life as they thought best. Either he quarrelled with his wife or she with him, or both of them with the children, or the latter among each other—between times the bass viol grumbled, for Schnorps was always hard at work developing his musical faculties—in short, their home life was a lively one.

If Schnorps had only been a little neater in his personal appearance!—but in this respect he did little honour to the Royal Orchestra. His shabbiness had grown proverbial. He had a special predilection for an enormous cravat to conceal the doubtful purity of his linen from the eyes of the curious. His coat was seldom brushed, and the lower part of his coat-sleeves shone like a mirror.

The pride of his heart was a dress-coat, which he donned only on extraordinary occasions. He had brought himself to purchase this piece of wearing apparel only by dint of the rigorous etiquette of the Royal Theatre, which authoritatively demanded the use of a dress-coat on certain days. It never occurred to him to have a new one, and he wandered from junk-shop to junk-shop until he found a specimen at Solomon Hoffa's, which he purchased for one thaler and some odd groschens, and which he thereafter wore to the horror of all respectable people, and to the annoyance of the entire orchestra.

It was really too shabbily old-fashioned. In fact, it was a disgrace to the corporation. The collar was of such goodly size as to almost completely hide the square head of Schnorps; the sleeves were so tight that Gottlieb could only with difficulty properly belabour his bass viol, and the broad tails stood out like the arms of a windmill from the lank legs of the wearer.

One morning he received a formidable-looking square letter, with the well-known official green seal, in which he was notified in the politest of language, but with all possible decision, that when taking part in the orchestra in future he was to appear in a coat which was more in harmony with the dignity of a Royal Theatre, and less likely to excite the risibility of the audience.

This left no room for doubt, it was certainly plain enough. Schnorps raged—talked about tyranny, interference with personal freedom, scolded his wife, and flogged all the young Schnorpses; but there was no help for it—the acquisition of a new coat loomed upon the horizon as an inexorable necessity.

And now occurred what had never occurred before. For several days in succession the townspeople saw the bass violinist Schnorps and his spouse walk about from one clothing shop to another. In each one they entered into lengthy negotiations, only to pass on after a time grumbling and scolding about the outrageous prices, until at last the firm of J. M. Lindenfeld had the good fortune to come to terms with Herr and Frau Schnorps about a new and handsome swallow-tail coat.

. . . . . .

"I'll tell you what, Sally," said the bass violinist one day to his better-half; "though I've been forced by pure tyranny to spend a sinful lot of money on that new dress-coat, there's no earthly reason why I shouldn't get all the good I can out of the old one. I wish you'd just send for

"IT WAS A DISGRACE TO THE CORPORATION."

old Peter and tell him to make Michel a jacket out of it; it will last the boy many a year."

Old Peter was a tailor whose chief art lay in mending and patching up old garments, and Michel was the eldest sprout and heir pretendent to the bass viol of the Schnorpses.

The tailor came, made a very close and conscientious examination of the old swallow-tail by the aid of a pair of enormous horn spectacles, and finally declared, with great decision, that the article in question had had its day, and that there was not the slightest possibility of renovating it.

This was a terrible shock for Schnorps, for Peter's judgment was considered quite incontrovertible, and when there was anything to be made out of an old garment he did it. This he had proved time and time again in the wardrobe of the Schnorpses. So there was nothing for it but to stow away the old dress-coat among other venerable relics, and it might have stayed there to this day if Frau Sally Schnorps had not hit upon a brilliant plan.

Hoods were quite the fashion just then, and why not make a hood out of a dress-coat? It might be trimmed with a quantity of ribbons and laces to conceal the shabbiness of the cloth, which latter could still further be improved upon by being turned. She was very proud of this idea, and forthwith called upon a deaf old seamstress, who often worked for her, and who was quite noted for her stupidity, but aside from that was a poor, unassuming woman who patiently worked for her living without expecting any generous remuneration. This last quality had served to gain her the good will of Frau Schnorps, into the mysteries of whose housekeeping she was thoroughly initiated.

She came and found the wife of the bass violinist at the door, about to go out, while Schnorps was rehearsing for the opera. In brief words Frau Sally explained to her that in the big wardrobe upstairs there was a dress-coat of her husband's which was quite worth the trouble of making over, and which she wished to be metamorphosed into a hood for herself.

"Very well, very well, I'll see to it all right, Frau Schnorps," replied the old woman; and while Frau Sally Schnorps went to market, her mind quite at rest, she entered the house where the youngest of the Schnorpses, who had been left to guard the domestic hearth, handed over the dress-coat, which she thereupon took home to "make over." And she did it. When she came back, after a day or two, the old dress-coat had become a new head-covering, which, to be sure, was rather heavily decorated with lace and various trimmings, but for this very reason exactly suited the taste of Madam Schnorps. It is true, her husband said, that now you could see that the dress-coat had really not been so bad, and that the money which went for the new one might have been put to some better use, but there was no use crying over spilt milk, the tyrannical intendant had decreed that it should be so, and he philosophically added—

> "For every evil under the sun
> There is a remedy or there's none.
> If there is one, try and find it,
> If there isn't, never mind it."

When autumn came the wife of the musician walked forth proudly in her new hood, and about the same time her husband received an invitation to spend the evening at the house of an old general, who was a great lover of music, and famous for his bachelor's suppers, which added a great attraction to his musical evenings. The old gentleman had a high opinion of Gottlieb Schnorps as a musician, and would have liked to ask him long ago, but he had never been able to bring himself to do so on account of Schnorps's shabbiness, and the bass violinist was indebted for this invitation chiefly to his new coat.

Schnorps was highly elated to receive it, and his mouth

watered at the thought of all the culinary delights which would await him after the music.

When the auspicious day came he devoted an unusual amount of care and attention to his toilet. Although it was only Thursday, he permitted himself the luxury of a clean shirt, bought himself—and this was the rarest of extravagances—a pair of white cotton gloves, even went so far as to brush his black trousers with a certain amount of energy, a thing he never did on ordinary occasions, so as not to wear out the cloth.

"Get my dress-coat out, Sally," he said in the evening, and she went upstairs in obedience to his behest.

Now it was that something horrible occurred!

As Schnorps's spouse opened the door of the wardrobe and put her hand in behind all the ancestral garments, she screamed aloud, for there, like a ghost of bygone days, the old swallow-tail grinned at her in the full glory of its invulnerable perfection. She turned it about again and again, and thought she was losing her reason—there was not a particle of doubt of it, it was undeniably the same coat which she had fondly believed she had been wearing on her head in the elaborated and decorative shape of a new hood. In wild excitement she turned the contents of the wardrobe topsy-turvy; trousers and coats were flung about to the right and to the left, but there was no vestige to be seen of the new dress-coat, and with convincing force the certainty came to her that the stupid old seamstress had cut up the new garment instead of the old to manufacture her head-gear therefrom.

So that was the reason it looked so well! Ah, now everything was clear.

"If Schnorps gets wind of this he'll murder me," sighed Frau Sally, and so much was certain, this affair must be hushed up for the time being.

But how was she to accomplish this?

She glanced out of the window at the neighbouring house, and a saving idea flitted through her mind. Stealthily she crept downstairs and out at the back door, and hastily entering the house across the way she poured out the sad tale of her misfortunes into the sympathetic ear of her neighbour, imploring her to help her out of her difficulties by lending her the dress-coat of her husband just for this one night.

The good-natured woman was easily won, and an hour later Schnorps, happily unconscious of the state of affairs, and attired in his neighbour's dress-coat, was on his way to the general, the servant of the latter walking behind him and dragging along his heavy bass viol.

The coat was somewhat tight, which fact caused its wearer to remark, as he was putting it on, that he was really growing stout in spite of his moderate way of living.

Poor innocent Schnorps!

The musical performance had passed off greatly to the satisfaction of the old general, and the ensuing excellent supper was no less to the satisfaction of his guests. The bass violinist indulged himself most freely in the good things set before him, and manifested a degree of steady perseverance as if he had fasted for a fortnight to fitly prepare himself for this special feast. He left nothing undone, plateful after plateful vanished, one glass of delicious wine after another disappeared in the bottomless pit of his eating apparatus, and whenever he thought himself unobserved he helped himself freely to generous handfuls of sweets, depositing them in the voluminous pockets of his dress-coat.

Ah, he was a kind father, when he had nothing to lose thereby, and he was quite willing to be a bringer of dainties to his dear ones at home.

The guests remained until very late, and of course Schnorps was the last to go. It was somewhere near two in the morning when he reeled home in a condition which really put every well-intentioned cab-driver under the moral obligation of turning out for him.

Arrived at the door of his house, he indulged in some profoundly philosophical reflections about the preposterous size of keys, and the smallness of the corresponding keyholes—so profound, in fact, that he sat for a long, long time upon the stone-steps, his head buried in his hands, and his eyes closed, until at dawn a cool breath of air roused him from his meditations, so that he rose shivering and passed into the house.

After several hours of refreshing sleep he awoke in no very enviable condition. He looked about him with wondering eyes, and suddenly he opened them to abnormal width as if to pierce the object upon which they fell.

It was the new swallow-tail. Merciful heavens, how it looked! During his *siesta* on the door-steps he had sat upon the cream-filled candies he had in his pocket, and the mixture of chocolate, sugar, and fruit had formed into a sticky crust on the tails of his coat which was truly horrible to behold.

The bass violinist jumped out of bed at a single bound, and examined the luckless coat, which in the very flower of its youth had been called upon to endure such hardships.

"When my old woman sees that, there'll be a row," he muttered, passing his hand desperately through his bristling locks. He seized a brush and began to belabour the swallow-tail with an amount of energy such as he had never before displayed; but although his perseverance was rewarded by the disappearance of some of the smaller stains, the large blurs which had been caused by the crushed chocolate-drops would yield to no amount of brushing, the less so as they were still moist, and by rubbing acquired a more formidable appearance.

Meanwhile he heard his wife beginning to stir in her room,

and poor terrified Schnorps, who at times quaked in his shoes before his fair spouse, puzzled his head to find some remedy for his trouble. Suddenly it occurred to him that years ago he had bought a bottle of benzine which he knew must be somewhere in his room.

"HE SEIZED A BRUSH AND BEGAN TO BELABOUR THE SWALLOW-TAIL."

He found a dozen bottles on top of the wardrobe, but how was he to know which was the one he wanted? He rummaged until he discovered one at the sight of which the certainty dawned within his dizzy brain that this was it. He spread out the unfortunate coat upon the table, poured a generous supply of the liquid supposed to be benzine upon it, and was about to rub it in with his handkerchief when a horrible sight appeared before him.

Wherever a drop of the fluid had fallen, the cloth turned red; and before the perplexed violinist could find an explanation for this remarkable metamorphosis, there appeared upon the coat an infinite number of large and small holes which sealed its doom for now and eternity.

It so happened that instead of benzine, Schnorps had laid hold of a bottle of sulphuric acid, which he had once used to clean the screws of his instrument.

When he realised what had happened, he certainly expected to go mad, and he weakly fell back in his chair, gazing fixedly upon his murdered swallow-tail. His head whirled—the new coat—his wife—the 15 thalers—the intendant—sulphuric acid—all was swallowed up in one wild eddy, and it was some time before he regained any self-possession.

Ye saints! it would never do to have his wife get hold of this! The first thing to do was to remove the article in question. Hastily he dressed himself, slipped on his felt slippers, hid the dress-coat beneath his dressing-gown, and stealthily crept upstairs, where he hid it, with many misgivings, in the utmost depths of the old wardrobe.

It was high time, for when he came back his better-half appeared upon the scene. Never had she inspired him with such terror as at this moment, and yet never since the days of their honeymoon had he bidden her good-morning as tenderly as he did to-day. She too was unusually amiable, a fact which only weighed the more upon his guilty conscience.

"Well, did you have a pleasant evening?" she asked.

"Oh yes, very nice—yes—quite nice!" he replied, in an embarrassed tone of voice.

"Oh, indeed!" she said, glancing about her as if she were looking for something, which caused poor Schnorps to tremble again.

"What are you looking for, dear?"

She gazed at him in surprise. Dear? He had only called her so once before, and that was when he asked her if she would have him.

"Nothing—that is—where's your new coat?"

"The coat," he answered, shaking in his shoes; "what do you want it for?"

"I should like to put it away," she said very gently.

"You needn't do that. I put it where it belongs."

"Where it belongs?" she asked in great excitement.

"Why yes," replied Schnorps; "upstairs in the wardrobe."

"Ah, so," she remarked, greatly relieved—"in the wardrobe! Yes, yes! Well, come and have your breakfast, Gottlieb; I am coming down in a minute."

With these words she walked out, and now it was Schnorps' turn to take a deep breath of relief.

He finished dressing and gradually became more tranquil—but it was the tranquillity that precedes a mighty storm.

The reader can readily imagine what followed.

After a pause of ten minutes, the shrill voice of Frau Sally rang through the house in a manner which made all the inmates start and tremble. Intending to return the borrowed coat to its rightful possessor, she had discovered the catastrophe, and raged like a lunatic.

At first Schnorps tried to defend himself and to comfort her, but when he began to understand all the details and complications of the hapless tale,—when he heard that he had ruined his neighbour's coat, and that his own had long ago gone to perdition by means of his wife's thoughtlessness and the old seamstress's stupidity, then his wrath knew no bounds.

It was really too much. To have to pay for *two* new

dress-coats, and to have none! it was death to him, it would bring him to an untimely grave.

I will cast the mantle of Christian charity over the ensuing scene; but to this day the neighbours talk about the row that took place at the house of the Schnorpses after the general's party.

Fritz Brentano.

THE MAN OF ORDER.

SO far as I am concerned, I must confess that I am not greatly interested either in painted Empresses, or in Cardinals, or in Pashas. My attention was riveted upon a lank, lean man, who must have been of unusual length when he was standing up, a man with white hair and a grey beard, round blue glasses before his eyes, beneath them a nose shaped like a potato, and a thin-lipped mouth drawn down at the corners in a sardonic smile. On his head there was a straw hat, the brim of which was of a width such as I had never before met with. This person sat upon a camp-stool, holding with his left hand a parasol lined with green over the afore-mentioned straw hat, and with his right hand guiding a small telescope screwed to a stick, which was fastened in the ground. There is no need to say that the ruler and guider of this telescope was reconnoitring the châlet across the way. What pleased me best was the fussiness, the apparatus, and the intensity of research which served the man's curiosity. Surely this was the last of the Mohicans, one of the last original characters which are disappearing more and more out of the insipid level of our most modern mediocrity and uniformity. Who was the man? The dear old village of Ragaz has, by no means to the delight of everybody, grown into a "fashion-

THE MAN OF ORDER.

"WHO WAS THE MAN?"

able" resort, and one meets queer enough figures there every summer. But one like the man with a telescope and camp-stool, who had improvised an observatory on the spur of the moment, is an exotic plant, even in the Ragaz of to-day, and is well worth the trouble of observation.

What a pity, I thought, that Amadeus Hoffmann is no more among the living, or Edgar Poe. For either of them this fellow would have been a find.

Gradually the spectators dispersed, as neither the empress, who had been turned out of her empire, nor the cardinal, who had taken the hint that he was superfluous, condescended to show themselves, and as it was getting rather dull to gaze upon the red fez of the pasha, which was just visible above the railing of the verandah at the right. At last there were only two left: the telescope man, who continued his observations, and my worthy self observing the obdurate observer.

Finally, we both accomplished our purpose—he in seeing Madonna Eugenia and the Prince-Cardinal leave the house in quick succession, I in being a witness to the geometrical correctness with which the discoverer took down his observatory.

His motions were as measured as if he felt it incumbent upon him to keep time to the music of the spheres. His very manner of getting up showed a man who never puts one foot before the other without having incontestably assured himself where he was about to tread. When his long bony figure had drawn itself out to its full length his first object was to see clearly. For this purpose he cautiously removed his spectacles from his potato-shaped nose and wiped the large, round blue glasses emphatically with a piece of soft leather he produced out of his right vest-pocket. Having put back the piece of leather and the spectacles to their original place, he commenced the work of packing up, without haste and without delay. At first the telescope was unscrewed, reduced to its smallest dimensions, wiped on all sides with a large red silk handkerchief, and enclosed in a leather case, out of which he had carefully blown the dust, and which he now laid down gently upon the camp-stool. Hereupon he pulled out the stick which had served as a holder for his telescope until now, but which, upon nearer acquaintance, proved to be a perfect miracle, a very encyclopædia of a stick, so to say. It was evidently the pride and joy of its happy possessor. There could be no doubt of that from the satisfaction with which he touched the various springs of the complicated apparatus to display the countless metamorphoses which made the stick appear in turn as a common cane, as an umbrella, as a hoe, as a geological hammer, as a pocket-dagger, as a candle-snuffer, as a reading-desk, as a corkscrew, as a cup, as a chisel, as an inkstand, and as various other things. At last I should really not have been surprised if this Chinese puzzle had suddenly put on the garb of a speaker in Parliament.

The man could read open admiration, the most unselfish of human sympathy, from my countenance, and consequently felt impelled to say, as he pointed to his stick, having reduced it to its most primitive form : " It is the result of five years of theoretic studies and three years of practical constructive experiments. Ay, sir, with genius and order one can accomplish some pretty good things upon this disorderly earth."

With that he leaned his miraculous staff carefully against a tree, buckled his telescope-case to a broad strap which hung across his right shoulder like a bandoleer, took up his camp-stool, devoted himself assiduously to reducing it to infinitesimal dimensions, and buckled the object, which in its present shape no person would ever have suspected of being a chair, to his strap. He then took up his encyclopædic stick, lightly pricked the ground with the point, and remarked, in the full consciousness of work well done: "All's in order! Cardinal, Pasha, Ex-empress, all done up in good order."

"Heilige Ordnung, segensreiche," I began, quoting Schiller.

"Yes, sir; that is the wisest word ever the immortal Marbach sage pronounced. To say that, he must have been a man of order himself. And that he was so is proved to-day by his printed note-book. Unfortunately his collection of pill-bills has not yet been published. Nor Goethe's Rhine-wine bills. Neither, I am sorry to say, have we as yet any printed proofs of the number of pipe-lighters which were twisted for Johann Heinrich Voss by his prudent housewife Ernestine. At the same time I must admit that gradually we are reducing our history of literature to something like order. There is nothing like a basis of scientific research. This alone will bring light into chaos. When we have once succeeded in establishing the relation of Goethe's digestion to his poetic production, then we may set to work to discover the relation of the first part of *Faust* to the second. Happily there are men living and working who know that the so-called minutiæ and bagatelles of life are in reality the most important things. I know a Leipsic professor who has brought together scientific proof to show that true literature is that which has been contemptuously dubbed waste-paper-basket-literature. I know another Alexandrian ditto of Leipsic who is to edit a work which his friends have signalled in advance as about to create a new epoch in literature, the title of which will be, 'The Wash-bills of our Classic and Romantic Poets, being a Collection of Records and Documents for a Prospective Inductive Analytical History of German Literature of the Eighteenth and Nineteenth Centuries.' I know a third Byzantian of Leipsic, who plans to bring the art of writing diplomatic history up to the acme of perfection. He has made the different kinds of snuff which Frederick the Great indulged in the objects of his preliminary investigations, in order to be able to furnish proof of the effect which each individual sort had upon the brain-nerves of said Frederick, and consequently upon the destiny of the human race. Do you see, sir, that is what I call a truly scientific spirit, a healthy realism that, a spirit of sterling accuracy! Three groans for anything like disorder! It is incredible what a mischief-maker disorder is in these days! There was a fellow the other day had the audacity to spell Goethe G-ö-t-h-e throughout an entire book! Would you believe it? Fortunately he got his fingers whacked right heartily with the academical rattan. 'Göthe'! what do you think of it? Of course it is idiotic in German to write the diphthongs *ä, ö, ü* as if they were *æ, œ, ue*—I'll admit that, and I dare say Goethe himself would to-day save himself the trouble of putting in the extra *e*, but the orthography of G-o-e-t-h-e has once been established, and in the interest of order I would advise none but anarchists and rebels to be so godless as to leave out the *e*. The law of order is supreme, in great and in the greatest, in small and in the smallest."

He stopped exhausted and gasped for breath. "On earth and in the heavens," I added at haphazard.

"In the heavens? Not that I know of!" he said, drawing down the corners of his mouth. At the same time he touched his lifted cane, allowing the candle-snuffers to protrude for a moment, as if he were about to snuff out all anarchic stars in the firmament. "Do you know, in the so-called heavens there is not much order? The disorderly conduct of the comets should have been interfered with long ago. And then this transit of Venus, what do you say to that? Do you call that order? Venus should go in a decent and orderly manner above or below the sun, but certainly not straight before his Majesty's very nose. Why, it is like snapping his fingers at the sun; it's disrespectful, it's opposed to all decorum, to all order."

So saying he darted away from me—we had meanwhile reached the hotel "Hof Ragaz," and entering the right wing had walked upstairs—and like a whirlwind he pounced upon a table standing in the hall, about which evidently there was something not in order.

"There it is again!" he muttered, slowly passing the tip of his fore-finger over the top of the table until upon the dusty surface the word "Dust" appeared in large type capitals.

"Hang those women!" grumbled the owner of the magic staff. "Will you believe me when I tell you that yesterday I wrote the same cry of warning upon the top of this table? All in vain!"

And setting down his elaborately-constructed cane with well-tempered force upon the first step of the staircase leading to the third storey, he continued: "Tell me, dear sir, did you ever in the course of your experience meet with a person of the feminine sex, be it child, girl, or matron, who could ever be prevailed upon by means of exhortation, kindness, severity, diplomacy, or force to fully shut the latch of a door, or turn down the bolt of a window-sash?"

"No, to tell the truth, I have never met a feminine person of that description."

"I thought so!" he continued, with a triumphant smile. "Oh, if you knew all the trouble, all the untold trouble, I have taken for years to teach the women-folks at home to properly shut doors and windows. All in vain! But do you know how I punish the disorderly batch at home? Whenever I find a door left upon the latch, or a window with the bolt but half-turned, I at once lift the door or the sash out of the hinges and lean it against the wall. This has the desired effect of vexing the women and giving them additional work, especially in winter. There's nothing like the law of order. But do you call that order, eh?"

And with a degree of moral indignation he pointed to a row of milk-stains upon the stairs. One of the chambermaids, hastening up or down stairs with a breakfast-tray, had not kept an eye properly upon the milk-pitcher.

What did our fanatic in the cause of order? Something I had never seen before. He pulled a piece of chalk out of his pocket, and step by step he marked a neat circle round about each drop of milk.

"You see," he said, "this is the way I do at home to call the attention of the women to such offences against all sense of decency and modesty, which of course they never see and correct of their own accord. Oh, disorder, thy name is woman."

Johannes Scherr.

THE LUXURY OF GOING ABOUT INCOGNITO.

FOR six years the couple had lived in a very small town, in which each inhabitant could furnish a detailed biography of his neighbour, possessed an intimate knowledge of his daily *menu*, and knew just when the post delivered a package to him—the size and shape of which package being made the subject of conversation at the next coffee-party, where also unfailing conclusions were arrived at as to the contents and sender of the object in question. Judge Schwarz, being a person of distinction in town, naturally suffered more than others under the zealous observation of his neighbours, and was quite sure that he could not have a button sewed on his coat without having his friends mention the fact to each other and make their comments upon it;—ay, he went so far as to believe himself particularly favoured by good fortune if the local paper did not get hold of the important event and retail it to its readers the next morning in a sprightly editorial.

This consciousness had in the course of years reached such a stage in the judge's mind as to become utterly unendurable; and as in certain individuals painful inner experiences seek to become personified in some external object, so all this small-town gossip, this puerile mutual observation and control, seemed to concentrate itself in the person of the Apothecary Lebermann, a good-natured but essentially prosy person, possessed of an insatiable curiosity, who was interested in the whole world, and wanted to know everything—on the other hand taking for granted that others had as lively a concern about him and the experiences of his daily life.

On the day on which our story begins the judge was returning from court in rather an irritable mood, and his face darkened perceptibly as he saw the apothecary coming to meet him.

While it was, as we have said, Herr Lebermann's justifiable peculiarity to desire to know everything, and with a rare toughness of purpose to work upon his neighbour with queries until the other would fling the desired information at his head in a fit of uncontrollable indignation, the judge was the most uncommunicative of mortals. It was his intention that no one should know what he did, or where he bought his things, or with whom he kept up a correspondence—ay, even his Christian name was to him a matter of deep secrecy; in fact, a sharp altercation between him and his wife had once been brought about by no other cause than that she had failed to fully understand his feelings in this respect, and unadvisedly addressing him one day on the railroad with the harmless remark, "See the charming view, Karl!" had unmasked him before his fellow travellers.

Here these two gentlemen, as unlike as possible in their peculiarities, met upon the street, and while the judge was as nimble as an eel in trying to escape the apothecary, the latter was equally assiduous in his efforts to detain him, and opened the conversation with the apparently unnecessary question, "Coming from court so early to-day, Herr Schwarz?"

"No!" replied the judge unkindly.

"No?" repeated Herr Lebermann, in a tone of surprise. "This is the way I generally see you come. Where have you been, then?"

Apparently the judge was deaf.

"Seems to me you generally come from court at this time of day," persisted Herr Lebermann; "Ah, I see, you don't care to tell me," he added pleasantly, "but I know all about it just the same!"

"If you know it there's no need of asking," growled the judge.

"And now you're on your way home," remarked Herr Lebermann, with the blissful serenity of a man who has accomplished his purpose of knowing all about the aims and intents of other people. "I'll walk along with you a bit. I am always out for a constitutional at this time of day!"

"That's a wise thing to do!" remarked Herr Schwarz with fatal indifference.

"And when I get home I eat my sandwich," the apothecary confidentially informed him; "only one, you know, so as not to take away my appetite for dinner! By the way, that reminds me—how does it agree with you to dine so much later?"

The judge gave him a scathing look. "How do you know that I dine later than usual?" he asked indignantly.

"You see, your cook is the sister of our maid, and she told her about it. You dine at half-past two, don't you?"

"Sometimes," cried the irritated judge, struggling to control his temper; "here we are at my house—good morning, Herr Lebermann!"

"One moment!" said the apothecary, taking possession of the judge's button-hole while the latter was angrily seeking to escape; "there seems to be company at your house."

"Why?" asked Schwarz, trembling with ire—he had fetched his sister-in-law from the station twelve hours ago, long after nightfall, and had hoped that the fact of her presence was as yet unknown.

"Well, I saw your maid buy *three* little tarts at the pastry-cook's this morning," said the apothecary innocently; "she generally takes only two—so I thought, perhaps——"

The judge darted a glance of utter contempt at his companion.

"Why did you not take it for granted I might desire to eat *two* tarts to-day?" he said with alarming politeness, and then walked into the house full of wrath.

Weighty decisions were ripening within him, and the result of his deliberation became apparent as he sat down to lunch with his ladies, and suddenly delivered himself of the astonishing words: "We'll start for Berlin this evening!"

Helen dropped her fork and gazed at her husband with wide-open eyes. "This evening?"

"When I say this evening I don't mean next year," growled the paterfamilias. "That's just like a woman! Here you've always been talking and begging to go and travel—to go and leave this miserable little place for awhile, and now when I offer to go, you raise objections!"

"My dear Karl!" began his wife soothingly, "I was only taken by surprise at your sudden resolve. What can have occurred to bring it about?"

"I'm tired of this small town gossip, and more especially of the apothecary!" said Karl, energetically. "Confound it—I can't blow my nose but that Lebermann sends to inquire if I have a cold! I want to go and see what life is like in a large town, where I can go about *incognito*. I can just manage to get away over Sunday. We'll take three round-trip tickets and go to Berlin this evening. Go and pack your things!"

He folded his napkin and got up. A low exclamation from Annchen interrupted him.

"*Three?*—shall I go too?"

"HELEN WAS SOFTLY CARESSING ON ONE SIDE, HIS LITTLE SISTER-IN-LAW PATTING HIS SHOULDER ON THE OTHER."

There was such an unmistakable expression of rapture upon her charming face that a smile stole across the features of her growling brother-in-law.

"Well, I should think so," he said; "did you suppose we would leave you at home?"

"Thank you, Karl—thank you!" cried Annchen, in a state of bliss; and while Helen was softly caressing her "bear" upon one side, his little sister-in-law was patting his shoulder upon the other, crying, "Thank you, Karl,—I think you are perfectly lovely!"

"Well, you're the first person that has told me so since I was two years old," remarked the judge, whose dudgeon was melting under the beams of the rapture he had been the cause of, like snow before the summer's sun. "Now I know how to tame such shy little birds. What, Helen? Perfectly lovely, am I?"

And with a half-ironical, half-flattered shrug of his shoulders he left the room to devote himself to assiduous studies of the time-table, which to him, as to most people who rarely travel, was a book of seven seals.

The day on which this memorable resolution was formed was a cold, windy autumn day, making it imperative to choose warm clothing for the night journey. All day the ladies were occupied with putting their wearing apparel in order, which, in the face of this journey, proved to be inadequate in many respects.

"We'll buy all that in Berlin," said Helen consolingly to her sister, who was putting on her plain little straw hat with a look of deep concern, quite unconscious of the fact how charmingly becoming it was to her rosy face. The judge walked up and down in the room, casting brief remarks at his ladies from time to time. "Don't take your entire outfit along just for two or three days," he remarked warningly.

Evening came fast enough; every moment was made the most of, and when the lamps were lit there was still this and that waiting to be attended to. At the last moment—they were just sitting down to tea—a thought struck the paterfamilias; he touched the bell.

"Did you attend to what I told you this morning?" he asked the maid in his mystifying fashion.

Pauline looked at her master with no very intelligent expression in her face.

"What do you mean, sir?"

"Did you get what I told you?" queried the judge.

Pauline was silent, thereby giving most decided expression to her bewilderment.

"Why, Karl, do tell her what you mean," implored Helen; "there's no time to be lost—we must be going!"

"Very well," replied the judge discontentedly; "of course it is more than you can endure not to know what I am referring to! Did you go and fetch my fur-lined great-coat from the furrier's?"

Pauline blushed guiltily.

"Oh, dear me, I forgot all about it, sir—I'll run there now as fast as I can!"

"Yes, and you'll run back no doubt when we are in the cars," said her master contemptuously. "Well, then, I shall take my death of cold on the journey—at any rate I shall be spared the trouble of telling Lebermann just how my funeral came off!"

"Well, well, Karl," said Helen, soothing his dismal forebodings; "seems to me there might be some other way out of your difficulty. Pauline can fetch the great-coat to the station and hand it to you there. Do you understand, Pauline?"

Pauline nodded humbly and departed, while the judge arose and took up the leather bag containing the money and tickets, and enjoined his ladies to make haste. "Put on your things, children—I think the carriage is coming!"

As the party reached the station their happy mood was somewhat dampened, for Pauline and the great-coat were not in sight. All in vain did eager eyes pierce the darkness of night, and all were about to succumb to fate and take their seats in the car, when the long-expected one, like Schiller's diver, appeared breathless upon the scene, holding the coat on high, and swinging it like a triumphal banner. The judge without delay slipped into the warmer garment, and indeed it was high time, for already the conductor was slamming to the doors of the other compartments,—a sharp whistle, and the train started.

Our three travellers were in the rosiest mood imaginable. Helen, who had not set foot outside of the provincial town, which was now her home, since her marriage, pictured to herself the glories of Berlin in the brightest of hues, and Annchen dreamed vague, golden dreams, and indulged in exquisite air-castles, in which at the decisive moment her unknown hero was always seen leaning out of some window.

The judge was gleefully rubbing his hands.

"Now then—at last we are free of that miserable place," he said, making himself comfortable in his corner of the compartment. "Now let us all go to sleep and open our eyes to-morrow morning in Berlin!"

The train sped through the night air; and it was not until it had reached Berlin that the Schwarzes awoke with the proud consciousness of being in the Imperial Capital.

The judge put his somewhat dishevelled head out of the window.

"See the hurry and bustle of the crowd," he said cheerfully. "This is rather different from the streets of Solau! Here the individual disappears like a drop in the ocean, and no one knows or cares what his neighbour is about. Come, children, we must get out!"

He stretched himself with lazy ease, and took his hand-luggage down out of the net, then jumped down himself after his ladies.

"Look you, there's not a person knows us here," he continued; "we can do exactly as we please for three days—it's like being at a grand masquerade!"

"Good morning, Herr Judge!" a voice cried at that moment behind him. "Shall I fetch you a cab?"

The addressed started perceptibly. A porter quite unknown to himself or his ladies stood before him and held out his hand for the luggage, with a peculiar, knowing smile upon his features, then quickly piled them upon his back with skilful dexterity.

"How do you know who I am?" asked the judge, somewhat irritated at this unexpected violation of his *incognito*.

His unknown friend, however, had already turned upon his heel in search of a cab, and was now storing his burden upon the top.

A glorious autumn morning was dawning over town, and the unknown splendour before them beckoned invitingly to our unsophisticated friends.

"Look here, Karl," began Helen, who had meanwhile conferred with Annchen as to their mutual wishes, "what do you say to going on foot to the hotel? As we are only to be here for so short a time, we should make the most of every moment, and seems to me, after last night's journey, a walk would be much more refreshing to us than a ride in a close cab!"

"Oh, yes!" cried Annchen, whose beaming eyes gazed upon the new world of wonders as a child might gaze upon fairyland.

"All right, go a-head!" replied the judge, whom the air of the metropolis had suddenly changed into a jovial fellow. "I'll run and buy a map of Berlin, and then join you!"

He paid for the cab while the ladies were walking slowly a-head, and gave a fee to make sure that the charioteer would safely deposit the trunks at the hotel; but as he was turning back to the station to buy the map the cab-driver called out—

"Thank you kindly, Herr Judge!"

That good gentleman was perceptibly taken aback; he cast a suspicious glance behind him,—there stood the porter who had addressed him in like manner, and the two men were grinning diabolically.

"Aha," said the judge to himself, "that fellow noticed

that his foolish speech vexed me, and now they are having a laugh at me in company. I suppose that's Berlin humour, and it has got to be endured!"

In possession of a Berlin town-map, which rivalled a moderate-sized bed-screen in size, the judge hastened to join his ladies, who had been caught by a shop window in the Friedrichstrasse as securely as flies caught in a fly-trap.

"That's right," said the judge indulgently, "take your time looking at these things. Where you are as utterly unknown as we are here, there is no harm in looking at show-windows."

He thereupon gave the objects in the window a close inspection.

"Well, Herr Schwarz, what is it that's taking your fancy?" suddenly cried a shrill voice, and a shoemaker's apprentice with undisguised mirth in his rogue's visage slipped by him laughing.

The judge was speechless.

"This is getting worse and worse!" he exclaimed; "there's something wrong here! Come, children, this is positively uncanny. This looks like the artful device of some scoundrel. Let us hurry up and go to the hotel. The next time any one calls me Herr Judge or Herr Schwarz, it will be the worse for him!"

The sisters were growing nervous also.

"Yes, yes," assented Helen, "we'll go to the hotel—it is very unpleasant here in the streets! I don't understand how it is, Karl," she added; "you must bear a striking resemblance to some popular town celebrity, whose name happens to be Schwarz into the bargain!"

"And who happens to be a judge as well?" asked Karl sarcastically. "That's very probable, my child! I have always said that no sooner do you set out to have a good time than immediately something occurs to frustrate your plans!"

They had walked on, eagerly discussing the possible cause of this unusual occurrence, and suddenly they discovered that they had lost their bearings.

"Where are we, anyway?" asked Annchen with a trembling voice. "I thought we were to be in Unter den Linden by this time?"

"That is so, Karl," added Helen; "you are taking us nobody knows where! These streets are not at all attractive, and I am tired out!"

Karl forthwith produced his tremendous map of the town.

"Wait one moment," he said with dignity; "I'll tell you immediately."

And he then and there unfolded the enormous sheet. A playful morning wind, however, mercilessly jerked it hither and thither, and there was nothing for it but to beg the ladies to stand on either side as banner-holders, and help him save it from destruction. But it took Karl longer than he thought to find his way about, and while he was still engaged in the effort, a tall, elegant-looking man walked down the street, and, with evident amusement, glanced at the conspicuous group, especially noting the charming person of little Annchen. The face of the stranger wore a pleasant, good-humoured expression, and, moreover, was so handsome and attractive that there was no perceptible reason why Annchen, raising her eyes at that moment, should suddenly blush to the roots of her hair, her hand at the same time trembling so that she could scarcely hold the map over which Karl and Helen were still chanting a woful duet in search of their hotel.

The stranger, evidently struck by the appearance of the lovely, embarrassed girl, walked on slowly and then turned and came back. There was undisguised merriment and a half-controlled laugh upon his lips as he passed around behind Karl and before the fair banner-holders.

"Good morning, Herr Judge Schwarz," he said, taking

his hat off low to the ladies, and turned to pass on his way.

But he had reckoned without his host. In a paroxysm of rage the judge darted after him.

"Sir, what does this mean? How do you know my name and title?" he cried, panting with indignation, while Helen vainly tried to appease him.

Karl shook off her hand impatiently.

"How can you have the effrontery to address me by my name?" he repeated in a tone of thunder.

"My dear sir," replied the stranger, laughing, "if your name is to be kept secret, allow me to call your attention to the fact that it would be the part of wisdom not to wear it plainly upon your back!"

Karl gazed upon the stranger in speechless astonishment. Helen turned her husband dexterously around. Ah, here was the solution of the riddle! That benighted furrier had forgotten, in the press of business, to remove the slip of paper from the judge's great-coat, by which that valuable garment had been distinguished from others entrusted to his keeping, and poor Karl had been walking about for an hour in Berlin with an enormous placard on his back bearing the inscription, "Herr Judge Schwarz!"

While Helen and Anna were occupied in removing this enemy of the much-desired *incognito* from the back of their liege lord and master, Annchen found time to whisper to her sister, "That was Kurt!"

"Nonsense!" cried Helen in surprise, now giving Karl's tormentor a scrutinising glance, while the latter was vainly endeavouring to pacify the enraged Karl—more likely, I regret to say, for the sake of the pretty damsel than for brotherly love. But Karl was obstinate, and would have nothing to do with forgiveness, and even the kind offer of the unknown to show him the way had no further effect than to extract a surly reply, "You may, for all I care!"

"WALKING ABOUT FOR AN HOUR IN BERLIN WITH A PLACARD ON HIS BACK."

"We want to go to the R—— Hotel," added the judge reluctantly, "if you know where that is?"

The stranger laughed again.

"Oh yes, I know perfectly well," he said; "it is not at all out of my way, if you will allow me to escort you there."

"No, thank you," said Karl curtly; "just tell me the way to go. My bump of locality is very well developed, but in this confounded town there's no finding one's way about."

"Allow me to mention my name," said the stranger after he had given brief directions as to the way, lifting his hat.

"Don't trouble yourself, thank you," growled the judge; "it is not my habit to make acquaintances upon the street. Come along, children."

And after a brief and not very reassuring farewell to the young man, he gave an arm to each of his ladies, and drew them along after him.

The stranger, thus brusquely dismissed, looked after the three departing figures for a moment, gave a low whistle, and went on his way still laughing.

Meanwhile Helen, touched by the look of disappointment on her sister's face, had smartly reproached her husband for showing so little politeness to the stranger.

"I don't understand you, Karl," she said. "How could you be so rude to the young man? It was only too natural that, under the circumstances, he indulged in the harmless joke of addressing you!"

"The impudence of it!" cried Karl in a rage.

"In fact, you ought to be grateful to him," Helen added boldly, "for without him and his explanation you would still be walking about with the slip on your back, like a book from the circulating library. The young fellow looked very nice!" Karl stood stock-still.

"I'll tell you what, children," he said energetically, "now leave me in peace about your unknown friend! That's the way all women are—that's what a woman's opinion is worth! Looked nice, did he? And such creatures are all for equality with men! If you are on the jury, and a convicted murderer has blue calf's eyes, every one of you would acquit him! I'd have you to know that it is my firm conviction the man was a sharper!"

"Shame on you, Karl!" cried Anna, her just ire getting the better of her shyness. Her hero a sharper,—this was too bad!

Her brother-in-law gave her a penetrating look.

"What business is it of yours, if I may be permitted to ask?"

"Annchen has seen him at D——!" said Helen, endeavouring to hide her sister's embarrassment.

"What?" asked Karl suspiciously, "you know the fellow? What's his name?"

That, as we know, was a very inconvenient question. That the unknown was called Kurt would scarcely suffice to satisfy the judge by way of personal information, and that was all Annchen knew about him. So she was silent, and confined herself to blushing once more, which, however pretty it might look, could scarcely be regarded as a satisfactory explanation, at least not to this unsentimental brother-in-law and judge.

"Aha!" said Karl, with a lordly air, "you are so well acquainted that you do not so much as know his name! Take my word for it, the man was a sharper—that is my firm opinion. Such fellows always look very elegant and well-bred. Not another word about him!"

Meanwhile they had safely reached the hotel, and it was time to yield to the imperious need for rest and sleep. This, to be sure, was not indulged in for long, for excitement and the wish to enjoy Berlin to the full soon drove the pleasure-seekers out again.

In the dining-room the question, "What now?" was

discussed at length by the couple, while Annchen listened to everything that was proposed with unmistakable indifference. To her Berlin had grown to be nothing but an enormous frame to hold the likeness of the adorable, who had crossed her path once more this morning in so surprising a fashion, and, alas! seemed utterly unconscious of the fact that he had ever seen her before.

The unknown, whom we will herewith introduce to our readers as Dr. Rüdiger, had meanwhile also reached the R—— Hotel, at which he too, as good luck would have it, had put up.

Himself unnoticed, he observed how the judge and his ladies, after a short parley with the *portier*, left the hotel, and no sooner had they turned the next corner than he too approached that personage.

"Has Herr Judge Schwarz gone out already?" he asked nonchalantly.

"Yes, sir, Herr Schwarz and the ladies have just gone," replied the *portier*, who in his person united the dignity of a Spanish grandee with eely suavity.

"That's too bad!" remarked the wily Rüdiger. "We were going to make an engagement for this evening!"

"Herr Schwarz ordered tickets to the opera for to-morrow night," said the *portier*.

"Ah! that's capital," replied Rüdiger. "You may procure a ticket for me in the same box; I will come and ask you for it."

He walked away cheerfully, and patiently did the principal sights of Berlin, in the secret hope that fortune would favour him and bring about a meeting between him and the Schwarz family. But for the present this hope came to naught.

Meanwhile our party had set out on their trip of pleasure. First they had devoted themselves to show-windows, and with many an admiring ejaculation had come to the conclusion that Berlin was the only place worth sojourning in. Then they pantingly followed two closed Imperial carriages, and endeavoured to make each other believe that they had caught a sight of the persons within. Finally, after the museum had been hurried through with profound awe and moderate comprehension, they all experienced decided pangs of hunger, and, with the intention of dining cosily together, they entered a superb restaurant on the ground floor.

The judge escorted his ladies to an inviting little table near one of the windows, from where one had a fine view of the streets and the busy crowds—not, to be sure, with the additional advantage mentioned in the well-known song—

> "Across the lands we gaze, oh!
> While we are all unseen——,"

for every glass of wine and every forkful of meat could be closely scrutinised by the passers-by.

But the pleasing knowledge of being quite unknown comforted the judge for this drawback of his position.

The waiter's question as to what they wished to have for dinner might have appeared as an insult to the judge in his exceeding love of secrecy; being, however, very hungry he generously forgave him, and the three together assiduously studied the *menu*, which sported a variety of names which might have been made to stand for almost *anything*, so that whatever one ordered there was always a pleasant surprise in view.

Soon a bottle with a promising silvery cork stood upon the table in a dainty cooler, and the judge was just raising his glass to drink the ladies' health: "Children," he said, "I can't tell you how delightful this is, to feel that one is sitting here free of all good friends and neighbours. Here's to our *incognito!*"

There was a playful tap at the window. Karl, poor

fellow, started as if he had beheld a ghost —indeed I know not but a ghost even would have been a more welcome sight at that particular moment than the smiling face of Herr Lebermann, who, with the unmistakable consciousness of giving the judge and his family a great and

"THE SMILING FACE OF HERR LEBERMANN."

unexpected pleasure, pressed his nose flat against the window-pane.

The judge dropped his fork. "For heaven's sake-- Lebermann!" he stammered with difficulty.

A further critical remark was suppressed, for the good

Lebermann, with a happy smile upon his face, stood before our pleasure-seekers.

"Well now, you'd never have supposed you'd find me here, would you?" he asked, full of rapture.

"No—that is the last thing I should have thought of," replied Karl mildly. "What brought you here?"

"I'll tell you all about it in a minute," replied Herr Lebermann, having given a chivalrous greeting to the ladies and proved himself thoroughly well-informed by looking at Annchen with the words, "Ah, this, I suppose, is your visitor that came the other night!"

He drew a chair up to the table and ordered a beef-steak.

The judge looked about him wildly, and was apparently so greatly in danger of indulging in unwary remarks, that Helen, to avert the storm, imprudently reminded the apothecary of his promised narrative.

"Well, you see," began the interesting arrival, "I noticed some time ago that there was something wrong with my molar tooth—the third in the upper row," he added, to expel every doubt. "I believe I mentioned it to you once, Herr Judge?"

"It's quite possible!" sighed Karl brokenly.

"Yes, yes, I remember it quite well! We were sitting at König's in the restaurant—it is not very long ago! Well, never mind! So, then, the day before yesterday, in the afternoon, that tooth began to hurt me."

"Too bad!" said Helen pitifully, feeling it incumbent upon her to say something polite.

"It wasn't very bad," said Herr Lebermann consolingly, "but still I felt it, you know! Yesterday, in the morning, the head-man had left open the back-door to the shop, and then there is always a draught; you have no idea how it blows. Time and time again I have said to him: 'Herr Semmler,' says I, 'don't leave that back-door unlatched,' but he can't get over the habit! You will say, you wouldn't be put upon!"

He looked at his victims expectantly.

"I don't say any such thing!" growled Karl, his soul burning within him. "Hurry up, children—we must be going!"

"I shall be through in a minute," said Herr Lebermann. "Where did I stop? Ah yes, I know! That miserable Semmler. When I tell him courteously it has no effect, and I don't like to be curt to him, for he is a decent enough fellow, and it's hard to find such another nowadays. He is quite to be depended upon. He has a little property too——"

"Yes, but Herr Lebermann," interrupted Helen, who already saw her husband in spirit rush at him with a knife, "you were going to tell us what brought you to Berlin!"

Herr Lebermann cut up his beef-steak with much deliberation.

"I was just about to tell you," he said with a courteous bow to Helen. "Well, you see, last night the door was left open again. I was somewhat heated. I had on a heavy over-coat,—perhaps I had walked faster than usual,—I shouldn't at all wonder if I had!—I entered the shop—and there was a tremendous draught! You really have no idea how bad it was—and at that very moment my tooth was at it again! I was quite beside myself, went upstairs to talk to my wife. It is really very convenient to have our lodgings in the same house now. 'Clara!' says I, 'my tooth!' 'The one that was stopped?' says she. 'Yes,' says I. Do you know my Clara, Frau Schwarz?"

Helen gave an affirmative nod—she felt her eyelids growing heavy. Karl nervously drummed on the table, and Annchen was the only one who was not bored, for she was looking out upon the street in feverish excitement, hoping to catch a glimpse of her unknown hero, and hearing never a word that was spoken about her.

"Well," continued Lebermann, "my wife, resolute as she is, said 'Lebermann'—she always calls me Lebermann now, since our youngest is not called Fatty any more, but Robert, and you know my name is Robert too, and there was everlasting confusion—Robert—Robert—there was no knowing which Robert was meant. Well, to make a long story short, she said, 'Lebermann,' says she, 'this is a serious matter. You'd best go to the right man at once!' No sooner said than done. I went and got a round-trip ticket—took the cars—came here—went to the dentist the first thing this morning—and now I'm free of all that, and I have had the rare good fortune of meeting you! This is delightful—really delightful!"

"So it is," said Karl, who was on the utmost verge of human endurance. "And now we must be going! Good-day to you, Herr Lebermann!"

"Where do you put up?" asked the apothecary.

"Nowhere as yet," lied Karl, with a bold brow, appeasing his conscience with the thought that they had not yet spent a night at the hotel. "Waiter—what's to pay?"

"And where shall we meet again?" asked this kind neighbour, who seemed fully determined to dog the steps of his countrymen like a fearful nightly apparition.

"Well, that's the last thing—I mean to say we haven't any definite plans as yet," said Karl, taking his hat from the hook, while the ladies, much cast down by the turn their happily-begun travels had taken, were also getting ready to go.

Ännchen was struggling with her mantelet, when suddenly she heard a very engaging voice behind her: "Permit me to be of assistance," and Dr. Rüdiger stood before the group with the happiest face in the world.

As far as the judge's expression at that particular moment

was concerned, it is only to be regretted that there was no photographer on the spot. He gave the uncalled helper a crushing look, offered his arm to his wife, beckoned Ännchen to his side, and without a word, bowed coldly to Lebermann and left the restaurant.

This was really too bad! After several hours' chase Rüdiger had at last succeeded in finding his lovely heroine once more, and at that very moment she was taken from him again. The only straw of refuge for him to cling to was Herr Lebermann, whom he had found in the company of the Schwarz family, and who might therefore be expected to give him some information.

"The judge was in a great hurry," he said, turning with an assumed air of placidity to the apothecary, who at once made room for the new-comer at his table.

"Yes, that's just like my friend Schwarz," he said deliberately, "he's always excited—always on the go. I'm not at all like him. I am much more quiet, and that's the very reason we get on so famously! My wife always says: 'Lebermann,'—my name is Lebermann, Apothecary Lebermann, from Solau——"

"Dr. Rüdiger!" remarked his new friend with a bow.

"Happy to meet you! Well, my wife says: 'Lebermann, you are the most imperturbable man I ever saw.' So you know my friend Schwarz, Dr. Rüdiger? Ah, by the way, I did not understand exactly whether he has found a hotel—do you know where he is staying?"

"At the R—— Hotel," replied Rüdiger innocently, thereby doing the worst service he could to the family to which he wished to make himself agreeable.

"Ah, I am glad to hear it; I shall go and order a room immediately," said Lebermann joyously; "he will be so pleased, I know."

The judge and his ladies had taken up their wanderings again not in the best of spirits. The fact that the world is round had never struck them as so vexatious as now, when, in consequence of this dire roundness, Herr Lebermann was always rolling towards them.

"What with this bad luck we are having," remarked the judge bitterly, "it's quite likely the fellow will cross our path again. After to-day's experience I am confident I could climb up on Mount Vesuvius to escape from men, and when I reach the top the volcano would be sure to spit out Lebermann. Hello! where are we now?" he added discontentedly. "We are always losing our way in this wretched town. In this respect really I prefer Solau!"

He disappeared once more behind his large map and began to search diligently for his hotel, or rather for the street that it was in.

A small street urchin, with a bright, saucy face, at this moment came singing and skipping along the side-walk. At sight of the deeply-absorbed family an expression of unalloyed bliss passed over his face, and with the exclamation, "Who lives behind there?" he put his finger straight through the map; thereupon he took flight with a perfect shriek of laughter ere the judge had recovered from his consternation sufficiently to take up the chase with any hope of success.

Helen and Annchen looked at their protector with some misgivings, in the uneasy expectation of seeing him beside himself with ire; but, lo and behold, he was quite the contrary! Herr Schwarz, who had been steadily regarding the injured map, strangely enough looked very well pleased, and taking a deep breath he said, "This *is* a good thing, now--if the lad hasn't punched a hole in the spot I have always had such a deal of trouble to find. This really simplifies matters greatly."

Hans Arnold.

THE INNER LIFE OF THE SECOND-CLASS CAB-DRIVER.

"A WRITER who would describe things that he has not seen with his own eyes is a feeble rhapsodist; his characters are unreal, and his productions will never touch the hearts of his readers!" Amen! My friend Otto put his glass down on the table with such vehemence that the red wine in it spattered on the table-cloth. I am very shy by nature; people who talk loud and set down their glass energetically, looking at me at the same time, as much as to say, "Any objections?" always awe me. That is the reason my friend Otto awed me. We sat opposite at the table in the Italian wine-room; while he was speaking he looked firmly at me; there was no doubt of it, he counted me in with these blameworthy authors. Our other friends who sat at table with us gazed at me in silence; it was evident that I was expected to say a weighty word in self-defence. I myself felt it incumbent upon me,—but unfortunately nothing appropriate occurred to me. After a lengthy pause I mildly remarked, "Quite true, one should dip down into the fulness of human life." My friend Otto laughed scornfully into his glass, our friends gave me a look of pity—I had undoubtedly made a fool of myself.

At the same time, the words of my friend Otto would never have made such an impression upon me if my conscience had not troubled me. A plan was ripening within me for a great social novel, delineating the life of the lower classes in Berlin. Realism—that was my programme. In spirit I saw my likeness in all the illustrated papers; behind my name I read, "The German Zola," in a parenthesis. I had not yet fully decided upon the contents of the novel; but so much was sure, the hero should be a second-class cab-driver,—if that didn't take, I didn't know what would.

"KEPT ME WAITING AT THE DOOR WHILE HE WAS AMUSING HIMSELF WITH HIS ADORED."

As I was walking home, I was tortured with tormenting doubts called forth by the words of my friend. "So you would delineate a second-class cab-driver?" I said to myself "What do you know about a second-class cab-driver? That in summer he wears a coat trimmed with galloons, and a cocked hat, and in winter a mantle, high boots lined with straw, and a fur cap—everybody knows that. But have you ever listened to the conversation with which at the stopping-places he makes time pass for himself and his colleagues? Have you ever followed him into the gin-shops where he refreshes himself with a glass of half-and-half and a sandwich? Do you know aught about his likes and dislikes? Or of the mutual relation between him and his horse? In a word, have you any knowledge of the inner life of a second-class cab-driver? Be honest with yourself, you have none; and here you are going to write a social novel about him! Well I never!" The last word I said half-audibly to myself while I was opening the street-door in a very ill humour.

I did not sleep well that night. I was perpetually pondering over the inner life of the second-class cab-driver.

When I arose, sighing, the next morning, I perceived that I should accomplish nothing by going on in this way, and I resolved to devote myself to practical studies. Armed with my note-book, I stepped out into the street.

It was a glorious spring morning, but I was indifferent to the fact; my eyes were riveted upon second-class cabs and their charioteers. At the next corner there was a stopping-place for six such; my heart beat faster as I beheld them. Heretofore these fellows had appeared to me in the light of ordinary mortals; now it struck me that there was a sly smile upon their faces, as if they were conscious of the fact of possessing something which they would take care not to divulge—the inner life of the second-class cab-driver.

I jumped into the foremost cab; it was open, and

sported cushions of red plush. The driver sat nodding upon the box, and for the present his inner life was hidden by the sound of a tremendous snoring.

"Thou shalt be my hero!" spoke a voice within me. After some fruitless efforts, I at last succeeded in waking him. I named some street at random, where he was to take me, and resolved to enter into conversation with him.

"Been on many trips to-day?" I asked in a winning voice, while he was putting his horse in motion. He did not seem to hear me, at least he paid no attention to my remark.

"Been on many trips to-day?" I repeated, still more pleasantly.

He turned his head about. "You're right there," he said. "It's a double trip."

I was taken back by this unexpected result of my speech. "Double trip?" I asked.

"Well, don't you believe it?" he asked indignantly. I was vexed that I had unwisely entered upon a double trip, and subsided.

"Pronounced faculty for justice," I put down in my notebook, "which occasionally amounts to unbending doggedness." As the note seemed too scant, I added, "Brusque and uncommunicative."

We had reached a part of the town which offered no possible attractions to me; so there was nothing for it but to drive back again. I jumped into the first cab I saw, and as I was just about to open conversation with the driver I perceived that it was a first-class cab. What was a first-class cab-driver to me? Besides, it cost me a shilling. I was terribly vexed with myself.

I now resolved to be more cautious in my choice of cabs. Long I strolled about the streets, keeping an eye on all the stopping-places I passed, until at last I beheld a young second-class cab-driver, who, as soon as he saw my gaze fixed upon him, leaped with jerky haste upon his box.

"At last," I said to myself while getting in, "this is a genuine wide-awake Berlin cab-driver, such as I want."

I tested his conversational powers with two or three casual remarks—my efforts were crowned with success. I told him to drive to the Thiergarten, as the most favourable place to listen undisturbed to his communications.

As we were jolting along the streets I silently gazed at my charioteer, who was enthroned with more audacity than grace side-wise upon his box, so that I could see his profile; I noticed certain dark shadows in his face, which looked as if he had inadvertently come into close contact with a bootbrush.

As soon as we had reached the shady precincts of the Thiergarten the sluices of his eloquence were opened, and indeed this worthy youth repaid me for all that I had heretofore missed.

"How is business going on?" I asked.

"Well, it's only just going so-so," he replied, "but up to last week it was going fine; we've had the whole town to sweep."

"Sweep?" I asked, somewhat puzzled.

"Well yes, you see," he said, "that's because all winter folks had to sit at home and have a fire, and now, you see, it's warm again——."

"Aha,—I understand," I interrupted; a rare point this for my note-book : "The second-class cab-driver manifests a surprising aptitude for simile; when the awaking springtime entices men to leave their dark houses and entrust themselves to his vehicle, he expresses this by saying that he has swept the whole town."

In the joy of my heart I offered him a cigar; he did not decline, at the same time remarking that he preferred snuff to tobacco, which, as he said, was better adapted to his calling.

Again I opened my note-book: "The second-class cab-driver does not disdain tobacco, preferring however to indulge in snuff."

"You see," I said, after having secured this important fact in writing for all future times, "how it is always well to open one's eyes to learn new things; up to this day I have never seen a cab-driver use snuff."

"Oh, as for them fellows——," he replied, shrugging his shoulders, "why should they snuff? I was talking about our business."

"How so?" I stammered, with a puzzled look. He leaned down to me. "I'm only taking this cab out to-day, because my father don't feel just right; the old hurdle belongs to him."

The trees in the Thiergarten began to dance before my very eyes.

"What is your calling?" I shrieked in mortal agony. With a smile he looked down upon me: "I'm a chimney-sweep," he said.

"Stop!" I called out to him in a voice of thunder; "I want to get out here!"

That afternoon I returned to my rooms with a bowed head; I had the feeling that everybody must know I had been out riding with a chimney-sweep.

As I entered the house I noticed that there was a gate-way beside the street-door bearing the inscription: "Cabs and carriages by the hour." I had only lived in that particular house for a few days, and so had paid no attention to this before. Now, as my eyes were resting thoughtfully upon this sign, I made the observation that it is in hours of deep contrition that the soul of man ripens to grand purposes; for a thought arose within me, the boldness of which almost made me grow dizzy.

In my unhappy experience with the chimney-sweep I had seen that one can be a cab-driver on time,—how would it be if for twenty-four hours I myself were to fill such a post?

I seized my hat, so that the sacred fire of my first decision should not be cooled off by pedantic considerations, entered the yard below, and the office of the cab-owner.

At first he was little inclined to favour my plan; then gradually it dawned upon him that I should certainly be a very cheap cab-driver, who would cost him nothing, and moreover put thirty shillings into his pocket, a sum which I then and there counted upon the table. He began to treat me with a certain air of gentle indulgence, such as one bestows upon a person who is not fully in his right mind, and whom it is best not to irritate. One favourable circumstance was that he had just had a new coat and a new pair of trousers made for one of his drivers; provided these garments fitted me, I should put them on to-morrow. As far as the hat was concerned, he would let me take the one belonging to Gustav, the driver whose place I was to take.

"So then,—to-morrow morning at five o'clock," he said, "right here in the yard!"

"I shall be here to-morrow morning at five o'clock," I replied with an easy air, as if it were a daily habit of mine to get up at five. I was turning to go, when he called after me, "But you must leave your eye-glasses at home!" and he pointed to my nose; "that will never do for a cab-driver!"

"You are right," I rejoined; "I shall get me a pair of steel spectacles."

With that I left him, and partook myself to a masquerade-shop, where I procured a large beard to cover the lower part of my face, and a wig; beside my original object of disguising myself as far as possible, the thought of Gustav's cocked hat made a special head-gear seem desirable. Beard and wig were sprinkled with grey, and must needs give me an air of homely dignity. In the shop of an optician I completed my outfit, looking through his entire stock of clumsy, old-fashioned spectacles. I could not find the desired steel spectacles, but there was a pair of horn ones with enormous circular glasses, by means of which my face gained an owl-like expression. That was what I wanted. Putting my treasures in my pocket, I stepped out upon the street, very well satisfied with myself. The energetic way in which I had seized upon this great enterprise pleased me; all my arrangements struck me as being exceedingly practical; I had a happy presentiment as to the success of my undertaking; this success I involuntarily carried into my thoughts of the novel that was to be, and I began to conjecture what remuneration I should demand. "I can't let you have it cheap, gentlemen," I said half-audibly with a triumphant smile, as I opened the door of the wine-room where I expected to meet my friends.

To evade every possibility of being recognised by them, I meant to tell them that I should be going out of town to-morrow.

This part of my programme also ran off smoothly. My friend Otto and all my other friends were present, and while my heart was leaping within me for proud joy over my new-discovered talent for adventure, I unfolded my fictitious plan of travel as coolly as possible.

The only person who seemed to be interested was my friend Otto.

"Going out of town?" he said. "Is it certain?"

"Quite certain," I replied; "I shall be leaving to-morrow morning."

"Where to?"

"Humph—a short trip to the country—to visit some relatives."

"For how long?" he queried further.

"That depends; two or three days at the most." It was really strange that he should be so inquisitive—and withal there was a peculiar look in his eyes. "He can't know?" I asked myself involuntarily, but I did not complete my sentence. "That is all nonsense," I said to myself; "he doesn't even know anything about the novel—how could he guess anything?" Indeed, he seemed quite satisfied at last, and when I had left them all I walked home with the consciousness that things were going finely.

"Are you the gentleman?" asked a deep, grumbling voice, when in the grey dawn of morning I entered the yard next morning.

Without breakfast, for I had not wished to betray myself to my landlady, with a false beard on my face and a wig on my head, and an enormous pair of horn spectacles on my nose—my feelings can readily be imagined. And with all that I felt it incumbent upon me to feign a cheerful manner to keep Gustav—for I judged him to be the possessor of the bass voice—in good spirits.

"The weather will be gorgeous to-day," I said, apparently in the best of humour, while my teeth were chattering with cold. Gustav grunted like a bear disturbed in his winter's sleep.

"Can I put on the things?" I asked.

Gustav pointed to the office. "In there," he said; "I'll be hitching up while you're about it."

Soon after I came forth attired as a cab-driver.

In the middle of the yard stood the cab with a horse before it, which in the light of early dawn looked like some antediluvian animal. Gustav was occupied with the harness, and seemed disinclined to take notice of me.

"Here we are," I said in a tone of assumed gaiety, which was not at all in keeping with my inmost mood. I seemed unspeakably ridiculous to myself.

Gustav looked at me askance, and made some inarticulate

ejaculation. His conduct was not particularly encouraging. Upon the box I saw some sort of a receptacle with an open top.

"Aha," I said, stepping up to it, "I presume this is the fodder-chest?"

Gustav looked at the receptacle and then at me. "That there?" he said; "sure, that's my hat."

"Ah, so——" I stammered in embarrassment; "your hat? Permit me."

It was with strange feelings that I took the hat from the box and held it in my hand.

"Number twelve thirty-two," said Gustav laconically.

"Twelve thirty-two," I repeated. It was the first time in my life that I felt I had a number.

"At noon you have to feed him the first time," Gustav informed me.

"Feed whom?" I asked involuntarily; my thoughts were occupied with the hat, and I thought that was what he was referring to.

Gustav seemed to consider it beneath him to answer my insipid question.

"Between four and five," he continued, "he gets his fodder again; do you know how to go to work to feed a horse?"

He held the nose-bag in his hands and looked at me as if he had strong doubts as to my efficiency.

"I have sometimes seen it done at the stopping-places," I replied dejectedly, "but we might as well make a trial."

"Well, then, go ahead," he said, handing the receptacle to me.

It was with some difficulty that I got the strap which held the bag adjusted around the horse's neck; Gustav stood behind me with a critical air.

"That ain't right," he said; "take the bit out first."

He now showed me how to take the bit out of the horse's mouth, and then made me do it.

The horse put his nose in the bag, and when he observed that there was nothing in it, he shook his ears, as much as to say, "I don't think much of such practical jokes!" The horse seemed to share his master's opinion of me, for Gustav was anything but satisfied, as his grunting tones proved.

"Well now, go ahead!" he said at last, scanning me once more from head to foot. From under the seat he produced a dark bundle, which upon being unfolded proved to be his mantle; he thereupon proceeded to put it around my shoulders.

"Bless us! This is heavy," I said, groaning under the burden.

As I seized the lines Gustav imparted his final instructions. "Here is the check," he said, putting a piece of metal with the number of my cab into my hand; "now drive to the Schlesische Bahnhof and wait there; maybe you'll get a job when the early train comes in. Give the check to the policeman; do you understand?"

"Yes, yes," I said; "I have often arrived by that station myself."

"And then when you're ready to start give him a good whack with your whip," he continued.

"Whom?" I was about to ask once more, for I thought he was still talking of the policeman, but fortunately I suppressed my dulness.

"For when he has been standing awhile," explained Gustav, "the nag gets awfully lazy and his bones get stiff; but when he's going he does very well, and then all you have to do is to let him jog along."

"Very well," I said, seizing the whip, which he handed to me; "I'll do precisely as you say."

Gustav opened the gateway preparatory to setting out. I jerked the reins and called out—"Go along!"

The steed in my cab, however, did not pay the least attention to my manipulations; so far as I could see, he had fallen asleep again.

I now began to belabour his back with the whip; even that was but half successful; he gave a little shrug of disdain, and stood still as if fastened to the ground.

"You must hit around further to the front!" cried Gustav from the gate; "he don't feel anything on his back any more!"

So I whipped him on the neck, but, lo and behold, he did not seem to approve of such treatment. He threw his head back, shook his ears as much as to say, "Have the goodness to desist from such foolishness!" And when I paid no attention to his objections, he suddenly lifted his hinder part and "thump" went his hoofs against the cab, making me shake and tremble upon my box.

Now Gustav came walking up to me slowly.

"Give it to me," he said, taking the whip out of my hand; "I'll have a talk with him."

The way Gustav "talked to him" seemed to make a decided impression upon the steed, for before I knew it he started in a canter, so that I was obliged to seize the reins convulsively in both hands.

"My hat," I shrieked, for I felt that the cocked hat was parting company with my head in a graceful curve. It was not until I was out on the street that I succeeded in quieting the excited nag.

"Dear me, this—is—a—malicious beast!" I called out breathless to Gustav, who was running after us with the hat and whip.

"He's only a bit ticklish," he replied consolingly.

I replaced the cocked hat upon the spot assigned to it. Gustav turned to go.

I passed along the quiet streets with my vehicle on the way to the Schlesische Bahnhof. I now had time to examine my steed more closely. He was white, with a tinge of yellow, corresponding to the colour a white beard assumes if its owner frequently moistens it with beer.

"THE WAY GUSTAV 'TALKED TO HIM' SEEMED TO MAKE A DECIDED IMPRESSION UPON THE STEED."

So we reached the Schlesische Bahnhof, where I joined the row of waiting cabs.

I had now reached my first station, and I sat upon my

box with attentive ears, so that no word of the conversation of my new colleagues should escape me.

For the present there was little hope of accomplishing my purpose, for the only thing I heard was a grand snoring-chorus—the assembled drivers were making up for their interrupted morning's sleep.

I tried to reason myself into the belief that the situation was very original and interesting, but the thought of my orphaned bed at home, and its discarded warmth and softness, would not be banished, and all at once the consciousness that I was cold and hungry and bored beyond endurance was borne in upon me with unrelenting sternness.

A vender of small sausages appeared upon the scene, and, although under ordinary circumstances the possibility of horse-meat would have caused me to abstain, I hastily came down from my box and purchased a pair of his charges.

"Can you give me some paper," I said, "to wrap them up in?"

The sausage-man looked at me in surprise. "Bless my buttons," he said,—"paper?"

I perceived that I was betraying myself. So I turned quickly away, and seeing the policeman at that moment, I handed him my check. Then I scrambled up on the box once more, and devoured the sausages. I thereupon moved into a corner of the box, wrapped myself up close in my mantle, and fell asleep. A tremendous uproar awoke me. The train had arrived; the cabs from the right and left were set in rattling motion; in the portico stood a man bellowing, 'One thousand two hundred and thirty-two," at the top of his voice. He seemed to have been occupied in this way for some time, for his face was purple with the exertion.

"Very good," I said, smiling to myself; "there is a passenger who can't find his cab; probably it will come to an altercation between him and the driver, and some of the most characteristic of Berlin phrases and expressions will

"IN THE PORTICO STOOD A MAN BELLOWING, 'ONE THOUSAND TWO HUNDRED AND THIRTY-TWO!'"

come to light. Novelist, prick up your ears; don't let anything escape you."

"One thousand two hundred and thirty-two!" called out the man once more. I looked at him closely; he seemed to be a travelling merchant; a medley of trunks, bandboxes, and travelling-bags were lying about him on the ground.

I looked about me smiling. "One thousand two hundred and thirty-two seems to be sleeping as sweetly as need be," I said to myself.

At that moment a voice struck my ear: "Twelve thirty-two—what's the matter, old noodle-head? Are you sitting on your ears?"

Quick as a flash I turned around. One of the small boys that hang around stations to help passengers find their cabs had pulled open the door of my cab.

My stars! It occurred to me then that I myself was number one thousand two hundred and thirty-two.

Before I had time to reprove the impudent lad, the passenger, who was quite blue in the face, began to fly at me.

"Look ye here," he cried in a loud voice, "it's likely you left your ears at home! Here I've been standing an hour injuring my lungs by yelling out your confounded number!"

I was trembling with rage. "Sir," I said, inclining my head to him from my box, "I must politely request you to address me in a more befitting manner!"

"I don't want any of your impudence," bellowed the azure-hued merchant. "It's your business to prick up your ears, that's all; and if you don't do it, I'll ask you to accompany me to the police-station!"

My blood was boiling with indignation, and, what was worse, I dared not reply, for fear my language would betray me.

"Boys, fetch my things!" the merchant called out to the

lads who were clustering about, and all the trunks, handbags, and bandboxes were set in motion.

Meanwhile my colleagues—as many of them as had not driven away—gathered about us, and I now heard my fill of the peculiarities of the Berlin vernacular that I had previously longed for.

"Better put your spectacles on your ears, so you'll hear better," cried one.

I tried to keep silent—but could I let such a brutal speech pass unchallenged? "It is very bad taste," I replied with dignity, "to reproach a person for physical infirmities; if my near-sightedness enjoins the necessity of wearing spectacles——"

"Don't lose your breath, cabby," cried a second, and a general laugh interrupted my speech.

"Cabby sees with his ears and hears with his eyes," shrieked one of the wretched boys. There was a laugh again; I was perspiring with indignation.

"Take that up on the box," cried my passenger in an insolent tone, thumping a heavy brass-nailed trunk down on my feet.

I was about to recommend greater caution when he handed me a couple of curtain-poles wrapped in paper and tied together with a cord.

"Take that too," he commanded, "and see that it doesn't slip down."

So it was a provincial upholsterer who was treating me thus! In spite of that, there was nothing for it but to obey his orders. I set the curtain-poles up on end and put my left arm around them.

Now there was an uproar among the boys once more. "Cabby, hold the crow-bars tight!" cried one. "Cabby with the crow-bars!" yelled the boys, shrieking, bellowing, and whistling in a diabolical chorus.

"To the tavern 'Green Tree' in the Klosterstrasse!"

cried the overbearing voice of the upholsterer. He got into the cab, and shut the door with a bang.

I seized the reins, the nag stood still, as if it were none of his concern.

"Go along with ye, you wretched beast! Hello there! Skip along!" I muttered between my teeth; the abominable quadruped persisted in stubborn indifference. I brought the whip down upon him "toward the front," as Gustav had advised me, and, sure enough, suddenly the cab quivered, struck with the hoofs of the balking steed.

An infernal concert of wild jubilations arose about me I sat upon my box in a state of wretched helplessness, and, to make matters worse, the travelling merchant put his head out of the cab.

"How long is it going to take you to get started?" he called out, following up his words with a perfect volley of oaths. "Did anybody ever see the like of this?"

One of my colleagues of the box was moved with brotherly pity, seized the malicious steed by the head, and put him in motion.

The other drivers sat on their boxes taking a nap, and there was no opportunity of entering into conversation with them. I was very much depressed, took off my mantle, for it was growing warm, climbed up into my seat, and drove away to try my luck elsewhere.

As we were jolting slowly across the Schlossplatz, there came straight across the square from the red Schloss a figure, the sight of which made my blood run cold—it was my friend Otto.

Supposing he should recognise me,—I dared not think the thought, I felt myself blush and then turn pale under my beard. I turned my head to the other side, toward the Schloss, but as I involuntarily looked at him askance, it seemed to me that he was standing still. In fact so he was,

—he stood there beckoning to me! I was seized with horror! "Beckon away as hard as you please," I said to myself, driving on. Now I heard his voice: "Hello there, cabman!" I pretended not to hear, and still drove on.

Then he came rushing with tremendous strides across the square.

"Confound you!" he cried. "Don't you hear me?"

There was no further possibility of escape; I must needs pull up.

Like a criminal over whom sentence of death has just been passed, I hung my head; with the corner of my left eye I saw that my friend Otto had on his best suit, and was carrying his summer overcoat over his arm.

"Kanonierstrasse No. ——," he said, jumping airily into the cab. I started involuntarily. What did he want to go to the Kanonierstrasse for? I knew that he did not live there—none of our boon companions lived there, I knew that also,—but some one dwelt within that house whom I knew very well, and that was Emma, my friend of the ballet, my Emma! That Emma was true, true as gold, I knew, thank Heaven! At the same time a vague unrest took possession of me, and in flying haste did I urge my steed in the direction of the Kanonierstrasse.

I riveted my eyes upon the house long before we reached it. Did my suspicion deceive me? Up there between the hyacinths did I not see some one look out? The wheels of my cab came rattling up before the door, no further mistake was possible; out of Emma's window inclined a head with raven curls—it was hers! At the same moment my friend Otto impetuously pulled open the door of the cab, jumped out, and threw kisses to her. Then he put his hand to his mouth and called out: "I'll wait for you down here with the cab. Come down, and we will have a drive in the Thiergarten."

I fell back into the corner of my seat. This was too

much! The wretch! My own faithless beloved I was to take on a drive in the Thiergarten!

Through my horn spectacles I cast one annihilating glance above; it fell upon no one, for Emma had left the window.

For a moment I considered—should I tear the wig, spectacles, and beard from off my face, and so drop my disguise before the traitors? But the ridicule, the eternal ridicule! It seemed to me the whole Kanonierstrasse would stand on its head in appreciation of the joke.

"Turn the top down," commanded my friend Otto. "It is stifling in here."

Worse and worse! But what could I do? I scrambled down and began to do as I was bid. Meanwhile the street-door opened and Emma floated across the threshold. A sombre oath escaped me.

"Now drive to the Thiergarten," said my friend Otto.

"Very well," I replied, with terrible irony in my savage voice.

The wretched couple behind my back seemed to be in the best of spirits, and as the cab was now open I could understand every word they spoke.

"Did you receive my post-card?" asked the villain.

"Of course I did," replied the faithless one. "I did not know he was going out of town. Are you quite sure he's gone? I'm in mortal terror."

"Never fear, my love," he replied; "I was in his rooms this morning. He must have left very early."

I was furious. So this was the meaning of his interested questions the night before!

Full of wrath I brought down my whip upon my horse.

"Don't beat that horse so!" cried my friend Otto from the cab; "we are in no particular hurry."

I burst into a roar of hysterical laughter. The villain! he was pitiful toward the horse, more than toward his friend. Again the nag was called upon to bear the brunt of my indignation at my friend Otto.

"The fellow must be mad," said my friend Otto.

"Don't talk so loud," begged Emma.

"Nonsense," he replied. "I told you that he is as deaf as a poker; moreover, look at him. I believe he has false hair!"

My wig had evidently become dislocated. I heard them giggle. For a moment I considered the propriety of turning my whip to good purpose behind me—but that of course would have betrayed me.

The noise of passing carriages on Leipzigerstrasse made it impossible for me to hear what was passing between the couple; it was not until we had reached more quiet streets that I again caught some bits of their conversation. I perceived that I was again the subject thereof.

"How do you get along with him?" asked my friend Otto.

"Oh well," responded Emma, "he's a good enough fellow."

Whack,—the nag caught it again then, for the tone in which she said it roused my ire.

"That's so," continued my friend Otto; "but he is a bore, an intolerable bore."

The knave! With bated breath I listened to hear what she would reply to this calumny.

Emma giggled; that was as much as to say, "You are right."

I was in a fever of wrath.

"Does he ever read any of his things to you?" asked my friend Otto.

"Does he write?" she queried in surprise. The uneducated goose! The superficial hussy! Did she not know that I had already published two volumes of lyrical poetry? And she asks if I write!

"I should think so," replied my friend Otto, with an infamous roar of laughter. "Every little while he hatches a new poem a yard or two long, and reads it to his friends."

Emma shook with laughter.

"So far he has spared me," she observed.

"Never fear, my love, never fear," I muttered into my false beard; "you shan't have any more opportunity to be bored by me!"

In my mind I was composing the crushing farewell-note I intended to write to the faithless one on the morrow.

After a time which seemed endless to me we reached the garden restaurant called "Charlottenhof."

"Hold on, driver!" bellowed my friend Otto, who, taking me to be deaf, considered it necessary to address me in his loudest tones. Then he turned to Emma.

"Come, sweetheart," he said, "we will have a glass of beer." He helped her get down. "Wait till we come back," he said to me. At the gate stood a waiter: "Fetch a glass of beer for the driver," he added, and before I had time to enter protest he had stepped into the garden, arm-in-arm with his lady-love.

Fully an hour and a half did my friend Otto see best to keep me waiting at the door, while he was amusing himself in the garden with his adored.

I occupied myself with writing my obituary in spirit, and tears of emotion over my sad fate trickled down my beard. "By the fickleness of a heartless woman"—thus read the last page of my obituary—"and the depravity of a man whom he took to be his friend, was this poet's heart broken, and this glorious possibility of immeasurable promise for Germany was nipped in the bud."

Ernst von Wildenbruch.

BON-MOTS.

EVERYBODY is a genius, at least once in his life. The only difference is that the so called geniuses have their good ideas thicker. This shows how wise it is to put everything on paper.

It always grieves me when a man of talent dies, for earth has more need of him than heaven.

This book had the effect which all good books have: it made the dull duller, the wise wiser, and the other millions remained unchanged.

One of the greatest discoveries which human reason has made in modern times is, in my opinion, the art of judging books without having read them.

He had a couple of warts on his nose in a position which made them likely to be mistaken for the heads of nails, by means of which that feature might have been fastened to his face.

It is no art to say a thing in few words when you have something to say, like Tacitus. But when you have nothing to say, and write a big book, that's what I call merit.

He combined the qualities of the greatest men in history: he carried his head on one side like Alexander the Great, he was always scratching his head like Cæsar, he could drink coffee like Leibnitz, and when he was comfortable in his easy-chair he would forget to eat and drink like Newton, and like him it was often necessary to wake him.

"Our forests are growing thinner, the supply of wood is declining, what shall we do?" Oh, when our forests are used up there is surely nothing to hinder our burning books until there is a new supply.

Of all commodities in the market there is none more remarkable than books. Printed by persons who do not understand them; sold by people who do not understand them; bound, reviewed, and read by people who do not understand them; and, best of all, written by people who do not understand them.

He was a most meritorious boy: before he was six years old he could say the Lord's Prayer backwards.

I have found throughout life that when all other means fail there is nothing that will give you a surer clue to a man's character than a joke which he takes amiss.

I suppose there is no man in the world who, if he turns thief for a thousand thalers, would not for half the money have preferred to remain the honest fellow he was.

Whosoever says he hates all kinds of flattery, and says it in good faith, has surely not become acquainted with all kinds, in matter or in form. To be sure, people of sense hate ordinary flattery, because they must necessarily feel mortified at the amount of credulity with which the flatterer credits them. That is, they hate ordinary flattery, because to them it is no flattery. According to my experience, there is no very great difference in human nature. Each has his own coin for which he will sell himself. It is human invention to differentiate between human beings; it is pride which supports these distinctions. Nobility of soul is very much of a piece with nobility of birth.

To make persons of discernment believe that you are somewhat which you are not is as a general thing more difficult than to become what you would appear to be.

IF you would know what other people think about an affair which concerns you, consider what you would think of them under like circumstances. Do not take any one for more moral in this matter than you are, or for more credulous. This remark is more than half true, and this is saying a great deal for a maxim which a person lays down in his thirtieth year, as I do this one.

ONE may rail at the faults of a great man, but one must not rail at the man for all that.

IT is safe to take it as a sure sign that you are growing better when paying your debts gives you as much pleasure as making money.

VIRTUE which is the result of good intention is not worth much. Impulse or custom is the thing.

THAT a false hypothesis is often to be preferred to the true one is shown by the theory of the freedom of human volition. Certainly we are not free, but it requires a very profound study of philosophy not to be misled by this knowledge. Freedom is the easiest explanation, and will remain the most popular one because appearances are for it.
—*Lichtenberg.*

THE story was told how St. Dionysius, after he had been beheaded, walked two miles with his head in his hand. "Two miles?" asked one of the company. "Yes, two miles; there is not the least doubt of it," was the reply. "I will gladly believe you," said a lady, wittier than the others; "on such occasions it is only the first step which is difficult."

THE French ambassador came to Charles V. with the request that Milan should be ceded to his master the king. Whereupon the emperor merely replied, "The wish of my brother, the King of France, is my own."

THE Duchess of Klingston desired to be admitted to the court circle at Berlin. She requested the Russian minister to take occasion to assure the king of her high esteem, and to tell him that she had been heard to say her fortune was in Rome, her fleet at Venice, and her heart in Berlin. When the king heard this he quickly responded with, "My compliments to the Duchess, and tell her I greatly fear she has favoured us with the least of her possessions."

A GREAT gentleman said to his servant in a moment of caprice, "Tell me, John, supposing the devil should come to get one of us, which one do you think he would take?"
"He'd take me, without a doubt, your honour."
"Why so, you absurd fellow?"
"Because he has some chance of losing me, but he is quite sure of you," was the reply.

A WITTY king, in travelling through his lands, passed a small provincial town in which great honour was shown him by the magistrate and burgomaster, the latter greeting the monarch in a solemn address. The most conspicuous thing about the portly little man was the well-rounded expansion of his spotless white vest. The day was very cold, and the speech was interminable. Suddenly the king interrupted the speaker, and, as if concerned about his health, pointing to the snowy vest, he graciously remarked, "My dear sir, I fear your *Mont Blanc* will catch cold!"

THE presence of a university makes the country stupid for miles about.—*Börne.*

WITH them (the troubadours) it is always the winter that goes and the spring that comes, and the *ennui* that remains.—*Schiller.*

IF called upon to choose between the pangs of conscience and the pangs of toothache I should unhesitatingly choose the former.

IN other countries when a citizen becomes dissatisfied with his government he emigrates, in France he requests the government to emigrate.—*Heine.*

THE EARLY DAYS OF A GENIUS.

THE ancients considered it as a piece of rare good fortune if the gods permitted a person to be born in a celebrated town. As, however, this good fortune has not befallen some very celebrated men, since Bethlehem, Eisleben, Stratford, Kamenz, and Marbach were not originally brilliant points in the thoughts of men, I trust Hans Unwirrsch was not put out by the fact of first seeing the light of day in a small town called Neustadt. There are not a few towns and boroughs bearing the same name; but they have never quarrelled over the honour of counting our hero among their citizens. Johannes Jakob Nikolaus Unwirrsch did not make his birthplace any more celebrated in the world.

Ten thousand inhabitants did this poor little town have in 1819; to-day it has one hundred and fifty more. It lay, and still lies, in a broad valley, surrounded by hills and mountains, down the sides of which the forest comes straggling into the precincts of the town. In spite of its name it is no longer new; painfully has it struggled along through stormy centuries, and is now enjoying a peaceful, sleepy old age. The hope of making a mark in the world it has gradually given up, and feels none the less contented for this. The sound of its church-bells makes an agreeable impression upon the wanderer, as he steps out of the woods on the nearest hill-top; and when it so happens that the sun is mirrored in the windows of the two churches and the houses, this same wanderer seldom remembers that all is not gold that glitters, and that evening-bells, fruitful fields, green meadows, and a pretty little town in a valley, is not enough by far to make an idyl. Amyntas, Palæmon, Daphnis, and Doris often lead anything but an idyllic life in the valley below. As the fleecing of lambs and sheep had gone somewhat out of fashion, people were reduced to pitching into each other's wool, and sometimes fleeced each other with a will. But there was much marrying and giving in marriage, and altogether people passed through life with a measure of comfort; that they found living not particularly dear, bore a part in this happy consummation. The devil take things when fruit and cider fail, and milk and honey is rare in Arcadia!

But we shall probably have further opportunity to lose words about this here and there, and if not it is no matter. For the present we must turn back to the young Arcadian, Hans Unwirrsch, and see how he finds his way about in life.

A very uneducated woman was the wife of the shoemaker. She could read and write in an exigency, but her philosophical education had been completely neglected; she wept easily, and with pleasure. Born in darkness, she remained in darkness; suckled her child, set him on his feet, and taught him to walk—put him on his feet for life, and taught him to walk for life. That is great praise, and the most cultured mother can do no more for her child.

In a low, dark room, into which but little fresh air and still less sunshine came, did Hans awake to consciousness;

and that was well in one respect. Later on he was not too much afraid of the caves, in which by far the greater part of humanity partaking of the blessings of civilisation are obliged to spend their lives. All his life he took light and air for what they are, luxuries which fate gives or denies, and which it seems to deny more willingly than to give.

The room on the street side, which had at the same time been Meister Anton's workshop, was kept unchanged in its former condition. With anxious care did the widow see to it that none of the tools belonging to the deceased were moved. Her uncle Grünebaum had declared his willingness to purchase all the unnecessary implements at an acceptable price; but Frau Christine could not bring herself to sell a single piece. In all her leisure hours she sat at her wonted seat beside the shoemaker's work-table, and in the evening it was, as we know, only by the light of the glass-ball that she could knit or sew or read her hymnal.

The poor woman worked hard to gain an honest living for herself and her child. In the little bedroom, the windows of which looked out into the yard, she lay many a night wakeful and anxious, while Hans Unwirrsch in his father's large bedstead was dreaming of the large rolls and buttered slices of bread that the neighbours' happy children enjoyed. Wise Meister Grünebaum did what he could by his relatives, but he was not very successful in his trade; he was too fond of delivering long speeches at the alehouse; and his customers were more willing to give him a pair of shaky boots to be mended than to order a new pair of him. It was with difficulty that he kept his head above water; but he was never chary about giving advice, indeed he gave it gladly and in large quantities, and unfortunately we must call attention to the not unusual fact that the quantity stood for the most part in no proper relation to the quality. Cousin Schlotterbeck, though by no means so wise as Meister Grünebaum, was more practical, and it was upon *her* advice that Frau Christine became a washerwoman, getting up in the morning between two and three, and returning at night tired and aching, to still the primary, physical hunger of her child, and translate his dreams into reality.

Hans Unwirrsch retained faint, odd, and uncertain memories of this period of his life, which he has reported to his nearest friends. He had a light sleep from early youth, and so he often awoke by the light of a match, with which in cold, dark nights of winter his mother lit her lamp to prepare for her early walk. He lay in his warm pillow, and did not stir until his mother bent over him to see if she had awakened the little sleeper by the pattering of her slippers. Then he would throw his arms about her neck and laugh, while she gave him a kiss and an exhortation to go quickly to sleep again, for the day was far distant. This exhortation he would obey at once, or else later. In the latter case he looked at the burning lamp through his half-closed eye-lids, and at his mother and the shadows on the wall.

Strange it is that all his recollections seem to be of winter; there was a misty atmosphere about the flame of the lamp; his breath made a cloud between him and the light; the frozen window-panes glittered, it was bitter cold, and the comfort he felt in his safe, warm bed was intermingled with terror of the bitter cold without, which made him pull the blanket over his nose.

He never could understand why his mother got up so early, while it was so dark and so cold, and while such queer, black shadows were gliding along the wall, nodding, rising, and bending. Still more vague were his thoughts about the places his mother went to; in accordance with his momentary mood, he pictured them more or less pleasantly, mingling in all sorts of details taken from fairy-tales, and fragments out of the conversations of grown persons that he had overheard, and which in these misty moments between sleeping and waking took on more and more of a gaudy colouring.

At last his mother was dressed, and once more she bent over the child's bed. Again he received a kiss, a great deal of good advice, and many enticing promises, if he would lie still, not cry, and go to sleep again. The assurance was added that the morning, and with it Cousin Schlotterbeck, would be coming ere long; the lamp was blown out, the room grew dark, the door creaked, the steps of his mother passed away; soon he was fast asleep, and when he awoke again Cousin Schlotterbeck was generally sitting by his bedside, and in the adjoining room he could hear the fire crackle in the stove.

Cousin Schlotterbeck, although she was not much older than Frau Christine Unwirrsch, had always been Cousin Schlotterbeck. No one in the Kröppelstrasse knew her by any other designation, and she was as well known in the Kröppelstrasse as the "old Fritz," as the Emperor Napoleon, and old Blücher, although she had no further resemblance to these celebrated heroes than that she used snuff like the Prussian king, and had a hooked nose like the "Corsican bloodhound."

Of right she should have filled a chapter by herself in this book, for she had a gift of which not every one can boast: to her the dead had not departed this earth; she saw them walk the streets, she met them on the market-place as one sees the living, and comes upon them unexpectedly around the corner. There was nothing weird about this to her; she spoke of it as of something quite natural and unsurprising, and to her there was no difference whatever between the Burgomaster Eckerlein, who had died in the year 1769, and often met her in his wig and red velvet coat near the apothecary's shop, and the grandson of this man, who owned this same apothecary's shop in the year 1820, and who was now looking out of the window with no faculty for seeing his grandfather walking below.

Even in the minds of Cousin Schlotterbeck's acquaintances this strange "gift" of hers no longer awakened horror. The unbelieving ceased scoffing at it, and the believing—of whom there was a goodly number—did not cross themselves any more. Upon the character of the good little woman this high favour had no perverting influence. She was not made supercilious by her marvellous seer's gift; she took it as an undeserved favour of God, and remained more humble than many other people who did not see nearly as much as the oldish spinster in the Kröppelstrasse.

As far as her external appearance is concerned, Cousin Schlotterbeck was of medium height, but she stooped perceptibly, and walked with a far-protruding head. Her clothes hung about her like something that does not belong there, and her nose was, as we have said, very sharp and very hooked. It would have impressed one disagreeably, this nose would, if it had not been for the eyes. But her eyes did penance for every sin her nose committed; they were remarkable eyes, and saw remarkable things. Clear and beaming they were up to her old age,—blue, young eyes in an old, old, dried-up face! Hans Unwirrsch never forgot them, although he looked into much more beautiful eyes in his life.

To learning, Cousin Schlotterbeck was devoted in a naïve way. She had a tremendous admiration for wisdom, and particularly for theological wisdom; little Hans was indebted to her for an introduction to all the erudition of which he made himself more or less a possessor in later times. She could tell fairy-tales which would have delighted the hearts of the Brothers Grimm, and when the wicked queen put the golden pin into her stepdaughter's head, Hans Unwirrsch felt the point of it piercing through to his very diaphragm.

Hans and the cousin were inseparable during the first

years of the boy's life. From early morning till late at night the ghost-seer took the part of a mother to the child; without her advice and help did nothing occur which related to him; many a time did she appease his hunger, and many a more subtle hunger did she awake in him.

Hans Unwirrsch was a precocious child, and learned to talk almost before he walked; reading was to him but play. Cousin Schlotterbeck understood this difficult art very well, and managed to stumble through the most incomprehensible big words.

She liked to read aloud, and indulged in a nasal eloquence which was very impressive to the child. Her library consisted principally of a Bible, a hymnal, and a long row of almanacs standing in unbroken line from the year 1790, each of which contained a touching, or comic, or sensational narrative, as well as a goodly stock of receipts and nostrums, and a fine collection of funny anecdotes. For a susceptible childish imagination there lay a world of rare wonder in these old pamphlets, and spirits of all kinds arose out of them, smiling, grinning, threatening, and leading the young soul through various horrors and delights. A still greater impression, however, did the "book of books," the Bible, make upon the boy. With shuddering rapture did Hans sit at the feet of his cousin, and dive into the mysteries of chaos; the earth was void and empty, until the light came dividing the darkness and the water under the land from the water over the land. When sun, moon, and stars began their dance, and signs, times, days, and years appeared, then he breathed anew; and when the earth brought forth grass, and leaves, and fruit-trees, and when the water, and the air, and the earth began to be peopled with moving and living animals, then he clapped his little hands, and felt ground under him once more.

But his days did not pass only with reading and listening to stories. As soon as Hans Unwirrsch did not throw his

"WITH SHUDDERING RAPTURE DID HANS SIT AT THE FEET OF HIS COUSIN."

hands about aimlessly any more, or put them into his mouth, his mother and cousin made haste to introduce him to the great principle of labour. Cousin Schlotterbeck was an ingenious woman, who managed to earn an extra penny by dressing dolls for a large factory, an occupation which was interesting enough for a child, and in which Hans liked to be helpful. Ladies and gentlemen, peasants and shepherds, and many other little personages of various social positions and ages, arose under the skilful fingers of his cousin, who worked away bravely with glue and with her needle, with bright bits of cloth and gilt paper, of which she gave a proper share to each, in exact proportion to the price. It was a philosophical occupation, which left one free to harbour a great many ideas, and Hans Unwirrsch took kindly to it, although, of course, his childish pleasure in the toys was soon lost. He who has grown up in a shop of Jack-in-the-boxes, takes little pleasure in each individual Jack-in-the-box, be he ever so gaudy and agile in turning up his toes.

After Martinmas, which momentous day unfortunately could not be celebrated with roast goose, Cousin Schlotterbeck devoted herself to independent fabrication. She could very profitably apply her talent to plastic art; she formed little men out of raisins, to be sold at Christmas, and for more humble minds she made churls out of dried plums. The first fellow of this latter kind, who was manufactured by Hans without help, gave him as much pleasure as the hopeful art student experiences at the sight of the picture which gained him the *prix de Rome*.

In his fifth year Johannes Jakob Nikolaus Unwirrsch was a little awkward fellow, in a pair of breeches which had been cut and designed for him to grow into. Out of bluish-grey eyes he looked merrily into the world and into the Kröppelstrasse, his nose had nothing characteristic as yet, his mouth promised fair to grow very large, and kept its promise. The yellow hair of the boy curled naturally, and was the prettiest thing about him. He had in every respect an excellent stomach, like all people who are designed to hunger a great deal in life; he got through with his A B C with no more difficulty than with the biggest slice of brown bread and with the fullest soup plate. The two women, his mother and his cousin, spoiled him, of course, to the best of their ability, and honoured him as crown-prince, hero, and world's wonder, so that it was well when the Government interfered, and declared him old enough to go to school. Hans Unwirrsch set his foot on the lowest round of the ladder, which stands by the fruitful tree of knowledge, the door of the poor-school opened to him, and Silberlöffel, the schoolmaster, promised Cousin Schlotterbeck at the door that her "precious boy" should neither be murdered by himself nor by the hundred and sixty good-for-nothings who were subject to his rule.

"Cousin" departed with a corner of her apron up to her eyes, and would not be comforted, until near the town well she met the pastor Primarius Holzapfel, who had died in the year eighteen hundred and fifteen, attired in his black surplice, with an enormous ruff about his neck, and a Bible in his hand. "Cousin" had been well acquainted with the pastor and his parents. His father had been a woodcutter, and his mother had died in the Hospital of the Holy Spirit; Primarius the pastor, with whose praise the town still rung, had occupied the very place in the poor-school to which Silberlöffel was taking little Hans.

In a dark street, in a one-storey building, which had once been an engine-house, the community had instituted a school for poor children, after having refused for a long time to give up any building for so superfluous an object. It was a damp hole; almost at any time of day you could see the water run down the walls; fungi flourished in the corners and under the teacher's desk. The tables and benches were moist and sticky, and during vacation they were always covered with a thin coating of mould. The windows it would be best not to mention; it was no wonder if in their vicinity there were also interesting growths of fungus. Neither was it a wonder if in the extremities of the teacher rheumatic knots formed, and in his lungs the most exquisite tubercles. It was no wonder if at times half of the pupils were ill with a fever. If the community had been called upon to put a marble monument on every child's grave which was dug in the churchyard by its guilt, it would soon have supplied a new building for the school.

Karl Silberlöffel was the name the teacher signed to the receipts for the enormous sums which he received quarterly from the State. Alas, the poor fellow had received this name as it were by the irony of fate; he had not been born with a silver spoon in his mouth. How can the Government be expected to bother about the schoolmaster Silberlöffel so long as the question as to what is the smallest possible amount of knowledge that may be permitted to the lower classes without harm and discomfort to the higher is still unsolved? For a long time to come the gentlemen puzzling over this question will consider the common schoolmasters as their enemies, and will look upon it as an absurd and altogether preposterous demand when dangerous and revolutionary idealists require them to do good unto their enemies, and at least dress them decently and feed them tolerably well.

Later in life our hero often invited the country schoolmaster at Grunzenow to his Sunday dinner or his Christmas punch, remembering these first school-days and the poor-teacher Silberlöffel. Neither did he object when the schoolmaster on the Baltic put some of the good, nourishing things set before him into his pocket for his seven boys at home; he himself would fetch him an old paper to wrap them in, and help him crowd the bundle into his coat pocket.

In the engine house at Neustadt the girls sat on the right-hand side and the boys on the left. Between these two divisions there was a passage from the door up to the teacher's desk, and in this passage Silberlöffel walked, coughing, up and down, without one of his charge being moved thereby to pity. Long, very long, was the poor fellow; thin, very thin, was he; very melancholy did he look, and he had good cause.

Another in his place would have raised his spirits, and warmed himself in the damp, cold room by lustily whipping the boys; but he was beyond that even. His faint ventures in this line were considered as a good joke merely; his authority was below zero. A pitiful reproach to all well-dressed people were the garments of this worthy man; especially the hat acted a perfect tragedy with its possessor. The point between the two was which should survive the other, and the hat seemed to know that it would carry the prize. A diabolical taunt seemed to grin from out of its boils and scratches. The villain knew that it would also survive the successor of the consumptive man; it was utterly indifferent to the mould and the dampness of the engine-house.

Hans Unwirrsch entered the swarm of poor scholars by no means with sentimental feelings. After having conquered the first surprise and embarrassment, after having made himself at home in his new surroundings, he proved himself to be no better than any other scapegrace, and to the best of his ability took part in the pleasures and pains of this praiseworthy public institution. Friends and enemies among the boys were soon discovered; congenial spirits attached themselves to him, the uncongenial tried to pull him out of his views of life by the hairs of his head, and in single combat as in general skirmish he often came to grief, which, however, he bore like a manly chap, without seeking refuge behind his teacher. As a manly chap he also had, at this period of his life, a healthy aversion toward the female sex upon the benches at the right of the passage. He was fond of putting shoemaker's wax on the girls' seats, and of coupling two and two of them together by firmly twisting the ends of their hair into a knot; he looked upon them with sovereign disdain as inferior creatures, who knew no other means of defence than shrieking, and through whom the schoolmaster was better informed about the left half of his school than the boys relished. At first there was not the least trace of chivalrous impulses and feelings within his bosom, but the time which

"COUPLING TWO AND TWO OF THEM TOGETHER BY FIRMLY TWISTING THE ENDS OF THEIR HAIR INTO A KNOT."

was to hail the first awaking dawn in this respect was not far distant, and soon there was *one* little creature on the other side of the school who made her influence felt upon Hans Unwirrsch. There came a time when he could not bear to see *one* little fellow-pupil cry, and when he felt a nameless longing, which was not directed toward the great slices of bread and butter and hunches of cake which he saw other children devour upon the street; but for the present he impudently put his hands in the pockets of his baggy breeches, set his legs far apart, put himself firmly on his feet, and sought to emancipate himself as far as possible from the absolutism of womankind. No more now did he sit quiet and patient at the feet of Cousin Schlotterbeck and listen reverently to her teachings and exhortations, her fairy-tales and almanac stories, and her Bible readings. To the great discomfort of the good old lady did he daily manifest a more critical spirit. The almanac stories he knew by heart; no sooner did the "Cousin" begin a fairy-tale than he interrupted her to suggest emendations and ask impertinently ironical questions; to her kind exhortations he always offered confusing objections, which more than once put the good lady quite out of countenance. When, as was her custom, the good soul got entangled in a long-breathed genealogical row of biblical names, Hans took a truly diabolical pleasure therein, and tried to drive the poor creature deeper into the thorns, so that she at last with angry virulence would clap the book to and call her quondam "little lamb" a "saucy good-for-nothing." Behind her back he was up to all sorts of trickery; yes, he went so far as to caricature her person before a select audience in the Kröppelstrasse, consisting of persons of his own age. In short, Hans Jakob Nikolaus Unwirrsch had now reached that stage in life during which loving relations with darkly melancholy looks and warning gestures prognosticated to this hopeful scion or youthful acquaintance a dark future, the beggar's staff, prison, penitentiary, and at last, as an agreeable conclusion, a disgraceful death on the gallows. It is well that prophecies usually are not fulfilled.

Naturally Hans now felt more drawn to his Uncle Grünebaum than to his mother and cousin. The original cobbler had much about him that was attractive to the youthful mind. To Hans, when in the company of this worthy man, time seldom seemed to drag.

Very dirty and neglected did the household and surroundings of Uncle Grünebaum look to any respectable woman. In his workshop it looked as if brownies had made their home, not with kindly intentions, but in the most bitter ire. A wilder topsy-turvy can scarcely be pictured. Uncle Grünebaum spent the greater part of his day and of

"READING THE 'TOWN AND COUNTRY HERALD' WITH A LOUD VOICE TO HIMSELF AND HIS BIRDS."

his work-hours in hunting for something or other. The tool he was in search of was never to be found, and rummaging for it did not benefit the general aspect of things. Over and above all there was a perpetual noise of whistling, singing, and screeching birds in large and small cages upon the walls; a tree-frog in a glass by the window foretold the weather. But as for the political weather, Meister Grünebaum foretold it to himself, reading the *Town and Country Herald* with a loud voice to himself and his birds, an occupation which also took up a good deal of his work-time. The worthy Uncle Grünebaum did only just so much cobbling as was necessary to keep him and his birds alive, and to pay for the *Herald*. His glass at the alehouse was oftener scored than is good for a respectable citizen and shoemaker.

During this period of his restless life Hans decidedly preferred the street and its details to domestic happiness, to the quiet undisturbed peace of his own home. Oh, thou blessed time of dirty hands and bleeding noses, of torn jackets and rumbled hair! Woe to the man who has never known thee! It were better for him if he had not known some other things which loving relations and friends with the darkly melancholy look blandly praised and recommended!

Wilhelm Raabe

NEWSPAPER HUMOUR.

Shoemaker's Apprentice (passing by a baker's stand): "Got any stale rolls?"

Baker: "Yes, my lad."

Apprentice: "Serves you right. You should have sold 'em when they were fresh."

IN COURT.—*Judge:* "How is it that you picked up a number of comparatively worthless articles, and left the money, which was close at hand, untouched?"

Criminal: "I hope your honour won't find fault with me for that. My wife has been hard enough on me about it."

Restaurant-keeper (to guest reading his paper): "I am very sorry, sir, to be obliged to ask you not to lunch here in future. You shake your head all the time. *I* know it's the politics, but others don't know it, and it's hurting my reputation."

AT A RESTAURANT. —"This beefsteak is so tough the knife won't go through."
Restaurant-keeper: "Waiter, another knife for the gentleman."

"GOODNESS, HOW YOU LOOK, CHILD!"

Father. "Goodness, how you look, child!"
Frankie: "I fell into the canal."
Father: "What! With your new trousers on?"
Frankie: "I didn't have time to take 'em off."

"ALLOW me, Mademoiselle, to present this to you."
"No, no, I do not wish to accept a present."
"It is a volume of my poems."
"Ah, that is different. I could not have permitted you to give me anything *valuable*."

Judge (to an individual notorious for thievish proclivities): "I was told you stole wood the other day. That is not true, is it, Peter?"

Peter: "Nay, Herr Judge."

Judge: "The policeman says he found the wood at your house. That can't be so?"

Peter: "Nay, Herr Judge."

Judge: "Well, Peter, I'll sentence you to six weeks in gaol. That's not too much, is it?"

Peter: "Nay, Herr Judge."

"I WONDER why that gentleman over there is holding the paper up before his face for such an interminable length of time?"

"The explanation is very simple. Because his tailor happens to be sitting at our table."

A CONSIDERATE YOUTH.—*Aunt:* "Well, Fritz, I hear you were flogged in school to-day?"

Fritz: "Yes, but it didn't hurt."

Aunt: "I thought I heard you cry."

Fritz: "I did that to please the teacher."

"YOU advertise your socks to have fast colours, and now I had on a pair for two days, and for a fortnight I have not been able to get the colour off from my feet."

"Well, don't you call that a fast colour? What more can you wish?"

AT THE LIVERY STABLE.—"How much do you ask for this horse by the hour?"

"One thaler."

"That is, I trust, counting up to the time when the horse returns? It is quite likely I shall be here somewhat later!"

Doctor: "I know just what will help you. You must drink two cups of very strong tea every morning."
Patient: "Why, that is just what I have done for years."
Doctor: "Then you must stop it."

"HENRY, my cigars are disappearing at a great rate. Is it possible that within the short time you have been in my service——"

"Never fear, sir; I have three boxes full left from my last master."

Lieutenant A. (relating his gallant adventures at the ball): "A crowd of ladies stood about me, waiting for me to say something very brilliant."
Lieutenant B.: "Of course you kept them in suspense."
Lieutenant A.: "Most certainly I did."

New Burgomaster: "No celebrity ever been born in this town?"
First Citizen: "Not yet, unfortunately; but all that will be different under your administration."

A. (to a young doctor): "How many rooms have you?"
B.: "First, there is a waiting-room."
A.: "Pardon me for interrupting you. What do you call a waiting-room? Is it a room in which your patients wait for you, or one in which you wait for patients?"

A.: "Dr. Krampel has saved my life."
B.: "I did not know that you were ever in his treatment."
A.: "No, when I consulted him he advised me to go to another physician."

POETRY AND PROSE.—"Tell me what it was that inspired you to write this glorious poem?"
Poet: "My youngest needed a new suit of clothes."

Lady (roguishly to her partner): "So you too are a conductor on the road to Hades?"

Young Physician: "You mistake, I am less than that — in fact, merely a brakesman!"

Baroness: "Your daughter will find a kind mistress in me. I trust she is accustomed to work and to early rising?"

Peasant: "That she is, ma'am. She can serve you as an example."

COQUETRY AVENGED.

COQUETRY AVENGED.—*Lady:* "Ah, Herr Lieutenant, I have rejected many addresses!"

Lieutenant: "Is that so? Well, you have had time to do so!"

Judge: "Prisoner, do you confess your guilt?"

Prisoner: "No. The words of my counsel have convinced me of my innocence."

Lady: "And so you are a friend of my son Edward? I shall be delighted to hear what news you can tell me about him. Is he enjoying his studies at the university, and has he grown accustomed to the intricacies of town-life? Has he learned to find his way about?"

Student: "Oh yes, he is all right so far as that is concerned. Only he has some difficulty in finding his way home from the tavern."

"Come, John, get up on the mare!"
"Pray, why should I make such a detour to get around to the other side?"

At the Ball.—*Gentleman:* "Do you play on the piano?"
Lady: "No."
Gentleman: "Ah, then you sing?"
Lady: "No, sir,—neither have I had the influenza."

Maid (to her young mistress, who has written a love-letter for her at her request): "Oh, thank you so much, Miss! The letter is beautiful. But please don't forget to put a postscript: Excuse bad writin' and spellin'!"

"It is very provoking that your wife should have read my last letter to you. I thought you said she never opens your letters?"
"She doesn't generally, but you committed the folly of writing 'Private' upon the envelope."

If you ask a man for the date of his birth, he tells you only the year; if you ask a woman, she never tells you more than the day.

Custodian of the Schloss at Heidelberg (explaining the functions of his office to stranger): "What the professors are to the university, that *we* are to the Schloss."

IN COURT.—*Defendant:* "Gentlemen, I have much to say in favour of my client. First——"
Prisoner (interrupting him): "You'd better not give yourself any trouble trying to pull me through, Herr Doctor. I take it the gentlemen haven't much faith left in either of us."

A.: "I wish I knew something to give my uncle for his birthday. He is such an old miser that no matter what I buy him, I'm sure he will not use it."
B.: "Why, that's glorious! All you have to do is to fill half-a-dozen of bottles with water, cork and seal them well, and stick on a label, 'Old Rhine Wine, 1780.'"

FREDERICK, a tailor's apprentice, has lent a shilling to Henry, a barber's journeyman. To show his gratitude, Henry says: "Frederick, if you should ever get into straits, if all your friends should fall off from you; if your father and mother, your sister and brother, should leave you in the lurch, then come to me, and take my word for it, *I'll shave you, and never charge you a penny!*"

Stranger: "Beg pardon, sir, will you tell me which road I must take to get to the university?"
First Student: "I don't know precisely myself. It is only two years since I came here. It is more likely you know, Bummer—you've been here for eight years."
Second Student: "I? I have forgotten long ago."

NOTE.

ACKNOWLEDGMENTS are here tendered to Herr Wilhelm Raabe, for his kind permission to include the translation from *Hunger-Pastor;* to Herr Julius Stinde, for his kind permission to translate from the *Familie Buchholz;* to Herr W. H. Riehl and his publisher, to translate from *Jörg Muckenhuber;* to Herr Friedrich Theodor v. Vischer, and to the Deutsche Verlagsanstalt, Stuttgart, to translate from Herr v. Vischer's *Auch Einer;* to Herr Ernst Eckstein, to translate from *Besuch im Carcer;* to Messrs. Kegan Paul, Trench, Trübner, & Co., Limited, and to Mr. Leland, for their kind permission to include Mr. Leland's translations of Scheffel and others (see *Gaudeamus*, published by Messrs. Kegan Paul). Best thanks are also to be accorded to various German authors and publishers, who have so courteously sanctioned translated extracts.

BIOGRAPHICAL INDEX OF WRITERS.

HUGO VON TRIMBERG is said to have been the rector of a school near Bamberg, 1260-1309. He wrote several books of a didactic and satirical type, including *The Runner* and *The Gatherer*, the latter of which he tells us was lost during his lifetime. He severely denounces everything and everybody pertaining to the younger generation, and chants the praises of the "good old times." His writings are somewhat desultory, and their chief interest lies in the inserted fables which serve him to spin out a moral.

HANS SACHS was born at Nuremberg, on 5th November 1494. In his fifteenth year he was apprenticed to a shoemaker, and was instructed in the elements of "master-singing" by the linen-draper Nunnenbeck. As a travelling journeyman in his trade he visited the schools of all the celebrated master-singers of Germany. Returning after five years to his native town, he devoted himself to his calling of shoemaker and to the art of song. His first poetic production was a hymn which he composed in Munich in 1514. The Reformation inspired him to an allegorical ode in honour of Luther, entitled "Die Wittembergisch Nachtigal," which was followed by a great number of short religious poems. He died at Nuremberg in 1576, his last years having been clouded by insanity. He was an extraordinarily prolific writer of songs, plays, and farces.

CHRISTOFFEL VON GRIMMELSHAUSEN (1620-1676) was born at Gelnhausen. During his youth he served in the army, and his experiences of life as a soldier in the Thirty Years' War are related in the romance of *Simplicius Simplicissimus*. During his later years he was mayor of the small town of Renchen, in the Black Forest. In his various writings he made use of a whimsical collection of *noms-de-plume*, thereby somewhat complicating the task of literary research.

LUDWIG TIECK (1773-1853) was the son of a rope-maker in Berlin. In his studies at the universities of Halle, Göttingen, and Erlangen, he devoted special attention to the Romanic languages, and later, at Berlin, to the history of art, Old German poetry, and modern literature. He soon found himself in opposition to the views of poetry then popular. After his marriage, he lived for a while in Jena on intimate terms with the two Schlegels, removing with them to Dresden, and later publishing an "Almanac of the Muses" in company with A. W. Schlegel. After 1840 he received a pension from Frederick William IV. of Prussia; he took up his residence at Berlin, where he died. He contributed a great deal to the Shakespeare literature of Germany, with the aid of historical and literary studies on this subject made during a visit to London in 1818, and wrote many dramas, lyrics, and novels, as well as works of severe literary criticism.

JEAN PAUL FRIEDRICH RICHTER, commonly called Jean Paul, was born in 1763 at Wunsiedel, in the Baireuth district. His writings abound in pleasing recollections of his youthful days, though these were spent in poverty. After passing through the gymnasium at Hof, and pursuing a course of studies at Leipsic, he made some attempts in satire, but without success. He was for some time employed as private tutor in several families, and after the publication of an incomplete romance entitled *The Invisible Lodge*, gained a reputation as a humorist. His later works include *Hesperus*, *The Life of Quintus Fixlein*, *Titan*, *Siebenkäs*, *Wild Oats*, and several other discursive romances. He was induced by his friendship for Herder to revisit Weimar in 1798, remaining there until 1800, when he went to Berlin. A few years afterwards he received a pension, which enabled him to live in modest and comfortable circumstances at Baireuth, where he died in 1825.

AUGUST FRIEDRICH FERDINAND VON KOTZEBUE (1761-1819) was born at Weimar, where his father held a high position at court. He studied at Jena, and subsequently held several political offices in Russia, as well as Germany. His first writings did much to rob him of public respect. In 1798 he went to Vienna to take charge of the court theatre. Soon after, when on his way to St. Petersburg, he was sent to Siberia. He continued to write during his exile, was recalled, and came to live at Jena, which place he left, however, because of his perpetual animosity for Goethe. He was intensely unpatriotic, and indulged himself repeatedly in his writings in pouring out invectives upon German Liberal politicians on the one hand, and upon the Romantic school and the reform of the drama attempted by Schiller on the other. His motives in literature, as in politics, were purely mercenary. So venomous was he in his attacks upon the ideals of the German "Burschenschaften" that he aroused the fanaticism of a young student, Ludwig Sand, who, moreover, suspecting him of acting as a Russian spy, assassinated him at Mannheim.

BIOGRAPHICAL INDEX OF WRITERS. 433

JOHANN HEINRICH DANIEL ZSCHOKKE (1771-1848), born in Magdeburg, and educated at the gymnasium connected with the monastery at that place. In 1788 he left his native town, and joining a company of actors, he roamed about as a playwright. He then studied philosophy, theology, history, and art at Frankfort-on-Oder, and became a tutor there. He filled several responsible political positions in Switzerland, until he retired in 1841 to his country-house near Aarau, where he died. He wrote a number of dramas, *Aballino, the Great Bandit, The Iron Mask*, etc., as well as countless romances, novels, and books of travel.

LOUIS CHARLES ADELBERT VON CHAMISSO (1781-1838) was a member of the old and aristocratic French family Chamisso de Boncourt, who were expelled from France by the Revolution, in which they lost their estates. Adelbert lived with his parents in Berlin, where he subsequently entered the Prussian army, accompanied the navigator Otto von Kotzebue on a voyage round the world, and then held for some years an appointment at the Botanic Garden in Berlin, where he died. He was a very versatile writer. Besides his lyrics and the fantastic story of *Peter Schlemihl*, which gained him a name in German literature, he wrote *De animalibus quibusdam e classe vermium Linnæi, Über die Hawaiisprache*, and *Bemerkungen und Ansichten auf einer Entdeckungsreise unter Kotzebue*.

HEINRICH HEINE (1799-1856) was born at Düsseldorf, of Jewish parents. He devoted himself to a mercantile calling at Hamburg for a while, then studied law at Berlin, Bonn, and Göttingen, adopted Christianity in 1825, edited the *Political Annals* in company with Murhard, lived at Berlin, Munich, and Hamburg, and finally in Paris, where he received a pension for his literary services up to his death.

MORITZ GOTTLIEB SAPHIR was born in 1795 at a small Hungarian town, where his grandfather, under the decree of the Emperor Joseph II. compelling the Jews to take family names, had adopted the name of Saphir. Intending at first to become a merchant, this idea soon grew distasteful to him. He went to Prague to study the Talmud; then began to devote himself entirely to literature, and soon wrote some verses, which showed his satirical talent. At Vienna his satirical muse made him so many enemies that he went to Berlin, where he wrote and edited a great many humorous books. He was obliged to leave Berlin also, and going to live at Munich, he got into trouble on account of some satirical passages which were supposed to refer to the King of Bavaria, and which resulted in his imprisonment. He died at Baden, near Vienna, in 1858.

WILHELM HAUFF was born at Stuttgart in 1802, studied theology at Tübingen, became tutor in a private family at Stuttgart, and subsequently edited a paper in that town. He aimed at improving the public taste, which had been greatly influenced by H. Clauren. With this object he wrote a novel, *The Man in the Moon*, purporting to be written by Clauren. Having lost the ensuing law-suit, Hauff wrote his celebrated *Controversy about the Man in the Moon*. He also wrote *Die Memoiren des Satans, Lichtenstein, Die Bettlerin von Pont des Arts, Die Phantasien im Bremer Rathskeller*, etc. He died at Stuttgart, September 18th, 1827.

EDUARD MÖRIKE (1804-1875), born at Ludwigsburg, studied at Tübingen, was pastor at Keber-Sulzbach, near Heilbronn, then teacher at Stuttgart. He belonged to the Suabian school of poets, wrote verses and novels, among the latter, *Das Stuttgarter Hutzelmännlein, Iris, Idylle am Bodensee*, etc.

FRIEDRICH THEODOR VON VISCHER (1807-1889), a celebrated writer on Æsthetics of the Hegelian school. He was born at Ludwigsburg, studied theology, and accepted a position as vicar at Harrheim. He went to Tübingen in 1833, and became first an extraordinary and then ordinary professor of æsthetics and German literature. On account of the too great liberality of his inaugural address he was at once suspended for two years. In 1848 he entered the Frankfort Parliament, where he occupied a position as an extreme radical. In 1855 he was called to the Polytechnical Institute at Zürich, and later filled a similar position at Stuttgart. Besides his greatest work, entitled *Æsthetics, or the Science of the Beautiful*, he wrote *The Sublime and the Comic*, and a third part to Goethe's *Faust*, a parody of Goethe's second part, as well as a great deal of prose and verse in a satirical and aphoristic vein, and many critical works on æsthetics.

FRITZ REUTER (1810-1874), born at Stavenhagen, in Mecklenburg-Schwerin, studied law at Rostock, went to Jena in 1832 and joined the Burschenschaft, which was then in very ill favour with the strongly Conservative government as promulgating Liberal tendencies. He was imprisoned, and after being in custody a year was sentenced to death. This sentence was modified by the king to lifelong imprisonment. He was taken to Fort Dömitz, and remained there until 1840, when he was released in consequence of the Prussian amnesty. He took charge of his father's estate at Stavenhagen, later going to Treptow as a tutor in a private family; later he devoted himself exclusively to literature at Neubrandenburg and then at Eisenach, where he died. His novels, comedies, and poems were all written in the Low-German dialect. Some of the best known are *Seed-Time and Harvest, Olle Kamellen, Ut mine Festungstid* (Aus meiner Festungszeit), *Die Reis'na Constantinopel*.

ERNST KOSSAK (1814-1880), born at Marienwerder, and died at Berlin. Wrote *Aus dem Wanderbuch eines litterarischen Handwerksburschen, Historietten, Berliner Silhouetten*, etc.

GOTTFRIED KELLER (1815-1887), born at Zürich, took up landscape-painting, and went to Vienna to continue his art studies. Returning to his native town in 1842, he gave up painting and devoted himself entirely to literary pursuits. Receiving some pecuniary aid from the Zurich Senate, he went to Heidelberg in 1848, and to Berlin in 1850, to study philosophy and dramaturgy. He then returned to Zürich. Among his novels, *Der grüne Heinrich* and *Die Leute von Seldwyla* are best known.

FRIEDRICH WILHELM VON HACKLÄNDER (1816-1877), novelist and comedy-writer, born at Burtscheid, near Aachen. Entered the mercantile profession, left it for the army, which he soon found distasteful. Discovering a talent for story-telling, he wrote many novels and sketches about military life, and some more ambitious works of fiction, as *Europäisches Sklavenleben*.

RICHARD VOLKMANN (*nom-de-plume* Richard Leander), 1830-1891, son of the celebrated physiologist Alfred Wilhelm Volkmann, resided at Halle, in the office of President of the Chirurgical Hospital and Medical Professor at the University. Besides a number of scientific works he wrote *Poems, Aus der Burschenzeit,* and *Träumereien an französischen Kaminen.*

HEINRICH SCHAUMBERGER (1843-1874), born at Neustadt-a-d-Heide, was a Common school-teacher; he was consumptive, and died at Davost. Wrote *Volkserzählungen, Vater und Sohn, Im Hirtenhaus,* etc.

PETRI KETTENFEIER ROSEGGER, born at Alpl in Obersteiermark, in 1843. He was the son of peasants, and received only a most elementary education. Being too delicate for a yeoman, he was apprenticed to a tailor in his seventeenth year. During the time of his apprenticeship he became interested in books, and tried his hand at literature. The editor of a paper to whom he had sent some of his work became interested in him, and through his intercession he was admitted to the Mercantile Academy at Graz. He subsequently received a stipend enabling him to complete his education. He then went to Graz, where he edited a monthly magazine and devoted himself to literary work. His novels, under the title of *Ausgewählte Schriften*, comprising twenty-three volumes, are published at Vienna.

WILHELM HEINRICH RIEHL, born 1823, at the little town of Biebrich on the Rhine. Studied at Marburg, Tübingen, Bonn, and Giessen. Edited several papers, and after having been made a member of the *Deutsche Nationalversammlung* founded the *Nassauische Allgemeine Zeitung*, at the same time undertaking the musical management of the Wiesbaden Theatre. In 1854 he was made Professor of Jurisprudence and Science of Government at Munich.

Later he became a member of the Academy of Science, and Director of the Bavarian National Museum. His books, published at Stuttgart, are mostly on historical subjects—*Civilised Society, Natural History of the German People*, etc.

FRANZ VON SCHÖNTHAN, born at Vienna in 1849, entered the navy, which he left after four years to go on the stage. After having written a number of novels and comedies he was engaged as comedy-writer for the Wallner Theatre at Berlin. He subsequently filled a position at the Vienna Theatre.

JULIUS STINDE, born 1841, at Kirch-Michel, in Holstein. Studied natural science. Occupied a position as chemist in a factory at Hamburg. Subsequently took charge of the Hamburg *Gewerbeblatt*, and devoted himself solely to literature, more especially to the popularisation of science. Later he wrote comedies in Low-German, which were very well received. Among his humorous writings, the *Familie Buchholz* has contributed most to his international popularity.

BOGUMIL GOLTZ (1801-1870), humorous and didactic writer, born at Warsaw; studied at Breslau. Bought several estates, in the management of which he was unsuccessful. Lost the greater part of his fortune and settled down at Thorn, to live the life of a literary recluse, though he often travelled. Wrote *Typen der Gesellschaft, Der Mensch und die Leute, Zur Physiognomie und Charakteristik des Volkes*, etc.

EDUARD PÖTZL, born 1851, at Vienna. Editor of *Neues Wiener Tageblatt*. Wrote humorous novels and sketches dealing with Vienna life and the Austrian courts of justice.

PAUL LINDAU, born in 1839, at Magdeburg. Editor of the well-known review, *Nord und Süd;* dramatic writer. Lived at Paris for several years as a literary correspondent to a number of German papers. Founded the *Gegenwart*. Has written many dramas and novels in a vein of caustic satire and wit. Also well known as a translator of French comedies.

ERNST ECKSTEIN, born 1845 at Giessen. Wrote many satirical epics and literary essays. Founded the humorous paper *Der Schalk*. Well known through his comedies and dramas, and as a prolific novelist.

JULIUS STETTENHEIM, born at Hamburg, 1831, now living at Berlin. Editor of the *Wespen* and of *Humoristisches Deutschland*. Wrote numberless *humoresques*, of which *Wippchen's sämtliche Kriegsberichte* is best known.

BIOGRAPHICAL INDEX OF WRITERS. 437

JOHANNES SCHERR, born 1817, at Hohenrechberg. After studying at Zürich and Tübingen, he taught for a while at Stuttgart, and took a prominent part in Liberal politics. In 1849 he fled to Switzerland on account of political difficulties, and in 1860, after an interval of literary activity, was made Professor of History and Literature at Zürich. His most prominent works are a number of histories dealing with certain tendencies and developments of civilisation. He also wrote humorous and other stories.

BABETTE VON BÜLOW (contemporary) writes under the *nom-de-plume* of Hans Arnold. Born at Warmbrunn, in 1850. Has written a number of stories, the subjects being mostly of child-life.

Cloth Elegant, Large 12mo,
Price $1.25 *per vol.*

INTERNATIONAL HUMOUR.

EDITED BY W. H. DIRCKS.

Each Volume will contain from 50 to 70 Illustrations and from 350 to 500 pages.

IN each of these volumes the object will be to give an anthology of the humorous literature of the particular nation dealt with. France, Germany, Italy, Russia, Spain, and Holland will each have their respective volumes; England, Ireland, and Scotland will each be represented, as will also America and Japan. 'From China to Peru' the globe will be traversed in search of its jokes, in so far as they have recorded themselves in literature. The word Humour admits of many interpretations; for the purposes of this Series it has been interpreted in its broadest generic sense, to cover humour in all its phases as it has manifested itself among the various nationalities. Necessarily founded on a certain degree of scholarly knowledge, these volumes, while appealing to the literary reader, will nevertheless, it is hoped, in the inherent attractiveness and variety of their contents, appeal successfully and at once to the interest of readers of all classes. Starting from the early periods of each literature—in Italy, for instance, from the fourteenth century, with Boccaccio, Sacchetti, and Parabosco; in France with the amusing Fabliaux of the thirteenth century; in Germany from Hans Sachs; characteristic sketches, stories, and extracts from contemporary European and other writers whose genius is especially that of humour or *esprit* will be given. Indicating and suggesting a view and treatment of national life from a particular standpoint, each volume will contain matter suggestive of the development of a special and important phase of national spirit and character,—namely, the humorous. Proverbs and maxims, folk-wit, and folk-tales notable for their pith and humour, will have their place; the eccentricities of modern newspaper humour will not be overlooked. Each volume will be well and copiously illustrated; in many cases artists of the nationalities of the literatures represented will illustrate the volumes. To each volume will be prefixed an Introduction critically disengaging and marking the qualities and phases of the national humour dealt with; and to each will be appended Notes, biographical and explanatory.

INTERNATIONAL HUMOUR.

Cloth Elegant, Large 12mo, Price $1.25 per vol.

Among the early Volumes will be the following:—

THE HUMOUR OF FRANCE. Translated, with an Introduction and Notes, by Elizabeth Lee. With numerous Illustration by Paul Frénzeny.

THE HUMOUR OF GERMANY. Translated, with an Introduction and Notes, by Hans Müller-Casenov. With numerous Illustrations by C. E. Brock.

THE HUMOUR OF ITALY. Translated, with an Introduction and Notes, by A. Werner. With 50 Illustrations and a Frontispiece by Arturo Faldi.

THE HUMOUR OF RUSSIA. Translated, with Notes, by E. L. Boole, and an Introduction by Stepniak. With 50 Illustrations by Paul Frénzeny.

THE HUMOUR OF HOLLAND. Translated, with an Introduction and Notes, by A. Werner. With Numerous Illustrations.

THE HUMOUR OF SPAIN. Translated, with an Introduction and Notes, by S. Taylor. With numerous Illustrations.

THE HUMOUR OF AMERICA. Edited, with an Introduction and Notes, by J. Barr (of the *Detroit Free Press*). With numerous Illustrations by C. E. Brock.

To be followed by volumes representative of ENGLAND, SCOTLAND, IRELAND, JAPAN, etc. The Series will be complete in about twelve volumes.

NEW YORK: CHARLES SCRIBNER'S SONS.

SPECIMEN ILLUSTRATION.

DOCTOR DECHAR: "AND YET YOU DECLARED THE OPERATION MUST BE DONE?"
DOCTOR RAPPASS: "OF COURSE. YOU MUST ALWAYS OPERATE."

NEW YORK: CHARLES SCRIBNER'S SONS.

AUTHORISED VERSION.

Crown 8vo, Cloth, Price 6s.

PEER GYNT: A Dramatic Poem.
BY HENRIK IBSEN.

TRANSLATED BY

WILLIAM AND CHARLES ARCHER.

This Translation, though unrhymed, preserves throughout the various rhythms of the original.

"In *Brand* the hero is an embodied protest against the poverty of spirit and half-heartedness that Ibsen rebelled against in his countrymen. In *Peer Gynt* the hero is himself the embodiment of that spirit. In *Brand* the fundamental antithesis, upon which, as its central theme, the drama is constructed, is the contrast between the spirit of compromise on the one hand, and the motto 'everything or nothing' on the other. And *Peer Gynt* is the very incarnation of a compromising dread of decisive committal to any one course. In *Brand* the problem of self-realisation and the relation of the individual to his surroundings is obscurely struggling for recognition, and in *Peer Gynt* it becomes the formal theme upon which all the fantastic variations of the drama are built up. In both plays alike the problems of heredity and the influence of early surroundings are more than touched upon; and both alike culminate in the doctrine that the only redeeming power on earth or in heaven is the power of love."—Mr. P. H. WICKSTEED.

London : WALTER SCOTT, LIMITED, 24 Warwick Lane.

Foolscap 8vo, Cloth, Price 3s. 6d.

THE INSPECTOR-GENERAL

(Or "REVIZÓR.")

A RUSSIAN COMEDY.

By NIKOLAI VASILIYEVICH GOGOL.

Translated from the original Russian, with Introduction and Notes, by A. A. SYKES, B.A., Trinity College, Cambridge.

Though one of the most brilliant and characteristic of Gogol's works, and well-known on the Continent, the present is the first translation of his *Revizór*, or Inspector-General, which has appeared in English. A satire on Russian administrative functionaries, the *Revizór* is a comedy marked by continuous gaiety and invention, full of "situation," each development of the story accentuating the satire and emphasising the characterisation, the whole play being instinct with life and interest. Every here and there occurs the note of caprice, of naïveté, of unexpected fancy, characteristically Russian. The present translation will be found to be admirably fluent, idiomatic, and effective.

London: WALTER SCOTT, LIMITED, 24 Warwick Lane.

GREAT WRITERS.

A NEW SERIES OF CRITICAL BIOGRAPHIES.
Edited by Prof. E. S. ROBERTSON and FRANK T. MARZIALS.
A Complete Bibliography to each Volume, by J. P. ANDERSON, British Museum, London.

LIBRARY EDITION.
Printed on large paper of extra quality, in handsome binding, Demy 8vo, price $1.00 each.

VOLUMES ALREADY ISSUED—

LIFE OF LONGFELLOW. By PROF. ERIC S. ROBERTSON.
"A most readable little work."—*Liverpool Mercury.*

LIFE OF COLERIDGE. By HALL CAINE.
"Brief and vigorous, written throughout with spirit and great literary skill."—*Scotsman.*

LIFE OF DICKENS. By FRANK T. MARZIALS.
"Notwithstanding the mass of matter that has been printed relating to Dickens and his works ... we should, until we came across this volume, have been at a loss to recommend any popular life of England's most popular novelist as being really satisfactory. The difficulty is removed by Mr. Marzials's little book."—*Athenæum.*

LIFE OF DANTE GABRIEL ROSSETTI. By J. KNIGHT.
"Mr. Knight's picture of the great poet and painter is the fullest and best yet presented to the public."—*The Graphic.*

LIFE OF SAMUEL JOHNSON. By COLONEL F. GRANT.
"Colonel Grant has performed his task with diligence, sound judgment, good taste, and accuracy."—*Illustrated London News.*

LIFE OF DARWIN. By G. T. BETTANY.
"Mr. G. T. Bettany's *Life of Darwin* is a sound and conscientious work."—*Saturday Review.*

LIFE OF CHARLOTTE BRONTË. By A. BIRRELL.
"Those who know much of Charlotte Brontë will learn more, and those who know nothing about her will find all that is best worth learning in Mr. Birrell's pleasant book."—*St. James' Gazette.*

LIFE OF THOMAS CARLYLE. By R. GARNETT, LL.D.
"This is an admirable book. Nothing could be more felicitous and fairer than the way in which he takes us through Carlyle's life and works."—*Pall Mall Gazette.*

New York: CHARLES SCRIBNER'S SONS.

GREAT WRITERS—continued.

LIFE OF ADAM SMITH. By R. B. HALDANE, M.P.
"Written with a perspicuity seldom exemplified when dealing with economic science."—*Scotsman.*

LIFE OF KEATS. By W. M. ROSSETTI.
"Valuable for the ample information which it contains."—*Cambridge Independent.*

LIFE OF SHELLEY. By WILLIAM SHARP.
"The criticisms . . . entitle this capital monograph to be ranked with the best biographies of Shelley."—*Westminster Review.*

LIFE OF SMOLLETT. By DAVID HANNAY.
"A capable record of a writer who still remains one of the great masters of the English novel."—*Saturday Review.*

LIFE OF GOLDSMITH. By AUSTIN DOBSON.
"The story of his literary and social life in London, with all its humorous and pathetic vicissitudes, is here retold, as none could tell it better."—*Daily News.*

LIFE OF SCOTT. By PROFESSOR YONGE.
"This is a most enjoyable book."—*Aberdeen Free Press.*

LIFE OF BURNS. By PROFESSOR BLACKIE.
"The editor certainly made a hit when he persuaded Blackie to write about Burns."—*Pall Mall Gazette.*

LIFE OF VICTOR HUGO. By FRANK T. MARZIALS.
"Mr. Marzials's volume presents to us, in a more handy form than any English or even French handbook gives, the summary of what is known about the life of the great poet."—*Saturday Review.*

LIFE OF EMERSON. By RICHARD GARNETT, LL.D.
"No record of Emerson's life could be more desirable."—*Saturday Review.*

LIFE OF GOETHE. By JAMES SIME.
"Mr. James Sime's competence as a biographer of Goethe is beyond question."—*Manchester Guardian.*

LIFE OF CONGREVE. By EDMUND GOSSE.
"Mr. Gosse has written an admirable biography."—*Academy.*

LIFE OF BUNYAN. By CANON VENABLES.
"A most intelligent, appreciative, and valuable memoir."—*Scotsman.*

LIFE OF CRABBE. By T. E. KEBBEL.
"No English poet since Shakespeare has observed certain aspects of nature and of human life more closely."—*Athenæum.*

LIFE OF HEINE. By WILLIAM SHARP.
"An admirable monograph . . . more fully written up to the level of recent knowledge and criticism than any other English work."—*Scotsman.*

New York: CHARLES SCRIBNER'S SONS.

GREAT WRITERS—continued.

LIFE OF MILL. By W. L. COURTNEY.
"A most sympathetic and discriminating memoir."—*Glasgow Herald.*

LIFE OF SCHILLER. By HENRY W. NEVINSON.
"Presents the poet's life in a neatly rounded picture."—*Scotsman.*

LIFE OF CAPTAIN MARRYAT. By DAVID HANNAY.
"We have nothing but praise for the manner in which Mr. Hannay has done justice to him."—*Saturday Review.*

LIFE OF LESSING. By T. W. ROLLESTON.
"One of the best books of the series."—*Manchester Guardian.*

LIFE OF MILTON. By RICHARD GARNETT, LL.D.
"Has never been more charmingly or adequately told."—*Scottish Leader.*

LIFE OF BALZAC. By FREDERICK WEDMORE.
"Mr. Wedmore's monograph on the greatest of French writers of fiction, whose greatness is to be measured by comparison with his successors, is a piece of careful and critical composition, neat and nice in style."—*Daily News.*

LIFE OF GEORGE ELIOT. By OSCAR BROWNING.
"A book of the character of Mr. Browning's, to stand midway between the bulky work of Mr. Cross and the very slight sketch of Miss Blind, was much to be desired, and Mr. Browning has done his work with vivacity, and not without skill."—*Manchester Guardian.*

LIFE OF JANE AUSTEN. By GOLDWIN SMITH.
"Mr. Goldwin Smith has added another to the not inconsiderable roll of eminent men who have found their delight in Miss Austen. . . . His little book upon her, just published by Walter Scott, is certainly a fascinating book to those who already know her and love her well; and we have little doubt that it will prove also a fascinating book to those who have still to make her acquaintance."—*Spectator.*

LIFE OF BROWNING. By WILLIAM SHARP.
"This little volume is a model of excellent English, and in every respect it seems to us what a biography should be."—*Public Opinion.*

LIFE OF BYRON. By HON. RODEN NOEL.
"The Hon. Roden Noel's volume on Byron is decidedly one of the most readable in the excellent 'Great Writers' series."—*Scottish Leader.*

LIFE OF HAWTHORNE. By MONCURE CONWAY.
"It is a delightful *causerie*—pleasant, genial talk about a most interesting man. Easy and conversational as the tone is throughout, no important fact is omitted, no valueless fact is recalled; and it is entirely exempt from platitude and conventionality."—*The Speaker.*

LIFE OF SCHOPENHAUER. By PROFESSOR WALLACE.
"We can speak very highly of this little book of Mr. Wallace's. It is, perhaps, excessively lenient in dealing with the man, and it cannot be said to be at all ferociously critical in dealing with the philosophy."—*Saturday Review.*

New York: CHARLES SCRIBNER'S SONS.

GREAT WRITERS—continued.

LIFE OF SHERIDAN. By LLOYD SANDERS.

"To say that Mr. Lloyd Sanders, in this little volume, has produced the best existing memoir of Sheridan, is really to award much fainter praise than the work deserves."—*Manchester Examiner.*

LIFE OF THACKERAY. By HERMAN MERIVALE and F. T. MARZIALS.

"The monograph just published is well worth reading, . . . and the book, with its excellent bibliography, is one which neither the student nor the general reader can well afford to miss."—*Pall Mall Gazette.*

LIFE OF CERVANTES. By W. E. WATTS.

"We can commend this book as a worthy addition to the useful series to which it belongs."—*London Daily Chronicle.*

LIFE OF VOLTAIRE. By FRANCIS ESPINASSE.

www.ingramcontent.com/pod-product-compliance
Lightning Source LLC
Chambersburg PA
CBHW031958300426
44117CB00008B/808